Police Officer Exam
FOR
DUMMIES®

by Raymond E. Foster and Tracey Vasil Biscontini

WILEY

Wiley Publishing, Inc.

Police Officer Exam For Dummies®

Published by
Wiley Publishing, Inc.
111 River St.
Hoboken, NJ 07030-5774
www.wiley.com

Copyright © 2011 by Wiley Publishing, Inc., Indianapolis, Indiana

Published simultaneously in Canada

For general information on our other products and services, please contact our Customer Care Department within the U.S. at 877-762-2974, outside the U.S. at 317-572-3993, or fax 317-572-4002.

For technical support, please visit www.wiley.com/techsupport.

Wiley also publishes its books in a variety of electronic formats. Some content that appears in print may not be available in electronic books.

Library of Congress Control Number: 2010941513

ISBN: 978-0-470-88724-0

Manufactured in the United States of America

10 9 8 7 6 5 4 3 2 1

WILEY

About the Authors

Raymond E. Foster was a sworn member of the Los Angeles Police Department for 24 years. He retired in 2003 at the rank of lieutenant. He holds a bachelor's degree in criminal justice management from the Union Institute & University and a master's degree in public financial management from California State University, Fullerton. He has also completed doctoral studies in business research.

Raymond has been a part-time lecturer at both the Fullerton and Fresno campuses of California State University, and he was the faculty advisor and chair of the criminal justice program at the Union Institute & University. His experience includes teaching upper-division courses in law enforcement, public policy, technology, and leadership. Raymond has published numerous articles in magazines such as *Government Technology, Airborne Beat,* and *Police Magazine.*

His first book, *Police Technology* (Prentice Hall), is used in more than 100 colleges and universities nationwide. His latest book, *Leadership: Texas Hold 'Em Style* (BookSurge Publishing), has been adopted by several universities for course work in leadership and several civil service organizations as required reading for promotion, and it has been well received in the wider market.

Tracey Vasil Biscontini is the founder, president, and CEO of Northeast Editing, Inc., a company specializing in the creation of test-preparation products. She holds bachelor's degrees in education and mass communications from King's College and a master's degree in English from the University of Scranton. Recently named one of the "Top 25 Women in Business in Northeast Pennsylvania," she is a former educator, journalist, and newspaper columnist whose award-winning writing has appeared in national magazines. Since founding Northeast Editing, Inc., in 1992, she has managed educational projects and authored test-preparation and library-reference content for some of the largest publishers in the United States.

Northeast Editing, Inc., is located in a former rectory in Jenkins Township, nestled between Wilkes-Barre and Scranton in northeastern Pennsylvania. Tracey's company boasts a relaxed work environment that serves as her staff's home away from home. When they're not hard at work, the editors and writers at Northeast Editing, Inc., enjoy breaks in a large backyard and welcome hugs from Prince, a stray cat that showed up one day and never left. Tracey lives in Avoca, Pennsylvania, with her husband Nick, son Tyler, and daughter Morgan.

Lindsay Rock is the managing editor of Northeast Editing, Inc., where she has written and edited test-preparation and trade books since 2003. She holds a bachelor's degree in journalism from Pennsylvania State University and is a member of Phi Beta Kappa, an academic honor society.

Lindsay currently resides in Exeter, Pennsylvania. She spends much of her free time riding her bright yellow quad through the woods, golfing, and watching Penn State and Pittsburgh Steelers football.

Dedication

To the men and women of law enforcement, who put their lives on the line every day.

Authors' Acknowledgments

Special thanks to Tracy Boggier, our acquisitions editor, who got the ball rolling; Elizabeth Rea, our incredible project editor, who offered advice and guidance every step of the way; our wonderful copy editors, Caitie Copple, Todd Lothery, and Christy Pingleton; and our knowledgeable technical editors, Stacy Bell and Richard Weinblatt.

Finally, more special thanks to everyone at Northeast Editing, Inc., who devoted countless hours of research and writing to help create this book.

Publisher's Acknowledgments

We're proud of this book; please send us your comments at http://dummies.custhelp.com. For other comments, please contact our Customer Care Department within the U.S. at 877-762-2974, outside the U.S. at 317-572-3993, or fax 317-572-4002.

Some of the people who helped bring this book to market include the following:

Acquisitions, Editorial, and Media Development

Project Editor: Elizabeth Rea

Acquisitions Editor: Tracy Boggier

Copy Editors: Caitlin Copple, Todd Lothery, Christine Pingleton

Assistant Editor: David Lutton

Technical Editors: Stacy Bell, Dr. Richard Weinblatt

Editorial Manager: Michelle Hacker

Editorial Assistant: Jennette ElNaggar

Art Coordinator: Alicia B. South

Cover Photos: ©iStockphoto.com/Tim McCaig

Cartoons: Rich Tennant (www.the5thwave.com)

Composition Services

Project Coordinator: Sheree Montgomery

Layout and Graphics: Carrie A. Cesavice, Melissa K. Smith

Proofreaders: Jacqui Brownstein, John Greenough

Indexer: Estalita Slivoskey

Publishing and Editorial for Consumer Dummies

Diane Graves Steele, Vice President and Publisher, Consumer Dummies

Kristin Ferguson-Wagstaffe, Product Development Director, Consumer Dummies

Ensley Eikenburg, Associate Publisher, Travel

Kelly Regan, Editorial Director, Travel

Publishing for Technology Dummies

Andy Cummings, Vice President and Publisher, Dummies Technology/General User

Composition Services

Debbie Stailey, Director of Composition Services

Contents at a Glance

Introduction 1

Part 1: The Road to Landing a Job as a Police Officer 7
Chapter 1: Signing Up, Getting Screened, and Other Prep Work................................9
Chapter 2: Preparing Yourself for the Police Officer Tests......................................23

Part II: Breaking Down the National Police Officer Selection Test (POST) and the NYC Test 31
Chapter 3: Solving Basic Math Questions on the POST..33
Chapter 4: Reading Between the Lines: Reading Comprehension 55
Chapter 5: Expressing Yourself with Proper Grammar, Punctuation, and Spelling........79
Chapter 6: Stretching Your Memory and Visualization Skills....................................99
Chapter 7: Reading and Writing Incident Reports..129
Chapter 8: Acing the Law Enforcement Essay Exam..147
Chapter 9: Completing the Personal History Statement...157

Part III: After the Written Test: Meeting Other Requirements 167
Chapter 10: Putting Your Physical Ability to the Test..169
Chapter 11: Presenting Yourself Well in the Oral Board Interview..........................181
Chapter 12: Preparing for Medical and Psychological Evaluations 189

Part IV: Practice Police Officer Exams.. 197
Chapter 13: Practice Test 1: The National Police Officer Selection Test (POST)...........199
Chapter 14: Answers and Explanations for Practice Test 1 221
Chapter 15: Practice Test 2: The National Police Officer Selection Test (POST)...........227
Chapter 16: Answers and Explanations for Practice Test 2 249
Chapter 17: Practice Test 3: The National Police Officer Selection Test (POST)...........255
Chapter 18: Answers and Explanations for Practice Test 3 277
Chapter 19: Practice Test 4: The New York City Police Department Police Officer Candidate Test 283
Chapter 20: Answers and Explanations for Practice Test 4 327

Part V: The Part of Tens 333
Chapter 21: Ten Tips to Help You Succeed on the Exam 335
Chapter 22: Ten Things to Expect at the Police Academy 339

Part VI: Appendixes 345
Appendix A: Law Enforcement Terminology and Resources.....................................347
Appendix B: Climbing the Law Enforcement Ladder 351

Index 355

Table of Contents

Introduction 1

About This Book 1
Conventions Used in This Book 2
What You're Not to Read 3
Foolish Assumptions 3
How This Book Is Organized 4
    Part I: The Road to Landing a Job as a Police Officer 4
    Part II: Breaking Down the National Police Officer
       Selection Test (POST) and the NYC Test 4
    Part III: After the Written Test: Meeting Other Requirements 4
    Part IV: Practice Police Officer Exams 4
    Part V: The Part of Tens 5
    Part VI: Appendixes 5
Icons Used in This Book 5
Where to Go from Here 5

Part 1: The Road to Landing a Job as a Police Officer 7

Chapter 1: Signing Up, Getting Screened, and Other Prep Work 9

Starting with the Notice of Examination (NOE) 9
Completing a Job Application 10
    Understanding what will get you disqualified 14
    Acting professionally 14
Taking the Written Test 15
    National Police Officer Selection Test (POST) 15
    New York City Police Department Police Officer Candidate Test 16
Completing the Personal History Statement 17
Taking the Law Enforcement Essay Exam 18
Passing the Physical Ability Test (PAT) 18
Making a Dynamite Impression during the Oral Board Interview 19
Undergoing the Medical and Psychological Evaluations 19
    Medical evaluation 20
    Psychological evaluation 20
What if I Get Eliminated during the Screening Process? 20

Chapter 2: Preparing Yourself for the Police Officer Tests 23

Knowing What You're Up Against on the Written Test 23
    The structure of the National Police Officer Selection Test (POST) 24
    The structure of the New York City (NYC) Police Department
       Police Officer Candidate Test 25
Getting the Lowdown on the Other Police Officer Tests 27
    Acing the physical ability test (PAT) 27
    Prepping for the oral interview 27
    Preparing for the psychological evaluation 28
    Getting ready for the medical exam 28

Part II: Breaking Down the National Police Officer Selection Test (POST) and the NYC Test 31

Chapter 3: Solving Basic Math Questions on the POST 33
What Do Math Questions Look Like? 34
   Addition questions 34
   Subtraction questions 36
   Multiplication questions 37
   Division questions 39
Determining Percentages 41
   What is a percent? 41
   How to find a percentage 42
Finding Averages 44
   What is an average? 44
   How to find an average 44
Picking an Answer if You Don't Know It 46
Practice Math Questions 47

Chapter 4: Reading Between the Lines: Reading Comprehension 55
Comprehending the Reading Comprehension Section on the POST 55
   Longer passages 56
   Definition passages 58
Examining the Reading Comprehension Questions on the New York City Test 59
   Written comprehension passages 60
   Information ordering passages 61
   Inductive reasoning passages 62
   Deductive reasoning passages 64
   Problem sensitivity questions 67
Practice Questions for the POST Reading Comprehension Section 67
Practice Questions for the NYC Reading Comprehension Section 71

Chapter 5: Expressing Yourself with Proper Grammar, Punctuation, and Spelling 79
Acing Grammar Questions 79
   Choosing the correct verb tense 80
   Watching out for subject-verb agreement 82
   Picking the correct pronoun 83
   Using the right adjective 86
   Identifying complete sentences and fragments 87
   Pluralizing nouns 88
Excelling at Spelling Questions 90
Practice Grammar and Spelling Questions 92

Chapter 6: Stretching Your Memory and Visualization Skills 99
Getting the Lowdown on Memory and Observation Questions on the NYC Test 99
   Digging deep for memorization questions 100
   Using your mind's eye for visualization questions 104
   Straightening out information ordering questions 110
   Determining the best course of action 113
   Getting your bearings 114
   Recalling letters and numbers 115
Practice Observation and Memory Questions 117

Chapter 7: Reading and Writing Incident Reports..**129**

  Tackling POST Questions about Incident Reports 129
    Demonstrating comprehension of incident reports on the POST 130
    Answering written questions about incident reports on the POST 134
  Mastering Questions about Incident Reports on the NYC Test 137
  Practice POST Incident Report Questions 140
  Practice NYC Incident Report Questions 144

Chapter 8: Acing the Law Enforcement Essay Exam **147**

  Following the Proper Steps to Craft a Winning Essay 147
    Prewriting 148
    Writing... 149
    Proofreading.. 150
  Understanding How Essays Are Scored... 152
  Warming Up to Sample Essay Prompts 153
  Practice Law Enforcement Essay Exam Question and Answer 154

Chapter 9: Completing the Personal History Statement **157**

  Becoming Familiar with the Personal History Statement.............................. 158
  Getting Ready to Complete the Personal History Statement......................... 162
    Gathering the necessary information.. 162
    Collecting the necessary documents 163
  Writing the Personal History Statement.. 163
    Understanding that honesty is the best policy.. 164
    Following directions and reading questions carefully 165
    Checking your work.. 166

Part III: After the Written Test: Meeting Other Requirements 167

Chapter 10: Putting Your Physical Ability to the Test.................................**169**

  Let's Get Physical: The Whys and Wherefores of the Physical Ability Test 169
    Understanding why police officers need the physical ability test 170
    Breaking down the skill areas of the typical test....................................... 170
    Getting the lowdown on the local test 171
  Getting in Shape before the Test 172
  What You Should Know and Do the Day of Your Test................................... 173
  Showing Them What You Can Do: Test Events 173
    One-minute sit-ups 174
    One-minute push-ups 175
    Vertical jump 175
    1.5-mile run 176
    440-yard mobility/agility run 176
    Modified squat thrust... 177
    Vehicle exit 178
    Stair climb 178
    Fence obstacles.. 178
    Trigger pull 178
    Dummy drag... 179

Chapter 11: Presenting Yourself Well in the Oral Board Interview 181
  Comporting Yourself Well 181
    Dressing professionally..182
    Acting professionally..182
    Speaking in front of others 183
  Honing Your Question and Answer Skills...184
    Expecting the right types of questions 184
    Knowing what the interviewers want to hear from you 185
  Sample Scenarios...186
    Interview 1 186
    Interview 2 187
    Interview 3 187
    Assessing the sample scenarios 187

Chapter 12: Preparing for Medical and Psychological Evaluations 189
  Getting Tested, Poked, and Prodded in the Medical Evaluation 189
    What can you see? Testing your vision 190
    Can you hear me now? Testing your hearing...191
    Not for the squeamish: Blood and urine tests 191
    Breathe in, breathe out: Checking your heart and lungs.........................192
    How low can you go? Monitoring muscular and skeletal disorders 193
    Other conditions...193
  Understanding What Happens during the Psychological Evaluation..........194
    Taking the personality test..194
    Interviewing with a psychologist 195

Part IV: Practice Police Officer Exams *197*

**Chapter 13: Practice Test 1: The National Police Officer
Selection Test (POST)**..199

Chapter 14: Answers and Explanations for Practice Test 1 221

**Chapter 15: Practice Test 2: The National Police Officer
Selection Test (POST)**..227

Chapter 16: Answers and Explanations for Practice Test 2 249

**Chapter 17: Practice Test 3: The National Police Officer
Selection Test (POST)**..255

Chapter 18: Answers and Explanations for Practice Test 3 277

**Chapter 19: Practice Test 4: The New York City Police Department
Police Officer Candidate Test**...283

Chapter 20: Answers and Explanations for Practice Test 4 327

Part V: The Part of Tens..*333*

Chapter 21: Ten Tips to Help You Succeed on the Exam **335**

Prepare Yourself..335
Get Plenty of ZZZs...336
Eat Healthfully...336
Arrive Early 336
Relax! 336
Carefully Read or Listen to Directions..336
Read the Questions First 337
Pace Yourself 337
Mark the Right Spot!..337
Take a Guess 337

Chapter 22: Ten Things to Expect at the Police Academy **339**

Rigorous Rule Enforcement..339
Physical Challenges...340
Strength Training...340
Firearms Training 341
EVOC Training..341
Academic Integrity 341
Language Training 342
Ethics Training...342
Human Relations 343
Field Training Program 343

Part VI: Appendixes...*345*

Appendix A: Law Enforcement Terminology and Resources...................**347**

Law Enforcement Terminology...347
Law Enforcement Codes 349
Additional Resources 350

Appendix B: Climbing the Law Enforcement Ladder...............................**351**

Starting on the Bottom Rung: Unranked......................................351
  Officer...351
  Detective/Investigator...351
  Sergeant 352
Moving to Middle Management: Bars 352
  Lieutenant...352
  Captain 352
  Major/Deputy inspector...352
Becoming the Top Dog: Stars...353
  Inspector/Commander 353
  Assistant chief...353
  Deputy chief..353
  Chief of police...353

Index..*355*

Introduction

Chances are that if you're reading this book, you're considering pursuing a career as a police officer. Good for you! Police work is both challenging and rewarding. As a police officer, you'll earn a good salary — police officers in the United States average about $53,000 a year. Police officers receive overtime pay and excellent benefits such as paid sick leave and vacation time, medical and life insurance, and outstanding retirement benefits.

A police officer's duties vary somewhat depending on the location of the police department. An officer in a small town may perform a variety of duties, while a cop in a large city may have more specific, routine duties. All police officers keep people safe by enforcing the law. Most spend at least part of their shift patrolling a designated area in a patrol car, on a motorcycle, or on foot. In some areas, police officers patrol on horses or bicycles. During patrols, officers are on the lookout for criminal activity. Their goal is to protect citizens and their property by catching thieves and other criminals and preventing crimes from taking place. They also direct traffic when necessary and issue traffic and parking citations. Police officers write incident reports and sometimes testify at hearings and trials. Other duties include responding to calls about burglaries, robberies, automobile accidents, fires, and domestic disturbances; conducting investigations by interviewing witnesses and gathering evidence; and making arrests.

The police officer hiring process is unlike that of any other job. It consists of much more than simply filling out a job application or sending a résumé and going on a job interview. The police officer screening process involves numerous tests and evaluations designed to ensure that you're ready to begin training to become a police officer. We wrote *Police Officer Exam For Dummies* to guide you through this screening process, from finding a Notice of Examination (NOE) to acing the oral board interview.

About This Book

Police work is challenging — and at times it can be stressful and dangerous. For the most part, though, police officers enjoy what they do. They know that their job is important, and they're proud to serve their communities by keeping them safe. The police officer hiring process involves many steps that we cover in this book, including these:

✔ Obtaining a Notice of Examination (NOE), which tells you that a written exam is being given because of a job opening or openings. This notice tells you where and when the exam will take place, what you have to do to register for the test, and what requirements you must meet to be a police officer in the specified area.

✔ Filling out a lengthy and detailed job application that asks you very specific information such as whether you've ever been a defendant in a court action and whether you've ever collected unemployment or worker's compensation insurance. The application also asks you to list each job you've held since you were 17 and every address you've lived at since elementary school.

✔ Taking and passing a written exam that may test your reading, math, and memory skills, and sometimes your writing skills. Though the written exam may vary a bit from one police department to the next, most departments give either the National Police

Officer Selection Test (POST) or a civil service exam such as the New York City (NYC) Police Department Police Officer Candidate Test. We help you review exam skills for both tests in this book.

✔ **Completing the Personal History Statement.** If you think the job application for a police officer job asks personal information, wait until you complete the Personal History Statement. Most police departments ask you to complete this document when you fill out the job application. The statement probes into your past and your personal life, asking questions such as, "Have you stolen anything?" and "Have you ever used marijuana or any other drug not prescribed by a physician?" You can't lie on the Personal History Statement — the police department uses it to investigate your background and requires you to complete a polygraph test about the information you provide.

✔ **Passing a physical ability test (PAT),** which determines whether you're in good enough shape to make it through the strenuous physical training at the police academy. Like the written test, the PAT may vary in terms of what you're asked to do — but rest assured that you won't be asked to go for a relaxing stroll. Expect to exert yourself doing sit-ups and push-ups, running, jumping vertically, climbing stairs, and dragging a dummy. Expect to sweat.

✔ **Completing the oral board interview,** a test to see how well you answer questions, use common sense, and handle yourself in stressful situations. Members of the oral board include senior police officers and sometimes community leaders. Expect to answer all kinds of questions about your personality and educational and work backgrounds during this interview, which typically lasts about two hours. Does this sound like an interrogation? You bet.

✔ **Undergoing a medical and psychological examination** to see whether you're healthy and mentally stable enough to work as a police officer. Expect to have both your body and brain poked and prodded.

In *Police Officer Exam For Dummies,* we give you all the information you need to make it through each step in the hiring process without being eliminated. We tell you how to prepare for each test and give you a chance to practice. Following the guidance in this book and completing the many practice exercises and tests is a great way to succeed and land a job as a cop.

Conventions Used in This Book

This book uses the following conventions to keep things consistent and easy to understand:

✔ We use the phrase *written police officer test* to refer to any kind of written test a police department may choose to give its job candidates. When we refer to the *National Police Officer Selection Test* — the *POST* — we call it by name. When we refer to a *civil service test,* we refer to the *New York City test* (NYC test) because this test is an excellent example of what you may see on a civil service test.

✔ When we discuss the physical test that police candidates take, we call it the *physical ability test (PAT).* Most police departments refer to this test as the PAT, but some also call it the *physical fitness test* or the *police officer physical exam.*

✔ We use the terms *medical evaluation* and *medical exam* interchangeably. We also do this with *psychological evaluation* and *psychological exam.*

✔ We use **boldface** to highlight keywords in bulleted lists and the action parts of numbered steps.

✔ We *italicize* any words you may not be familiar with and provide definitions.

✔ All Web sites and e-mail addresses appear in monofont. When this book was printed, some Web addresses may have needed to break across two lines of text. If that happened, rest assured that we haven't put in any extra characters (such as hyphens) to indicate the break. When you use one of these Web addresses, just type exactly what you see in this book, pretending that the line break doesn't exist.

What You're Not to Read

Of course, we'd love it if you read every word of this book — we wrote it, after all. We also understand, however, that life is hectic and time is limited, so here are some portions that you're able to skip over without putting yourself at a serious disadvantage:

✔ *Sidebars* are the shaded boxes you see throughout the book that provide extra information or detailed examples. Though you'll likely enjoy the gems of knowledge in the sidebars, they don't necessarily give you an edge on the exams, so feel free to read them later.

✔ If you know you're going to take the National Police Officer Selection Test (POST), you can skip the information in this book about the New York City (NYC) Police Department Police Officer Candidate Test — and vice versa. If you know you're going to take a civil service test, concentrate on the NYC test information.

✔ The same holds true for the practice tests. If you know you're going to take the POST, complete the practice tests in Chapters 13, 15, and 17. If you know you're going to take the NYC test, complete the practice test in Chapter 19.

✔ Part V contains tips to help you succeed on police officer exams and tells you what to expect at the police academy. You don't need this information to pass either the POST or the NYC test.

✔ We include the information in the two appendixes in the back of this book because we think you'll find it interesting. However, you don't need it to become a police officer.

Foolish Assumptions

We all know what happens when we assume, but while writing this book, we decided to live dangerously and make the following assumptions about you, our reader:

✔ You're interested in becoming a police officer, and you want to know more about the job and the hiring process.

✔ You want to take some police officer practice tests so that you know what to expect and what to focus on when studying.

✔ You want to prepare yourself for each step of the police officer hiring process to help ensure your chances of overall success.

✔ You understand that successfully completing all exams, interviews, and evaluations means that you qualify to begin training to become a police officer. You know that patrolling the beat doesn't occur until after you've received extensive training at a police academy.

✔ You can read, speak, and understand the English language reasonably well. (Writers of police officer exams assume this, too.)

How This Book Is Organized

This book is divided into six parts and 22 chapters. The table of contents outlines the specifics, but the following is an overview of what you can expect to see.

Part I: The Road to Landing a Job as a Police Officer

It's not easy to become a cop. The screening process is long and difficult. You have to pass several tests to be considered for a job. Before you can start, you have to obtain a Notice of Examination (NOE). In Part I, you find details about the NOE and an overview of the various tests you have to take — either the National Police Officer Selection Test (POST) or the New York City Police Department Police Officer Candidate Test, the physical ability test (PAT), the medical and psychological evaluations, and so on.

Part II: Breaking Down the National Police Officer Selection Test (POST) and the NYC Test

If the written exam makes you a bit nervous, turn to Part II, where you find details about and practice questions for two common written police officer tests: the POST and the NYC Police Department Police Officer Candidate Test (sometimes called the NYC test for short). Subjects on these tests include basic math; reading comprehension; grammar, punctuation, and spelling; memory and visualization; and incident reports. In Part II, we devote a chapter to each of these subjects to prepare you for the written exam, and we also discuss the Law Enforcement Essay Exam and the Personal History Statement.

Part III: After the Written Test: Meeting Other Requirements

The written police officer test is just the tip of the iceberg — police officer candidates must also pass a physical ability test (PAT), shine during an oral board interview, and undergo medical and psychological evaluations. We cover each of these tests in Part III. Chapter 10 tells you what you have to do to ace the PAT — and no, eating doughnuts isn't a category on the PAT. Chapter 11 tells you what to expect during the oral board interview, and Chapter 12 gives you a heads-up on the medical and psychological evaluations.

Part IV: Practice Police Officer Exams

Want to try your hand at taking a written police officer exam? Part IV includes four practice exams: three POSTs and one NYC test. And because practice exams aren't much good to you unless you can check your answers, we include answer and explanation chapters for each exam.

Part V: The Part of Tens

The Part of Tens is a standard element of *For Dummies* books. Chapter 21 gives you some tips to help you succeed on police officer tests. Chapter 22 tells you what you can expect at the police academy — lots of studying and physical training.

Part VI: Appendixes

Although the information in Part VI isn't mandatory — you don't need it to pass any of the police officer exams — you may find it interesting and helpful. Do you know the difference between a *burglary* and a *robbery?* Are *homicide* and *first-degree murder* the same thing? Appendix A defines these terms and many others, along with codes such as *FTA* (failure to appear) and a *10-80* (a chase in progress).

Appendix B guides you through the law enforcement chain of command.

Icons Used in This Book

To make this book easier to read and simpler to use, we include some icons that can help you find key ideas and information. Keep an eye out for them.

This icon appears next to information that may benefit you during the various steps of the hiring process. This information can save you time and effort.

When you see this icon, you know the information that follows is especially important to keep in mind.

This icon highlights information that may pose a threat to your success on the police officer exams.

This icon points out sample questions that appear in the review chapters.

Where to Go from Here

The great thing about *For Dummies* books is that you can start wherever you want and still find complete information. Want to know how you'd perform on a police officer exam without any preparation? Turn to Chapter 13 and take a practice test, and then check your answers in Chapter 14 to see how well you did. Are you more interested in a specific subject, like incident reports? Check out Chapter 7. The point is that you don't have to read this book from cover to cover. You can start wherever you think you need the most work, using the table of contents and the index to help you find particular topics.

If time is of the essence, find out whether you're taking the POST or a civil service exam such as the NYC test, and turn to the appropriate chapter for information relating to the test you're going to take. If you're not sure where to start, we suggest Part I, which outlines the police officer hiring process from locating a Notice of Examination (NOE) to passing the medical and psychological evaluations.

Part I

The Road to Landing a Job as a Police Officer

The 5th Wave   By Rich Tennant

"This maitre d' job is only temporary until I take my police officer exam."

In this part . . .

To apply for most jobs, you simply send in a résumé or fill out an application. Then you're called for a job interview. If you're qualified for the job and make a good impression, you may receive a job offer. If only becoming a police officer were this easy! To land a job as a cop, you must undergo a lengthy screening process during which you complete at least one written test, a physical ability test (PAT), an oral board interview, and medical and psychological evaluations — and you're still not finished. After you make it through the screening process, you're on your way to the police academy.

In this part, we guide you through the police officer screening process, or what you need to do to become a police officer. We tell you where you can find a Notice of Examination (NOE), which tells you how to register for the written test. We also explain how to fill out an application for a police officer job and how to prepare for the police officer tests.

Chapter 1

Signing Up, Getting Screened, and Other Prep Work

• •

In This Chapter

▶ Taking the beginning steps to become a police officer

▶ Completing tests — written, physical, oral, medical, and psychological

▶ Giving it a second try if necessary

• •

The job of a police officer isn't easy. Police officers investigate crimes, arrest criminals, assist citizens in emergencies, collect and secure evidence, write reports, and testify in court. They keep a community safe by enforcing the law. Their job is an important one, so police departments carefully screen job applicants.

To land a job as a cop, you have to undergo a lengthy screening process. You must be able to solve quadratic equations and bench press 500 pounds. Okay, we're just kidding, but the screening process to become a police officer does involve passing several tests. The good news is that getting a good score on these tests is within reach for most individuals.

In this chapter, we tell you about the screening process to become a police officer. To get a job as a cop in most police departments, you must obtain a Notice of Examination (NOE), complete an application, pass a written exam and a physical ability test (PAT), and undergo a background investigation, an oral board review, and a medical and psychological evaluation. But hold on! You're not finished yet. You still have to contend with the police academy. Whether you must do this on your own before the screening process or after you pass the medical and psychological evaluations depends on the city and state where you're applying for a job.

In some parts of the country, a police department will pay for you to attend a police academy. In other areas, you must enroll in a state-certified academy at a community college, and you have to pay for this academy yourself. Should you do this before you apply for a job? You could, but keep in mind that some large cities, such as Los Angeles and New York City, still require you to attend their academies even if you have attended a state-certified academy at a community college. The moral of the story? Find out what's required in your city and state before you apply for a job and begin the screening process.

Starting with the Notice of Examination (NOE)

The first step to becoming a police officer is to find a *Notice of Examination* (NOE), which is also called an *Exam Announcement*. While many police departments post an NOE because they have job openings, other departments give the written test every so often, and the NOE may simply announce the time and place of the test. If the NOE is posted because of job openings, it indicates where and when you should submit a job application, the time and place of the test, and the test registration fee. You can see an example NOE for a job opening in Figure 1-1.

POLICE OFFICER NOTICE OF EXAMINATION

The city of Happyville will conduct a written examination on June 10 at 9:30 a.m. at Happyville High School, 200 Mountain Road, Happyville, to fill existing vacancies at the Happyville Police Department. Applications for the position are available at Happyville Town Hall, 123 Main Street, Happyville, between the hours of 8 a.m. and 5 p.m., Monday through Friday, or on the Happyville City's Web site (www.happyville.com). A $100 nonrefundable fee is required to process the application. Fees must be in the form of a check or money order. Cash will not be accepted. Completed applications with signatures and the $100 fee must be received at Happyville Town Hall by 5 p.m., Friday, May 30, 2010, to participate in the examination. Applications will not be accepted at the exam location.

Salary range is from $22,000 to $26,000 with excellent benefits. Police officers should expect to work overtime, weekends, holidays, and various shifts.

To be considered for a position within the Happyville Police Department, an applicant must

- be a U.S. citizen
- speak fluent English
- have a high school diploma or a GED
- have a valid Social Security number
- possess a valid driver's license
- be at least 21 years of age and not older than 34 years of age
- possess good moral character
- pass a written examination
- pass a polygraph test
- pass a background investigation
- meet a vision requirement of uncorrected 20/100 to correctable 20/20 and not be color blind
- pass a medical evaluation
- pass a psychological examination

For questions or additional information, contact the Happyville Police Department at 123-4567 or visit www.happyville.com.

The city of Happyville is an Equal Opportunity Employer (EOE).

Figure 1-1:
A sample Notice of Examination for a police officer position.

How do you find an NOE? The easiest way is to periodically check the Web sites of nearby police departments. Another option is to access a national police officer Web site such as PoliceOne.com (www.policeone.com/careers), where you can search police officer job openings by state, city, and zip code.

Completing a Job Application

Before taking a written police officer test, you must pay a fee and submit a completed job application like the one shown in Figure 1-2. You must complete the application in black ink or type it, depending on the instructions on the application. The application should be neat and complete, and the information on it should be accurate. Read all the directions *before* you fill out the application.

Make a few copies of the application and practice completing it. After you finish the final copy, photocopy it. You may need the information on the application later in the screening process.

Remember that neatness counts — if a police department can't read your writing, you're not likely to receive a job offer. An application for a police officer job is different from most other job applications because it asks for very detailed specific information, such as the address of every home you've ever lived in since elementary school. Why do police departments make their job application so difficult to complete? Think about it — a police officer carries a gun. Should a police department give a gun to an unstable individual who has had past run-ins with the law? Absolutely not.

Gather the following information before you complete an application for a job as a police officer:

- Birth certificate.

- Driver's license.

- Education information (names of your high school, college, and/or business school; the years you attended; and the diploma or degree you received).

- Employment information, as shown in Figure 1-3 (list of your former employers, the position and type of work you did, the dates during which you were employed, and your reasons for leaving). Follow the directions to see how far back you must go. Some applications ask you to list each employer you had during the past ten years.

- The names, addresses, and telephone numbers of co-workers at each job to include as references.

- If you served in the military, your date of entry (month, day, and year) and your date of discharge (month, day, and year).

- All former convictions, including traffic tickets.

- The address of each residence you have lived at since graduating from elementary school (about sixth grade); the month and year you moved into each residence, and the month and year you left.

- The names, addresses, and telephone numbers of five personal references, other than family members.

- An itemized list of your debts, including the names and addresses of banks or places that have given you loans, the amount you owe on each loan, your monthly payment, any overdue payments, and the nature of the debt, such as a mortgage or new car loan.

Some police officer job applications require you to submit copies of the following documents along with the application:

- Birth certificate

- Valid driver's license

- Certified copy of your driving record

- Social Security card

- High school diploma or GED certificate

- College transcripts

- Selective Service registration form

- Form DD214, Certificate of Release or Discharge from Active Duty, for each term of service if you served in the U.S. Armed Forces

- Marriage license, divorce decree, and/or legal separation papers

 If you're a male applicant born after January 1, 1960, you must show proof of your registration with the Selective Service (SSS Form 3A). If you don't have this document, you can get a copy by calling the Selective Service at (847) 688-6888 or toll-free at (888) 655-1825, or go to www.sss.gov for more information.

Figure 1-2:
A sample application for a police officer job.

APPLICATION FOR EMPLOYMENT

CST pass	
PHY qual	
To AIS	
Agility	

INSTRUCTIONS: TYPE OR PRINT. SIGN IN INK. EACH REQUEST FOR APPOINTMENT REQUIRES A SEPARATE APPLICATION.

Before completing this application, read the position announcement to be sure you have the minimum qualifications for this position. Then complete the application fully. Read and sign affirmation.

OMISSIONS MAY RESULT IN REJECTION OF APPLICATION

APPLICATION FOR APPOINTMENT TO THE POSITION OF _____

1. Name in full: _____
   Last   First   Middle

   Phone number (including area code): _____

   What other names have you been known by? _____

   Female applicants must furnish maiden name: _____

2. Address: _____
   Street   City   State   Zip Code

   How long have you lived in [city]? _____

   How long have you lived in [state]? _____

3. Date of Birth: _____   Present age: _____

4. Are you a citizen of the United States? _____

5. Proof of Citizenship attached ☐No ☐Yes   (IE: Copy of Birth Certificate)

6. Do you possess a valid Operator's License? ☐No ☐Yes
   _____
   State   Number

7. Education:

Name & Address of School	Years Attended From	Years Attended To	Course Diploma or Degree
High School			
College			
Business School			

THIS SECTION CONTINUED ON ATTACHED PAGES ☐YES ☐NO

8. Employment Records:
   Social Security Number: _____

Name & Address of Employer	Position & Type of Work	Employed From	To	Reason for leaving

9. United States Military Service: ☐No ☐Yes Branch of Service: _____

   Date of Entry: _____   Date of Discharge: _____
   Month/Day/Year   *Month/Day/Year*

   Type of Discharge: _____   Serial No.: _____

10. Have you ever previously applied for any position in the [city] Police Department or any other Law Enforcement Agency or Correctional Institution?
    ☐No ☐Yes What Agency? _____ When? _____
    What Position? _____

11. List all convictions (include traffic arrests): _____

12. Have you ever been a defendant in any court action? ☐No ☐Yes
    Describe _____

13. Are you now or have you ever been a member of any organization, corporation, company, partnership, association, trust, foundation, fund, club, society, committee, political party, or any group of persons, whether or not incorporated, which engages in or advocates, abets, advises or teaches, or follows a purpose which is to engage in or advocate, abet, assist in the overthrow, destruction or alteration of the Constitutional form of government of the United States or of the State of XX, or of any political subdivision of either of them, by revolution, force, violence or other unlawful means?
    ☐No ☐Yes Describe _____

14. I hereby affirm that there are no intentional misrepresentations or falsifications in the foregoing statements and answers to questions. I am aware that should investigation disclose any such misrepresentations or falsifications, my application shall be rejected or, if already employed, my employment may be terminated.

    _____
    Applicant's Signature   Date

THIS SECTION CONTINUED ON ATTACHED PAGES ☐YES ☐NO

EMPLOYMENT HISTORY

STARTING WITH THE DATE YOU LEFT HIGH SCHOOL, ACCURATELY ACCOUNT FOR ALL PERIODS OF EMPLOYMENT AND UNEMPLOYMENT IN DATE ORDER, INCLUDING YOUR PRESENT EMPLOYER. INCLUDE ALL SEASONAL, TEMPORARY, OR PART-TIME JOBS YOU HAVE HELD WHILE FURLOUGHED OR LAID-OFF FROM YOUR PERMANENT JOB. *ANSWER ALL QUESTIONS*.

PLEASE PRINT OR TYPE

Have you ever applied for or collected unemployment compensation? ❑Yes ❑No

Have you ever applied for or collected workman's compensation? ❑Yes ❑No

Have you ever filed for bankruptcy? ❑Yes ❑No

Social Security Number: _____

EMPLOYER: _____ PHONE: _____

ADDRESS: _____

CITY: _____ STATE: _____ ZIP: _____

EMPLOYED FROM: _____ TO: _____ SALARY: _____

REASON FOR LEAVING: _____

POSITION: _____ DUTIES: _____

CO-WORKER: _____ PHONE: _____

ADDRESS: _____

CITY: _____ STATE: _____ ZIP: _____

CO-WORKER: _____ PHONE: _____

ADDRESS: _____

CITY: _____ STATE: _____ ZIP: _____

SIGNATURE: _____ DATE: _____

PAGE _____ OF _____

Figure 1-3:
You may see several Employment History boxes like this one attached to a police officer job application.

Understanding what will get you disqualified

Not everyone may participate in the police officer screening process. If you've done something in your past that prevents you from obtaining a permit to carry a concealed firearm, you'll be knocked out of the competition to win a job as a police officer. You may be disqualified from becoming a police officer if you

- Are a fugitive from justice
- Have been admitted to a mental health facility
- Have been convicted of a felony
- Were dishonorably discharged from the Armed Forces
- Entered the United States illegally
- Are currently on parole or probation
- Have been convicted of a crime involving domestic violence or stalking
- Are currently subject to a restraining order or protection from abuse order
- Have an addiction to drugs or alcohol
- Have been judicially declared incompetent or insane

Acting professionally

Suppose you obtain a Notice of Examination (NOE) that says you need to drop off a completed application at the police department the week before the written test. You're in the midst of painting your apartment that week but stop by the police department to hand in your application. Your clothes aren't clean and they're splattered with paint. You're perspiring and notice that a line of candidates is waiting to hand in applications. You see an old high school friend ahead of you in line. "Hey, Joe!" you shout, slap the man on the back, and shake his hand. The officer behind the front desk is on the phone and motions for you to keep it down. Are you making a good first impression? Are you behaving professionally? No! Always act professionally — when you hand in your application, when you take your written test, and when you arrive for an oral interview.

Employment outlook

The employment outlook for police officers is good — and it's expected to get better. The U.S. Bureau of Labor Statistics estimates that by 2018, the number of law-enforcement jobs will increase by 10 percent. Why the increase? The population is growing, and older employees are expected to retire.

Local police departments will likely do the most hiring, particularly those in urban areas with high crime rates.

Candidates who are bilingual, have military training, or have college degrees have the best chance of landing a job as a local cop.

Jobs in state and federal law enforcement will be harder to find. But candidates who are bilingual, have military experience, or hold college degrees have the best shot at these jobs as well. Those with investigative experience also have a leg up on the competition.

Taking the Written Test

After you find a Notice of Examination (NOE), complete a job application, and register for the written test, you have to take and pass this test. Were you a good test-taker in school? Don't panic if you weren't. Most of the written tests police officers must take are fairly basic. You can easily pass them with some practice and preparation.

Not all police departments in the United States give the same written test. Some give a test called the National Police Officer Selection Test (POST). Others give a civil service test, such as the New York City Police Department Police Officer Candidate Test. We address both of these tests in this book.

 Before you take a written police officer test, find out as much as you can about the test by contacting the police department and visiting its Web site. Many police departments offer study guides that you can download from their Web site. But if you can't find what you're looking for, don't be afraid to ask questions.

A few departments also require candidates to pass a video-based examination. During this test, you watch videos of scenarios instead of reading about them and then answer multiple-choice questions about the scene you've just witnessed.

Some police departments interview candidates about two to three weeks after they pass the written exam. This is an initial interview. Don't confuse it with the oral board interview, which is much longer.

National Police Officer Selection Test (POST)

The National Police Officer Selection Test, better known as the POST, has four sections, and each section is timed. The first three sections are Mathematics, Reading Comprehension, and Grammar. These sections have both multiple-choice and true-and-false questions. Most multiple-choice questions have five answer options — A, B, C, D, and E. You blacken the oval that corresponds to the answer choice that you believe is correct. The fourth section is called Incident Report Writing. You have to write out your answers to the questions in this section.

 You should attempt to answer every question on the POST because there's no penalty for guessing. Your score is based only on the number of questions you answer correctly. When you don't know the answer to a question, eliminate answer options that you know are incorrect and make a good guess.

The following is a brief rundown of what to expect in each section of the POST. To find out more about the POST, turn to Chapter 2.

✔ **Section 1: Mathematics.** The questions in the mathematics section of the POST require you to use basic arithmetic — addition, subtraction, multiplication, and division. You also have to determine averages on this test. You can't use a calculator on the POST, but the test booklet has scratch paper you can use to figure out your answers. For more information about the kind of mathematics questions that are on the POST, turn to Chapter 3.

✔ **Section 2: Reading Comprehension.** On this section of the POST, you read passages or several paragraphs about a subject and answer questions about the information in the passage. Passages are about police duty, but you don't need any knowledge of police duty to answer the questions. Everything you need to know to answer the questions is in the passage. Both multiple-choice and true-and-false questions are in the reading comprehension section of the POST. To find out more about answering reading comprehension questions, see Chapter 4.

✔ **Section 3: Grammar.** The grammar section of the POST tests your knowledge of grammar, punctuation, and spelling. This section has two types of questions. To answer the first type of question, you choose the word that best fits in a blank in a sentence. To answer the second type of question, you choose the word in a sentence that's misspelled. We tell you more about grammar, punctuation, and spelling in Chapter 5.

✔ **Section 4: Incident Report Writing.** Incident report writing tests your writing skills. In this section of the POST, you're given a completed (filled-out) incident report and asked questions about it. Though the information you need to answer the questions is right in the incident report, you're judged on how you write out your answer. Your answers should be complete sentences that are grammatically correct. To read more about incident reports, turn to Chapter 7.

New York City Police Department Police Officer Candidate Test

Though many police departments give the National Police Officer Selection Test (POST), others give a civil service test, such as the New York City (NYC) Police Department Police Officer Candidate Test. This exam contains about 85 questions testing your ability in these areas:

✔ **Inductive and deductive reasoning:** Inductive reasoning questions give you a set of details and ask you to draw a conclusion based on these details. Deductive reasoning questions do just the opposite — they give you a conclusion and ask you to choose details supporting the conclusion. You can find out more about inductive and deductive reasoning questions in Chapter 4.

✔ **Information ordering:** These questions test your ability to follow directions. You're given a series of steps that you must follow to correctly answer the questions. The questions explain that an officer has completed some steps and ask you what the officer should do next. Chapter 6 tells you more about information ordering questions.

✔ **Memorization:** Memorization questions on the NYC test assess your ability to remember details about what you've seen. You're given ten minutes to study a photograph or an illustration. Then, when a page is turned and you can no longer see the picture, you must answer questions about details within it.

✔ **Problem sensitivity:** To answer these questions, you have to predict whether something is likely to go wrong in a given situation. For example, you may be given a guideline as to when police officers should evacuate persons in a building, and then you may be asked questions about information in this guideline. For more about problem sensitivity questions, turn to Chapter 6.

✔ **Spatial orientation:** To answer spatial orientation questions on the NYC test, you read a description and determine where you are in terms of direction (north, south, east, or west). Some spatial orientation questions include a map indicating one-way streets and roadway obstructions. To answer these questions, you have to choose the most efficient route to get from one place to another while obeying all traffic regulations. For more about memorization and spatial orientation questions, turn to Chapter 6.

✔ **Visualization:** Imagine the street on which you live. Now imagine what this street looks like if you were standing behind the houses or buildings. Visualization questions on the NYC test ask you to envision what something looks like from a different angle or perspective. We discuss visualization questions in detail in Chapter 6.

✔ **Written comprehension:** Written comprehension questions on the NYC test are similar to reading comprehension questions on the POST. You read a passage containing information about police duty and answer questions about the information in the passage. To read more about these types of questions, review Chapter 4.

✔ **Written expression:** These questions assess your knowledge of grammar. You choose the sentence that presents information clearly, accurately, and completely. For more about grammar questions, see Chapter 5.

Completing the Personal History Statement

Most police departments require candidates to complete a Personal History Statement, a long document in which you respond to questions about your past and your character. Although some departments ask you to complete this statement after the written test, many allow you to complete it at home and require that you have it notarized by a notary public before you turn it in.

Honesty is the only policy when responding to questions on the Personal History Statement. A background investigator checks your responses, and if this person discovers that you lied or omitted something important, the police department will disqualify you from the screening process. Therefore, it's better to tell the truth and explain the reasons for your actions. You can view a sample Personal History Statement in Chapter 9.

A Personal History Statement asks questions such as these:

✔ Have you ever been arrested or convicted of an offense? If your answer is "yes," explain the incident in concise detail on a separate sheet of paper, giving the dates and nature of the offense, the name and location of the court, and the disposition of the case. A conviction may not disqualify you, but a false statement will.

✔ Have you ever been on probation or parole? If "yes," explain the details on a separate sheet of paper.

✔ Have you been involved as a party in a lawsuit? If "yes," explain the details on a separate sheet of paper.

✔ Have you ever driven a motor vehicle within the past three years without the proper insurance?

✔ Have you ever had your driver's license placed on probation for receiving an excessive number of traffic violations?

✔ Have you ever been placed as an assigned risk for vehicle insurance?

✔ Have you filed for bankruptcy?

✔ Are you under obligation to pay child support? If "yes," are you current with payments?

✔ Describe in your own words the frequency and extent of your use of alcoholic beverages.

You also have to provide the following information on a Personal History Statement:

✔ Contact information (name, address, and telephone numbers)

✔ Driver's license information (driver's license number, state, expiration date, height, weight, eye color, hair color, scars, tattoos, or other distinguishing marks)

✔ Traffic record (list of all traffic citations you've received, except for parking tickets; list of all accidents you've been involved in as a driver; and list of all motor vehicles you own or operate)

- Military service (dates of service, branch of service, and type of discharge)

- Family members (names, addresses, and telephone numbers of immediate family members and other persons living in your home)

- Education (names of schools/colleges, locations, dates attended, areas of study, and type of degree)

- References (names, addresses, telephone numbers, years known, and occupations of four persons who are not relatives)

- Employment history (list of all employers back to 17 years of age; a brief summary of your duties in each position)

- Residences (list of all addresses, including city, state, and zip code, where you've lived during the last ten years, beginning with your present address; list must include names of landlords and neighbors)

- Financial obligations (list of name/location of institutions or banks, type of accounts, and average balance; list of credit cards and names of issuing institutions)

- Professional, fraternal, or civic association memberships (list of organizations, period of time you belonged, and the office you held)

In addition to conducting a background investigation, many departments also require candidates to take a *polygraph test,* also called a *lie detector test.* Some agencies use a lie detector test called a *computerized voice stress analyzer* (CVSA). The questions you'll be asked are often the same as those you answered on the Personal History Statement. Be honest and consistent and you'll do fine.

Taking the Law Enforcement Essay Exam

Because police officers complete so many written reports — they must write an incident report each time they respond to a scene — police departments consider good writing skills essential to good job performance. And many of the documents police officers write wind up in court as evidence, so good writing skills are a must. Some police departments require candidates to take the Law Enforcement Essay Exam in addition to the written police officer test. This exam measures your ability to write clearly and correctly.

The Law Enforcement Essay Exam isn't long. You respond to a single writing prompt that isn't about police work — it's personal. A prompt may ask you to recall a specific experience in your life and then reflect upon what you learned from that experience. You have 40 minutes to write your response to the prompt. You can read some sample prompts and a sample essay in Chapter 8.

Passing the Physical Ability Test (PAT)

If you pass the written police officer test, you then take the PAT, the physical ability test. Police work is often physically demanding. At the police academy, recruits are trained so that they're in good enough condition to chase and cuff suspects, quickly climb stairs and fences, scale walls, and defend themselves from criminals when necessary. The physical fitness training at the academy is *tough.* The PAT assesses whether you're in good enough shape to undergo this training. If you fail the PAT, you're eliminated from the screening process. To discover how to prepare for the PAT, read Chapter 10.

The type of exercises on the PAT depends on the police department. However, many police departments test candidates' ability to do the following in a given time period:

- 440-yard mobility/agility run
- 1.5-mile run
- Dummy drag
- Fence obstacles
- Modified squat thrust
- Push-ups
- Sit-ups
- Stair climb
- Trigger pull
- Vehicle exit
- Vertical jump

If you fail either the written exam, the PAT, or the background investigation, you'll be notified by mail. If your oral board interview has been scheduled, it will be canceled.

Making a Dynamite Impression during the Oral Board Interview

The oral board interview is similar to a job interview, but it's much more intense. Many candidates are eliminated based on their performance in this interview. During an oral board interview, you face a panel of interviewers who ask you personal questions and questions based on the background investigation that was conducted after you submitted a Personal History Statement. Who are these interviewers? Many are high-ranking police officers. Community members and a psychologist may also serve on the panel. In some departments, a representative from the human resources department may also be in the room as an observer.

The panel judges your appearance, professionalism, and honesty in response to questions such as, "Why do you want to be a police officer?" and "Why do you want to work for this police department?" Members of the panel try to discover whether you exercise good judgment and common sense during stressful situations. They try to determine whether you're mature, compassionate, and — above all — honest. Read about the types of questions asked during an oral board interview in Chapter 11.

Undergoing the Medical and Psychological Evaluations

If a police department asks you to undergo a medical and psychological evaluation, you're very close to landing a conditional job offer. These evaluations are simply another final test to ensure that you're healthy and psychologically stable so that you can perform well as a police officer. Turn to Chapter 12 to find out about these tests in detail.

Medical evaluation

Before a physician examines you, he or she will ask about your family's health history, measure your height and weight, and take your temperature and blood pressure. The physician will then perform these tests, among others:

- ✔ Vision
- ✔ Hearing
- ✔ Blood and urine
- ✔ Heart and lungs
- ✔ Muscular and skeletal

Psychological evaluation

Psychological evaluations are designed to test your mental stability and evaluate how you handle stress. During this evaluation, you're asked to respond to a list of questions. Don't lie or try to figure out how you "should" answer these questions. Be honest and consistent. The same questions may be asked several times but phrased differently. Be sure to respond the same way each time you're asked the same question. Some departments also require candidates to meet with a psychologist, who may ask about any problems revealed on the Personal History Statement or during your background investigation.

What if I Get Eliminated during the Screening Process?

You don't want to think about it, but it's possible you may be eliminated at some point during the screening process for a police officer job. Being eliminated doesn't mean you have to give up your dream of becoming a police officer, though. You can try again when another Notice of Examination (NOE) is posted on a police department's Web site. Most departments have a minimum waiting period before you can try again. Here are the typical waiting periods for the tests:

Written test (second attempt)	90-day wait
Written test (third attempt)	1-year wait
PAT (second and third attempts)	You may retest during the next scheduled test. You don't need to submit a new application.
PAT (fourth attempt)	1-year wait
Interview	1-year wait
Background/polygraph	1-year wait

Organization of municipal, county, and state departments

When you decide to become a cop, you probably picture yourself working for a municipal, or city, police department. This is certainly a good option, but law-enforcement agencies range from small, country police departments to large federal agencies. Note that some of these law-enforcement agencies have different hiring requirements than municipal police departments.

✔ **Municipal police officers:** Municipal, or local, police departments are generally divided geographically, with each department providing basic law enforcement for a city, town, or other municipality. In some cases, one local police force may serve several small communities.

These departments are staffed by uniformed police officers who patrol the area and respond to calls. These officers perform basic police duties, such as arresting criminal suspects, directing traffic, investigating crimes, and more. Officers in larger police departments are often assigned to carry out a specific duty.

Local police agencies typically organize their service areas into geographic districts. Officers are assigned to specific districts and are expected to familiarize themselves with their patrol area and be watchful for anything out of the ordinary. Some local police agencies serve unique jurisdictions that entail special enforcement responsibilities. These special police forces include college campus police, public school district police, and transportation system security. Local police officers may serve in specialized fields, such as fingerprint identification, chemical analysis, or police training. Others may also serve with special police units, such as canine units, motorcycle units, harbor patrol, or special weapons and tactics (SWAT).

✔ **County sheriffs and deputy sheriffs:** Police departments at the county level consist of sheriffs and deputy sheriffs. Most sheriffs are elected officials with job requirements comparable to those of a local police chief. Sheriff's departments are generally small, employing fewer than 50 officers. Deputy sheriffs share many of the same law enforcement responsibilities of officers in urban police departments. Some 911 call-response centers are staffed by county police departments.

✔ **State police officers:** Officers of state police agencies, often known as *state troopers* or *highway patrol officers,* have statewide jurisdiction for arresting criminals and enforcing traffic laws on state highways. These officers also have special functions at the scene of traffic accidents. In these situations, state police officers may direct traffic, provide first aid, summon additional emergency support, and write accident reports. State police agencies may also provide assistance for local police forces, particularly in rural areas and small towns, and provide executive protection for the governor and other dignitaries.

Chapter 2

Preparing Yourself for the Police Officer Tests

- -

In This Chapter

▶ Preparing for the POST and the NYC exam

▶ Understanding the different types of questions on the POST and NYC exam

▶ Getting ready for the physical, medical, and psychological tests and the oral interview

- -

To become a police officer, you have to take and pass several tests. The type of tests and what's on them depends on the police department — a police department can ask you about the weather if it chooses to do so, but don't worry, this is highly unlikely. Though the exams that most departments give aren't all the same, they're similar. Most police departments require police officer candidates to take and pass written, physical, medical, and psychological exams.

Why do you have to take so many tests to become a police officer when other jobs require only an interview or two? Police officers are often responsible for saving lives, so police departments want to hire only the best candidates. One way to find these candidates is to make them take different kinds of tests and then interview them.

In this chapter, we give you an overview of each type of police officer test. For a written exam, many police departments give either the National Police Officer Selection Test (POST) or the New York City (NYC) Police Department Police Officer Candidate Test. Read on to find out what to expect on both of these written tests.

Knowing What You're Up Against on the Written Test

To become a police officer, you have to take and pass a written test. Not all police departments give the same written test — that would be much too easy. The two most common written tests given to police officer candidates are the National Police Officer Selection Test (POST) and the New York City (NYC) Police Department Police Officer Candidate Test. Fortunately, these written tests and other written tests are fairly similar.

Most written police officer exams take one to three hours to complete. On test day, give yourself adequate time to take the exam. Avoid scheduling appointments or making other time commitments on this day so that you can give your full attention to the test. Dress comfortably but professionally, as high-ranking law-enforcement officials will likely monitor the test, and you don't want to make a bad impression. Arrive at the center well-rested, on time, and prepared to do your best. To get you through the entire test, have multiple pencils, pens, erasers, and, if allowed, calculators.

The structure of the National Police Officer Selection Test (POST)

Though not all police departments give the same written test, many give the National Police Officer Selection Test, which is commonly called the POST. The POST is different from most other written police officer tests because it's divided into sections, and each section has a specific number of questions and a time limit.

Your answers on the POST are scanned and scored by a computer. When you mark your answers on the answer sheet, blacken only one oval for each question. If you mark two ovals, the computer scores your answer as incorrect, even if one of the ovals is the correct answer.

Sections of the POST

The POST has four sections: Mathematics, Reading Comprehension, Grammar, and Incident Report Writing. Although many questions include details about scenarios that many police officers encounter every day, you don't need knowledge of police proceedings to answer them. As a candidate, you're not expected to know exactly how a police officer should act in every situation — that's what the academy is for, after all. The POST gives you hypothetical situations, and you use the information in these situations to answer the questions. Table 2-1 lays out the sections of the POST, along with the number of questions in each section and how long you have to complete it.

Table 2-1	POST Test Questions and Time Limits		
Section	*Test*	*Number of Items*	*Time Allowance*
1	Mathematics	20	20 minutes
2	Reading Comprehension	25	25 minutes
3	Grammar	20	15 minutes
4	Incident Report Writing	10	15 minutes

Types of questions on the POST

Three types of questions are on the POST:

- ✔ Multiple-choice questions
- ✔ True-and-false questions
- ✔ Short-answer questions

Expect to answer multiple-choice questions in the Mathematics, Reading Comprehension, and Grammar sections of this test. The questions in the Mathematics section require you to solve problems using basic math — addition, subtraction, multiplication, and division. Then you fill in the oval for the answer choice (A, B, C, D, or E) with the correct answer. To brush up on your arithmetic, flip to Chapter 3.

You're not penalized for guessing on the POST. If you don't know the answer to a question, eliminate answer choices that you know are incorrect and make a good guess based on what remains.

To answer the multiple-choice questions in the Reading Comprehension section, you read a paragraph or a group of paragraphs. This passage contains all the information you need to answer the questions. Though these reading passages are about police duty, you don't need to know anything about law enforcement to answer them. For more information about reading-comprehension questions on the written police officer test, turn to Chapter 4.

Some questions in the Reading Comprehension section of the POST are true/false. Again, all the information you need to determine whether a statement is true or false is in the passage before the question. Some of these questions contain a blank incident report and an incident description, such as a complaint filed by the owner of a business that has been burglarized. You indicate whether a statement about this description and report is true or false.

The multiple-choice questions in the Grammar section are a bit different. For some of these questions, you choose the answer choice that best fills in a blank in the sentence. This type of question has two or three answer choices — A and B, or A, B, and C. Other questions in the Grammar section ask you to choose the word that's misspelled. These questions have five answer options (A, B, C, D, and E). Chapter 5 has more about grammar questions.

Section IV of the POST is the Incident Report Writing section. The questions in this section are open-ended, which means that you write out your answers in your answer booklet. You must answer in a complete, grammatically correct sentence that's free from spelling errors. You may be asked simple questions like, "What is the name of the suspect?" and, "What is the location of the incident?" Finding the answer is easy — it's right in front of you in the incident report. Organizing that answer into a sentence that gets you the maximum amount of points on the exam is the challenging part. To find out more about incident reports, turn to Chapter 7.

Tips for the POST

Here are some simple tips to help you prepare for the POST:

- ✔ Buy textbooks or get a tutor if you're not confident about your reading, writing, or math skills.
- ✔ Get at least eight hours of sleep the night before the test.
- ✔ Don't wait until the night before your exam to start studying.
- ✔ Read every question thoroughly, and be sure you understand what it's asking you before you select your answer.
- ✔ Answer every question on the test — you don't lose points for wrong answers!

The structure of the New York City (NYC) Police Department Police Officer Candidate Test

Unlike the POST, the NYC exam isn't divided into specific sections with a time limit on each section. With the exception of the memory questions, which appear in the beginning of the test, questions designed to test various skills and abilities are integrated throughout the test.

You take the NYC exam using a computer at the testing center. Cellphones, calculators, and other electronic devices aren't allowed in the center. You need to answer at least 70 percent of the questions on this exam correctly to receive a passing score.

Types of questions on the NYC exam

The NYC exam includes many different types of questions designed to test various abilities that police officers must have to succeed on the job. All questions on the NYC exam are multiple-choice, with four answer options (A, B, C, and D). Expect to see the following types of questions on this test:

- **Observation and memory:** Police officers must remember details, such as what a suspect looks like and what he or she was wearing. To test your observation and memory skills on the NYC exam, you're asked to look at a picture and study its details. You have ten minutes to memorize as much as you can about the picture. Then the picture is sealed tightly in your test booklet, and you have to answer 10 to 20 questions about it based only on what you can recall from memory. To practice answering observation and memory questions, turn to Chapter 6.

- **Written comprehension:** These questions test your ability to understand written sentences and paragraphs. You read a long passage about a subject and then answer questions about specific details from that passage. Chapter 4 can help you brush up on your written-comprehension skills.

- **Written expression:** These questions give you information about an incident that a police officer has responded to. This information may indicate the place and time of an accident, the vehicle involved, the driver, and the damage incurred during the accident. You read this information and choose the answer option that expresses the information in a clear, accurate, and complete manner. Read Chapter 7 for more on these types of questions.

- **Information ordering:** These questions test your ability to follow rules based on the order in which they're presented. You read a list describing the steps required to complete a task — such as how to apprehend a suspect — and then you read a scenario in which an officer must follow these steps. The questions ask you what the officer should do *before, after, first, next,* or *last.* Chapter 6 covers information-ordering questions.

- **Inductive reasoning:** These questions present you with details and ask you to make an inference or a generalization about them. You must think about how and why these details fit together to form a conclusion. We look at these questions in more detail in Chapter 4.

- **Deductive reasoning:** Deductive-reasoning questions test your ability to apply general rules and procedures to specific scenarios. Deductive reasoning is the opposite of inductive reasoning. Chapter 4 examines deductive-reasoning questions.

- **Visualization:** These questions ask you to envision what a diagram, illustration, or pattern looks like from a different perspective. For example, you may look at a diagram of a row of buildings and answer a question about the view from the back of the buildings. Turn to Chapter 6 to practice answering these types of questions.

- **Problem-sensitivity:** Police officers must often determine whether something is likely to go wrong. They must be able to identify problems, such as when to place a barricade on a roadway to warn motorists of danger. Problem-sensitivity questions typically include a sentence or two stating a procedure or protocol that officers normally follow during a specific event. To answer these questions, you need to decide what, if anything, is likely to go wrong in that particular situation and how an officer should respond. Chapter 6 guides you through problem-sensitivity questions.

- **Spatial orientation:** Police officers must have a good sense of direction and be able to follow directions. Spatial-orientation questions on the NYC exam may ask you to visualize turning north on a street, taking a right, and then traveling south. Then they ask you in which direction you're now traveling. You can brush up on spatial-orientation skills in Chapter 6.

Tips for the NYC exam

Here are some tips for preparing for the NYC exam:

- ✔ Get at least eight hours of sleep the night before the test.

- ✔ Eat a full meal before taking the exam, being careful not to overeat.

- ✔ Listen carefully to the directions provided by the person proctoring the test. The proctor may make announcements regarding how much time you have left to complete the exam.

- ✔ Read every question thoroughly, and be sure you understand what it's asking you before you select your answer.

- ✔ If you're unsure of a question, mark it and then go back to it later.

- ✔ Keep a positive attitude.

Getting the Lowdown on the Other Police Officer Tests

In addition to the written exam, most police officer candidates are required to complete physical, psychological, and medical tests and then an oral interview. Any one of these tests has the potential to disqualify you from a career as a police officer, but knowing what to expect can help you impress your judges and pass your exams.

Acing the physical ability test (PAT)

The physical ability test (PAT) is demanding and is designed to reveal whether you're physically fit enough to successfully complete the physical training at the police academy. The physical exam doesn't necessarily test your ability to perform specific police tactics; rather, it helps departments determine whether you have the potential to develop the range of motion, flexibility, strength, and endurance that police officers need to be successful in the field.

Although the main purpose of the PAT is to assess your physical abilities, the PAT also tests your ability to make smart and quick decisions and to keep your cool during stressful situations. Expect to do sit-ups and push-ups, exit a vehicle, climb stairs, fence obstacles, and drag a dummy. Some departments require you to complete an agility course, in which you run from station to station performing different exercises such as climbing stairs. For more information about the PAT, refer to Chapter 10.

Before you go to the testing location, find out as much as you can about the PAT you're about to take. Ask what events are on the test and whether each event has a time limit. Don't be afraid to ask questions; the more you know, the more you can prepare and the better you'll perform on test day. Also, wear appropriate clothing. Most agencies require you to wear physical training clothing. Be sure to choose conservative clothing without law-enforcement logos or offensive law-enforcement slogans or cartoons.

Prepping for the oral interview

Like the physical test, the oral interview requires you to think on your feet — but you "perform" using words and phrases instead of sit-ups and hundred-yard dashes.

Most police departments require you to face a hiring board that includes veteran police officers and others such as community leaders and representatives from the city council or county human resources department. The interviewers have a copy of your résumé or application and rating sheets to grade your performance. As you answer their questions, they record their thoughts on the rating sheets and later translate those thoughts into points.

Expect to be asked questions about your education, interpersonal relations, and work history. The interviewers ask you questions that require you to show reasoning, decision-making, and problem-solving skills. Be prepared for questions such as, "Why do you want to be a police officer?" and, "Do you like to take risks?" Turn to Chapter 11 for more of a preview of the types of questions you may be asked.

The interviewers rate you on your behavior during the interview, so keep your cool. Answer the questions concisely, but don't rush. If you appear confused or frustrated, they may award you a low grade. Be honest, friendly, and patient.

Preparing for the psychological evaluation

The psychological exam (covered in Chapter 12) is designed to test whether candidates can mentally handle the stress and pressure that come with being a police officer. The department uses the psychological evaluation to be sure that it doesn't hand a loaded gun to anyone who may be unstable.

The psychological exam is similar to the medical exam (covered in the next section) in the sense that you can't study for it. Though it's possible to gather information about the types of questions on this test, be careful that your answers don't sound rehearsed.

The psychological exam, like the other exams, varies from one department to the next, but many departments give the exam in two parts. The first is a questionnaire designed to bring to light underlying psychiatric problems that you may not be aware of or that you may not want to talk about with a therapist or psychologist. The questionnaire is long and may seem repetitive, but departments use it to identify your personality traits and how you respond to conflict and stress.

Don't try to figure out what the questionnaire on the psychological exam is "really" asking you. Just read the questions, fill in your honest answers, and move on. Take your time, tell the truth, and complete the entire exam.

After your questionnaire has been reviewed, you move on to the second part of the evaluation: a meeting with a psychologist who interviews you and asks you about your responses on the questionnaire. The psychologist will most likely explain the results of the exam and discuss any conclusions about your personality, coping methods, and stress level. The psychologist may ask you about your relationships with your friends and family or your childhood. Regardless of the topic, always be honest and open with the psychologist. If the psychologist feels as though you're hiding something or lying, you may receive a poor grade on this exam.

Getting ready for the medical exam

After the Americans with Disabilities Act (ADA) was passed, it became illegal for employers to request medical and psychological exams without first offering a position to the candidate on conditional grounds. So you'll most likely receive a job offer before you need to prep for the medical exam — pass this last test and you're on your way to the police academy!

You may wonder why you have to take a medical exam when you've already passed a physical exam. Some health conditions can hinder your ability to save lives. A physician looks for signs of these conditions during the medical exam.

The medical exam, like the psychological evaluation, is one of the few exams that don't require studying. Though you can make smart lifestyle choices, eat right, and exercise daily, you can't make a predetermined or hereditary condition go away. Don't try to hide a medical condition, no matter how insignificant it may seem to you. Be completely honest with the doctor during your medical exam — your life isn't the only one depending on your good health.

During the medical exam, the physician tests your range of motion, reflexes, spine curvature, and muscle resistance. The doctor will also examine your ears, nose, and throat and check your vision, your ability to see colors, and your hearing. The physician may request that you complete additional tests for diabetes and heart and lung disease. To find out more about the medical evaluation, read Chapter 12.

Most departments require a drug test prior to the medical examination. If traces of prescription drugs show up in your system, you'll be asked which medications you're taking and why. If illegal drugs are detected in your system, your conditional offer of employment will be revoked. Police officers must always be drug-free.

Part II

Breaking Down the National Police Officer Selection Test (POST) and the NYC Test

The 5th Wave   By Rich Tennant

In this part . . .

As part of the police officer screening process, you have to take and pass a written test. Not all police departments give the same written test, but fortunately, most police departments require candidates to take a written test called the National Police Officer Selection Test (POST) or a civil service test such as the one given in New York City.

In this part, we break down the types of questions you'll see on each of these tests. We also supply plenty of practice exercises to prepare you for the real thing. We even explain an additional test some police departments give called the Law Enforcement Essay Exam.

Chapter 3

Solving Basic Math Questions on the POST

In This Chapter

▶ Surveying different types of math sample questions

▶ Working on problems involving percentages and averages

▶ Narrowing down your answer choices

▶ Practicing math problems

Suppose you've just returned to the station after responding to a reported burglary at a local business. At the scene of the crime, the company president tells you that eight computers, valued at approximately $500 each, are missing. Two phones, valued at about $20 each, and four printers, valued at $320 total, were also taken. As you make your way around the office, one of the employees claims that his MP3 player was taken from his desk. He remembers paying $120 for it a few months ago. Before leaving the scene, the president tells you that she found one of the stolen computers behind the building but also noticed that a stack of books is missing from her office. She estimates the value of the missing books as $60.

At the station, you sit at your desk and pull out your notes. You have to write an incident report about what happened. You have to indicate where the crime occurred, who was involved, and what was stolen. You have to figure out the total value of all the missing items, but it isn't easy. According to your notes, items originally reported stolen were discovered, and items first thought to be in the office were later determined missing. You need to be able to perform basic mathematical operations to complete the incident report. Even if you use a calculator, you need to know when to add, subtract, multiply, and divide.

Police officers work with numbers every day to determine the total value of stolen goods and the total number of miles traveled. You must be confident in your basic math skills to be able to do this.

The National Police Officer Selection Test (POST) and some other written police officer exams include questions that require you to use basic math operations. (The POST has 20 math questions, while the NYC test has only a few, very basic math problems.) You have 20 minutes to answer these questions. You can't use a calculator, but you can use scratch paper to figure out your answers. Don't be intimidated by these questions, even if you haven't taken a math course in years. In this chapter, we show you how to recognize, solve, and answer these types of questions correctly.

Ditching your calculator

When taking the POST and some other police exams, you won't be allowed to use a calculator to figure out the answers to the math problems. Instead, you must use a piece of scrap paper and work the answers out by hand. Don't be intimidated by the thought of doing math problems without a calculator. Maybe you're used to using a calculator to find out how much you should tip the server at your favorite restaurant or to divide the cable bill with your roommate, but this doesn't mean you can't find the correct answers without one.

Instead of relying on your calculator to find the answers to everyday problems, practice using only some scrap paper and your brain power. While you're at the grocery store, add together the items in your order before you check out — round up or down if your order is large and see how close you come to figuring out your actual bill. When you have a project to complete, add together the amount of time each part of the project will take to find the total amount of time you'll spend on it. Find reasons to practice math problems every day, and don't cheat yourself by using a calculator — stick to scrap paper and your mind.

What Do Math Questions Look Like?

If you take the POST or a similar test, you have to answer many math questions. Don't worry — these questions don't require you to memorize or use complex math formulas. They're fairly simple and based on real-life scenarios that police officers encounter on the job. All the information you need to answer these questions appears in the sentence or passage that goes with the question. Math questions on the POST are multiple choice.

Addition questions

To answer some questions on the POST, you need to use simple addition. These questions often ask for the *total* number of hours, prices, miles, and so on. To solve these problems, you have to combine all appropriate numbers.

The *sum* (answer) of an addition problem should always be greater than the *addends* (numbers added together) in the equation. Suppose you're asked to find how many prized goldfish were stolen from a pet store. You're told that 2 goldfish were stolen from one tank and 3 were stolen from another tank. You should automatically eliminate any answer choices that involve the numbers 3, 2, and 1. The sum of the equation 2 + 3 is 5. The number 5 is clearly greater than 2 or 3.

Addition questions on the POST normally appear as a short passage, or paragraph, containing information to help you solve the problem. The passage includes numbers and keywords to signal that addition is the correct operation to use when answering the question. These keywords include *sum, more, greater, total,* and *all together.*

On the POST, you may see a question like this:

In preparing a report on a burglary in a doctor's office, Sergeant Cruz listed the following stolen items and their value:	
Computer	$800
Paper shredder	$150
Digital camera	$400

What is the total value of the stolen goods?

(A) $550

(B) $950

(C) $1,250

(D) $1,350

(E) $1,450

To find the total value of the stolen goods, add the value of the computer, the paper shredder, and the digital camera: $800 + $150 + $400 = $1,350. Choice (D) is correct.

That wasn't so bad, was it? Remember that you need only basic math skills to pass this test — the kind of math skills you learned in elementary school.

Now try some more sample questions based on the following information:

> Having responded to a burglary at a local jewelry store, Sergeant Lombardo begins completing an incident report. He lists the following stolen items and their value:
>
> | | |
> |---|---|
> | Necklace | $350 |
> | Earrings | $85 |
> | Charm bracelet | $290 |
> | Diamond ring | $760 |

What is the total value of all the stolen goods?

(A) $1,135

(B) $1,385

(C) $1,485

(D) $1,505

(E) $1,585

The correct answer is Choice (C). You determine the total value of the items stolen from the jewelry store by adding the values of each piece of jewelry: $350 + $85 + $290 + $760 = $1,485.

What is the total value of all the stolen goods *except* for the charm bracelet?

(A) $1,135

(B) $1,195

(C) $1,295

(D) $1,485

(E) $1,775

The correct answer is Choice (B). You determine the total value of the items stolen from the jewelry store with the exception of the charm bracelet by adding the value of each piece of jewelry without the value of the charm bracelet: $350 + $85 + $760 = $1,195. You can also use subtraction to solve this problem. Deduct the charm bracelet's value from the total value of the stolen goods: $1,485 − $290 = $1,195.

Be on the lookout for words that may complicate your understanding of the task. For example, the preceding sample question asks you to find a total, but it includes the word *except*. If you miss this word, you'll answer the question incorrectly. Luckily, on the test the word *except* normally appears in capital letters and is difficult to overlook.

Subtraction questions

Subtraction questions on the POST look similar to addition questions, but instead of *combining* numbers to determine a total, you're asked to take numbers *away* from a total.

Just as in addition problems, use common sense when solving a subtraction problem. Your *difference* (the answer to a subtraction problem) shouldn't be greater than your *minuend*, or largest number. For instance, if 11 fish are stolen from a pet store but the owner finds the 6 fish that were taken from one of the tanks, then the number of fish that are now missing shouldn't be any greater than 11. You can now eliminate all answer choices that are larger than your largest number.

Specific words used in math questions alert you to use subtraction to find the answers. Watch for these words on the POST: *difference, less, fewer, remain,* and *left over.*

On the POST, a subtraction question looks like this:

Each week, Officer Mills drives his police cruiser approximately 200 miles, which is about 40 miles a day. This week, he spent an entire day in the station and didn't have to drive at all. What is the total number of miles Officer Mills drove this week?

(A) 120

(B) 140

(C) 160

(D) 200

(E) 240

Because Officer Mills spent an entire day in the police station and didn't drive at all, you have to subtract the miles he would have driven that day from the number of miles he typically drives in one week: 200 miles – 40 miles = 160 miles. This week, Officer Mills drove 160 miles, or Choice (C).

Did you notice that this sample question used the word *total?* As you can see, addition questions aren't the only questions that ask you to find the total miles, value, or hours. Pay close attention to the passage's other details to answer this type of question correctly.

Now, try a few more subtraction questions. Remember to read the passages carefully to figure out what the question is really asking.

Officer Greene patrols the park 30 times a week, which is about 6 times a shift for 5 shifts. This week, however, he took a vacation day. How many times did he patrol the park this week?

(A) 20

(B) 24

(C) 30

(D) 36

(E) 42

Choice (B) is correct. Because Officer Greene took off one day this week, and he normally patrols the park 6 times a day, subtract 6 patrols from his total number of daily patrols: 30 – 6 = 24. This week, he patrolled the park 24 times.

The next two questions are based on the following information.

> Having responded to a burglary in a local library, Officer Washington lists the following stolen items and their value:
>
> | | |
> |---|---|
> | 2 hardcover books | $20 each |
> | 3 paperback books | $10 each |
> | 4 audio books | $60 each |
> | 1 laptop computer | $450 |
> | Total | $760 |

What is the total value of the stolen items *except* for the computer?

(A) $110

(B) $310

(C) $450

(D) $760

(E) $1,210

To solve this problem using simple subtraction, subtract the computer's value from the total value of all the stolen items: $760 – $450 = $310. The value of the stolen items except for the computer is $310, Choice (B).

While tidying up, the librarian finds that the burglar stole only 2 audio books, not 4. What is the new total value of the items stolen from the library?

(A) $540

(B) $580

(C) $640

(D) $700

(E) $820

The easiest way to solve this problem is to break it down into two equations. First, figure out what the total would be if the librarian only discovered one audio book. Each audio book is $60, so subtract the audio book's cost from the original total: $760 – $60 = $700. Because the librarian found 2 books, subtract the cost of another audio book from the new total: $700 – $60 = $640. The new total value of the items stolen from the library is $640. Choice (C) is correct.

Multiplication questions

Multiplication questions that appear on the POST and similar written police officer exams may look like addition questions at first. As you reread the passages and questions and perhaps even attempt to solve a few using addition, you may realize that it would be easier and quicker to use multiplication.

When using multiplication, don't forget two very easy rules:

✔ Any number multiplied by 0 always equals 0. Example: $2 \times 0 = 0$

✔ Any number multiplied by 1 always equals itself. Example: $4 \times 1 = 4$

Just as with addition and subtraction questions, keywords may help you decide to use multiplication to find an answer. Remember, the answer to a multiplication equation is called the *product,* and the numbers you're multiplying are called *factors.* Look for the words *of, product,* and *times* to signal that you may need to use multiplication.

On the POST, a multiplication question looks like this:

Officer McDonald completes 7 incident reports each week. If she takes two weeks of vacation each summer, how many incident reports does she complete in one year?

(A) 84

(B) 210

(C) 336

(D) 350

(E) 364

To answer this question, multiply the number of weeks Officer McDonald works each year by the number of incident reports she writes each week. Because she takes two weeks of vacation in the summer, she works a total of 50 weeks: $50 \times 7 = 350$ reports. Choice (D) is correct. Officer McDonald completes 350 incident reports each year.

You may need to rely on what you already know to answer some math problems. For example, a question on the POST may not tell you that there are 52 weeks in a year, 7 days in a week, or 24 hours in a day. This is common knowledge.

The next two questions are based on the following information.

In preparing a report on a burglary in an apartment, Officer Walker lists the following stolen items and their value:

2 MP3 players	$120 each
1 laptop computer	$500
6 DVDs	$20 each
3 cellphones	$80 each

What is the total value of the stolen DVDs?

(A) $60

(B) $120

(C) $240

(D) $300

(E) $320

To answer this question, multiply the number of DVDs stolen by the value of each DVD: $6 \times \$20 = \$120$. The total value of the stolen DVDs is $120. Choice (B) is correct.

What is the total value of the stolen computer and the cellphones?

(A) $340

(B) $420

(C) $580

(D) $660

(E) $740

To solve this problem, you need to use both addition and multiplication. First, you have to figure out the cost of the stolen cellphones. Because 3 phones were stolen, each valued at $80, multiply these two numbers: $80 × 3 = $240. The value of the stolen cellphones is $240. Next, add the total value of the cellphones to the computer's value: $240 + $500 = $740. The total value of the stolen cellphones and laptop computer is $740. Choice (E) is correct.

During one day, Officer Robinson patrolled approximately 9 miles on foot. If he patrolled the same route 8 more days in the next two weeks, how many miles total did he patrol?

(A) 17

(B) 72

(C) 81

(D) 90

(E) 107

You can solve this problem easily using simple math, but you have to be careful. It may seem like this question is asking you to multiply 8 days by 9 miles, but because it asks for the *total* miles, you have to include the first day's travel. So, 8 days plus the first day is 9 days, and 9 days × 9 miles = 81 miles. Choice (C) is correct. Officer Robinson patrolled approximately 81 total miles in two weeks.

Division questions

Expect to see a few division questions on the POST and on similar written police officer tests. Division questions typically provide you with a large number and ask you to break it down in various ways. These questions may appear in reference to groups of people, values of stolen goods, or even miles driven in a police cruiser.

When you see the word *each* in a division problem, you know you're required to come up with a number that applies to every member of the whole group. Using our earlier example, if the pet shop owner tells you that the total value of the missing goldfish is $165, and 11 goldfish valued at the same price were stolen, you'd have to figure out how much *each* gold-fish costs: $165 ÷ 11 goldfish = $15. Every stolen goldfish in the group is worth $15.

Division may be the most complicated mathematical operation of the four we've discussed so far. For many people, learning division in school was confusing. The math questions on the POST generally don't require uneven division, meaning you don't have remainders or decimals in your division problems. As you may have noticed in many of the passages in this chapter, many of the values given are approximates or estimates. This makes it easier to add, subtract, multiply, and especially divide.

When you think you're dealing with a division question on the POST, look for the word *per*. This word may be substituted for *each* and typically appears in phrases such as "per hour," "per gallon," or "per teaspoon."

A division question on the POST looks like this:

Last year, Officer Hernandez made 96 arrests. She made the same number of arrests each month. How many arrests did she make each month?

(A) 2

(B) 4

(C) 8

(D) 16

(E) 24

Choice (C) is correct. You should already know that there are 12 months in a year. If Officer Hernandez made 96 arrests last year, arresting the same number of people each month, then you simply divide 96 arrests by 12 months: $96 \div 12 = 8$. She made 8 arrests per month.

You're not allowed to use a calculator on the math section of the POST, but you can use scrap paper. Having scrap paper comes in handy when you're dividing numbers, especially when you're using long division. Take your time, check your math, and ask for more paper if you need it.

In one week, Sergeant Turner drove his police cruiser 420 miles. If he drove the same route for 5 days, how many miles did he travel per day?

(A) 84

(B) 105

(C) 210

(D) 380

(E) 425

Use simple division to answer this question. Sergeant Turner drove 420 miles this week and worked 5 shifts, so those are the numbers you need to work with: 420 miles $\div$ 5 = 84 miles. Sergeant Turner drove 84 miles each day. Choice (A) is correct.

Burglars broke into an electronics store and left with 25 digital readers with a total retail value of $4,950. What is the value of each digital reader?

(A) $110

(B) $125

(C) $198

(D) $990

(E) $1,238

Don't let a large number like 4,950 intimidate you. If you use long division, it won't take you much time to solve the equation. The passage gives you all the numbers you need: $4,950 and 25. So, $4,950 $\div$ 25 = $198. Each digital reader has a value of $198, so Choice (C) is correct.

In the past two weeks, Officer Amos patrolled the local park 20 times. If he typically works 5 shifts each week and visited the park an equal number of times during each shift, how many times did he patrol the park each day?

(A) 1

(B) 2

(C) 4

(D) 5

(E) 10

To solve this problem, you have to perform two simple division equations. First, you need to find out how many times Officer Amos visited the park in one week. Divide 20 patrols by 2 weeks: 20 ÷ 2 = 10. Now, you know that Officer Amos visited the park 10 times each *week*. The next step is to find out how many times per *day* he patrolled the park. You find this by dividing the number of times he visited each week by the number of shifts he works each week: 10 ÷ 5 = 2. He patrolled the park 2 times a day for the past two weeks. Choice (B) is correct.

Determining Percentages

Although math questions involving percentages are a bit more complicated than the questions in this chapter so far, they're not really all that difficult. To solve a math question asking you to find a percentage of something, you need only the basic skills you've been reviewing, especially multiplication and division.

What is a percent?

Percents are fractions that always have a denominator of 100. The word *percent* is defined as "per 100 parts." If you think about it, the word *century* means 100 years because *cent* means *100*. Even a quick glance at the word *percent* may lead you to believe that it has to involve something with the number 100.

Percents may appear on the POST and other tests in three different ways:

- As a percent: 30%
- As a fraction: $\frac{30}{100}$
- As a decimal: 0.30

Fractions have numerators and denominators. The *numerator* is the number on the top of the fraction, and the *denominator* is the number on the bottom of the fraction. In the fraction ½, the number 1 is the numerator and the number 2 is the denominator.

How to find a percentage

Finding percentages isn't difficult, but you have to be comfortable working with fractions before you can do this. Remember that a percent is a fraction with a denominator of 100.

Suppose you're asked to find 10% of 50. One way to find the answer to this question is to cross-multiply. Cross-multiplication involves multiplying two fractions. One fraction is always your percentage, or a number over 100. Use x to represent whichever number you need to find — in other words, the number you don't know.

You already know that 10 is $\frac{10}{100}$. This is your first fraction. The other is $\frac{x}{50}$. You then need to solve for x.

Start with your equation: $\frac{10}{100} = \frac{x}{50}$.

Next, multiply diagonally: $10 \times 50 = 500$ and $100 \times x = 100x$; so, $500 = 100x$.

Then, divide by 100 to find x: $\frac{100x}{100} = \frac{500}{100}$.

Finally, $x = 5$.

So, 10% of 50 is 5.

The part of a percentage you need to find to answer a math question determines which technique you use to solve the problem. Sometimes it's easier to use decimals and multiplication, and other times it's easier to use fractions and cross-multiplication. Occasionally, you also need to add and subtract.

You can use decimals to find 10% of 50. You already know that 10% is 0.10. All you have to do is multiply 50 by 0.10 to find your answer: $50 \times 0.10 = 5$.

Now, let's try a question similar to one you may see on the POST.

During a recent drug bust, Officer Martin logged 40 baggies of drugs. At the lab, it was discovered that only 25% of the baggies were filled with a pure substance. How many baggies were filled with pure drugs?

(A) 5

(B) 10

(C) 15

(D) 20

(E) 30

You can use either cross-multiplication or multiplication of decimals to find this answer. You can view 25% as 0.25 or $\frac{25}{100}$. If you use cross-multiplication, you set up your equation and multiply diagonally. Then, you divide by 100 to find x. Your work should look like this:

$$\frac{25}{100} = \frac{x}{40}$$
$$\frac{100x}{100} = \frac{1000}{100}$$
$$x = 10$$

If you want to find the answer using decimals, you multiply the total number of baggies by 25%: $40 \times 0.25 = 10$. Whether you cross-multiply or multiply decimals, if you choose Choice (B), you're correct.

Determining the answers to math questions that involve fractions is easiest when you do the process on paper. Because you can't use a calculator on the POST and you may not be able to do all the necessary steps in your head, use your scrap paper. Erase or scratch out mistakes, use the front and back, and draw boxes and images. Do whatever you need to do to answer the question.

Now, let's try a few more math problems involving percents. Solve them using whichever method is most comfortable for you.

Yesterday, Sergeant Gibson arrested 8 gang members. A total of 32 known members are in this particular gang. What percentage of the gang did Sergeant Gibson arrest?

(A) 10%

(B) 15%

(C) 20%

(D) 25%

(E) 40%

This question asks you to find the percentage; therefore, you know that you're looking for the numerator in the fraction. You already know that the denominator is 100 and that Sergeant Gibson has arrested 8 of the 32 known gang members. If you cross-multiplied to find the percentage, your work would look like this:

$$\frac{x}{100} = \frac{8}{32}$$
$$\frac{32x}{32} = \frac{800}{32}$$
$$x = 25$$

You can also solve this problem by dividing 8 by 32: $8 \div 32 = 0.25$. You know that 0.25 is 25%. Choice (D) is correct.

Normally, 75% of the police officers in your department put in overtime each week. If there are 150 officers in your department who work overtime, how many members are in the department in all?

(A) 150

(B) 175

(C) 200

(D) 225

(E) 250

Choice (C) is correct. This question asks you to find the total number of police officers that work for your department. It tells you that 75% of the officers is equal to 150 officers. Cross-multiplication is the easiest and quickest way to find this answer. Your work should look like this:

$$\frac{75}{100} = \frac{150}{x}$$
$$\frac{15,000}{75} = \frac{75x}{75}$$
$$200 = x$$

If one-quarter of the tickets Officer Lewis writes each day are for parking violations and she typically writes 60 tickets per day, how many tickets does she write for violations other than parking?

(A) 15

(B) 20

(C) 30

(D) 45

(E) 60

To find the answer to this question, you need to work with 75%, not 25%. The question asks you to find the number of tickets Officer Lewis writes that are *not* for parking violations. If 25% of them *are* for parking violations, then 75% of them are *not* for parking violations. To find how many tickets Officer Lewis writes that are not for parking violations, cross-multiply:

$$\frac{75}{100} = \frac{x}{60}$$
$$\frac{100x}{100} = \frac{4500}{100}$$
$$x = 45$$

You can also use decimals to find this answer: $60 \times 0.75 = 45$. Choice (D) is correct.

Finding Averages

Police officers often deal with averages. They may be asked to determine the average number of arrests they make each month, the average number of miles they drive a police motorcycle each week, or the average number of calls they respond to each month. Because averages are so commonplace, some math questions on the POST ask you to find averages.

What is an average?

An *average* is the sum of a group of values divided by the number of values. For example, to find the average of 2, 4, 6, and 8, add together the values: $2 + 4 + 6 + 8 = 20$. Then, divide by the number of values: $20 \div 4 = 5$. The average of those numbers is 5.

Averages may be whole numbers or may have a remainder, which may be a decimal or a fraction. Sometimes, questions on written police officer exams ask you to estimate or round to the nearest value, so you don't have to worry about remainders.

How to find an average

Calculating an average isn't difficult. To find an average, add all values and then divide by the number of values you added. For example, to find the average of 3, 4, and 5, you add those numbers and divide by 3. So, $3 + 4 + 5 = 12$, and $12 \div 3 = 4$. The average of 3, 4, and 5 is 4.

Think back to the pet store that was robbed. Recall that 6 fish were stolen from one tank and 5 were stolen from another. The average number of fish stolen from a single tank was 5.5, because $6 + 5 = 11$ and $11 \div 2 = 5.5$, or 5½. An average of 5½ fish were taken from each tank in the pet store.

You know that you have to determine an average when you see the word *average* in the question. As soon as you see the word *average,* be ready to add and divide!

A typical question on the POST dealing with averages looks like this:

The number of incident reports that Officer Davis wrote each week for the past two months was 8, 9, 7, 6, 11, 8, 5, and 8. What is the average number of incident reports he wrote each week?

(A) 6

(B) 7

(C) 7¾

(D) 8½

(E) 10

To answer this question, add the numbers of incident reports provided and then divide by that many: 8 + 9 + 7 + 6 + 11 + 8 + 5 + 8 = 62. Because you added 8 numbers, you then divide 62 by 8: 62 ÷ 8 = 7.75. Because 0.75 is ¾, Choice (C) is correct.

Try not to become distracted by other numbers in the questions. In this sample question, you were told that these numbers were collected over a two-month period, but you didn't need to involve the number 2 in any of the math you used. After you read the question, try going back to the passage to see which numbers you need to find the right answer and which numbers you can disregard. Put a line through those that you don't need.

Try a few more math questions asking you to find an average.

Officer Polanski had 6 overnight protective detail shifts over the past two weeks. They lasted 6 hours, 8 hours, 5 hours, 7 hours, 10 hours, and 8 hours. What is the average length of time she spent working protective detail each night? Round to the nearest whole number.

(A) 4

(B) 5

(C) 6

(D) 7

(E) 8

To find the answer to this math question, just add and divide. You know how many hours Officer Polanski worked each night and how many nights she worked. Begin by adding: 6 + 8 + 5 + 7 + 10 + 8 = 44. Then divide: 44 ÷ 6 = 7.333. Because .333 is not above .5, the nearest whole number is 7, not 8. So each protective detail shift lasted approximately 7 hours. Choice (D) is correct.

After a class of recruit officers complete their first exam, their professor tells them that the females averaged a score of 90 and the males averaged a score of 85. Fifteen females and 25 males are in the class. What is the average score of the entire class?

(A) 85.33

(B) 86

(C) 86.88

(D) 87

(E) 87.50

This question requires either a long string of addition, or some multiplication. If you choose to multiply, you multiply the number of female students by their average score and the number of male students by their average score. So, 90 × 15 = 1,350 and 85 × 25 = 2,125. Next, you have to add the scores of the females and males: 1,350 + 2,125 = 3,475. (If you had added fifteen 90s and twenty-five 85s, this would be the total you'd get.) Now, divide the total scores of the tests by the total number of students who took the test: 3,475 ÷ 40 = 86.875. Because you weren't asked to round to the nearest whole number, your answer wouldn't be Choice (D). Instead, the answer closest to 86.875 is Choice (C).

During a five-day period, Officer Barrett drove his patrol motorcycle 425 miles. If he drove 75 miles in one day, how many miles did he average on each of the other days? Round to the nearest whole number.

(A) 84

(B) 85

(C) 86

(D) 87

(E) 88

You have to be careful with this question and think about what it's actually asking you to find. You don't want to find the average miles Officer Barrett drove every day during the five-day period, just the four other days. Your first step is to subtract the number of miles he drove in one day from the total number of miles: 425 − 75 = 350. Now, divide 350 by the four other days: 350 ÷ 4 = 87.5. Rounded to the nearest whole number, the average miles he drove in a four-day period was 88 miles per day. Choice (E) is correct.

Picking an Answer if You Don't Know It

You may occasionally run into a math question on the POST that completely stumps you — you don't know which operations to use, what order to use them in, or even whether using so much time to figure out the answer to that one problem is worth it in the end. You may be tempted to skip the problem altogether, but don't! It's important not to leave any questions unanswered. On the POST, you're not penalized for answering incorrectly. You only get credit for correct answers, so make an educated guess.

When you don't think you can answer a question in a reasonable amount of time, work backwards. Instead of trying to find the answer, plug the answer choices into the word problem. See whether they make sense and whether you can make one of them work for you. If the first choice you try seems too large, try a smaller one. Keep going until you find one that works.

Working backwards is typically only effective when you're asked to find simple numbers. It may work if you're attempting to find a product, difference, or sum, but it's not guaranteed. Always make an attempt to solve a problem before deciding to guess.

Suppose you see a question like this on the POST:

Officer O'Malley wrote ⅓ of her incident reports on Tuesday. On Thursday, she wrote ¾ of the remaining reports, which left 10 for her to finish on Friday. How many reports in all did she have to write this week?

(A) 60

(B) 80

(C) 90

(D) 120

(E) 140

If you aren't sure how to set up an equation or even where to begin to solve a problem such as this, then you should pick an answer choice and plug it in to the question. It's always best to start with the middle number (in this case, 90) so you know whether you have to go bigger or smaller on your next guess.

Plugging Choice (C) into the word problem results in the following:

Officer O'Malley wrote ⅓ (90 × ⅓ = 30) of her incident reports on Tuesday, which left 60 to finish. On Thursday, she wrote ¾ (60 × ¾ = 45) of the remaining reports, which left 15 (60 − 45 = 15) for her to finish on Friday.

The original question states that she has 10 reports to finish on Friday, not 15. Because Choice (C) results in a number that's too high, eliminate Choices (D) and (E). This leaves Choices (A) and (B).

In this problem, Choice (A) is correct. If Officer O'Malley had 60 incident reports to begin with and wrote ⅓ of them (60 × ⅓ = 20) on Tuesday, then she'd have 40 left to complete on Thursday. On Thursday, she wrote ¾ of the remaining 40 (40 × ¾ = 30), so 40 − 30 = 10.

Practice Math Questions

The following passages and question sets are designed to help you practice answering questions involving the use of basic math skills. For all questions, choose the answer that *most correctly* answers the question.

1. In one day, Officer Ramos drove his police cruiser 85 miles. If he patrolled the same route three more days that week, how many miles total did he travel?

(A) 275

(B) 340

(C) 355

(D) 400

(E) 425

The correct answer is Choice (B). 85 + 85 + 85 + 85 = 340 miles, or 85 × 4 = 340 miles.

2. While working on an incident report of a burglary, Officer Owens receives a call from the homeowner who states that she found some of the jewelry she reported missing. Officer Owens must now adjust the total value of missing items in his report. The original total was $2,240, but the homeowner has discovered a necklace worth $740 and a pair of earrings worth $320. What is the new total value?

   (A) $1,060

   (B) $1,180

   (C) $1,270

   (D) $1,500

   (E) $1,920

   The correct answer is Choice (B). $740 + $ 320 = $1,060; $2,240 − $1,060 = $1,180.

3. In a single day, Officer Davila is able to patrol approximately 12 miles on foot. If she patrols the same route 12 more times in the next three weeks, how many miles total did she patrol?

   (A) 48

   (B) 96

   (C) 108

   (D) 144

   (E) 156

   The correct answer is Choice (E). 12 miles × 12 patrols = 144 miles; 144 + 12 miles = 156 miles.

4. The number of arrests that Sergeant Porteus made each week for the past three months was 2, 5, 8, 4, 7, 8, 9, 14, 3, 10, 5, and 6. What is the average number of arrests she made per week?

   (A) 5.5

   (B) 6

   (C) 6.75

   (D) 7

   (E) 8

   The correct answer is Choice (C). 2 + 5 + 8 + 4 + 7 + 8 + 9 + 14 + 3 + 10 + 5 + 6 = 81; 81 ÷ 12 = 6.75 arrests.

5. If three-quarters of the calls that Officer Weiss responds to each week are for motor vehicle accidents, and he typically responds to 40 emergency calls per week, how many calls does he respond to for emergencies other than car accidents?

   (A) 5

   (B) 10

   (C) 15

   (D) 20

   (E) 30

   The correct answer is Choice (B). 40 × 0.25 = 10, or 40 × 0.75 = 30; 40 − 30 = 10 calls.

6. While responding to a burglary at a bookstore, Officer Myers overhears the owner tell another officer that the thieves stole 30 audio books. The owner estimates that the total value of the stolen items is approximately $1,260. What is the value of an individual audio book?

   (A) $42

   (B) $44

   (C) $45

   (D) $46

   (E) $50

   The correct answer is Choice (A). $1,260 ÷ 30 = $42.

Questions 7 and 8 are based on the following information.

In preparing a report on a burglary in a home, Officer Lewis listed the following stolen items and their values.

3 laptop computers	$450 each
2 MP3 players	$120 each
1 HD television	$700
Cash	$1,100
Total	$3,390

---

7. What is the total value of the stolen items *except* for the computers?

   (A) $450

   (B) $900

   (C) $1,350

   (D) $1,800

   (E) $2,040

   The correct answer is Choice (E). $450 × 3 = $1,350; $3,390 − $1,350 = $2,040.

8. While cleaning the house, the homeowner finds that the burglars only stole two laptop computers, but they took another $2,800 in cash from the bedroom safe. What is the new total value of the stolen items?

   (A) $2,490

   (B) $2,800

   (C) $2,940

   (D) $5,740

   (E) $6,190

   The correct answer is Choice (D). $3,390 − $450 = $2,940; $2,940 + $2,800 = $5,740.

9. During a drug bust, Officer Harrison logged 120 baggies of a white powder. At the lab, it was determined that only 45% of the baggies were filled with illegal drugs. How many baggies were filled with illegal drugs?

    (A) 48

    (B) 54

    (C) 58

    (D) 66

    (E) 72

    The correct answer is Choice (B). $120 \times 0.45 = 54$ baggies.

10. After a class of recruit officers complete their first exam, their professor tells them that the students in the first two rows averaged a score of 95 while the students in the back of the room averaged a score of 75. Normally, 10 students sit in the front rows and 14 sit in the back. What is the average score of the entire class? Round to the nearest whole number.

    (A) 75

    (B) 79

    (C) 81

    (D) 83

    (E) 85

    The correct answer is Choice (D). $95 \times 10 = 950$; $75 \times 14 = 1,050$; $1,050 + 950 = 2,000$; $2,000 \div 24 = 83.333 = 83$.

11. During the past two weeks, Officer Coleman worked on old incident and aid reports. The first week, he finished 6 reports before lunch and 5 more after lunch. The second week, he completed 10 reports before lunch, but only managed to finish 4 after lunch. How many reports did he write during the past two weeks?

    (A) 15

    (B) 16

    (C) 20

    (D) 22

    (E) 25

    The correct answer is Choice (E). $6 + 5 + 10 + 4 = 25$ reports.

12. In the past three weeks, Officer Maroni has patrolled the local cemetery 90 times. If she worked five shifts each week and visited the cemetery an equal number of times during each shift, how many times did she patrol the cemetery each day?

    (A) 3

    (B) 4

    (C) 5

    (D) 6

    (E) 7

    The correct answer is Choice (D). $3 \times 5 = 15$; $90 \div 15 = 6$ times.

> *Questions 13 and 14 are based on the following information.*
>
> In preparing a report on a robbery outside of a convenience store, Officer White listed the following stolen items and their values.
>
> | | |
> |---|---|
> | Cellphone | $100 |
> | Watch | $220 |
> | Cash | $50 |
> | Total | $370 |

13. Officer White later received a call from the victim saying that, in addition to his own cellphone, he also had his wife's cellphone on him when he was robbed. This cellphone is worth three times as much as the victim's. What is the new total value of the stolen items?

    (A) $300

    (B) $470

    (C) $570

    (D) $670

    (E) $700

    The correct answer is Choice (D). $100 × 3 = $300; $370 + $300 = $670.

14. As Officer White finalizes his report, he receives a call from the victim's wife. She says she found the $50 he thought was taken from him in the back pocket of his jeans. What is the new total value of the items taken from the victim?

    (A) $100

    (B) $200

    (C) $320

    (D) $420

    (E) $620

    The correct answer is Choice (C). $370 – $50 = $320.

15. During a two-week period, Officer Lokuta drove his police cruiser 840 miles. If he patrolled the same route for eight days, how many miles did he average per day?

    (A) 52

    (B) 105

    (C) 210

    (D) 315

    (E) 420

    The correct answer is Choice (B). 840 miles ÷ 8 days = 105 miles.

16. Officer Miller had 11 security detail shifts over the past three weeks. They lasted 6 hours, 5 hours, 4 hours, 6 hours, 8 hours, 5 hours, 7 hours, 10 hours, 4 hours, 3 hours, and 8 hours. What is the average length of time she spent working security detail each night?

    (A) 4

    (B) 5

    (C) 6

    (D) 7

    (E) 8

    The correct answer is Choice (C). 6 + 5 + 4 + 6 + 8 + 5 + 7 + 10 + 4 + 3 + 8 = 66; 66 ÷ 11 = 6 hours.

Questions 17 and 18 are based on the following information.

In the past six months, crime rates have both increased and decreased. In January, 25 incidents of domestic violence were reported. By June, 40 incidents of domestic violence were reported. At the beginning of the year, only 4 home burglaries were reported. In June, 10 people reported that their homes had been broken into. However, in January there were 8 reported arsons while June only saw 4.

---

17. How many assaults, burglaries, and arsons were reported in June?

    (A) 37

    (B) 41

    (C) 43

    (D) 52

    (E) 54

    The correct answer is Choice (E). 40 + 10 + 4 = 54.

18. By what percent did the reports of domestic violence increase from January to June?

    (A) 40%

    (B) 46.5%

    (C) 50%

    (D) 60%

    (E) 70%

    The correct answer is Choice (D). 40 – 25 = 15; 15 ÷ 25 = 60%.

19. The court house and the police station are approximately 5 miles apart. If Officer Devers made three trips to the court house this week, how many miles in all did he travel?

    (A) 5

    (B) 10

    (C) 15

    (D) 20

    (E) 30

    The correct answer is Choice (E). $5 + 5 + 5 + 5 + 5 + 5 = 30$, or $5 \times 6 = 30$, or $5 \times 2 = 10$; $10 \times 3 = 30$ miles.

20. While working on the last incident report of the evening, you receive a call from the owner of a convenience store that was robbed earlier that day. Although he originally reported that the suspect took $900 from the register, he has just discovered about $120 under the register that belonged in the drawer. How much did the suspect actually take from the store?

    (A) $120

    (B) $500

    (C) $780

    (D) $900

    (E) $1,120

    The correct answer is Choice (C). $900 – $120 = $780.

Chapter 4

Reading Between the Lines: Reading Comprehension

In This Chapter

▶ Understanding the purpose of reading comprehension questions

▶ Surveying the types of reading passages on the POST

▶ Preparing for reading comprehension questions on the NYC test

All police departments give a written test to screen applicants for police officer jobs, but they don't all give the same test. A police department can give you a test asking questions about the weather, automobiles, or fashion — don't worry; we're just kidding. Most written police officer tests are similar. Many departments give applicants the National Police Officer Selection Test, also called the POST. Other departments give a police officer test similar to the one given in New York City. Both of these tests ask reading comprehension questions in which you read and then recall details about what you've read. In this chapter, we tell you what you need to know to answer reading comprehension questions on the POST and the New York City tests.

Comprehending the Reading Comprehension Section on the POST

The reading comprehension section of the POST asks you to read a passage and remember details in this passage. What the heck is a reading passage, you ask? A reading passage is simply a few paragraphs about a subject. The reading passages on the POST are about police duties, but you don't need to know anything about law enforcement to understand them. This reading passage is an example of the kind you might see on the POST:

To reduce the number of speeding vehicles in Middlebury and keep residents safe, the Middlebury Police Department has formed a partnership with a group called the Neighborhood Speed Watch. Members of this group are residents of Middlebury who have expressed an interest in reducing the number of speeding vehicles.

Members of the Neighborhood Speed Watch receive a portable radar unit. When they witness a vehicle speeding, they use the portable radar unit to determine the vehicle's speed. They then log the vehicle's speed into a book, along with the vehicle's license plate number and a description of the vehicle.

Police will place a speed monitoring awareness trailer (SMAT) unit in areas where many speeding vehicles have been logged in the book. These large units display the speed of passing vehicles as they pass by. SMAT units have been proven effective in getting vehicles to slow down. Police will also enforce the speed limit in these areas by ticketing vehicles traveling above the speed limit.

Now that's not so bad, is it? Most police departments include passages about police duty, but a police department may include any type of reading material to test your reading comprehension skills. So although it's not likely you'll read about Shakespeare, it's possible.

According to the passage, Middlebury police will place an SMAT unit in areas where many

(A) tickets have been issued.

(B) accidents have occurred.

(C) speeding vehicles have been logged.

(D) speeding vehicles have been warned.

(E) residents have filed complaints.

Choice (C) is the correct answer to this question. If you look back at the passage, you'll see that SMAT units will be placed in areas where members of the Neighborhood Speed Watch have logged many speeding vehicles into the book.

The great part about answering questions on the reading comprehension section of the POST is that you can look back at the passage to find the information you need. In fact, it helps to read the questions *first,* so you know what to look for as you read.

Not all questions on the POST are multiple-choice. Some are true-or-false. A true-or-false question about the previous passage might look like this:

Members of the Neighborhood Speed Watch must be residents of Middlebury.

(A) True

(B) False

Choice (A) is correct. The passage says that members of the Neighborhood Speed Watch are residents of Middlebury who have expressed an interest in reducing the number of speeding vehicles.

Not all reading passages on the reading comprehension section of the POST are the same. Some passages are fairly long. These passages are usually followed by three or four multiple-choice questions and one or two true-or-false questions.

Other passages contain statements or definitions. To answer the multiple-choice question following this type of passage, you have to correctly interpret part or all of this statement or definition. For example, such a passage might contain several amendments to the United States Constitution and ask you a multiple-choice question interpreting one of them.

A third type of passage on the POST has to do with incident reports. An incident report is simply a report a police officer completes after investigating an incident, such as a burglary or a domestic violence complaint. Questions about incident reports appear on both the POST and the New York City (NYC) police officer tests, so we devote Chapter 7 to incident reports and everything you need to know about them.

The reading comprehension section of the POST contains 25 questions. You have 25 minutes to complete this section of the test. There's no penalty for guessing on the POST, so if you're not sure which answer is correct, make a good guess.

Longer passages

The following is an example of a longer reading comprehension passage on the POST. Read this passage carefully and answer the questions that follow. Don't be afraid to read the questions *before* you read the passage. If you do this, you'll know what to look for as you read.

To keep the community safe and beautiful, Smithtown has made the building code and the regulation of building permits more stringent. These new requirements apply to all people living and working in buildings in the city of Smithtown.

Residents planning to develop, remodel, or add additions to commercial or multifamily property must apply for a *Commercial/Multifamily Building Permit.* Applicants for Commercial/Multifamily Building Permits *must* complete a Building Permit Application Form. Applicants for Commercial/Multifamily Building Permits *must* complete one or more of the following forms:

> Commercial and Multifamily Building Permit Checklist
> Plumbing Fixture Count Form
> Site Plan
> Industrial/Commercial Environmental Information Form

Residents planning to build or add additions to residential property must apply for a *Residential Building Permit.* Applicants for Residential Building Permits *must* complete a Building Permit Application Form. Applicants for Residential Building Permits *must* complete the following forms:

> Site Plan
> Plumbing Fixture Count Form

Those planning to do sign work must apply for a *Sign Permit.* Applicants for Sign Permits *must* complete a Sign Permit Application Form. Applicants for Sign Permits *must* complete the following forms:

> Site Plan
> Right-of-Way Permit Application Form

Those planning to do right-of-way work or work in an easement must apply for a *Right-of-Way Permit.* Applicants for Right-of-Way Permits *must* complete a Right-of-Way Permit Application Form. Applicants for Right-of-Way Permits *must* complete the following forms:

> Site Plan
> Traffic Control Plan
> Right-of-Way Contractor License Application Form

Now answer the following example questions about the passage you just read. All the information you need to answer these questions is in the passage.

According to the passage, a person planning to construct a commercial building must complete

(A) a Commercial and Multifamily Building Permit Checklist.

(B) an Industrial/Commercial Environmental Information Form.

(C) a Building Permit Application Form.

(D) a Plumbing Fixture Count Form.

(E) a Site Plan.

According to the passage, a person planning to construct a commercial building must complete a Building Permit Application Form, so Choice (C) is correct.

The importance of reading comprehension

Although some people think police officers spend all their time chasing down hardened criminals, the truth is that police officers are responsible for a lot of reading and writing on the job. As a police officer or any other type of law enforcement officer, you'll most likely be reading and writing every day. That's why the POST, the NYC test, and other police exams test your ability to remember and interpret what you've read. The reading comprehension section of the exam isn't there to remind you of high school English class or bore you with pointless reading — it's there to make sure you can handle the reading and writing aspects of the job.

According to the passage, both someone working on an easement and someone working on a sign must complete a

(A) Building Permit Application Form.

(B) Sign Permit Application Form.

(C) Traffic Control Plan.

(D) Plumbing Fixture Count Form.

(E) Right-of-Way Permit Application Form.

Individuals working on an easement and working on a sign need to complete a Right-of-Way Permit Application Form, so Choice (E) is correct.

According to the passage, a person planning to add an addition to a residential building must complete an Industrial/Commercial Environmental Information Form.

(A) True

(B) False

The statement is false, so Choice (B) is correct. A person planning to add an addition to a residential building would not have to complete an Industrial/Commercial Environmental Information Form. This person would have to complete a Building Permit Application Form.

Definition passages

Some reading comprehension passages on the POST give a definition of something related to the law. To answer the multiple-choice question that follows this type of passage, you have to correctly interpret the meaning of part of this definition. Remember to read the question *before* you read the passage. To answer questions on this part of the test, you usually don't need to read the whole passage. Here's an example of a definition passage:

Someone charged with or convicted of the *possession* of drugs is one who has been found with illegal drugs, the chemicals used to make particular drugs, or the devices needed to use the drugs (paraphernalia). This charge implies that the person was aware that he or she was in possession of these items.

Although the amount of drugs one must possess to be charged with *possession with the intent to sell* is different in each state, a person who has been charged with or convicted of this crime has been found to possess a large amount of drugs. This amount is typically more than the average user could use in a day. This charge also implies that the person was aware that he or she was in possession of the drugs.

A person accused of *distributing* or *trafficking* drugs is one who has tracked, sold, traded, or moved illegal drugs of any type into the United States from another country.

One is charged with or convicted of *manufacturing* drugs if he or she has been caught in the production process of making illegal drugs either for distribution or for self-use.

Drug dealers are often convicted of *selling*. This involves receiving money, favors, material items, or services in exchange for any type of illegal drug.

When you're completing the reading comprehension portion of the POST, remember that you shouldn't make marks in your test booklet. Although you should make mental notes about where certain pieces of information are located in the passages, you shouldn't underline or otherwise mark them. If you're taking an exam other than the POST, read the directions at the beginning of your test to find out whether you can make stray marks in your test booklet.

Now answer the following example question about the passage you just read:

Which of the following best describes *possession with the intent to sell?*

(A) During a routine traffic stop, Officer Lloyd discovers a small baggie of marijuana in the pocket of John's jeans. After searching his car, he finds a pipe and another small baggie in the glove compartment containing approximately one ounce of pot.

(B) Having raided the rest of Marco's home, police officers enter his basement. They find thermometers, plastic tubes, funnels, coffee filters, hot plates, and an assortment of jugs and jars filled with a variety of chemicals.

(C) After receiving a call about two suspicious men who had stopped for food at a Texas diner, the police track down their pickup truck and pull them over. One man tells the officers that they have just returned from a trip to Mexico. In the bed of the truck, police find multiple suitcases stuffed with crystal meth hidden beneath a few layers of blankets and clothing. The men say they did not know what was in the suitcases.

(D) On her way home from school, Lila stops by Frank's apartment. Frank is a friend of Lila's older brother who often parties with her on weekends. Lila gives Frank cash and leaves with a dime bag of marijuana in the pocket of her purse.

(E) Having received a noise complaint from neighbors, Officers Rodriguez and Stacks enter Brandon's home and spot 15 to 20 plastic baggies filled with marijuana on his coffee table. In his bag near the door, they find several blunts and more baggies. Upon searching what Brandon referred to as his guest bedroom, they find five marijuana plants, a list of names, and a shoebox of cash hidden in the closet.

To answer this question, read or reread the part of the passage that discusses the definition of possession with the intent to sell. According to the passage, a person charged with this crime was in possession of a large amount of drugs — more drugs than the average user could use in a day. The person was also aware that he or she was in possession of the drugs. Based on this information, Choice (E) is the best answer. Because the drugs were throughout Brandon's home, he must have known they were in his possession.

Examining the Reading Comprehension Questions on the New York City Test

New York City gives its own written test for police officer applicants, and some police departments in other areas model their tests after this test. The content of the NYC test isn't all that different from the POST, but the NYC test uses different names for the reading passages within its test. While the information in these passages on the NYC test is about police duty, you don't need knowledge of law enforcement to answer the questions. The following types of passages are in the reading portion of the NYC test:

✔ Written comprehension

✔ Information ordering

✔ Inductive reasoning

✔ Deductive reasoning

✔ Problem sensitivity questions

Written comprehension passages

The written comprehension passages on the NYC test are similar to the longer reading passages on the POST. These passages test your ability to understand written sentences and paragraphs. The written comprehension passages on the NYC test usually contain details about an incident. The following is an example of this type of passage on the NYC test:

> Police officers Jeffrey Hirsch and Dana Holtz were patrolling their area driving down Glendale Road in Hudson at 7:25 p.m. on September 13, 2008, when they made a left turn onto First Avenue. Officers Hirsch and Holtz observed a woman signal toward them from the SaveMoney grocery store parking lot. At 7:26 p.m., the officers made a right turn onto Carrey Avenue and into the store parking lot. The woman identified herself as Ms. Sylvia Roth, age 36, of Riverside. Ms. Roth then reported her vehicle as stolen.

> Ms. Roth told the officers that she parked her car outside the grocery store at 6:45 p.m., and then she and her daughter, Megan Roth, age 6, went into the store. Ms. Roth said she noticed a green sedan and a yellow compact car in the lot as she entered the store. She returned to the parking lot at 7:23 p.m. to find the car missing. At 7:24 p.m., Ms. Roth called her husband.

> Ms. Roth's vehicle was a red 2005 Chevrolet Malibu with no other distinguishing characteristics. It had the New York license plate number 4902PT. Ms. Roth said she locked the car before entering the store, and she still had her keys in her possession. Ms. Roth told the officers that besides her key, her husband had the only other key to the vehicle.

> At 7:31 p.m. Mr. Martin Roth, Sylvia Roth's husband, arrived at the scene. Mr. Roth drove a blue 2001 Volkswagen Jetta with the New York license plate number TY20P2.

> Officer Hirsch began an investigation of the scene. Hirsch noticed a small amount of broken glass near the spot in which Ms. Roth's vehicle had been parked. Officer Hirsch collected some of the glass, but did not find any other evidence. Then, officers Hirsch and Holtz obtained statements from Mr. and Ms. Roth, who left the scene at 7:36 p.m. Officer Holtz entered the vehicle into the station database as a stolen vehicle.

You probably noticed that this passage contains many details. Even if you're a reading whiz, you won't be able to remember specific details in this passage such as license plate numbers. To answer questions about this passage, you have to look back at the passage. It's a good idea to read the questions in this section *before* you read the passage. This way you can easily identify the information you need as you read.

Following are the type of multiple-choice questions you'll see on the NYC police officer test. Look back at the passage to find the correct answers.

Which one of the following is the correct license plate number and description of Ms. Roth's vehicle?

(A) NY plate #TY20P2, yellow 2001 Volkswagen Jetta

(B) NY plate #4902PT, blue 2001 Volkswagen Jetta

(C) NY plate #TY20P2, green 2005 Chevrolet Malibu

(D) NY plate #4902PT, red 2005 Chevrolet Malibu

Don't get the license plate number and description of Ms. Roth's car confused with the license plate number and description of her husband's car. Ms. Roth's car was a red 2005 Chevrolet Malibu with the New York license plate number 4902PT. Choice (D) is the correct answer.

At what time did Ms. Roth notice her car was missing?

(A) 6:45 p.m.

(B) 7:23 p.m.

(C) 7:25 p.m.

(D) 7:36 p.m.

According to the passage, Ms. Roth first noticed her car was gone at 7:23 p.m., so Choice (B) is correct.

How many keys did the Roths have for the missing vehicle?

(A) 0

(B) 1

(C) 2

(D) 3

The passage says that Ms. Roth had a key and her husband had the only other key. Therefore, Choice (C) is correct.

Who first noticed the broken glass in the parking lot?

(A) Martin Roth

(B) Officer Holtz

(C) Sylvia Roth

(D) Officer Hirsch

The passage says that Officer Hirsch noticed a small amount of glass near the spot where Ms. Roth's car had been. Therefore, Choice (D) is correct.

Information ordering passages

Some reading passages on the NYC police officer test contain a series of steps about something related to law enforcement. These passages are called information ordering passages. A single multiple-choice question follows this type of passage. This question gives you a brief scenario about a person, often a police officer. Then the question asks you what the person should do next based on the information in the passage. The purpose of this section is to test your ability to follow a rule or set of rules in a certain order. The following passage is an example of an information ordering passage you might see on the NYC police officer test.

When officers obtain alcohol as evidence, they should

1. Collect the suspected alcohol in its original container.

2. Pour the suspected alcohol into a plastic specimen bottle. If the suspected alcohol is no longer in its original container, remove any ice to prevent dilution. Seal the plastic specimen bottle with evidence tape. Initial and date the bottle's seal. If possible, seal, initial, and date the bottle in front of the suspect.

3. Place the specimen bottle in an evidence bag. Seal the plastic bag with evidence tape. Initial and date the bag's seal. If possible, seal, initial, and date the bag in front of the suspect.

4. Place the alcohol's original container in another evidence bag and seal the bag with evidence tape. Initial and date the bag's seal. If possible, seal, initial, and date the bag in front of the suspect.

5. Complete an evidence form for each piece of evidence and attach the forms to the evidence bags.

6. Drop off the evidence and evidence forms at the proper location.

Note that this passage contains specific steps that must be followed in a certain order. The following question involves a situation in which an officer must follow these steps.

Officer Link placed a suspect under arrest on DUI charges. Upon inspection of the vehicle, Officer Link located what appeared to be an open can of beer. Officer Link removed the beer can from the car in front of the arrested suspect. She poured the remaining beer into a plastic specimen bottle. Officer Link sealed the bottle with evidence tape in front of the suspect. What should Officer Link do next?

(A) Place the specimen bottle in an evidence bag.

(B) Initial and date the bottle's seal.

(C) Drop off the evidence and evidence forms.

(D) Place the alcohol's original container in an evidence bag.

According to the passage, Officer Link completed these steps: She collected the alcohol in its original container; she poured the alcohol into a specimen bottle; and she sealed the bag with evidence tape. Next, she should initial and date the bottle's seal. Choice (B) is correct.

Inductive reasoning passages

The NYC police officer test contains inductive reasoning passages. These passages contain general details that apply to many individuals, such as procedures police officers must follow. To answer the questions for this type of passage, you need to use inductive reasoning — you must move from the general to the specific. For example, you might be expected to apply police procedures to an incident an officer is investigating.

To better understand inductive reasoning, consider this example: You're probably familiar with the symptoms of a common cold, which include a red, stuffy nose; watery eyes; sneezing; and coughing. Suppose you notice that your co-worker Bruce has all of these symptoms.

You can apply the general symptoms of the common cold to the specific — Bruce. In other words, you can use inductive reasoning to conclude that Bruce has a cold.

You don't find the answer to a question about an inductive reading passage spelled out in the passage. Instead, you must choose the most logical conclusion. Consider the following example.

Recruit officers were intrigued when they discovered that a guest speaker would be lecturing during their class last Monday. With more than 25 years of experience in the NYPD, Assistant Chief Pat O'Carroll's accomplishments are impressive; however, his goal was not to impress the class of young students. Instead, Chief O'Carroll wanted to teach them the proper way to begin an investigation into a traffic accident. O'Carroll stated that police must adhere to the following steps when responding to the call:

1. Arrive on the scene quickly but safely.

2. Carefully access and survey the scene.

3. Patiently and carefully interview all witnesses and those involved in the accident to gather facts.

4. Objectively review all personal observations and witness statements.

5. Be patient, and consider multiple options.

The following example question requires you to choose the most logical answer based on the passage:

Based on the information provided in the preceding passage, it would be most correct for recruits to assume that the main reason responding officers should follow these steps at the scene of an accident is

(A) to keep pedestrians and bystanders away from any broken glass.

(B) to ensure that all information obtained is as accurate as possible.

(C) to determine the cause of the accident as quickly as possible.

(D) to be prepared to search the vehicle for weapons, drugs, or stolen goods.

You won't find the answer to this question in the passage. You have to use the information in the passage to draw a conclusion. Reread the steps given in the passage. Think about what would happen if an officer did not bother to interview witnesses and those involved in the accident. Think about what would happen if the officer let his or her opinions get in the way instead of reviewing information objectively. Would the officer's assessment of the accident scene be accurate? No! The main reason officers must follow these steps is to ensure that the information they obtain is as accurate as possible. Therefore, Choice (B) is correct.

To answer some questions on the NYC police officer test, you must read information in a table and draw a conclusion about this information using inductive reasoning. The following is an introduction to a table along with a table like one you might see on the test.

Officers studying the law are learning about traffic and moving violations in the state of Pennsylvania. To understand how drivers accumulate enough points to have their licenses suspended (11), the class receives a handout containing the following information.

VEHICLE CODE	DESCRIPTION OF VIOLATION	POINTS
3112	Failure to stop at a red light	3
3304 (5)	Improper passing on left or right	3
3310	Following too closely	3
3323	Failing to stop at a stop sign	3
3332	Illegal U-turns	3
3341	Failure to comply with train crossing gate	4 (and 30-day suspension)
3345	Failure to stop for a school bus with lights on	5 (and 60-day suspension)
3362	Exceeding speed limit	2–5
3542	Failure to yield at cross walk	2

After reviewing the preceding table, it would be most correct for an officer to conclude that

(A) a driver stopped for speeding may receive points based on how many miles he or she was traveling over the speed limit.

(B) a driver stopped for passing a school bus that is flashing red lights will receive a lecture about child safety.

(C) a driver stopped for following the car in front of him or her too closely and then passing the car will receive a license suspension.

(D) a driver stopped for ignoring a red light who already has 5 points on his or her license will receive a license suspension.

The answer to this question isn't stated in the table; you have to use the information in the table to figure out the correct answer. You may begin by eliminating answer choices that you know are incorrect. Nothing in the table indicates that a driver will receive a lecture about child safety, so Choice (B) isn't correct. A license suspension is mentioned only for failing to comply with a train crossing gate and failing to stop for a school bus with lights on, so you can eliminate Choice (C). The same is true for Choice (D) — nothing in the table leads you to conclude that a driver with 5 points will receive a license suspension for ignoring a red light. Choice (A) makes sense based on the information in the table. A range of points (2–5) is listed for exceeding the speed limit. Therefore, it's possible that a driver may receive points based on how many miles he or she was traveling over the speed limit.

Deductive reasoning passages

The NYC test contains deductive reasoning passages. These passages are the opposite of inductive reasoning passages — they contain specific information that you have to apply to a general situation.

Using deductive reasoning is easier than you may think. Consider this statement: "All birds have feathers." Your friend Burt has a parakeet named Squeaky. A parakeet is a kind of bird.

You can use deductive reasoning to draw this conclusion: "Squeaky has feathers." See how it works? You moved from the general (all birds) to the specific (Squeaky).

Read through the following example of a deductive reasoning passage and then test yourself with the example question.

In December 2006, the State of New York modified its laws regarding residential and commercial swimming pools to ensure the safety of unsupervised children. The following are ordinances, or regulations, the state altered or added to its Uniform Fire Prevention and Building Code. Spas and hot tubs are the only exceptions to these rules.

1. Every pool must be equipped with an alarm that should be turned on when the pool is not in use. This alarm will sound if someone enters the water when the pool is closed. Anyone in the vicinity of the pool should be able to hear the alarm. This alarm may be shut off when the pool is in use.

2. Every pool must be surrounded by a 4-foot-high (48-inch-high) barrier/fence. If the pool is above ground and the barrier only partially surrounds the structure, the ladder should be removed when the pool is not in use.

3. While a new pool is under construction, the entire area should be surrounded by 4-foot-high barriers at all times. The only people allowed to enter the area are members of the crew in charge of construction or renovations.

4. All pools must be covered when not in use by a material that fits the standards listed in ASME/ANSI A112.19.8M (Suction Fittings for Use in Swimming Pools, Wading Pools, Spas, Hot Tubs, and Whirlpool Bathtub Appliances).

According to the preceding information, which of the following is the best example of a residential pool that adheres to the State of New York's swimming pool ordinances?

(A) Melanie's pool is above ground. A 4-foot fence surrounds three-quarters of the structure and an alarm sounds when her children break the surface of the water to wash their feet after playing in the sandbox. Each night, they place a fitted cover on the pool.

(B) Brian is having a company install a new in-ground pool in his backyard. A 4-foot wooden fence surrounds the pool, and Brian has talked to workers about installing an alarm to detect movement on the surface of the water once they fill the pool. Sometimes Brian approaches the pool to inspect the work the crew is doing; last night he touched up some paint around the border of the steps in the shallow end.

(C) Because one part of Regina's above-ground pool is so close to the side of her garage, her 4-foot fence only surrounds half of the structure. She feels that her young children are safe when they play on the deck near the pool, however, because an alarm sounds if they enter the water when she isn't there. At night, she stores the ladder in her shed and places a fitted cover on the pool.

(D) Tom and Patti love their new pool. When they lie beside it and close their eyes, all they can hear is the splash of water as their children jump in from all sides. Because the pool has a heater, they didn't want to spend money on a cover they would never use. The barrier that surrounds the in-ground pool is approximately 3 feet high and is decorated with various potted plants.

Choice (C) is the only answer option that meets the major criteria in the passage: The pool has an alarm, a 4-foot barrier, a ladder that is removed at night, and a cover that is placed over the pool at night.

Not all deductive reasoning questions on the NYC test are about information in passages. To answer some questions, you have to use deductive reasoning to draw a conclusion based on information given in a brief definition.

When answering questions on the NYC test about definitions, look for key words or phrases. Incorrect answer options do not take key words and phrases into account.

The multiple-choice question following this type of passage will give you four scenarios. You have to choose the one that best matches the information in the definition. The key is to use only the information in the definition — don't base your answer on personal knowledge. Following is an example of such a definition and question:

> *Disorderly Conduct:* The crime of engaging in socially unacceptable, unruly behavior that disturbs the peace of others.

According to the definition given, which one of the following is the best example of disorderly conduct?

(A) Terry Ames spends several hours at a bar and then tries to drive home intoxicated. She hits a tree and destroys her car but is not seriously hurt.

(B) Santo LaToy robs a convenience store by threatening a clerk with a knife. The clerk is not injured, and LaToy runs off with more than $100 in cash.

(C) Jamie Ketron is drunk and shouting obscenities outside a restaurant full of people. When the owner of the restaurant asks him to leave, he begins shouting at the owner.

(D) Samantha Brown leaves her children home alone so she can buy beer and cigarettes. One child tries to light a candle and starts a fire in the home. No one is injured.

When you choose an answer, consider that the crime of disorderly conduct is to engage in behavior that is considered socially unacceptable. Choice (C) best fits this definition. Jamie Ketron's behavior definitely disturbs the peace of those dining in the restaurant.

Other types of deductive reasoning questions give you a description of a suspect and ask you to choose the item that an officer would consider most helpful in identifying the suspect. Always choose the most outstanding item or characteristic. This type of question looks like this:

> On October 10, several drug-related homicides were committed at different locations. Based on the descriptions of eyewitnesses, it is believed that the same person committed all the homicides. Police officers have compiled this description: The suspect is a white male, with short brown hair cut close to his head, approximately 140 pounds, with a tattoo of a dragon on his left cheek, and is wearing a red, hooded sweatshirt.

Officer Roland has stopped four white males for questioning. Which one of the items of information provided by the witnesses should Officer Roland consider the most helpful in identifying the suspect?

(A) The suspect has short brown hair.

(B) The suspect weighs approximately 140 pounds.

(C) The suspect has a tattoo of a dragon on his cheek.

(D) The suspect is wearing a red, hooded sweatshirt.

Choice (C) is the best answer because the suspect's hair may have grown longer, Choice (A); his weight may have changed, Choice (B); and he could have changed his sweatshirt, Choice (D). However, it's unlikely that he would have been able to have the tattoo removed from his cheek.

Some of the reading comprehension questions on the NYC test ask about basic police procedures, but you aren't expected to know anything about these procedures before you take the exam. The passages on the exam include all the information you need to know. To answer the question correctly, you use the information from the exam and your own common sense and good judgment.

Problem sensitivity questions

Problem sensitivity questions on the NYC test ask you to eliminate answer choices that would create a problem and choose the answer option that would not create a problem. Problem sensitivity questions are often based on information in a sentence. The answer choices are scenarios relating to the sentence. You choose the scenario that would not create a problem. The important thing to remember is to use only the information in the sentence, which might look like this:

> A police officer has the right to search abandoned property and take custody of such property to find its owner.

For which one of the following would an officer have the right to search property?

(A) A duffle bag left behind at an airport

(B) A car parked illegally in a parking lot

(C) A drug dealer's suitcase

(D) A home that has been foreclosed

The word *abandoned* is the key to choosing the correct answer in this sentence. The only item in the answer choices that is definitely abandoned is the duffle bag in the airport. Therefore, Choice (A) is correct. The car in Choice (B) may or may not be abandoned; the same holds true for the drug dealer's suitcase in Choice (C). A foreclosed home is owned by a bank or mortgage company, so Choice (D) is incorrect.

Practice Questions for the POST Reading Comprehension Section

The following passages and question sets are designed to help you practice your reading comprehension questions. For all questions, choose the answer that *most correctly* answers the question.

> *Read the passage and answer Questions 1 through 4.*

To reduce the risk of injury, the state of Pennsylvania enforces the following bicycle laws. A bicycle, or bike, is considered a vehicle — and drivers must follow the rules of the road. Rules for bicycle drivers are the same as rules for vehicles. For example, bicycle drivers must stop at stop signs, stop at traffic lights, and yield to pedestrians. Police in Hightown are also enforcing these additional bicycle regulations:

All signals should be made with the left arm.

> When turning left, extend the hand and arm horizontally.

> When making a right turn, extend the left hand and arm upward.

> When reducing speed and stopping, extend the left hand and arm downward.

A person riding on a bike must sit on the seat, not on any other part of the bike.

No bike should be used to carry more persons than the number for which it is designed. An exception is an adult rider transporting a child in a child seat that is securely attached to the bike.

Bicycles may be driven on the shoulder of a road or on the roadway.

Bicyclists at night should have headlamps and reflectors.

Bikes should have a braking system that stops 15 feet from an initial speed of 15 miles per hour on clean, dry pavement.

Bikes must be equipped with a horn or bell to warn others in an emergency situation.

Bicyclists cannot ride a bike on a sidewalk in a business district.

Persons under 13 must wear a helmet when riding on a bike.

Bicyclists who do not obey these regulations should expect to be fined $40 for a first offense and up to $100 for a second or subsequent offense. Parents or guardians of children who are in violation of the new bike regulations will be fined.

1. According to the passage, a bicyclist making a right turn should

    (A) use a horn or bell to warn others.

    (B) extend the left hand and arm downward.

    (C) extend the left hand and arm upward.

    (D) get off the roadway and onto the sidewalk.

    (E) extend the left hand and arm horizontally.

According to the passage, all signals should be made with the left arm. When making a right turn, the left hand and arm should be extended upward, so the correct answer is Choice (C).

2. According to the passage, which of the following is acceptable?

    (A) Riding on the sidewalk in a business district

    (B) Sitting on the handlebars of a moving bike

    (C) Driving on the shoulder of the road

    (D) A 10-year-old riding without a helmet

    (E) Riding a bike at night without a headlamp

The passage says that bicycles may be driven on the shoulder of a road or on a roadway, so Choice (C) is correct.

3. According to the passage, which of the following statements would be accurate?

   (A) The parent or guardian of a child who violates the bicycle ordinances for the first time should expect a fine of $40.

   (B) A parent who transports a child in a seat attached to a bike will be fined at least $40.

   (C) Both parents and children riding bicycles in Hightown must wear helmets.

   (D) It is sometimes acceptable for two people to ride on a bike designed for one person.

   (E) A person who repeatedly violates the biking ordinances should expect to pay a fine in excess of $100.

   The last paragraph of this passage explains the penalties for not following the bicycle regulations. According to this paragraph, parents or guardians of children who are in violation of the new bike regulations will be fined, and the fine for a first offense is $40. Therefore, Choice (A) is correct.

4. According to the passage, a person riding a bicycle in Hightown must stop at stop signs.

   (A) True

   (B) False

   This statement is true, Choice (A). According to the first paragraph, bicycle drivers must follow the same rules that vehicles must follow, and this includes stopping at stop signs.

Read this passage and answer Question 5.

Murder in the first degree involves the taking of another person's life intentionally. This charge or conviction implies that the accused planned the murder. Those accused of killing law enforcement officials or members of the court are often charged with first-degree murder, because their crime is seen as a special circumstance.

Murder in the second degree involves the taking of another person's life intentionally but assumes that the act was not planned. This charge or conviction implies that the accused possessed an understanding that he or she was about to commit murder but did not stop himself or herself from doing so.

Voluntary manslaughter involves the taking of another person's life unintentionally. This charge or conviction is normally applied to someone who has killed another person during a fit of rage or passion or in the process of committing another, less serious crime. It is assumed that the accused was distracted by his or her emotions or the task at hand and could not control the outcome of the incident.

Involuntary manslaughter is defined as the taking of another person's life unintentionally while behaving carelessly or not paying attention to the situation at hand. If the accused injured a person during the act and that person dies within one year of the injury, the accused may be convicted of involuntary manslaughter.

5. Which of the following best describes *voluntary manslaughter?*

   (A) While changing the radio station in her car, Mary does not see that the car in front of her has slowed to make a left turn. She crashes into the vehicle in front of her. Two weeks later, the driver of the car she hit dies from internal injuries assumed to be caused by the crash.

   (B) Last week, Luke discovered that his business partner, George, had been stealing money out of their business's bank account. When confronted, George adamantly denied Luke's claims. When more money was removed from the account the following day, Luke took his gun to George's house and shot him when he answered the door.

   (C) Starving and without money to buy food, Mark decides to rob the next woman that walks past him carrying a purse. As he waits around the corner of a deserted street, he plans his attack. When the opportunity finally comes, he grabs an elderly woman's purse and, in the struggle, she falls to the ground and hits her head. Later that night, she dies.

   (D) Lucy has just walked in on her husband, Max, abusing their 3-year-old daughter. Enraged, she turns on Max. They argue, and she picks up the lamp on her daughter's dresser and hits Max in the head. Twenty minutes later, Max is still unconscious and not a threat to Lucy or her child. Despite this fact, Lucy packs some of her belongings, turns the gas on in the kitchen, and leaves the house with her daughter. Max is discovered by a neighbor the next morning, but dies at the hospital from carbon monoxide poisoning.

   (E) Jeremy has never liked his grandfather. After an argument with him one night, Jeremy goes down to the basement to sulk. He sees the open gun rack and devises a plan. When his grandmother goes grocery shopping the next morning, he will kill his grandfather. The next morning, Jeremy's grandmother comes home to find her husband dead and her grandson in the basement, cleaning the gun.

   In the scenario described in Choice (C), Mark is in the process of committing another crime when he unintentionally kills the woman. This is voluntary manslaughter.

Read the passage and answer Questions 6 through 8.

In an effort to ensure that local businesses have ample parking for customers, the Sandy Town Police Department is enforcing the following new regulations regarding parking meters:

> No vehicle is allowed to park at a parking meter for longer than six hours, even if coins have been deposited in the meter.

> Vehicles taking up more than one parking space will be fined $10 for a first offense, and $40 for each subsequent offense.

> No person shall willingly break a parking meter or deposit slugs, buttons, or anything other than coins in a parking meter.

> Persons must now deposit coins in a parking meter beginning at 8:00 a.m. on weekdays instead of at 9:00 a.m.

> Persons must now deposit coins in a parking meter until 7:00 p.m. instead of until 5:00 p.m.

> Parking on Saturday and Sunday is no longer free. Coins must be deposited in parking meters from 9:00 a.m. until 7:00 p.m.

The Sandy Town Police Department wants to ensure residents and visitors that all money deposited in parking meters will be used to maintain meters and public streets.

6. According to the passage, on weekdays, those using parking meters must begin depositing coins at

    (A) 7:00 a.m.

    (B) 8:00 a.m.

    (C) 9:00 a.m.

    (D) 9:30 a.m.

The passage explains that on weekdays coins must now be deposited in parking meters beginning at 8:00 a.m. instead of at 9:00 a.m. Therefore, Choice (B) is correct.

7. According to the passage, which of the following will be fined $10 for a first offense?

    (A) Vehicles taking up more than one space

    (B) Persons breaking a parking meter

    (C) Vehicles parked at meters on the weekend

    (D) Persons who deposit slugs in a parking meter

The passage states that vehicles taking up more than one parking space are fined $10 for a first offense and $40 for subsequent offenses. The correct answer is Choice (A).

8. A vehicle is only allowed to remain at a parking meter for six hours.

    (A) True

    (B) False

This statement is true, Choice (A), and is explained in the first item of the list in the passage.

Practice Questions for the NYC Reading Comprehension Section

The following passages and question sets are designed to help you practice your written comprehension, information ordering, inductive reasoning, deductive reasoning, and problem sensitivity skills. For all questions, choose the answer that *most correctly* answers the question.

> *Answer Questions 1 through 4 on the basis of the following written comprehension passage.*

On October 17, 2009, police officers McGrane and Douglas responded to a call at 84 South St. at 3:45 p.m. in response to a botched home invasion reported by a Mrs. Anderson. They arrived at the apartment at 3:55 p.m., rang the doorbell, and were greeted by Mrs. Anderson's neighbor, Mrs. Wilson. Mrs. Anderson was shaken up, so Mrs. Wilson attempted to tell the officers what she knew. She told them that Mrs. Anderson, a stay-at-home mom, was in her backyard with her 6-year-old daughter hanging clothing on the line when someone broke into her house through the side door. According to Mrs. Wilson, Mrs. Anderson went back in the house around 3:30 p.m., unaware that a trespasser was inside, and discovered the door to her husband's office open. Gaining composure, Mrs. Anderson then told the officers that she knew something was wrong because her husband never leaves his office door unlocked and open. She grabbed her youngest daughter and ran quickly past the door to the staircase. She did not want to leave the house without her 11-year-old daughter, who was upstairs working on a project for school. Although she tried to pass the door to the office without being seen, an intruder took notice. He chased her up the stairs, but she got to her daughter's room and locked the door before he caught her. She used her daughter's cellphone to call the police. When she was sure the intruder had left the house, she ran to Mrs. Wilson's house with her children.

While Officer McGrane interviewed Mrs. Anderson and Mrs. Wilson, Officer Douglas walked through the house. Other than a few papers strewn across the floor, Mr. Anderson's office did not look disturbed. However, one of the desk drawers was open. She made note of this and then proceeded upstairs to the 11-year-old's room to check on the children.

Catherine, Mrs. Anderson's eldest daughter, told Officer Douglas that her father is a lawyer, but she didn't know what kind. She told Officer Douglas that when her mother ran into her room, she told her to be quiet and move away from the door. Catherine took a seat by her window, which overlooks the backyard. There was some pounding on the door, but then it stopped. They heard the suspect run down the stairs, and Catherine watched him run through their backyard. He hopped the fence that separates their yard from their neighbors' and ran through their neighbors' yard and onto their driveway. She saw him turn right at the end of the driveway. She lost track of him after that. Catherine told the officer that he was wearing a black winter hat, blue jeans, and a brown, long-sleeved shirt. Catherine did not see the man's face. Officer Douglas thanked Catherine for talking to her and then returned to the living room.

Officer McGrane told Officer Douglas that Mrs. Anderson had identified the suspect as an approximately 28-year-old white male, 5 feet 10 inches and 170 pounds. Mrs. Anderson confirmed her daughter's description, but also added that he was wearing leather gloves. Despite a noticeable mole on the suspect's left cheek, she could not describe his face, but she claimed that she would recognize him if she saw his face again. She told the officers that she would not know if anything was missing from her husband's office, because she rarely spends time in the room. She said her husband was out of town, but when she had called him about the break-in, he said he would be home early the next morning.

Officers McGrane and Douglas returned to the station to complete their crime report. They planned to interview Mr. Anderson the next day.

1. At what time did Mrs. Anderson go back into the house after hanging clothes on the line?

   (A) 3:30 p.m.

   (B) 3:43 p.m.

   (C) 3:55 p.m.

   (D) 3:57 p.m.

If you read the first paragraph of this passage carefully, you'll see that Mrs. Wilson said that Mrs. Anderson went back into the house around 3:30 p.m., Choice (A).

2. What color shirt was the suspect wearing?

   (A) Black

   (B) Blue

   (C) White

   (D) Brown

The third paragraph of the passage says that the suspect was wearing a black winter hat, blue jeans, and a brown, long-sleeved shirt. The correct answer is Choice (D).

3. How did Mrs. Anderson know that an intruder was in the house?

    (A) The door to her husband's office was open.

    (B) An upstairs window was open.

    (C) She heard a loud noise near Catherine's room.

    (D) She heard someone walking up the stairs.

    The first paragraph says that Mrs. Anderson knew that something was wrong when she saw her husband's office door open; she said he never leaves it unlocked and open. Choice (A) is correct.

4. When did Mr. Anderson say that he would be home?

    (A) In a few minutes

    (B) The next morning

    (C) That night

    (D) The next evening

    The last sentence of the fourth paragraph says that Mr. Anderson is planning to come home early the next morning, Choice (B).

> *Answer Question 5 solely on the basis of the following information ordering passage.*

When officers allow nonemployees into the police station they should

1. Ask for the visitor's identification.

2. Verify the identification and ensure that the person is not a known threat.

3. Require the visitor to complete a visitation form that describes the reason for the visit.

4. If the visitor is doing maintenance, ask for the visitor's work order. Make a copy of the work order, which will be filed with the visitation form.

5. Create a visitor pass that includes the visitor's name and the name of the employee the visitor is there to see.

6. Require the visitor to wear the pass on an outermost piece of clothing so that it is in plain sight.

7. Ask the employee who is meeting with the visitor to escort the visitor from the public area to other sections of the building. (*Note*: Do not allow unattended visitors to go into other sections of the building.)

8. When the visitor is ready to depart, ask the visitor to sign out on the visitation form.

9. File all visitation forms and accompanying documents in the proper location.

5. A nonemployee visitor comes to the station while Officer Torres is working. The visitor, Hector Martin, tells Officer Torres that he is there to fix a broken copy machine. Officer Torres asks for the visitor's identification, verifies its validity, and determines that Mr. Martin is not a known threat. Officer Torres asks Mr. Martin to complete a visitation form. What should Officer Torres do next?

    (A) Ask an employee to accompany Mr. Martin through the building.

    (B) Create a visitor pass for Mr. Martin with his name.

    (C) File Mr. Martin's visitation form and work order in the proper place.

    (D) Ask to see a copy of Mr. Martin's work order.

The passage says that after asking the visitor to complete a visitation form describing the reason for the visit, the officer should ask to see the visitor's work order if the visitor is doing maintenance work. Therefore, Choice (D) is the next step.

Answer Question 6 solely on the basis of the following inductive reasoning passage.

After learning about different kinds of drug crimes, recruit officers attended a class about using specially trained police dogs to track down hidden drugs. They witnessed Officer Jim Garza and his beagle, Hank, find a bag of marijuana on an undercover cop and locate another hidden in an old locker in the back of the classroom. Officer Garza then explained how he trained Hank to find illicit substances, especially those hidden in the baggage of airline passengers. He noted that Hank first had to pass obedience, endurance, and agility tests. Officer Garza, Hank's handler, explained that he then followed these steps when training Hank to locate marijuana:

1. The handler plays tug-of-war with the dog using a plain, unscented towel. The towel becomes the dog's favorite toy.

2. Once the dog favors the towel, the handler hides a bag of marijuana in the center of the towel and introduces it to the dog. The dog soon identifies the scent of the marijuana as the scent of his towel.

3. After the dog familiarizes itself with the scent of the marijuana, the handler hides the towel containing the hidden drugs in a variety of places nearby. The handler then instructs the dog to find his toy.

4. When the dog finds the towel, the handler rewards the dog with a game of tug-of-war. The dog soon will eagerly track down the scent because he associates the smell of marijuana with his favorite toy.

6. Based on the preceding information, the recruits would be correct to conclude that

(A) a police dog can learn to find any kind of drug.

(B) a police dog would rather work than play.

(C) beagles are most often used as police dogs.

(D) most dogs can be trained to be police dogs.

The way in which Officer Garza trained Hank to find marijuana could be used with any kind of drug. Therefore, Choice (A) is the best answer.

Answer Question 7 solely on the basis of the following inductive reasoning passage and table.

Officers studying the law are learning about the frequency of traffic accidents. To understand how the presence of a traffic light affects the number of accidents that may take place at high-volume intersections per year, the class receives a handout containing the following information:

Intersection	Incidents (2009)	Traffic Light
1st St. and Ocean Dr.	5	Yes
5th St. and Elm St.	9	Yes
Hill St. and Cedar Ave.	12	No
6th St. and Lake St.	6	Yes

Intersection	Incidents (2009)	Traffic Light
Park Ave. and Oak St.	14	No
Main St. and Joseph Ave.	16	No
9th St. and Maple St.	7	Yes
3rd St. and Washington Ave.	1	No

7. After reviewing the preceding table, it would be most correct for an officer to conclude that

(A) traffic lights are necessary at all high-volume intersections.

(B) traffic lights at intersections result in fewer accidents.

(C) traffic lights do not affect the number of accidents at intersections.

(D) traffic lights at intersections result in more accidents.

Most of the intersections with traffic lights had fewer accidents; therefore, Choice (B) is the best answer.

Answer Question 8 solely on the basis of the following deductive reasoning passage.

Kleptomania is an impulse-control disorder. Those who suffer from kleptomania cannot stop themselves from stealing items of little or no value. Kleptomaniacs experience a sense of relief or liberation once they have successfully completed their task. The diagnostic criteria that mental health professionals use to diagnose kleptomania are as follows:

- The inability to resist the urge to steal an item that one does not need for any practical use and does not plan to exchange for money.

- The presence of a tense, anxious feeling in the time leading up to the act of stealing.

- The presence of relief, satisfaction, or pleasure once the item is in one's possession.

- The lack of anger or vengeance influencing the decision to steal.

- The lack of a conduct disorder, manic disorder, or antisocial personality.

8. According to the preceding description, which one of the following is the best example of a kleptomaniac?

(A) William, a young man short on cash, feels that he must steal two small electronic items each day to resell them so he can pay his rent.

(B) Rose, a young woman, frequently breaks the law by stealing, defacing private property, and purposely speeding through stop signs and red lights.

(C) Matthew, an elderly man who despises the owner of the small shop next door to his house, purchases a newspaper from the shop each day, but hides candy, greeting cards, or magazines inside the pages. He does this because he wants to hurt the shop's owner.

(D) Alex, a middle-aged woman, steals paper clips, chocolate bars, sale markers, and pens off the desks of her co-workers or while waiting in line at stores to achieve a feeling of bliss that will calm her nerves for a little while.

The middle-aged woman who steals to achieve a feeling of bliss, Choice (D), best matches the definition of a kleptomaniac.

> *Answer Questions 9 and 10 solely on the basis of the definition given before each question.*

Juvenile delinquency: A person, usually under the age of 18, who has violated the law with antisocial behavior that is beyond what his or her parents can control and therefore must be dealt with by law enforcement.

9. According to the definition given, which one of the following is the best example of juvenile delinquency?

   (A) Ricky, a 17-year-old, has started smoking but has not yet been caught by his parents.

   (B) Lori, a 15-year-old, dresses in black and paints her face white when she goes out with her friends at night.

   (C) Tony, a 16-year-old, has been involved in many fights and has recently seriously injured a boy.

   (D) Pam, a 17-year-old, has been suspended because she skipped school with her friends.

Tony, the boy described in Choice (C) who fights and has now seriously injured a boy, meets the definition of a juvenile delinquent because he is the most likely to have legal charges against him.

Second-degree murder: Nonpremeditated killing resulting from an assault but not from a vicious crime such as rape or armed robbery; the killing may have been caused by dangerous conduct and the killer's lack of concern for human life.

10. According to the definition given, which one of the following is the best example of second-degree murder?

   (A) Amy shoots and kills a classmate because the girl stole Amy's boyfriend.

   (B) While holding up a liquor store, Ray shoots and kills the clerk.

   (C) Jerome speeds in his car and hits a tree. He and a passenger are killed.

   (D) Carrie gets into a fight and beats another girl, who dies.

Choice (D) is the best example of second-degree murder because Carrie's killing of the girl she fights with is not premeditated, but she continues to hit the girl until she dies.

> *Answer Question 11 on the basis of the following passage.*

A police officer may not frisk someone during a routine encounter unless the police officer has reason to suspect that the person is involved in criminal activity and is armed and dangerous.

11. An officer should frisk which of the following?

   (A) A man getting on a train who is believed to have a gun

   (B) A woman boarding an airplane who is of Middle Eastern descent

   (C) A young man who is smoking a cigarette

   (D) A young woman who has blood on her shirt

According to the statement, officers have the right to frisk anyone they suspect is armed. Therefore, they should frisk the man who may be carrying a gun, depicted in Choice (A).

Answer Question 12 on the basis of the following passage.

Police officers may shoot and kill a dog if they see the dog pursuing, seriously wounding, or killing a human being or a domestic animal, such as another dog or a cat. This is true regardless of whether or not the dog in question is licensed.

12. An officer is justified in shooting a dog in which of the following instances?

(A) A police officer shoots a pit bull because it is growling and he is afraid of it.

(B) A police officer shoots a German shepherd that has chased and is killing a cat.

(C) A police officer shoots a dog because it is roaming a neighborhood unlicensed.

(D) A police officer shoots a dog after it has bitten a man's hand.

The officer who shoots the dog that is killing a cat, Choice (B), is justified according to the definition.

Answer Question 13 solely on the basis of the following information.

13. While Officer Garcia is on patrol, an alarm is transmitted over the police radio regarding a robbery that occurred an hour ago. The suspect is described as a black male, about 300 pounds, with brown hair and brown eyes, wearing a purple jacket. The suspect has a mustache and a beard. Police Officer Garcia stops four black males for questioning. Which one of the pieces of information provided by the victims should Officer Garcia consider the most helpful in identifying the suspect?

(A) The suspect is wearing a purple jacket.

(B) The suspect weighs 300 pounds.

(C) The suspect has a mustache and a beard.

(D) The suspect has brown hair and brown eyes.

The piece of information that would most likely identify the suspect is his weight. He is a large man. Therefore, Choice (B) would best identify him.

Chapter 5

Expressing Yourself with Proper Grammar, Punctuation, and Spelling

In This Chapter

▶ Brushing up on the various parts of speech and their usage

▶ Improving your spelling skills

▶ Answering practice grammar and spelling questions

*P*olice officers need to be able to write clearly and correctly so that others understand their meaning and don't misinterpret the facts. Police officers must keep meticulous records relating to crime scenes. While police officers investigate crimes and arrest individuals, they don't charge these individuals with a crime — other law-enforcement officials, such as prosecuting attorneys, do this. These law-enforcement officials rely on a police officer's records to effectively perform their jobs. Police officers must also create arrest reports and incident reports that must be complete and correct, without grammar and spelling errors. Police officers are often called upon to testify in court that the information in their reports is accurate.

Both the National Police Officer Selection Test (POST) and the New York City (NYC) exam assess your knowledge of grammar and spelling.

Imagine seeing the following written on a police report:

Because the suspect's has read hair and were whereing a blew jaket.

What's wrong with this sentence? For starters, it's a sentence fragment and not a sentence — a sentence is a complete thought. This group of words has other problems as well. It's not grammatically correct, and words are spelled incorrectly. The writer's meaning is clearer in the following revision:

The suspect had red hair and was wearing a blue jacket.

In this chapter, we address what you need to know to ace grammar and spelling questions on the POST and NYC test as well as on other written police officer tests. We begin with a review of the basics to get you up to speed.

Acing Grammar Questions

Do you use correct grammar when you speak? While grammatical slips are often acceptable in speech, they're more noticeable — and more inappropriate — in writing. Brush up on your grammar to ace the grammar questions on the POST and NYC test. You may see questions assessing your knowledge of the following:

- ✔ Verb tense
- ✔ Subject-verb agreement
- ✔ Pronouns
- ✔ Comparative and superlative adjectives
- ✔ Complete sentences versus fragments
- ✔ Pluralizing

Choosing the correct verb tense

Suppose you were to tell your spouse, "Today I am playing a round of golf. After this, I had gone to the grocery store. I will buy steak for dinner." Your spouse would likely give you a look that said, "Huh?" The sentences are confusing because the verb tenses don't agree. You would more likely say, "Today, I played a round of golf. After this, I went to the grocery store. I bought steak for dinner." Now, the verb tenses agree. The sentences are written in the past tense. Keep in mind that sometimes it's necessary to switch tenses. For example, it's okay to say, "I have been sleeping later because I am tired." This sentence contains a verb in the present perfect progressive tense *(have been sleeping)* and a verb in the present tense *(am)*. But in this sentence, the change in tense is essential to the meaning.

Some questions on written police officer tests are about verb tense. These questions may ask you to read a sentence with a blank in it and then choose the verb that best fits in the blank. Before you tackle some sample questions, you may find it helpful to review the different verb tenses.

Verb tenses fall into one of three primary categories — present, past, and future — with each category representing the time frame suggested by the verb. For example, verbs in the future tense refer to actions that haven't taken place yet, but will in the future. Within each main category are several types of more specific verb tenses. Tables 5-1, 5-2, and 5-3 show the types of verb tenses found in each of the three main categories, along with examples.

Note that verbs in the progressive tenses and the present perfect, past perfect, future, and future perfect tenses include words such as *am, are, have, had, has*, and *will*. These additional words are called *auxiliaries*.

Table 5-1	Present Tenses
Tense	*Example*
Present	allow(s)
Present progressive	am/is/are allowing
Present perfect	have/has allowed
Present perfect progressive	have/has been allowing

Table 5-2	Past Tenses
Tense	*Example*
Past	allowed
Past progressive	was/were allowing
Past perfect	had allowed
Past perfect progressive	had been allowing

Table 5-3	Future Tenses
Tense	*Example*
Future	will allow
Future progressive	will be allowing
Future perfect	will have allowed
Future perfect progressive	will have been allowing

When you answer questions on a written police officer test about verb tense, look for clues in the sentence. Clues are words that help you choose the correct tense. Read this sentence:

We _____ ice cream from the new ice cream shop last week.

Notice how the words "last week" help you figure out that the verb should be past tense. If this were a test question, you would choose a verb in the past tense, such as *ate* or *had*. Now, try this question:

Next year, I _____ culinary school.

(A) attend

(B) attended

(C) will attend

(D) had been attending

(E) had attended

The words "next year" are clues in this sentence. They tell you that this is something that has not happened yet. Choice (C) is the correct answer.

Watching out for subject-verb agreement

Some grammar on the police officer written test asks you to choose a verb that agrees with the subject of a sentence. To correctly answer these questions, study the following rules and the accompanying examples:

- ✔ Use a singular verb with a singular subject.

  The dog barks.

- ✔ Use a plural verb with a plural subject.

  The dogs bark.

- ✔ Use a plural verb when two or more subjects are connected by *and.*

  Bill and Jose eat snacks after practice.

- ✔ Use a singular verb with *either/or* or *neither/nor.*

  Neither Umberto nor Marianna knows where their mother has gone.

- ✔ Use a singular verb when two singular subjects are connected by *or* or *nor.*

  A ball or a bat broke the window.

- ✔ Use a singular verb in sentences with *each, everyone, every one, someone, somebody, anyone,* and *anybody.*

  Everyone stands in line over there.

- ✔ Use a singular verb with sums of money or periods of time.

  Ten minutes is not a long time to wait for the doctor.

  Fifty dollars is too much money for that purse.

- ✔ Use a singular verb with collective nouns such as *team* and *group.*

  The team is ready for the game.

  The group knows which bus to ride.

- ✔ If a phrase is between the subject and the verb, make sure the verb agrees with the subject and not the phrase.

  The women who work at the hospital are attentive.

- ✔ When a compound subject has both a singular and plural subject joined by *or* or *nor,* the verb should agree with the part of the subject that is closest to the verb.

  Her son or her nurses are going to help her eat dinner.

- ✔ In sentences beginning with *there* or *here,* the subject of the sentence follows the verb. The verb should agree with the subject.

  There are three detectives on their way to the crime scene.

Now, try these questions:

Every football player _____ after school each day.

(A) practice

(B) will practices

(C) has been practices

(D) practices

(E) have practice

The correct answer is Choice (D). *Every* is singular, so it requires a singular verb.

There ____ many different flavors of coffee at the store.

(A) is

(B) are

(C) was

(D) will

(E) had

The correct answer is Choice (B). Remember that the subject is *flavors*.

Picking the correct pronoun

Pronouns make writing easier to read. A *pronoun* is a noun substitute, and the noun a pronoun refers to is called the *antecedent*. To see the difference pronouns make, first read the following paragraph, which doesn't use pronouns:

> Julio rode Julio's bike to soccer practice today. First, Julio stopped at the store for a drink. Julio parked Julio's bike, but Julio forgot to lock Julio's bike. When Julio came out of the store, Julio's bike was missing. Julio was in big trouble!

Now read the following version, which takes advantage of pronouns:

> Julio rode his bike to soccer practice today. First, he stopped at the store for a drink. He parked his bike, but he forgot to lock it. When he came out of the store, his bike was missing. He was in big trouble!

Some questions on the verbal expression section of the police officer written test ask you to choose the correct pronoun in a sentence. In this section, we review some pronoun basics so you can answer these questions correctly.

Subject and object pronouns

For starters, a pronoun may be either a subject pronoun or an object pronoun:

- ✔ **Subject pronouns:** *I, you, he, she, it, we, you, they, who*
- ✔ **Object pronouns:** *me, you, him, her, it, us, you, them, whom*

Think about what a *subject pronoun* might do. Take the place of the subject in the sentence, you say? Correct! The same holds true for an *object pronoun* — it takes the place of the object in a sentence. In most sentences, the subject of the sentence comes before the verb, and the object of the sentence comes after the verb. Read these sentences:

> Shar baked a cake for her grandmother. (*Shar* is the subject of the sentence.)

> She baked a cake for her grandmother. (The subject pronoun *she* is now the subject.)

Now read these sentences:

> Phillip burned his hand. (*Hand* is the object of the sentence.)

> Phillip burned it. (The object pronoun *it* is now the object.)

Now that you know the difference between subject and object pronouns, the next step is to review some rules about pronouns. Study each of the following rules and consider the examples. They'll help you correctly answer questions about pronouns on the police officer test.

✔ Use a subject pronoun when the pronoun is the subject of the sentence. This rule also applies when a compound subject contains a noun and a pronoun.

Dwayne and I asked to enter Mrs. Hernandez's room.

✔ Use an object pronoun when the pronoun is the object of the sentence. Also use an object pronoun when a compound object contains a noun and a pronoun.

Mrs. Hernandez gave Dwayne and me permission to enter.

✔ Use a subject pronoun to rename the subject.

This is he.

It is I who would like to see the new movie.

✔ Use a subject pronoun after the words *than* or *as*.

Josie bakes tastier treats than I. (It helps to mentally complete this sentence: *Josie bakes tastier treats than I do.*)

She is more attractive than I. (Same here: *She is more attractive than I am.*)

✔ Use an object pronoun as the object of a prepositional phrase.

My mother yelled at me.

Possessive pronouns

Possessive pronouns show ownership. They include *its, yours, his, hers, ours, theirs,* and *mine.* A possessive pronoun never needs an apostrophe.

The cat injured its tail. (not *it's*)

The torn jeans are his. (not *his's*)

Use possessive pronouns before nouns ending in *ing,* such as *running, jumping, thinking,* and *reading.*

Your (not *you*) coming home late has caused you to get grounded for a week.

Their (not *them*) calling the police resulted in the robbery suspect's arrest.

Reflexive pronouns

Reflexive pronouns include *myself, yourself, yourselves,* and *ourselves.* Only use reflexive pronouns when they refer back to another word in the sentence.

I fixed the leaky faucet myself. (*myself* refers back to *I*)

He got up and walked all by himself. *himself* refers back to *he*)

Indefinite pronouns

Indefinite pronouns don't refer to a specific person or thing. They can be singular or plural.

✔ **Singular indefinite pronouns** include *another, anybody, anyone, anything, each, either, everybody, everyone, everything, nobody, no one, nothing, somebody, someone,* and *something.*

✔ **Plural indefinite pronouns** include *both, few, many, others,* and *several.*

If a singular indefinite pronoun is used in a sentence with another pronoun, the other pronoun should also be singular.

> Each employee knew it was time for his or her evaluation. (not *their*)

> Everyone in the department should write down his or her emergency contact information. (not *their*)

Singular pronouns are even singular when they're used in combination with one another.

> Anything and everything is on sale today. (*is* not *are*)

> Each and every flower is in full bloom. (*is* not *are*)

> Anybody and everybody is invited to my party. (*is* not *are*)

Demonstrative pronouns

Demonstrative pronouns often refer to the pronouns that come after them. *That, this, those,* and *these* are demonstrative pronouns.

> Is this cheese still fresh? (*this* refers to *cheese*)

> Those shoes are too tight on me. (*those* refers to *shoes*)

Now try answering these questions:

My brother Henry is shorter than _____.

(A) me

(B) I

(C) us

(D) all of them

(E) we be

The correct answer is Choice (B). Use a subject pronoun after *than* or *as.*

Every child in the class needs to be accompanied by _____ parents.

(A) their

(B) his or her

(C) its

(D) he or she

(E) them

The correct answer is Choice (B). A singular indefinite pronoun refers to a singular subject pronoun.

Officer Parker and _____ patted down the suspect before placing him in handcuffs.

(A) you

(B) me

(C) we

(D) I

(E) us

The correct answer is Choice (D). The subject pronoun *I* is correct because the pronoun is part of the compound subject of the sentence.

Using the right adjective

You may be asked a question or two about positive, comparative, and superlative adjectives on the police officer test. Follow these guidelines when choosing an answer:

- Use a *positive adjective* when the adjective isn't being used for comparison purposes; in other words, it isn't comparing the noun or pronoun it modifies to any other noun or pronoun.

  Contrary to the way it may sound, the word *positive* in this context doesn't mean the opposite of *negative*.

  Chen is a good-looking man. (The positive adjective is *good-looking*. Chen's appearance isn't being compared to that of anyone else.)

- Use a comparative adjective to compare only two items, ideas, or people.

  Comparative adjectives usually end in *er*.

  LaShonda is prettier than Julia. (The comparative adjective is *prettier*. LaShonda and Julia are the only two nouns being compared in this instance.)

- Use a superlative adjective when comparing three or more items, ideas, or people.

  Superlative adjectives usually end in *est*.

  Sheila is the tallest girl in the room. (The superlative adjective is *tallest*. The presumption here is that there are more than two girls in the room.)

- For adjectives with three or more syllables, use *more* and *most* to form the comparative and the superlative.

  Chen is more interesting than Paul. (*Interesting* has four syllables.)

  Chen is the most interesting guy in the room.

- For the two-syllable adjectives *clever, gentle, friendly, quiet, common, cruel, handsome, polite,* and *simple,* you may use either *er* and *est* or *more* and *most* to form the comparative and superlative.

  LaShonda is the friendliest girl in the room.

  LaShonda is the most friendly girl in the room.

Now try answering the following practice question.

Officer Martin is often asked to reach high shelves in the police station because he is the _____ of all the police officers on the force.

(A) tallest

(B) most tallest

(C) taller

(D) more taller

(E) tall

The correct answer is Choice (A). This question compares Officer Martin to all the police officers on the force — three or more people — so the superlative form is used. Because the word *tall* is only one syllable, you don't need to use the word *most*.

Identifying complete sentences and fragments

A *complete sentence* contains a subject and a verb and expresses a complete thought. Following are two examples of complete sentences.

> Jorge ran home.

> Suzie watched television.

Fragments are incomplete sentences that stand by themselves. They're usually missing information such as a subject, a verb, or punctuation. The following sentence is incomplete:

> Driving down the street.

The sentence is missing a subject. It doesn't tell you who is driving down the street, and thus it's an incomplete thought. Fragments can also be dependent clauses, or phrases that follow a main clause. Consider the following:

> Rose works in her garden. Throughout the day.

Throughout the day is a dependent clause because it depends on *Rose works in her garden* to give it meaning. Easy ways to correct fragments are to add information or to remove the period between the fragment and the main clause, like this:

> Rose works in her garden throughout the day.

Now try a practice question. One of the following sentences contains a fragment. Choose the answer that best fixes the error.

While the department in the neighboring community has the ability to have at least four full-time officers patrolling the streets after midnight. Our department cannot afford to have more than two full-time officers patrolling the area after midnight.

(A) The department in the neighboring community has the ability to have at least four full-time officers patrolling the streets after midnight. Our department cannot afford to have more than two full-time officers patrolling the area after midnight.

(B) While the department in the neighboring community has the ability to have at least four full-time officers patrolling the streets after midnight, our department cannot afford to have more than two full-time officers patrolling the area after midnight.

(C) While the department in the neighboring community has the ability to have at least four full-time officers patrolling the streets after midnight, therefore, our department cannot afford to have more than two full-time officers patrolling the area after midnight.

(D) While the department in the neighboring community has the ability to have at least four full-time officers patrolling the streets after midnight, however, our department cannot afford to have more than two full-time officers patrolling the area after midnight.

(E) While the department in the neighboring community has the ability to have at least four full-time officers patrolling the streets after midnight, and our department cannot afford to have more than two full-time officers patrolling the area after midnight.

The correct answer is Choice (B). Changing the period to a comma after the first sentence eliminates the sentence fragment and connects the dependent clause with the main clause.

Pluralizing nouns

Just as in spelling, the rules for forming plural nouns aren't foolproof; there are exceptions to every rule. The most common way to make a noun plural is to add *s* to the end. For example, the plural of *boy* is *boys,* and the plural of *plate* is *plates.* However, there are many exceptions to the rule, including the following:

✔ **For words that end in *ch, x, s,* or *s*-like sounds, add *es* to the end of the word.**

Examples: *match/matches, tax/taxes, witness/witnesses*

✔ **Some nouns have irregular verb forms.**

Examples: *child/children, mouse/mice, person/people*

✔ **Some irregular forms include nouns that keep their Latin or Greek forms.**

Examples: *syllabus/syllabi, fungus/fungi*

✔ **For words that end in a consonant and *y,* change the *y* to *i* and add *es.***

Examples: *baby/babies, story/stories*

✔ **To words that end in *o,* add *s* or *es.* There's no simple rule to explain when to use *s* versus *es.***

Examples: *hero/heroes, potato/potatoes, auto/autos, photo/photos*

✔ **For words that end in *f* or *fe,* replace the *f* with a *v* and add *es.***

Examples: *leaf/leaves, self/selves, knife/knives*

✔ **For words that end in *is,* replace the *is* with *es.***

Examples: *diagnosis/diagnoses, crisis/crises*

✔ **For words that end in *um,* replace the *um* with *a.***

Examples: *datum/data, medium/media*

✔ **For words that end in *on*, replace the *on* with *a*.**

Examples: *criterion/criteria, phenomenon/phenomena*

✔ **Words that end in *a* are pluralized by adding an *e*.**

Examples: *alga/algae, vertebra/vertebrae*

✔ **For words that end in *ex*, replace the *ex* with *ices*.**

Examples: *index/indices, vortex/vortices*

✔ **For words that end in *us*, replace the *us* with *i* or *ora*.**

Examples: *alumnus/alumni, stimulus/stimuli, corpus/corpora*

✔ **Words that end in *eau* are pluralized by adding an *x*.**

Examples: *beau/beaux*

✔ **Nouns that usually come in pairs are plural.**

Examples: *pants, glasses, tweezers*

✔ **Some nouns have no singular form. These are usually plural.**

Examples: *snow, amends*

✔ **Some nouns have the same singular and plural form.**

Examples: *deer, sheep, salmon*

A noun is never made plural by adding *'s* or *s'* to the end of the word. Nouns that end in *'s* or *s'* are possessive nouns and must possess something. Consider these examples: *Mary's sister is 5 years old. The students' books were destroyed in the fire.*

Now try some practice questions.

There were seven _____ involved in the accident on the interstate.

(A) vehicle's

(B) vehicle

(C) vehicles

(D) vehicles'

(E) vehicleses

The correct answer is Choice (C). This sentence should contain the plural noun *vehicles*, not the singular noun *vehicle*, the possessives *vehicle's* or *vehicles'*, or the incorrect plural noun form *vehicleses*.

During a search, _____ and other paraphernalia were seized by the police officers.

(A) drugs'

(B) drug's

(C) drugs

(D) drug

(E) drugses

The correct answer is Choice (C). This sentence should contain the plural noun *drugs*, not the possessives *drugs'* or *drug's*, the singular noun *drug*, or the incorrect plural noun form *drugses*.

A grammar question may ask you to choose the word or words that should go in the blank. This type of question may look like this:

The officer shouted to the suspect, "Put _____ hands in the air."

(A) your

(B) you are

(C) you're

(D) his

(E) their

The correct answer is Choice (A). This sentence should contain the possessive pronoun *your*, not *his* or *their*. *You're* is the contraction for *you are* and is a homophone for the correct answer, *your*.

Lieutenant Herron pulls over a man driving without a license. He fills out a Seized Driver's License Receipt/Report, which contains the following two sentences:

1. The suspect produces a valid registration and insurance card for the vehicle, that is up-to-date.

2. The suspect is compliant with police orders, and he parks the car on the side of the road and waits until his ride arrives.

Which of the following choices best explains the preceding sentences?

(A) Only Sentence 1 is grammatically correct.

(B) Only Sentence 2 is grammatically correct.

(C) Neither Sentence 1 nor Sentence 2 is grammatically correct.

(D) Both Sentence 1 and Sentence 2 are grammatically correct.

The correct answer is Choice (B). Sentence 2 is correct, but Sentence 1 has a misplaced comma. A comma is not needed before the restrictive clause *that is up-to-date*.

Excelling at Spelling Questions

The content of the written police officer test can vary, but some tests have spelling questions. Now, we know what you're thinking: "Why do I have to know how to spell words when I can just use a spell-checker to check my work?" Read this report:

Monday, September 20

The incident at the Holy Cross Cematery ocurred sometime between 8 p.m. Sunday and 6 a.m. Monday. The groundskeeper reported that more than 50 stones had been overturned and dozens of grave cites valdelized.

Do you think a spell-checker would catch all the errors in this note? Probably not. It's important to be able to express yourself like a professional, which means you need to be able to correctly spell most words in the English language. While you can't memorize the dictionary before you take this test, you can study some common spelling rules and learn the correct spelling of some commonly misspelled words.

Spelling rules aren't foolproof — often there are exceptions to a rule. However, applying spelling rules can help you eliminate incorrect answer options. Following are ten such rules to keep in mind:

✔ **The letter *i* comes before *e* except after *c* and when a word sounds like *ay*.**

Examples: *friend, thief, believe, neighbor, sleigh*

Exceptions: *weird, protein, foreign*

✔ **When the letter *c* follows a short vowel, it's usually doubled.**

Examples: *tobacco, raccoon, stucco, occupy*

✔ **The letters *ck* are used instead of *cc* if the letter following the *c* sound is *e, i,* or *y*.**

Examples: *frolicked, blackest, lucky*

✔ **If the *j* sound follows a short vowel, it's usually spelled *dge*.**

Examples: *dodge, judge, budget*

✔ **The *ch* sound is spelled *tch* after a short vowel.**

Examples: *witch, kitchen, catch, hatchet*

✔ **If a word has a short vowel sound and ends in *le*, there must be two consonants between the vowel and the *le* ending.**

Examples: *tickle, little, bottle, angle*

✔ **If a word has a silent *e*, you must drop the *e* before adding a vowel suffix.**

Examples: *force/forcing, age/aging, ride/riding, convince/convincing*

✔ **When the *ee* sound comes before a vowel suffix, it's usually spelled with the letter *i*.**

Examples: *ingredient, zodiac, material*

✔ **The ending *ist* is usually used to refer to someone who does something, whereas the ending *est* is used to create superlative adjectives.**

Examples: *machinist, druggist, strongest, longest*

✔ **The ending *cian* always refers to a person, whereas the endings *tion* and *sion* are not used to refer to people.**

Examples: *musician, electrician, condition, expression*

The rules presented in this chapter will help you spell many words correctly, but some words don't follow specific rules. If you're stuck trying to determine the correct spelling of a particular word, try sounding it out by its syllables. For example, when spelling the word *disappearing*, break down the word into syllables to spell it correctly: *dis-ap-pear-ing*. That was pretty simple, right?

Have a friend read aloud the words in Table 5-4. Write down each word when you hear it. Use the table to check your spelling.

Table 5-4		Commonly Misspelled Words	
Word	**Hint**	**Word**	**Hint**
acceptable	not *exceptable*	intelligence	not *intelligance*
accommodate	double *c* and double *m*	jewelry	not *jewlry* or *jewelery*
amateur	not *amature*	judgment	not *judgement*
apparent	not *aparent*	kernel	not *kernal*
argument	no *e* before *ment*	leisure	not *liesure*
calendar	not *calender*	license	*c* first, then *s*
category	not *catigory*	lightning	not *lightening*
cemetery	no *a*	maintenance	not *maintenence*
changeable	keep the *e* before *able*	millennium	double *l* and double *n*
collectible	not *collectable*	miniature	not *minature*
committed	double *m* and double *t*	misspell	double *s* and double *l*
conscience	both *s* and *c*	noticeable	*e* before *able*
discipline	both *s* and *c*	occasionally	double *c*, single *s*, and double *l*
embarrass	double *r* and double *s*	occurrence	double *c*, double *r*, and *ence*
equipment	not *equiptment*	pastime	single *t*
exceed	not *excede*	personnel	double *n* and single *l*
existence	not *existance*	questionnaire	double *n*
gauge	not *guage*	recommend	single *c* and double *m*
grateful	not *greatful*	referred	single *f* and double *r*
guarantee	not *guarranty*	relevant	not *relevent*
harass	single *r* and double *s*	rhythm	*rh* and then *th*
height	not *heighth*	separate	not *seperate*
ignorance	not *ignorence*	sergeant	not *sargent*
indispensable	not *indispensible*	supersede	not *supercede*
inoculate	single *n* and single *c*	vacuum	double *u*

Practice Grammar and Spelling Questions

The questions in this section are designed to give you some good practice for the verbal expression components of the written police officer exam. Remember, the more you practice vocabulary, spelling, and grammar, the more you'll improve these skills.

The POST (National Police Officer Selection Test) contains 20 questions about grammar and spelling. You have 15 minutes to answer these questions. Note that some grammar questions on the POST have only two answer options while others have three. In this practice section, Questions 1 through 12 reflect the types of grammar and spelling questions you'll see on the POST. Questions 13 through 17 are similar to those you'll see on the NYC test.

> *For Questions 1 through 3, choose the correct word to fill in the blank.*

1. Let's keep this information between you and _____.

   (A) I

   (B) me

   The statement calls for an objective pronoun, so Choice (B) is correct.

2. _____ coat is on the back of that chair.

   (A) You're

   (B) Your

   You're is a contraction for *you are,* so Choice (B) is correct.

3. The _____ are open to the public in June and July.

   (A) beach's

   (B) beaches

   (C) beaches'

   There's no need to make the noun possessive in this sentence. Choice (B), the plural *beaches,* is correct.

> *In Questions 4 and 5, which word in the sentence is misspelled?*

4. In many towns, a person riding a bycicle must follow the same rules as someone who is driving an automobile.

   (A) riding

   (B) bycicle

   (C) someone

   (D) driving

   (E) automobile

   Choice (B) is the correct answer. The correct spelling is *bicycle.*

5. On Wednesday morning, Officer Samson investigated a burglery on Main Street in which a stereo and two television sets were stolen.

   (A) Wednesday

   (B) investigated

   (C) burglery

   (D) stereo

   (E) television

   Choice (C) is the correct answer. *Burglary* is the correct spelling.

> *For Questions 6 through 9, choose the correct word or words to fill in the blank.*

6. The recruit officers lined up with _____ backs turned to the audience.

   (A) their

   (B) they're

   (C) there

   Choice (A), the possessive pronoun *their,* is correct here. *They're* is a contraction for *they are,* and *there* is an adverb used to show placement. Both are homophones for the correct answer, *their.*

7. Officer Jones and _____ are on duty this week.

   (A) me

   (B) I

   The pronoun *I,* Choice (B), is correct here because it refers to the subject *(Officer Jones and I)* performing the action *(are).*

8. The officers removed their _____ out of respect to the family.

   (A) hat

   (B) hat's

   (C) hats

   The plural noun *hats,* Choice (C), is correct here, not the singular noun *hat* or the possessive *hat's.*

9. The robbery suspect hopped into a car, stopped at a stoplight, and yelled to the woman driving, "Put on _____ seatbelt, because we're going on a wild ride!"

   (A) your

   (B) you're

   (C) you are

   Choice (A), the possessive pronoun *your,* is correct here. *You're* is the contraction for *you are* and is a homophone for the correct answer, *your.*

> *For Questions 10 through 12, choose the word that's spelled incorrectly.*

10. As the victim recounted the events of the evening, she became irrational and began assalting the police officer asking her questions.

    (A) victim

    (B) recounted

    (C) irrational

    (D) assalting

    (E) officer

    Choice (D) is the correct answer. The correct spelling is *assaulting.*

11. In the past month, thirtheen lives have been lost because of careless drivers not paying attention while driving through construction zones.

    (A) thirtheen

    (B) because

    (C) careless

    (D) attention

    (E) construction

    The correct answer is Choice (A). The correct spelling is *thirteen*.

12. The visbly shaken resident told police officers that her purse, jewelry, and other irreplaceable items had been removed from her house by an unknown individual.

    (A) visbly

    (B) resident

    (C) jewelry

    (D) irreplaceable

    (E) individual

    Choice (A) is the correct answer. The correct spelling is *visibly*.

For Questions 13 through 17, choose the answer that best explains the sentences.

---

13. After talking to everyone at the accident scene, Officer Hernandez fills out the incident report, which contains the following two sentences:

    1. The driver of the Honda Civic was traveling north when it veered off the roadway and struck a guardrail.

    2. The driver of the Honda Civic was cite for careless driving.

    (A) Only Sentence 1 is grammatically correct.

    (B) Only Sentence 2 is grammatically correct.

    (C) Neither Sentence 1 nor Sentence 2 is grammatically correct.

    (D) Both Sentence 1 and Sentence 2 are grammatically correct.

    Choice (C) is the correct answer. Neither sentence is correct. In Sentence 1, the pronoun *it* should be replaced with either *he* or *she* because the pronoun modifies the driver, not the vehicle. In Sentence 2, the wrong verb tense is used. The present tense of the verb *cite* should be replaced with the past tense *cited*.

14. A recruit officer has written a special report about the rise of drug crimes in the small community where he lives. Before he turns it in, he reviews the report, which contains the following two sentences:

    1. Drugs are destroying the small town of Hughesville, and residents no longer feel safe in their own community.

    2. The influx of drugs in Hughesville has brought not only crime and violence but also death.

    (A) Only Sentence 1 is grammatically correct.

    (B) Only Sentence 2 is grammatically correct.

    (C) Neither Sentence 1 nor Sentence 2 is grammatically correct.

    (D) Both Sentence 1 and Sentence 2 are grammatically correct.

    Choice (D) is the correct answer. Both sentences are correct. Sentence 1 correctly uses a conjunction to link two sentences. Sentence 2 correctly uses the correlative conjunctions *not only* and *but also.*

15. Officer Frederickson fills out an accident report after responding to the scene. Later he reads though the report, which contains the following two sentences:

    1. While proceeding through the intersection, the driver of vehicle B noticed another vehicle approaching his vehicle, but could not stop in time.

    2. The driver of vehicle A was traveling north through the intersection at a high rate of speed when it failed to stop at the posted stop sign.

    (A) Only Sentence 1 is grammatically correct.

    (B) Only Sentence 2 is grammatically correct.

    (C) Neither Sentence 1 nor Sentence 2 is grammatically correct.

    (D) Both Sentence 1 and Sentence 2 are grammatically correct.

    Choice (A) is the correct answer. Sentence 1 is correct, but Sentence 2 contains an incorrect pronoun. The pronoun *it* should be replaced with either *he* or *she* because the pronoun modifies the driver, not the vehicle.

16. A recruit officer is preparing a statement to read in front of her class. The statement contains the following two sentences:

    1. After conduct research for the past six months, I have determined that Pine Hill residents are not satisfied with their refuse pick-up requirements and schedule.

    2. Mrs. Jagger complained that the refuse on hers street is picked up at a different time each week, and sometimes her street is missed entirely.

    (A) Only Sentence 1 is grammatically correct.

    (B) Only Sentence 2 is grammatically correct.

    (C) Neither Sentence 1 nor Sentence 2 is grammatically correct.

    (D) Both Sentence 1 and Sentence 2 are grammatically correct.

    Neither sentence is grammatically correct, so Choice (C) is the correct answer. In Sentence 1, the incorrect verb tense is used. The present tense of the verb *conduct* should be replaced with the present participle tense *conducting*. In Sentence 2, the indefinite pronoun *hers* is used incorrectly. *Hers* should be replaced with the possessive pronoun *her.*

17. An officer fills out an incident report after responding to a domestic abuse call. Later he reads through the report, which contains the following two sentences:

    1. The victim is visibly shaken and bleeding from her left eye, refuses medical treatment.

    2. The suspect has left the house, and the victim is not going to file any charges at this time.

    (A) Only Sentence 1 is grammatically correct.

    (B) Only Sentence 2 is grammatically correct.

    (C) Neither Sentence 1 nor Sentence 2 is grammatically correct.

    (D) Both Sentence 1 and Sentence 2 are grammatically correct.

    The correct answer is Choice (B). Sentence 2 is correct, but Sentence 1 is missing a conjunction, such as *and,* to link the last part of the sentence, *refuses medical treatment,* to the first part of the sentence.

Chapter 6

Stretching Your Memory and Visualization Skills

....

In This Chapter

▶ Committing details to memory

▶ Sharpening your observation skills

▶ Getting everything in the right order

....

Suppose you and your partner are on patrol and see a man fleeing from a convenience store. A clerk bursts from the store and shouts, "Help! Get him! He just robbed the store!" The thief dashes through a nearby yard, so you and your partner exit the patrol car and chase him. However, the thief scales a fence and then vanishes. You suspect that someone was waiting for him on the other side of the fence.

You and your partner radio dispatch to alert nearby patrol to the area to help you find the suspect, but you have one big problem: You can't remember what he looks like. You can't recall his facial features or his approximate height and weight. And you can't remember what he was wearing. That's not good!

Police officers must be able to remember what they see. This includes people, buildings, roads — you name it. They must remember a suspect's scars and tattoos as well as the location of emergency exits in apartment buildings and one-way streets in neighborhoods. They must also remember what they hear, such as their supervisors' directions for correctly handling emergencies. And they must often recall these details under stressful conditions.

The New York City (NYC) test and other written police officer tests ask questions that require you to observe and recall details. Don't panic if you think this is difficult. We give you tools for remembering and recalling details in this chapter, and you get plenty of opportunities to practice, too.

Getting the Lowdown on Memory and Observation Questions on the NYC Test

If you take the New York City (NYC) police officer test or a similar test, expect to answer many memory and observation questions. Some of these questions ask you to look at a photograph and memorize details. Other questions may require you to envision which direction a suspect is traveling based on a description, follow directions in order, interpret maps, and remember numbers and letters in a particular order.

Digging deep for memorization questions

The NYC test contains memorization questions. To answer these questions, you're given ten minutes to study a photograph and file away in your memory as many details about it as you can. Ten minutes may seem like a long time to stare at a photograph — and it is! The questions ask you for very specific information, such as what item a person is carrying or what words appear on a sign on a particular building. It takes time to memorize this much information. Use these categories and questions to help you memorize important details in any photograph:

- **People:** Are there people in the photo? If so, how many? What are they wearing? Are they standing or sitting? What are they holding?

- **Buildings:** Are there buildings in the photo? If so, study the order in which they appear. Note their color and size. How many floors does each building have? If a store window is shown, what can you see in the window? If one or more buildings have signs, what do these signs say?

- **Other details:** Are there cars in the picture? If so, note their color and location. Are there animals in the picture? If so, where are they, and what are they doing?

When trying to memorize details in a photograph, focus on the most important details and try to connect them with your prior knowledge. For example, do the buildings in the picture look like they're in a country town or a large city? Making connections helps you remember information when you start to answer questions.

You may see a photograph like the one that follows on the NYC test. Study this photograph for ten minutes. Time yourself, and try to memorize as many important details about the photograph as you can. Don't write down any details or take any notes. Then cover the photo and answer the following example questions:

Photo courtesy National Photo Company Collection (Library of Congress)

What animal is sitting beside the woman?

(A) A squirrel

(B) A bird

(C) A dog

(D) A cat

The animal sitting beside the woman is a dog, Choice (C). The small dog sitting beside the woman is the only animal in the photograph, so the other choices are not correct.

Where is the woman's hat?

(A) Under her arm

(B) On her lap

(C) In her hands

(D) On her head

The woman in the picture is holding her hat on her lap, so Choice (B) is correct. The woman is not holding anything under her arm, so Choice (A) is incorrect. The woman has one hand on her lap and the other is motioning toward the dog, so Choice (C) is incorrect. You can also eliminate Choice (D), because the woman is not wearing anything on her head.

Which of these objects is beside the woman in the picture?

(A) A statue

(B) A door

(C) A shrub

(D) A lamppost

A dog sits to one side of the woman and a shrub is located on her other side, so Choice (C) is correct. The picture does not contain any of the items in the other choices.

Which of these is the woman wearing?

(A) A scarf

(B) A vest

(C) A necklace

(D) A jacket

The woman is wearing a jacket, along with a shirt and a skirt, so Choice (D) is correct. Choices (A), (B), and (C) are incorrect because the woman is not wearing a scarf, a vest, or a necklace.

For more practice, study the following photograph for ten minutes. Then cover the photograph and answer the questions. Don't look back at the photograph to determine your answers.

Photo courtesy www.public-domain-image.com

Which letter is NOT on the sign in the foreground of the photograph?

(A) A

(B) B

(C) C

(D) E

Although partially cut off, the sign hanging in the foreground of this photograph features information about the platforms, lines, and trains available at this specific stop. The letters A, C, and E appear in circles on the sign, whereas B does not. Choice (B) is correct.

How many exit signs are in this photograph?

(A) 1

(B) 2

(C) 3

(D) 4

This photograph features one exit sign positioned slightly to the left of the tiled wall, so Choice (A) is correct. It is above the head of the only person, a woman, in the photograph.

The sign hanging from the ceiling in the middle of the picture reads "Boarding Area." What does the symbol to the left of these words indicate?

(A) An entrance

(B) An exit

(C) No shoes, no service

(D) Handicap accessibility

The symbol to the left of the words "Boarding Area" on the sign hanging from the ceiling in the middle of the picture is one that signals handicap accessibility, Choice (D). It is a person in a wheelchair — the universal symbol for handicapped.

How many people are in this photograph?

(A) 1

(B) 2

(C) 3

(D) 4

Choice (A) is correct; one woman appears in this photograph. She appears to be wearing a hooded sweatshirt and has a purse over her right shoulder.

The right side of the photograph shows a close-up view of tiles on a wall. How many full wall tiles are in this photograph?

(A) 2

(B) 4

(C) 6

(D) 10

Including all partials, the total number of wall tiles that appear in this photograph is ten. However, only four are full tiles, which makes Choice (B) correct. The others are cut out by the photographer's zoom, angle, and perspective.

Which of the following letters appears in a circle above the door of the train?

(A) H

(B) J

(C) K

(D) L

The letter L appears in a circle above the door of the train; therefore, Choice (D) is correct. It appears to be a light that is signaling something about that specific train.

Which of the following numbers appears repeatedly along the walls of the station in this photo?

(A) 2

(B) 4

(C) 6

(D) 8

Choice (D) is correct. The number 8 appears at least twice to the left of the train in this photograph. It appears to be part of a patterned border along the wall of the station.

Which shape appears above the flag on the front of the train?

(A) Circle

(B) Square

(C) Octagon

(D) Triangle

Above the image of the American flag is a white circle with black writing. Choice (A) is correct.

Using your mind's eye for visualization questions

Imagine that you're in pursuit of a suspect who enters the third house on a street. Your supervisor tells you to position yourself in the alley directly behind this house. How do you remember which house the suspect entered when you're looking at the houses from the back? You have to envision the house — note its color and shape — and picture what the houses on the street look like from the alley behind them. To answer some questions on the NYC test, you have to envision what a diagram would look like from a different perspective.

Make the most of your memory

The memory and visualization questions on the police officer exam test how well you remember what you see and read. Memory and observation are vital to success in law enforcement. Officers must be able to observe and remember suspects' physical traits, the make and model of vehicles, and the time and place that incidents occur. Preparing thoroughly for memory and visualization questions will help you succeed on the police exam and excel as a police officer.

Imagine you're on a routine patrol when you walk past the buildings shown in the following diagram.

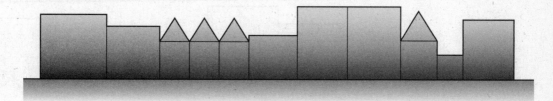

As you turn the corner, your view of the buildings changes. Which of the following most accurately represents your view from the back of the buildings?

(A)

(B)

(C)

(D)

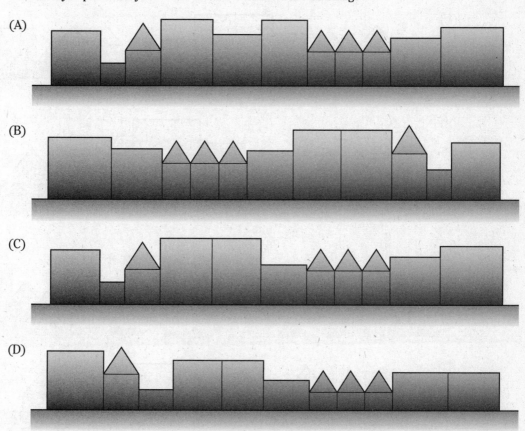

Your view from the back should be the exact opposite of your view from the front. The buildings should be in the same order, only reversed. None of the roofs should be switched on any of the buildings, and none of the bigger buildings should suddenly appear between the smaller ones. Choice (C) is correct because it shows the buildings in the correct order but reversed. The third building from the left when you're facing the buildings from the front is the third building from the right when you're facing the buildings from behind.

Now imagine you're on a routine patrol when you walk past the rear view of the buildings pictured in the following diagram.

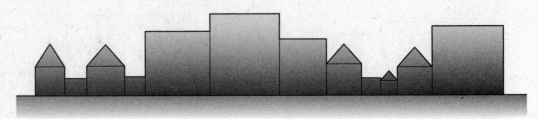

Which of the following most accurately represents your view from the front of the buildings?

(A)

(B)

(C)

(D)

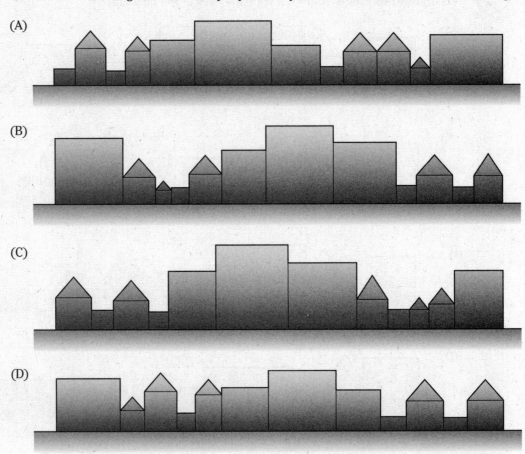

Your view from the front should be the exact opposite of your view from the back, so Choice (B) is correct. In Choice (B), none of the roofs have been misplaced and the buildings are all in their original positions, but reversed. The second house from the left when you're looking at the buildings from the back is the second house from the right when you're looking at the building from the front.

Other visualization questions ask you to interpret maps. Police officers must be able to do this well because they spend a good part of their day patrolling. Although you've most likely memorized the streets in your town, when you're working as a police officer in unfamiliar territories, you may rely on maps or directions to help you find your way.

On the NYC test and other written police officer tests, the maps may include symbols and words, such as a compass rose or street names, to help you answer the questions correctly. The following information may appear on a map:

- ✔ **Keys or legends:** A key or legend gives you the meaning of pictures or symbols that appear on the map. For example, in a map of city streets, you may see directional arrows in a single or double form. The key for this map explains that a single arrow indicates a one-way street and the direction in which it runs. Two arrows, one on top of the other, may signal a two-way street, indicating that the street allows traffic to travel in both directions (north/south or east/west). Legends and keys for maps may also include symbols that distinguish houses from apartment buildings and streetlights from stop signs.

- ✔ **Captions:** A caption is a word, phrase, or sentence explaining the purpose of the map. The caption may include additional information about streets, signs, or buildings.

- ✔ **Labels:** Labels are words or phrases identifying something on a map, such as the name of a building. Sometimes a line or an arrow extends from the label to the part of the map it identifies. Other times, the label may be placed on top of or inside the image it represents. Labels on maps often indicate the names of streets and buildings. Without a label on a map, you might have trouble finding specific locations, such as Dan's Deli located on the corner of Main Street and South Street.

- ✔ **Directional cues:** Many maps have arrows indicating direction. Some have a compass rose to show which directions are north, south, east, and west.

When you're answering questions based on maps, pay close attention to one-way streets and other information about the proper flow of traffic. When completing the test questions, you should choose answers that follow normal traffic patterns. Even police officers should refrain from going the wrong way down a one-way street!

Now, try answering questions about the following map.

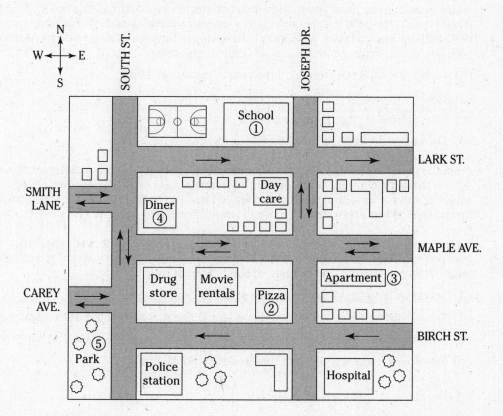

If you are located on Smith Lane and travel north on South Street, and then turn east on Lark Street and south on Joseph Drive for two blocks, you will be closest to Point

(A) 1.

(B) 2.

(C) 3.

(D) 4.

After traveling north on South Street, east on Lark Street, and south on Joseph Drive, you arrive at the pizza shop, Point 2, on the corner of Birch Street and Joseph Drive. Choice (B) is correct. While the apartment building on Maple Avenue (Point 3) is close, it requires an additional turn.

If you are located at Point 3 and travel west, and then turn south onto Joseph Drive and west on Birch Street for one block, you will be closest to the

(A) hospital.

(B) park.

(C) pizza shop.

(D) diner.

If you start at Point 3, the apartment building on Maple Avenue, and travel south on Joseph Drive and west on Birch Street, you eventually reach the park, Point 5. Choice (B) is correct. The pizza shop, Point 2, is located on Birch Street. However, the directions you are given state that you should travel one block on Birch Street, so you would face the park when you arrived at the corner of Birch and South streets. You would arrive at the hospital if you traveled east instead of west on Birch Street.

While patrolling the park, you receive instructions to respond to an emergency that has taken place at the school. After snatching a woman's purse outside the school, the suspect fled south on Joseph Drive. Which of the following is the most direct route for you to take in your patrol car, making sure to obey all traffic regulations?

(A) Travel east on Birch Street and then north on Joseph Drive.

(B) Travel north on South Street and then east on Lark Street.

(C) Travel north on South Street and then east on Maple Avenue.

(D) Travel east on Birch Street and then south on Joseph Drive.

From the park, you are most likely to encounter the suspect, who is moving south on Joseph Drive, by traveling north on South Street and east on Maple Avenue. Choice (B) would position you behind the suspect, while Choices (A) and (D) are incorrect because Birch Street is a one-way street, traveling west. Therefore, Choice (C) is correct.

After finishing a drug-safety lecture at the school, you receive orders to report to a disturbance at the diner. Which one of the following is the most direct route for you to take in your patrol car, making sure to obey all traffic regulations?

(A) Travel west on Lark Street and then south on South Street.

(B) Travel south on Joseph Drive, west on Maple Avenue, and then north on South Street.

(C) Travel south on Joseph Drive, east on Maple Avenue, and then north on South Street.

(D) Travel east on Lark Street and then south on South Street.

If you obey all traffic regulations, the quickest route is south on Joseph Drive, west on Maple Avenue, and then north on South Street. Choice (B) is correct. Had you responded to the call on foot, you could have easily traveled west on Lark Street and south on South Street.

TIP

Always pay close attention to one- and two-way streets on maps. Sometimes, the quickest route means traveling the wrong way on a one-way street. Only choose answer options giving routes that obey traffic regulations.

Now answer the questions about the following map.

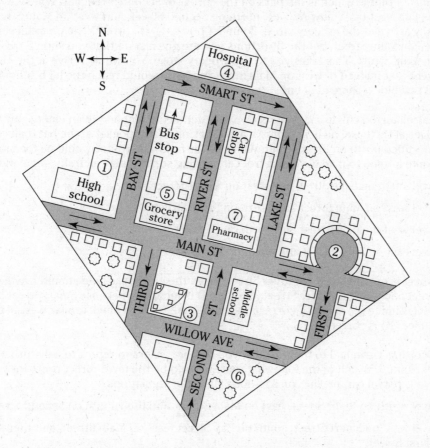

EXAMPLE

If you are located on Second Street and travel west on Main Street, and then turn north on Bay Street and east on Smart Street, you will be closest to Point

(A) 3.

(B) 4.

(C) 5.

(D) 6.

After traveling west on Main Street, north on Bay Street, and east on Smart Street, you arrive at the hospital, Point 4, which is located in the center of Smart Street. While the car shop on River Street is close, it requires an additional turn. Choice (B) is correct.

If you are located at Point 6 and travel west, and then turn north onto Second Street and west on Main Street for one block, you will be closest to the

(A) high school.

(B) park.

(C) grocery store.

(D) cul-de-sac.

Beginning at Point 6, which is the park on the corner of Second Street and Willow Avenue, and traveling west on Willow Avenue, north on Second Street, and west on Main Street, you eventually arrive at the grocery store, Point 5. Choice (C) is correct. The pharmacy, Point 7, is located on Main Street, but the directions you are given state that you should travel one block on Main Street. This takes you to the grocery store. You would arrive at the cul-de-sac if you went east instead of west on Main Street, and you would reach the high school if you traveled two blocks instead of one.

While patrolling the cul-de-sac, you receive instructions to respond to an emergency that has taken place at the baseball field, Point 3. After picking a fan's pocket at the baseball game, the suspect fled north on River Street. Which of the following routes would be the most direct route for you to take in your patrol car, making sure to obey all traffic regulations?

(A) Travel north on Lake Street and west on Smart Street.

(B) Travel west on Main Street and north on River Street.

(C) Travel west on Main Street and north on Bay Street.

(D) Travel east on Main Street and north on River Street.

The suspect is moving north on River Street. From the cul-de-sac, you should travel west on Main Street and north on River Street. Choice (A) is incorrect because Smart Street is a one-way street. Choice (C) is also incorrect, because it takes you a block too far west of the suspect. Choice (B) is correct.

After escorting a criminal to the hospital, you receive orders to report to a disturbance at the park, Point 6. Which of the following routes would be the most direct route for you to take in your patrol car, making sure to obey all traffic regulations?

(A) Travel south on River Street, east on Main Street, and then south on Second Street.

(B) Travel west on Smart Street, south on Bay Street, east on Main Street, and then south on First Street.

(C) Travel south on River Street, west on Main Street, south on Third Street, and then east on Willow Avenue.

(D) Travel east on Smart Street, south on Lake Street, east on Main Street, and then south on First Street.

The quickest route for you to take is east on Smart Street, south on Lake Street, east on Main Street, and south on First Street. While Choice (C) also leads you to the park, following all traffic regulations, the distance you have to travel is farther, so this route would take longer. Choice (D) is correct.

Straightening out information ordering questions

Police officers must follow proper procedures when performing their jobs, which often means completing steps in a specific order. Information ordering questions assess your ability to do this. These questions contain a reading passage with a list of steps, which you use to answer one or more questions. While you don't need to memorize the steps, you should read them several times and then refer back to them as you answer the questions.

An information ordering question on the NYC test looks like this:

> During a lecture, recruit officers learn the proper procedure to follow when making a routine traffic stop. They learn that while most traffic stops are routine and safe, a traffic stop may escalate into something dangerous — especially if the driver has something to hide. Before stopping a car, recruits are instructed to be sure that the driver has broken a law or that they have reasonable suspicion to believe that the driver will soon do so. After they have confirmed that a law has been or will be broken, they should follow these steps:
>
> 1. Run the license plate: Before stopping a car, a police officer should enter the car's plate into the state's motor vehicle database.
>
> 2. Code 3: After the driver's information has been obtained, a police officer should change his or her status to a Code 3 to signal other officers on the radio that he or she is taking action.
>
> 3. Stop: Once the driver has pulled the car to the side of the road, a police officer should park his or her vehicle no more than 20 feet behind the car.
>
> 4. Approach: As a police officer nears the car, he or she should take notice of how many people are in the vehicle, how they are behaving and moving, and how they respond to the officer's questions. The officer must be cautious and aware at all times.

Now take a look at the following example question.

> While practicing a traffic stop during training, Officer Michaels watches a vehicle run a red light and begins to pursue the car. He radios in a Code 3 and turns on his lights. The car pulls to the side of the road, and Officer Michaels parks approximately 15 feet from the car and prepares a careful approach. Which step did Officer Michaels skip?
>
> (A) Confirm the driver broke the law.
>
> (B) Run the license plate in the database.
>
> (C) Stop the car safely and efficiently.
>
> (D) Notice how many passengers are in the car.

Choice (B) is correct. Before Officer Michaels pursued the vehicle and reported a Code 3, he should have run the license plate in the state's motor vehicle database to obtain information about the owner of the car. This information may contain the owner's name and history with the law (arrest records, time served in jail, outstanding warrants, and so on). Running the license plate may alert a police officer to a potentially dangerous situation or allow the officer to discover that the vehicle is stolen.

Now, try two more information ordering questions. Remember to read the passage several times before answering the questions.

> In class, recruit officers learn the importance of following protocol during the preliminary investigation into a domestic violence case. At the beginning of the investigation, officers should be sure to attain the names and ages of everyone involved in the case, including all children, regardless of whether they were present in the home during the incident. Officers should conduct all interviews separately. They are strongly encouraged to record all conversations in addition to taking notes. The recruit officers receive a handout with the following steps for conducting a preliminary investigation into a domestic violence case:
>
> 1. Ask the victim if he or she is in pain, and document any visible injuries, especially those indicative of strangulation. Be sure to ask the victim whether he or she was forced to have sex.
>
> 2. Note if the victim's clothing is torn or makeup is smeared. Note whether the victim appears to be under the influence of drugs or alcohol. If the victim is pregnant, include this in the documentation.

3. Note whether the suspect has sustained any injuries and whether the suspect is under the influence of drugs or alcohol.

4. Note the size difference between the victim and the suspect. Attempt to determine who instigated the fight.

At the end of the lesson, the group's instructor describes a domestic violence investigation he took part in years ago. He tells the group that the victim had a broken arm and her shirt was torn at the sleeve, while the suspect did not sustain any injuries. He says the suspect was about a foot taller than the victim and roughly 50 pounds heavier. As the officer conducting the interview attempted to figure out who was responsible for starting the fight, the victim and suspect shouted over each other, placing blame on one another. According to this information, what should the officer have done differently at the beginning of this preliminary investigation?

(A) Asked the victim if she was pregnant or had children

(B) Checked the victim's neck for evidence of strangulation

(C) Conducted the interviews with the victim and suspect separately

(D) Asked the victim and suspect to take turns speaking

As the paragraph before the question states, officers should always conduct separate interviews with victims, suspects, children, and witnesses in domestic violence cases. Choice (C) is correct. The presence of another person involved in the incident may interfere with an officer's attempt to obtain accurate information. For example, if a victim feels threatened by a suspect, she may not speak honestly about what led to the dispute. Officers should work to secure honest and accurate information about each case they investigate.

Information ordering questions are not always based only on the list provided. Some may ask about information in the paragraph accompanying the list. Pay attention to both the paragraph and the list when reviewing information ordering questions.

Despite all the precautions parents may take to keep their children safe, occasionally children stray from their parents' line of sight. In class, recruit officers learn what to do when a child approaches them claiming to be lost. Officers should follow these steps in the order they are given:

1. Report the incident to the desk officer and the radio dispatcher.

2. Question people who may be in the area. Ask whether they have any information about the child that may be useful in reuniting the child with his or her parents.

3. Take the child to the police station if his or her parents or caregiver cannot be located.

4. Create and submit an aid report detailing the assistance provided to the child.

The recruits are provided with the following example:

A small child named Regina approaches Officer Rodriguez's patrol car outside the entrance of an amusement park. She tells the officer that she cannot find her mother and begins to cry. After Officer Rodriguez reports that he was approached by a lost child, his next step should be to

(A) put Regina in the cruiser and take her to the station.

(B) question Regina and use her responses in his aid report.

(C) leave Regina at the park entrance while he searches for her family.

(D) question people in the area who may have seen Regina or her family.

Choice (D) is correct. After Officer Rodriguez reports that Regina has approached him and claims to have been separated from her mother, he should question people in the area who may have witnessed Regina step away from her family. Common sense should tell you that he should not leave her alone, neither in his car nor at the park's entrance. Witnesses may be able to point him in the direction of the group Regina was with or may recognize the little girl and know how to contact her mother.

Determining the best course of action

The NYC test contains problem sensitivity questions in which you're asked to observe a situation and decide whether something is likely to go wrong.

Problem sensitivity questions typically include a sentence or two stating a procedure or protocol that officers normally follow during a specific event, such as an automobile accident. For example, under certain circumstances, officers must place traffic cones or a barricade on a busy road as a warning to drivers. The question then asks you to choose the answer choice that gives a situation requiring this action.

Although a person may be in clear violation of the law, sometimes police officers need to delay arrest because of medical emergencies or life-threatening conditions.

For which of the following should an officer call for an ambulance or medical assistance before making an arrest?

(A) A woman who is intoxicated in public and has twisted her ankle

(B) A man who suffered a black eye while running from police

(C) A man who will not wake with an empty syringe in his hand

(D) A woman who has first-degree burns on her arm

The correct answer is Choice (C). When a person is not responsive, regardless of any drugs that may be in his or her system, it is vital to request medical assistance. A man who will not wake with an empty syringe in his hand should receive medical assistance before he is arrested and taken to the station for possession of an illegal narcotic.

For which of the following should an officer make an arrest instead of calling for medical assistance or an ambulance?

(A) A man who was stabbed twice during a domestic dispute with his wife

(B) A woman who is vomiting from alcohol after attacking someone in a bar

(C) A man who was shot in the arm while attempting to rob a store

(D) A teenager who broke his leg after being caught defacing private property

Choice (B) is the correct answer. Multiple stab or gunshot wounds are life-threatening medical emergencies. While a broken leg may not be life-threatening, it's doubtful that the teenager would be able to walk once arrested, and it would be inhumane to allow him to sit in a jail cell or be booked without first being treated. A woman who is vomiting from consuming alcohol after starting a fight in a bar should be arrested, however. Unless she is experiencing symptoms of serious alcohol poisoning, an officer should take her to the station rather than to a hospital.

Imagine performing the action you are asked about in each answer choice for a problem sensitivity question. Which one seems like it would work best under the circumstances? In which situation do you think the action you are performing is necessary for a positive outcome?

Now, try one more set of problem sensitivity questions. Remember to use the information in the sentence provided and a combination of common sense and previous knowledge to answer the questions.

Many police departments across the country appreciate undercover investigations and consider them beneficial. However, in some situations, uniformed police officers may be of more use than undercover officers.

In which of the following situations would uniformed officers be most appropriate or helpful?

(A) Arresting prostitutes

(B) Uncovering drug rings

(C) Preventing after-school fights

(D) Tracking stolen goods

Choice (C) is the best answer to this question. If a uniformed police officer is present at a playground or the entrance/exit of a school after hours, students may be less inclined to start a fight or pick on their peers.

In which of the following situations would undercover officers be most appropriate or helpful?

(A) Acting as security at a sporting event

(B) Escorting a high-profile celebrity

(C) Directing traffic after a large concert

(D) Investigating a known sexual predator

You can assume that an undercover police officer would be more effective in investigating a known sexual predator, because this person would likely run from a uniformed officer. Choice (D) is correct.

Getting your bearings

Spatial orientation questions on the NYC test ask you to determine a location based on a description. Consider this scenario:

When I came home from work yesterday, my dog Flea slipped out the front door and headed north down the street. Flea looked back at me happily as if to say, "Catch me if you can." Well, I tried to catch him. I ran behind him and watched him make a left turn and then a right turn. Finally, Flea stopped to sniff a fire hydrant and I caught him.

Based on this information, what direction was Flea traveling in before he was caught: north, south, east, or west?

The paragraph tells you that Flea first traveled north. Then, Flea turned left. Now Flea is traveling west. Then the dog turned right. This means Flea is traveling north again. It helps to draw a map on a piece of scrap paper and include a small compass rose.

Now take a look at the following passage and the question that pertains to it.

While questioning a witness to a purse snatching, you are told that the suspect shoved the victim against a wall and then ran up the street, heading north. He dashed across a busy intersection, ran one more block, and then turned right, disappearing around the corner of a brick office building.

According to the information you received, you would be most correct if you reported that the suspect was last seen traveling

(A) north.

(B) south.

(C) east.

(D) west.

If the suspect was last seen turning right and had originally been running north, then it would be most correct to report that he was last seen traveling east. If you look at a compass rose, you can see that the direction on the right side of the compass is "east." Choice (C) is correct.

Now, try one more spatial orientation question. Memorize the directions on a compass rose and draw one on scratch paper. Also draw a map on scratch paper according to the information in the question.

> While questioning a crime victim, you are told that Suspect 1 held a knife to the victim while Suspect 2 took his wallet. Both suspects, white males, headed south after robbing the victim. The crime victim chased them for three blocks and then they split up. Suspect 1 turned left and Suspect 2 got into a car that made a right turn.

According to the information you received, you would be most correct if you reported that Suspect 2 was last seen traveling

(A) north.

(B) south.

(C) east.

(D) west.

If the suspect were traveling south and took a right turn, then he would be traveling west. Does this sound backwards? Consider this: If you are facing south, and you stick out your right hand, it will point west. If you're facing north and stick out your right hand, it will point east. In this case, the suspect was facing south and got into a car, which made a right turn. Choice (D) is correct.

Recalling letters and numbers

Some written police officer tests include number and letter recall questions, although the NYC test and the POST (National Police Officer Selection Test) do not. These questions are designed to test your visual perception and your short-term memory skills.

All the information you need to answer number and recall questions appears in the key featured before the questions. This key is comprised of random combinations of letters and numbers. Each three-letter combination corresponds with a double-digit number combination. Although these questions are called "recall questions" on the test, the challenge here isn't really to recall the letters and numbers; rather, the questions test your ability to interpret the information in the key.

The following is an example of a key you might see on a written police officer test:

Key

PUR	BLU	DER	YEL	ORA
48	87	98	75	27

Tips to improve your memory

As you prepare for the written police officer exam, use these tips to improve your memory:

✔ **Pay close attention to your environment and any disruptions around you.** If you're easily distracted, work on one thing at a time — no multitasking! It takes approximately eight seconds for memories to form, so try to maintain your focus as you attempt to learn new things.

✔ **If you're an auditory learner, which means you learn better when you hear things rather than see them, try reading aloud when you're studying for the exam.** During the exam, whisper to yourself as you read.

✔ **Write down details you need to remember, and then rewrite them again (and again, if need be).** The act of rewriting makes the learning process active, rather than passive, and helps to imprint the information in your memory.

✔ **Associate information you need to learn with senses.** Think of how something may look, smell, touch, or taste. Imagine colors, odors, sounds, and textures.

✔ **Use what you already know and draw connections between new material and familiar names, faces, and locations.** If a character or a store in a scenario reminds you of a family member or a shop near your house, use it to your advantage.

✔ **Keep a positive attitude.** If you're open to new ideas, you'll remember more than if you attempt to close off your mind with negative moods and energy.

Questions 1 through 4 are examples of number and letter recall questions. Determine the correct answers to the following questions, based on the preceding key.

What is the number value for DER, based on the key?

(A) 48

(B) 75

(C) 98

(D) 27

Look at the key to figure out the number that goes with DER, the third set of letters. According to the key, DER goes with the number 98, so the correct answer is Choice (C).

What is the number value for YEL, based on the key?

(A) 87

(B) 48

(C) 75

(D) 98

The letters YEL correspond to the number 75, so Choice (C) is correct.

What is the number value for BLU, based on the key?

(A) 27

(B) 87

(C) 48

(D) 75

Choice (B) is correct, because the letter combination BLU corresponds with the number 87.

What is the number value for PUR, based on the key?

(A) 98

(B) 48

(C) 87

(D) 75

Choice (B) is correct because the letter combination PUR is paired with number 48 in the key.

Practice Observation and Memory Questions

The following passages and question sets are designed to help you practice your memory and visualization skills. For all questions, choose the answer that *most correctly* answers the question.

> *Answer Question 1 solely on the basis of this information ordering passage.*

During a lecture on writing comprehension and grammar, recruit officers receive a handout explaining the correct way to complete an incident report. Their instructor reminds them to write in chronological order. She also reminds them that the person reading the incident report most likely will not have accompanied them to the incident. Therefore, their report should be detailed, accurate, concise, and clear. Incident reports should be written in the first person. The handout includes the following steps for completing an incident report:

1. Begin with the date, time, location, type of incident, and name of responding officer(s).

2. Record the information the dispatcher provided when the call was received (for example, suspect description, location, summary of incident, and injuries).

3. Begin the second paragraph with details of arrival including when officers arrived on the scene, what they observed as they approached the scene, and whom they first spoke to.

4. Describe all conversations and events that may have occurred after arrival.

1. The instructor asks the recruits to draft an incident report for the next class. Officer Martin's first line reads, "On Monday, January 10, 2009, at 10:30 a.m. Officer Morgan and I (Officer Sanchez) responded to a noise complaint at 414 Market Street." His next line should read:

(A) Officer Morgan did not wish to get out of the car when we got to the scene, so I went alone.

(B) When we arrived on the scene, we noticed that all lights in the house were on, and we could hear loud music playing from the street.

(C) The 911 dispatcher reported that the report came from an older man residing at 410 Market Street who claimed that the music was too loud and he could hear screaming and laughter occasionally.

(D) When I knocked on the door, no one answered, so I went around to the back and discovered multiple intoxicated co-eds engaged in a snowball fight.

After adding a sentence stating the time, date, location, incident, and names of the responding officers, Officer Martin should report information about the call, so Choice (C) is correct. This information comes from the dispatcher and, following chronological order, should appear in the report before any events that happened after the officers received the call.

> *Answer Question 2 solely on the basis of this information ordering passage.*

In class, a guest lecturer speaks to recruits about making a citizen's arrest. He tells the group that before a citizen makes an arrest, the citizen should attempt to notify authorities and get permission from police. If the citizen has the driver's license number, address, or detailed description of the person to be arrested, the lecturer claims that it would be safer for the citizen to give that information to the police instead of making the arrest alone. He then gives the class instructions, which they are to pass on to any citizen they may encounter who wants to make a citizen's arrest. The instructions include the following steps:

1. After notifying authorities, evaluate the situation as thoroughly as possible. Is a crime truly being committed? What is the severity of the crime? Is anyone injured?

2. Tell the suspect to stop what he or she is doing using a loud, forceful voice. If the suspect is holding a weapon, tell the suspect to put the weapon on the ground.

3. Let the suspect know, firmly, that he or she is now under citizen's arrest. The suspect should not leave the scene of the crime until police arrive. Physical restraint may be used, but only if the suspect attempts to leave.

4. Do not question the suspect or touch evidence. The police will arrive shortly to take care of those responsibilities.

5. Have a bystander or eyewitness call authorities once again to let them know the citizen's arrest either has been successful or has failed. Be honest and thorough with the details you give.

2. In a role-playing exercise later that day, one recruit is assigned the role of a citizen wanting to make a citizen's arrest. After notifying authorities and evaluating the situation, the recruit decides he needs to stop the suspect. Which of the following steps should the recruit take next?

(A) Have an eyewitness call authorities to tell them he is going to try to stop the suspect.

(B) Move the suspect's weapon out of reach with his foot, being careful not to touch or tamper evidence.

(C) Speak loudly and firmly. Tell the suspect to stop what he is doing and put his weapon on the ground.

(D) Use physical restraint to stop the suspect as he tries to leave the scene.

After notifying authorities and evaluating the situation thoroughly, the citizen should tell the suspect to stop what he is doing and put his weapon on the ground in a clear, strong, and loud tone. Therefore, Choice (C) is correct. Once this step is complete, the tasks in Choices (B) and (D) may be completed.

> *Answer Questions 3 and 4 on the basis of the following statement.*

Occasionally, police officers find that they are unable to handle a situation alone and must contact another government agency for help.

3. For which of the following circumstances should a police officer most likely refer to another agency?

(A) A man who is threatening his neighbors with a shovel

(B) A woman who has thrown a brick through her boyfriend's window

(C) A dog who will not stop barking and is a disturbance to the neighborhood

(D) A teenager who is caught spray painting local playground equipment

Choice (C) is correct because, although police may be able to control situations where people are involved, they are not typically experts in animal control. A dog that is constantly barking and has become a disturbance to the neighborhood is not the sole responsibility of police; instead, police officers may want to call Animal Control or a veterinarian's office.

4. For which of the following circumstances should a police officer most likely *not* refer to another agency?

   (A) A 10-year-old who is constantly bruised and appears hungry at school

   (B) A 15-year-old who skips school frequently and does not do his homework

   (C) A 14-year-old who shows signs of depression and self-destructive behavior

   (D) A 17-year-old who has been caught shoplifting from various mini markets

Choices (A), (B), and (C) may require the additional attention of school counselors, psychologists, and other mental health professionals. Choices (A) and (B) may also benefit from a reference to Social Services. However, the teenager in Choice (D) is a repeat juvenile offender. He or she should remain the concern of the police department because of his or her criminal behavior.

Answer Questions 5 through 8 on the basis of the following key.

Key

MTN	LUC	PRI	KEL	ELC
36	93	69	63	96

5. What is the number value for PRI, based on the key?

   (A) 93

   (B) 69

   (C) 63

   (D) 36

After referring to the key, you can see that letter combination PRI corresponds with the number 69. Choice (B) is correct.

6. What is the number value for MTN, based on the key?

   (A) 96

   (B) 93

   (C) 63

   (D) 36

After referring to the key, you can see that letter combination MTN corresponds with the number 36. Choice (D) is correct.

7. What is the number value for ELC, based on the key?

   (A) 63

   (B) 69

   (C) 93

   (D) 96

After referring to the key, you can see that letter combination ELC corresponds with the number 96. Choice (D) is correct.

8. What is the number value for KEL, based on the key?

   (A) 36

   (B) 93

   (C) 63

   (D) 60

   After referring to the key, you can see that letter combination KEL corresponds with the number 63. Choice (C) is correct.

   Answer Questions 9 through 12 on the basis of the following photograph. Study the photograph for ten minutes. Then cover it and answer the questions.

Photo courtesy of Library of Congress, Prints & Photographs Division, Detroit Publishing Company Collection

9. What type of business is located on the second floor of the building?

   (A) Screen printer

   (B) Shirt maker

   (C) Shoe cobbler

   (D) Cabinet maker

   In the photograph, the writing on the second floor window reads "Fullencamp and McGonigal Tailors and Shirt Makers," which suggests that the second floor houses a shirt-making business, Choice (B).

10. How many photographs are displayed in the window on the first floor?

    (A) 2

    (B) 3

    (C) 4

    (D) 5

    The window of the first floor shows a display containing four photographs, so Choice (C) is the correct one.

11. What address number is shown in the photograph?

    (A) 129

    (B) 199

    (C) 222

    (D) 229

    On the left side of the photograph, a door is marked with the address number 229, Choice (D).

12. What is the name of the company on the first floor of the building?

    (A) Detroit Photographic Co.

    (B) Randall Publishing Co.

    (C) Smith and Jones Shirt Co.

    (D) Des Moines Plate Co.

    Choice (A) is the correct one. The name of the business on the first floor is indicated in two places: above and below the window. The business in the photograph is the Detroit Photographic Co.

Answer Question 13 based on the following passage.

While questioning a crime victim, you are told that the suspect held a gun to the victim and demanded the cash the victim had just withdrawn from an ATM. The suspect, a white male, headed north after robbing the victim. The crime victim chased him, following close behind as the suspect made a right, a left, and another left. He then went into the subway and the victim lost him.

13. According to the information you received, you would be most correct if you reported that the suspect was last seen traveling

    (A) north.

    (B) south.

    (C) east.

    (D) west.

    You would be accurate if you reported that after traveling north and making a right (east), a left (north), and another left, the suspect was last seen traveling west, Choice (D).

Answer Questions 14 through 17 solely on the basis of the following map. The flow of traffic is indicated by the arrows. Points 1 through 7 are also indicated on this map. You must follow the flow of traffic.

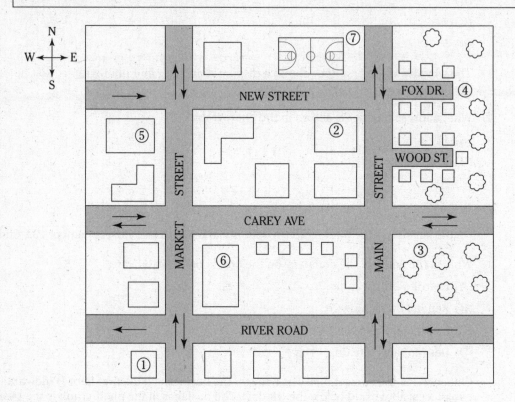

14. If you are located on Wood Street and travel south on Main Street, and then turn west on River Road and north on Market Street, you will be closest to Point

    (A) 1.

    (B) 2.

    (C) 5.

    (D) 6.

    After traveling south on Main Street, west on River Road, and north on Market Street, you arrive at Point 6. Choice (D) is correct. While Point 1 on the corner of River Road and Market Street is close, it would require traveling farther west or turning south.

15. If you are located at Point 2 and travel east, and then turn south onto Main Street and east on Carey Avenue, you will be closest to Point

    (A) 3.

    (B) 4.

    (C) 5.

    (D) 6.

    Starting at Point 2, the building on the corner of New Street and Main Street, and traveling south on Main Street and east on Carey Avenue, you eventually arrive at the park, Point 3. Choice (A) is correct. The building at Point 6 is also located on Carey Avenue, but the directions you are given state that you should travel east, not west.

16. While patrolling the buildings on River Road, you receive instructions to respond to an emergency that has taken place in the development at Fox Drive. After attempting to break into a home, the suspect fled north on Main Street. Which of the following choices is the most direct route for you to take in your patrol car, making sure to obey all traffic regulations?

    (A) Travel east on River Road and north on Main Street.

    (B) Travel west on River Road, north on Main Street, and east on Fox Drive.

    (C) Travel west on River Road, north on Market Street, east on New Street, and north on Main Street.

    (D) Travel west on River Road, north on Market Street, west on New Street, and north on Main Street.

    From your position on River Road, you are most likely to encounter the suspect, who is moving north on Main Street, by traveling west on River Road, north on Market Street, east on New Street, and north on Main Street. Therefore, Choice (C) is correct. Choices (A) and (D) are incorrect because River Road and New Street are one-way streets.

17. After stopping at the soccer field, Point 7, you receive orders to report to a disturbance at Point 1. Which one of the following choices is the most direct route for you to take in your patrol car, making sure to obey all traffic regulations?

    (A) Travel west on New Street and south on Market Street.

    (B) Travel south on Main Street, west on Carey Avenue, and north on Market Street.

    (C) Travel west on New Street, south on Market Street, and east on River Road.

    (D) Travel south on Main Street and west on River Road.

    From your position on New Street, you'll most likely arrive at Point 1 in the shortest amount of time if you drive south on Main Street and west on River Road. Choice (D) is correct.

> *Answer Questions 18 and 19 on the basis of the following statement.*

Police officers are always on the lookout for suspicious behavior, or actions by others that may lead them to believe a crime has been committed or is in the process of being committed.

18. Police officers patrolling a city block in the afternoon would be *most* suspicious of which of the following?

    (A) An abandoned lemonade stand at the end of a driveway

    (B) A house with its side windows open and multiple newspapers on its porch

    (C) A house with multiple garbage bags and recycling cans on its front lawn

    (D) A car with its windows down, sunroof open, and no driver inside

    Police officers patrolling a city block in the middle of the day should be suspicious of a house with its side windows open and multiple newspapers on its porch, so Choice (B) is correct. The newspapers on the porch indicate that the owners of the house have not been around to take the papers inside. This may signal that they are on vacation or staying elsewhere for a few days. If the house is empty, it may be a target for burglars. If no one is home, someone from the outside may have opened the windows on the side of the house.

19. Police officers patrolling a city block at night would be *least* suspicious of which of the following?

    (A) Loud music, screaming, and laughter coming from a house on the corner

    (B) Two women in tight clothes and heels pacing in and out of an empty alleyway

    (C) A ladder propped up against the back of a house, raised to reach a second story window

    (D) A small group of teenagers, gathered on a front porch, talking and laughing

    Police officers patrolling a city block at night should most likely not be concerned with a group of teens hanging out on the front porch of a house, so Choice (D) is correct. If they aren't too loud, don't appear to be bothered by the appearance of a police cruiser, and are behaving, they most likely aren't committing any criminal acts. Choices (A), (B), and (C), however, may lead to criminal acts of underage drinking or noise violations, prostitution, and home invasion, respectively.

20. You are on a routine patrol when you walk past the buildings shown in the following illustration.

    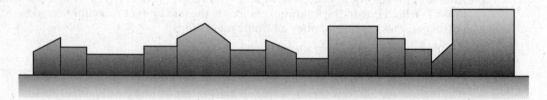

    As you turn the corner, your view of the buildings changes. Which of the following most accurately represents your view from the back of the buildings?

    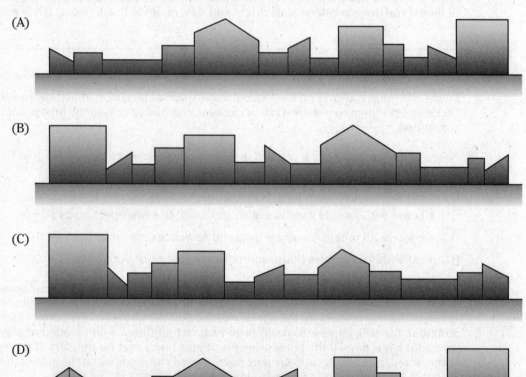

Your view from the back should be the opposite of your view from the front. All the buildings should be in the same order; none of the roofs should be switched on any of the buildings and none of the buildings should move from their original locations. Choice (C) is correct because it shows the street in the correct, reversed order.

Answer Questions 21 through 24 on the basis of the following key.

Key

BER	JEF	LNE	NIC	THO
50	15	01	05	10

21. What is the number value for NIC, based on the key?

   (A) 15

   (B) 10

   (C) 50

   (D) 05

After referring to the key, you can see that letter combination NIC corresponds with the number 05. Choice (D) is correct.

22. What is the number value for THO, based on the key?

   (A) 10

   (B) 50

   (C) 01

   (D) 15

After referring to the key, you can see that letter combination THO corresponds with the number 10. Choice (A) is correct.

23. What is the number value for BER, based on the key?

   (A) 10

   (B) 15

   (C) 05

   (D) 50

After referring to the key, you can see that letter combination BER corresponds with the number 50. Choice (D) is correct.

24. What is the number value for LNE, based on the key?

   (A) 50

   (B) 05

   (C) 01

   (D) 10

After referring to the key, you can see that letter combination LNE corresponds with the number 01. Choice (C) is correct.

Answer Question 25 based on the following passage.

While gathering witness statements at the scene of an aggravated assault, you are told that the suspect knocked the victim to the ground and kicked her repeatedly. The suspect ran when she noticed a crowd had formed. The suspect, a black female, headed south. One of the witnesses chased her, following close behind as the suspect made a left, a right, another right, and then a left. She then hailed a cab and the witness lost track of her.

25. According to the information you received, you would be most correct if you reported that the suspect was last seen traveling

(A) north.

(B) south.

(C) east.

(D) west.

You would be most correct if you reported that after traveling south, making a left (east), a right (south), another right (west), and a left, the suspect was last seen traveling south. Choice (B) is correct.

Answer Questions 26 through 29 solely on the basis of the following map. The flow of traffic is indicated by the arrows. Points 1 through 8 are also indicated on this map. You must follow the flow of traffic.

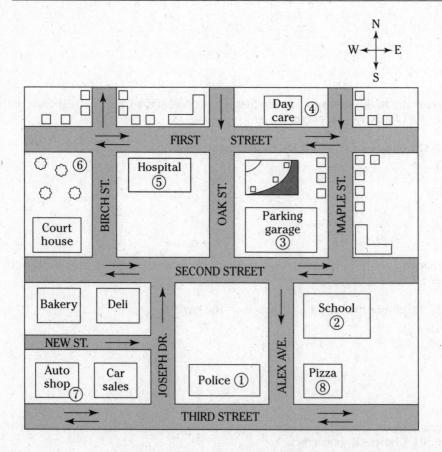

26. If you are located on Second Street and travel south on Alex Avenue, and then turn west on Third Street and north on Joseph Drive, you will be closest to the

    (A) hospital.

    (B) auto shop.

    (C) deli.

    (D) police station.

    After traveling south on Alex Avenue, west on Third Street, and north on Joseph Drive, you are closest to the deli. While the hospital is straight ahead, you can't reach it using Joseph Drive. You pass the police station on Third Street, but the directions include a turn onto Joseph Drive, so you don't stop there. Choice (C) is correct.

27. If you are located at Point 2 and travel west, and then turn north onto Birch Street and east on First Street, you will be closest to Point

    (A) 5.

    (B) 4.

    (C) 6.

    (D) 7.

    Starting at Point 2, the school located on the corner of Second Street and Alex Avenue, and traveling west on Second Street, north on Birch Street, and east on First Street, you arrive at the hospital at Point 5, Choice (A). The park at Point 6 is also located on First Street, but the directions you are given state that you should travel east, not west.

28. While patrolling the area around the bakery and the deli on Second Street, you receive instructions to respond to an emergency that has taken place at the pizza shop, Point 8. Which of the following choices is the most direct route for you to take in your patrol car, making sure to obey all traffic regulations?

    (A) Travel south on Joseph Drive and east on Third Street.

    (B) Travel west on Second Street, south on Alex Avenue, and east on Third Street.

    (C) Travel north on Birch Street, east on First Street, south on Oak Street, east on Second Street, and south on Alex Avenue.

    (D) Travel east on Second Street, south on Alex Avenue, and east on Third Street.

    From your position on Second Street, you will most likely arrive at the pizza shop in the shortest amount of time if you drive east on Second Street, south on Alex Avenue, and east on Third Street. Therefore, Choice (D) is correct. Choice (A) is incorrect because Joseph Drive is a one-way street going in the opposite direction indicated. Choice (C) is incorrect because it would take longer to reach the pizza shop using that route.

29. After stopping at the park, Point 6, you receive orders to report to a disturbance at Point 3. Which one of the following choices is the most direct route for you to take in your patrol car, making sure to obey all traffic regulations?

    (A) Travel east on First Street, south on Oak Street, and east on Second Street.

    (B) Travel north on Birch Street, east on First, south on Maple, and west on Second.

    (C) Travel south on Birch Street and east on Second Street.

    (D) Travel south on Birch Street and west on Second Street.

From your position on First Street, you'll most likely arrive at the parking garage in the shortest amount of time if you drive east on First Street, south on Oak Street, and east on Second Street. Therefore, Choice (A) is correct. Choice (B) would also lead you to Point 3, but would require an additional block of travel.

> *Answer Question 30 based on the following passage.*

While speaking with a witness at the scene of a crime, you are told that the suspect left the jewelry store clutching a necklace. The suspect, an Asian male, headed north and then hailed a cab. The cab turned right at the next intersection.

30. According to the information you received, you would be most correct if you reported that the suspect was last seen traveling

   (A) north.

   (B) south.

   (C) east.

   (D) west.

You would be correct if you reported that after traveling north and hailing a cab that turned right, the suspect was last seen traveling east. Choice (C) is correct.

Chapter 7

Reading and Writing Incident Reports

• •

In This Chapter
▶ Answering reading comprehension questions about incident reports on the POST
▶ Acing the POST incident report writing section
▶ Responding to questions about incident reports on the NYC test

• •

Both the National Police Officer Selection Test (POST) and the New York City (NYC) test ask questions about incident reports. "What's an incident report?" you ask. It's simply a report about an incident that a police officer has investigated. Imagine this scenario: Officer Grant responds to a call about a stolen vehicle in a mall parking lot and investigates the situation. He gathers information from the car's owner, Mr. Ramirez. Officer Grant jots down a description of the car and its license plate. He then interviews witnesses who remember seeing a car with two men inside parked next to Mr. Ramirez's car. Officer Grant discovers some broken glass in the spot where Mr. Ramirez's car used to be. What do you think Officer Ramirez does when he returns to police headquarters? He completes an incident report describing the situation, most likely on an incident report form.

Some questions about incident reports on police officer exams are based on a description of an incident and a blank incident report form. These questions may ask you whether the description contains enough information to complete the incident report. You may see true-and-false questions about details in the description. For other questions, you look at a completed incident report and answer questions about it.

You need to write your answers clearly, using complete sentences and correct grammar. In this chapter, we teach you everything you need to know to answer questions about incident reports on both the POST and the NYC test.

Tackling POST Questions about Incident Reports

The POST uses incident reports in both the Reading Comprehension section and the Incident Report Writing section. In the Reading Comprehension section, you're given a blank incident report with a paragraph describing the incident underneath. The "questions" are actually statements. You have to determine whether these statements are true or false based on the incident report and the paragraph. A statement may look like this: "The incident report can be fully completed based on the information in the paragraph."

The Incident Report Writing section tests your writing skills. You're also given an incident report in this section, but this time it's filled out, not blank. You have to write out your answers to the questions in this section, and grammar and spelling count.

Demonstrating comprehension of incident reports on the POST

The Reading Comprehension section of the POST contains true-and-false questions about incident reports. These questions are based on a description of an incident and a blank incident report. Figure 7-1 shows what a blank incident report looks like.

INCIDENT REPORT — POLICE DEPARTMENT

1. ADDRESS OF INCIDENT	2. OFFENSE	3. CODE	4. DATE

5. NAME OF VICTIM: INDIVIDUAL OR BUSINESS	6. ADDRESS	PHONE

7. ASSIGNED OFFICERS/BADGE NUMBERS	8. AGE OF VICTIM	9. RACE OF VICTIM	10. VICTIM'S DATE OF BIRTH

11. NAME OF SUSPECT	12. ADDRESS

13. AGE	14. RACE	15. SEX	16. DATE OF BIRTH	17. HEIGHT	18. WEIGHT

19. HAIR	20. EYES	21. PHYSICAL DESCRIPTION

22. CHARGES

23. ITEM	24. BRAND	25. SERIAL NUMBER	26. VALUE
27. ITEM	28. BRAND	29. SERIAL NUMBER	30. VALUE
31. ITEM	32. BRAND	33. SERIAL NUMBER	34. VALUE

35. _____
SIGNATURE OF OFFICER/BADGE NUMBER

Figure 7-1: A blank incident report.

Take a moment to look over this incident report. Note that it's divided into many small sections. As we go through these sections, imagine you're completing the report on the job. In Section 1, you include the address of the incident. For example, if a house was burglarized, you add the address of the house here. In Section 2, you indicate the offense; for example, burglary. In Section 3, you include a police code for the offense. Police departments use many codes to represent all kinds of information, such as "10-4" to indicate "okay." The police code for residential burglary might be 62r. If that were the case, you'd include this code in Section 3. You don't need to know police codes until you're on the job. All the information you need to answer the questions on the POST is in the description of the incident. You note the date of the incident in Section 4.

The incident reports on the POST are all set up in the same way. This means that the first section is always for the address of the incident, the second section is always for the offense, and so on. It helps to be familiar with the sections of this form before taking the POST.

In Sections 5 and 6, you add information about the victim: the victim's name and whether the victim is an individual or a business (Section 5), and the victim's address and telephone number (Section 6). In the next row, Sections 7–10, you indicate the assigned officers — when you're on the job, you'll be one of these officers — and their badge numbers, plus the age, race, and date of birth of the victim.

In the next row, Sections 11 and 12, you indicate the name and address of the suspect. In the following row, Sections 13–18, you add descriptive details about the suspect — his or her age, race, sex, date of birth, height, and weight. In Sections 19–21, you add additional descriptive details, including the suspect's hair and eye color, and a physical description. You also include what the subject was wearing in the physical description. If the suspect has a tattoo or a noticeable scar, you include this information as well. In Section 22, you indicate the charges the suspect faces, such as assault and battery. In the last three lines of the incident report form, you include information about any items that were stolen. Lastly, you sign the report (Section 35) and include your badge number.

The officer who signs the form in Section 35 is the one who has completed the form.

You may not have all the information you need to complete the entire incident report form. For example, you may not have a suspect, and even if you do, you may not know the suspect's birthday, age, height, and weight. If items were stolen, the victim may not know the serial numbers of those items. Some true-and-false statements on the POST state that the incident report can be fully completed based on the information in the paragraph, which is the description. You indicate whether this statement is true or false.

Now read the following incident description:

> Trevor Madden, age 31, of 251 Park Street, called police headquarters at 5:50 p.m., Tuesday, April 4, to report that his car had been stolen from a parking garage at 205 101st Street. Officers Emily Hex and Ken Thomas arrived on the scene at 5:55 p.m. The officers found broken glass and tire marks in the space where Madden claimed to have parked his car. Madden's car is a silver 2006 Chevy Impala.

Does this paragraph contain all the information you need to fully complete the incident report? No! It contains some of the information, such as the address of the incident, the offense, the victim's name and address, the assigned officers, and a description of the car. But it's missing the badge numbers of the officers and the victim's age, race, and date of birth. It also doesn't contain any information about a suspect.

Take a look at the following incident report form, read the incident description, and answer the questions accordingly.

INCIDENT REPORT — POLICE DEPARTMENT			
1. ADDRESS OF INCIDENT	2. OFFENSE	3. CODE	4. DATE
5. NAME OF VICTIM: INDIVIDUAL OR BUSINESS		6. ADDRESS PHONE	
7. ASSIGNED OFFICERS/BADGE NUMBERS	8. AGE OF VICTIM	9. RACE OF VICTIM	10. VICTIM'S DATE OF BIRTH
11. NAME OF SUSPECT		12. ADDRESS	

13. AGE	14. RACE	15. SEX	16. DATE OF BIRTH	17. HEIGHT	18. WEIGHT

19. HAIR	20. EYES	21. PHYSICAL DESCRIPTION

22. CHARGES

23. ITEM	24. BRAND	25. SERIAL NUMBER	26. VALUE
27. ITEM	28. BRAND	29. SERIAL NUMBER	30. VALUE
31. ITEM	32. BRAND	33. SERIAL NUMBER	34. VALUE

35. _____
SIGNATURE OF OFFICER/BADGE NUMBER

Stephen Ferguson, owner of Ferguson's Pub (75 Twelfth Avenue), called police headquarters at 2:15 a.m., Sunday, August 4, to report an assault that occurred outside his bar. Officers Leonard Parker and Renee Sanders arrived at the pub at 2:20 a.m. to investigate the incident. Mr. Ferguson explained that Bernard Nelson, 32, and Jeffrey Carter, 30, had an altercation outside the pub, and Nelson assaulted Carter. Carter was treated at the scene for minor injuries.

Section 11 can be fully completed based on the information in the paragraph.

(A) True

(B) False

To answer this question, find Section 11 on the blank incident report. It says "Name of Suspect." The description says Bernard Nelson assaulted Jeffrey Carter, so Nelson is the suspect. The correct answer is Choice (A), True. If you were an officer completing a report about this incident, you would include Bernard Nelson in Section 11.

Officers Parker and Sanders arrived at the scene at 2:15 a.m.

(A) True

(B) False

This question asks you about a detail in the description of the incident. Go back to the description to find out when Officers Parker and Sanders arrived at the scene. The description says the owner of Ferguson's Pub called police headquarters at 2:15 a.m. and that the officers arrived at the pub at 2:20 a.m. The answer to Question 2 is Choice (B), False.

On both the POST and the NYC test, looking back at a reading passage or an incident report to find the information you need is acceptable. Reading the questions first and then looking for the answers as you read is also acceptable.

Now try another set of questions.

INCIDENT REPORT — POLICE DEPARTMENT			
1. ADDRESS OF INCIDENT	2. OFFENSE	3. CODE	4. DATE
5. NAME OF VICTIM: INDIVIDUAL OR BUSINESS	6. ADDRESS PHONE		
7. ASSIGNED OFFICERS/BADGE NUMBERS	8. AGE OF VICTIM	9. RACE OF VICTIM	10. VICTIM'S DATE OF BIRTH
11. NAME OF SUSPECT	12. ADDRESS		
13. AGE	14. RACE	15. SEX	16. DATE OF BIRTH	17. HEIGHT	18. WEIGHT
19. HAIR	20. EYES	21. PHYSICAL DESCRIPTION	
22. CHARGES			
23. ITEM	24. BRAND	25. SERIAL NUMBER	26. VALUE
27. ITEM	28. BRAND	29. SERIAL NUMBER	30. VALUE
31. ITEM	32. BRAND	33. SERIAL NUMBER	34. VALUE
35. SIGNATURE OF OFFICER/BADGE NUMBER			

Olivia Wentz, owner of Café Wentz at 483 Vermillion Drive, called police headquarters at 10:35 a.m. to report that her restaurant had been robbed at gunpoint. Officers Terrance Greene (badge number 243) and William Martin (badge number 906) arrived at the restaurant at 10:50 a.m. to investigate the incident. Ms. Wentz reported that the suspect took $280 from the cash register and an MP3 player. The suspect is Randall Smith, a homeless man with a heroin addiction.

The incident report can be fully completed based on the information in the paragraph.

(A) True

(B) False

The suspect took $483 from Café Wentz's cash register and an MP3 player.

(A) True

(B) False

While the description of the incident contains a lot of information, it doesn't contain enough to fully complete the incident report form, so the answer to Question 1 is Choice (B), False. The incident description says that the suspect took $280 from the cash register, so the answer to Question 2 is also Choice (B), False.

Answering written questions about incident reports on the POST

The POST tests your writing skills. It asks you questions about a completed incident report form, and you have to write your answer in the space provided. To receive points for your answer, your answer has to be correct (no kidding!). It also has to be written in one or more complete sentences. You need to use correct grammar and spelling.

Consider this question:

What color hair does the suspect have?

You might be tempted to write the word "brown" in response to this question, but your answer will be marked incorrect if you do — even though the suspect may have brown hair. The following is a better answer:

The suspect has brown hair.

Be sure to include all necessary words in your answer. Consider this question and answer:

What is the victim's date of birth?
Victim's date of birth is March 30, 1982.

This answer makes sense, but it isn't grammatically correct. A better response is this:

The victim's date of birth is March 30, 1982.

Be sure that all the words in your response are spelled correctly. Read this question and answer:

What was the suspect wearing?
The suspict was whereing blu jeans and a blak t-shirt.

Four words are misspelled in this answer, so it would be marked incorrect. What do you do if you don't know how to spell a word? Don't use it! Choose a word that you're certain is spelled correctly. The preceding sentence should read:

The suspect was wearing blue jeans and a black t-shirt.

A sentence expresses a complete thought. Most sentences have a subject, a verb, and an object. The car (subject) struck (verb) a telephone pole (object). When in doubt, keep it simple, but make sure it's correct.

Now, read the following incident report, questions, and sample answers.

INCIDENT REPORT — POLICE DEPARTMENT			
1. ADDRESS OF INCIDENT	2. OFFENSE	3. CODE	4. DATE
45 Abernathy Street	Assault	T7-2424	08/09

5. NAME OF VICTIM: INDIVIDUAL OR BUSINESS	6. ADDRESS	PHONE
Adrian Reese	98 Eighth Avenue	555-289-4895

7. ASSIGNED OFFICERS/BADGE NUMBERS	8. AGE OF VICTIM	9. RACE OF VICTIM	10. VICTIM'S DATE OF BIRTH
Derrick White #1999 Jeremiah Fitzpatrick #4252	39	Black	09/04

11. NAME OF SUSPECT	12. ADDRESS
Simon Slade	293 Clapper Drive

13. AGE	14. RACE	15. SEX	16. DATE OF BIRTH	17. HEIGHT	18. WEIGHT
36	White	Male	04/15	6'2"	210

19. HAIR	20. EYES	21. PHYSICAL DESCRIPTION
Brown	Brown	Wearing blue pants, white shirt, and blue baseball cap

22. CHARGES
Assault

23. ITEM	24. BRAND	25. SERIAL NUMBER	26. VALUE
27. ITEM	28. BRAND	29. SERIAL NUMBER	30. VALUE
31. ITEM	32. BRAND	33. SERIAL NUMBER	34. VALUE

35. *Derrick White #1999*
SIGNATURE OF OFFICER/BADGE NUMBER

What is the victim's name?

_____

The victim's name is Adrian Reese.

What is the suspect's address?

_____

The suspect's address is 293 Clapper Drive.

What is the victim's age?

_____

The victim's age is 39.

Now try to answer the following questions on your own. Then read the sample answers.

INCIDENT REPORT — POLICE DEPARTMENT

1. ADDRESS OF INCIDENT	2. OFFENSE	3. CODE	4. DATE
6345 Brickman Road	Trespassing	H1-9890	01/21

5. NAME OF VICTIM: INDIVIDUAL OR BUSINESS	6. ADDRESS PHONE
Megan Lee	6345 Brickman Road 555-247-9372

7. ASSIGNED OFFICERS/BADGE NUMBERS	8. AGE OF VICTIM	9. RACE OF VICTIM	10. VICTIM'S DATE OF BIRTH
Natasha Bowman #4087 Raymond Monroe #2138	22	Asian	03/09

11. NAME OF SUSPECT	12. ADDRESS
Bryan Ming	45 108th Street

13. AGE	14. RACE	15. SEX	16. DATE OF BIRTH	17. HEIGHT	18. WEIGHT
28	Asian	Male	11/12	5'10"	160

19. HAIR	20. EYES	21. PHYSICAL DESCRIPTION
Black	Brown	Wearing a red shirt and blue jeans

22. CHARGES
Criminal trespass

23. ITEM	24. BRAND	25. SERIAL NUMBER	26. VALUE
27. ITEM	28. BRAND	29. SERIAL NUMBER	30. VALUE
31. ITEM	32. BRAND	33. SERIAL NUMBER	34. VALUE

35. _Natasha Bowman #4087_
SIGNATURE OF OFFICER/BADGE NUMBER

What charges are being brought against the suspect?

_____

The charge being brought against the suspect is criminal trespass.

What is the suspect's physical description?

_____

The suspect was wearing a red shirt and blue jeans.

Where did the incident take place?

_____

The incident took place at 6345 Brickman Road.

What is the suspect's date of birth?

_____

The suspect's birthday is November 12.

What are the name and badge number of the officer who completed the incident form?

_____

The officer who completed the form is Natasha Bowman. Her badge number is 4087.

Mastering Questions about Incident Reports on the NYC Test

Some questions on the NYC test are about incidents. These questions give you details about the incident such as the place of the crime, the time of the crime, the victim, the crime — such as car theft — and the suspect, if a suspect is identified. These details look like this:

Place of Crime: 35 Washington Terrace

Time of Crime: 9:35 p.m.

Victim: Sarah Holmes

Crime: Purse snatching

Suspect: Unidentified

The actual question following these details says something like:

Officer Roman is completing a report about the incident. Which one of the following expresses the preceding information *most clearly, accurately, and completely?*

The key to answering this type of question is to choose the answer option that

- ✔ Uses all the details
- ✔ Uses the details correctly and doesn't change their meaning
- ✔ Is grammatically correct

 When answering questions about incidents on the NYC test, rule out answer options that change the meaning of the details given in the question. The correct answer choice will clearly state the victim and what happened to him or her, where, and when. It will also include the name of the suspect, if one has been identified.

The following is a clear, accurate, and complete expression of the details noted earlier in this section:

An unidentified person snatched Sarah Holmes's purse in front of 35 Washington Terrace at 9:35 p.m.

Now read this sentence, which might be an answer option on the test:

An unidentified person snatched a purse at 9:35 p.m. in front of 35 Washington Terrace. Sarah Holmes has a purse.

Do you see what's wrong with this answer option? The information is correct, but it's not clear that the woman whose purse was stolen is Sarah Holmes. Try to find the problem with this sentence:

A purse was snatched in front of Sarah Holmes at 9:35 p.m. in front of Washington Terrace by an unidentified person.

This sentence has the same problem as the previous sentence: It's not clear that Sarah Holmes was the person whose purse was stolen.

Now read the following information and question:

While on patrol, Officer Jerome Walker responded to a report of aggravated assault. The following details were obtained at the scene:

Place of Crime: 293 45th Street

Time of Crime: 10:35 a.m.

Victim: Mildred Ingles

Crime: Aggravated assault (assault with a weapon)

Injuries to Victim: Minor

Suspect: Felix Sutton

Officer Walker is completing a report of the incident. Which one of the following expresses the preceding information *most clearly, accurately, and completely?*

(A) Felix Sutton assaulted Mildred Ingles with a weapon at 10:35 a.m. at 293 45th Street. The victim received minor injuries.

(B) Mildred Ingles, who received minor injuries, was at 293 45th Street at 10:35 a.m. Felix Sutton assaulted someone with a weapon.

(C) At 10:35 a.m. at 293 45th Street, Felix Sutton was involved in an assault with a weapon. The victim in the incident received minor injuries.

(D) Mildred Ingles and Felix Sutton live at 293 45th Street. At 10:35 a.m. an assault with a weapon occurred there.

Choice (A) is the best answer because it restates all the information in a clear, coherent way. Choice (B) is incorrect because this choice doesn't indicate that Mildred Ingles was the victim of the assault. Choice (C) is incorrect because it doesn't indicate who the victim was, and Choice (D) is incorrect because it doesn't indicate that Mildred Ingles and Felix Sutton were involved in the assault at the residence.

Now read the following reports and try answering the questions that follow.

While on patrol, Officer Cynthia Ricks responded to a burglary. The following details were obtained at the scene:

Place of Crime: 787 Sugar Lane

Time of Crime: Between 8:00 p.m. and 10:00 p.m.

Victim: Emil Hunter

Victim's Address: 787 Sugar Lane

Items stolen: $200, gold ring

Suspect: Unidentified

Officer Ricks is completing a report of the incident. Which one of the following expresses the preceding information *most clearly, accurately, and completely?*

(A) At 8:00 p.m. or 10:00 p.m., an unidentified person or Emil Hunter burglarized 787 Sugar Lane and took $200 and a gold ring.

(B) An unidentified person took $200 and a gold ring. Between 8:00 p.m. and 10:00 p.m., Emil Hunter was at his residence, 787 Sugar Lane.

(C) An unidentified person burglarized Emil Hunter's residence, 787 Sugar Lane, between 8:00 p.m. and 10:00 p.m. and took $200 and a gold ring.

(D) Between 8:00 p.m. and 10:00 p.m. an unidentified person burglarized 787 Sugar Lane. Emil Hunter has $200 and a gold ring.

Choice (C) is correct because it describes the incident clearly and coherently. Choice (A) is incorrect because this answer states that Emil Hunter may be the suspect, but he isn't. Choice (B) is also incorrect because the information doesn't indicate that Emil Hunter was in his residence between 8:00 p.m. and 10:00 p.m. Choice (D) is incorrect because this choice doesn't say that the cash and the ring were taken by the burglar.

While on patrol, Officer Jennifer Ross responded to a reported arson. The following details were obtained at the scene:

Place of Crime: 54 Washburn Avenue (Peterman's Coffee Warehouse)

Time of Crime: Between 2:00 a.m. and 3:00 a.m.

Victim: Peterman's Coffee Warehouse

Damage: Second floor destroyed; first floor sustained smoke and water damage

Crime: Arson

Suspect: Unidentified

Officer Ross is completing a report of the incident. Which one of the following expresses the preceding information *most clearly, accurately, and completely?*

(A) The first floor of Peterman's Coffee Warehouse sustained smoke and water damage, and the second floor was destroyed between 2:00 a.m. and 3:00 a.m. An unidentified person committed arson at 54 Washburn Avenue.

(B) At 54 Washburn Avenue, between 2:00 a.m. and 3:00 a.m., the first floor of the building sustained smoke and water damage and the second floor was destroyed. An unidentified person committed arson at Peterman's Coffee Warehouse.

(C) Between 2:00 a.m. and 3:00 a.m., an unidentified suspect damaged the first floor and destroyed the second floor at 54 Washburn Avenue. The arson occurred at Peterman's Coffee Warehouse.

(D) An unidentified arsonist set a fire at Peterman's Coffee Warehouse, located at 54 Washburn Avenue, between 2:00 a.m. and 3:00 a.m. The first floor of the building sustained smoke and water damage, and the second floor was destroyed.

Choice (D) is correct because it restates all the information correctly. Choice (A) is incorrect because it doesn't state that the arson occurred at the warehouse. Choice (B) is also incorrect because it doesn't indicate that 54 Washburn Avenue and the warehouse are the same location. Choice (C) is incorrect because it doesn't state that the suspect committed arson.

Practice POST Incident Report Questions

The following passages and question sets are designed to help you practice interpreting incident reports and answering questions about them. Choose or write the answer that *most correctly* answers the question.

Questions 1 and 2 are based on the following incident report form and incident description.

INCIDENT REPORT — POLICE DEPARTMENT

1. ADDRESS OF INCIDENT | 2. OFFENSE | 3. CODE | 4. DATE

5. NAME OF VICTIM: INDIVIDUAL OR BUSINESS | 6. ADDRESS PHONE

7. ASSIGNED OFFICERS/BADGE NUMBERS | 8. AGE OF VICTIM | 9. RACE OF VICTIM | 10. VICTIM'S DATE OF BIRTH

11. NAME OF SUSPECT | 12. ADDRESS

13. AGE | 14. RACE | 15. SEX | 16. DATE OF BIRTH | 17. HEIGHT | 18. WEIGHT

19. HAIR | 20. EYES | 21. PHYSICAL DESCRIPTION

22. CHARGES

23. ITEM | 24. BRAND | 25. SERIAL NUMBER | 26. VALUE

27. ITEM | 28. BRAND | 29. SERIAL NUMBER | 30. VALUE

31. ITEM | 32. BRAND | 33. SERIAL NUMBER | 34. VALUE

35. _____
SIGNATURE OF OFFICER/BADGE NUMBER

Marie Hudson, 48, of 786 Palm Avenue called police headquarters at 7:50 p.m., Friday, March 7, to report that her purse had been stolen in front of 547 Baltimore Drive. Officers Justin Forest and Ryan Morris arrived at the scene at 8:00 p.m. to investigate the incident. Ms. Hudson told police that her purse contained her credit cards and approximately $150 in cash.

1. Sections 23 and 26 can be fully completed based on the information in the paragraph.

   (A) True

   (B) False

   The correct answer is Choice (A), True. Sections 23 and 26 should contain the name of a stolen or missing item and its value, and the paragraph contains this information.

2. Marie Hudson's address is 547 Baltimore Drive.

   (A) True

   (B) False

   According to the paragraph, Marie Hudson's address is 786 Palm Avenue. The paragraph states that the incident occurred in front of 547 Baltimore Drive. Therefore, the correct answer is Choice (B), False.

Questions 3 and 4 are based on the following incident report form and incident description.

INCIDENT REPORT — POLICE DEPARTMENT

1. ADDRESS OF INCIDENT	2. OFFENSE	3. CODE	4. DATE

5. NAME OF VICTIM: INDIVIDUAL OR BUSINESS	6. ADDRESS PHONE

7. ASSIGNED OFFICERS/BADGE NUMBERS	8. AGE OF VICTIM	9. RACE OF VICTIM	10. VICTIM'S DATE OF BIRTH

11. NAME OF SUSPECT	12. ADDRESS

13. AGE	14. RACE	15. SEX	16. DATE OF BIRTH	17. HEIGHT	18. WEIGHT

19. HAIR	20. EYES	21. PHYSICAL DESCRIPTION

22. CHARGES

23. ITEM	24. BRAND	25. SERIAL NUMBER	26. VALUE
27. ITEM	28. BRAND	29. SERIAL NUMBER	30. VALUE
31. ITEM	32. BRAND	33. SERIAL NUMBER	34. VALUE

35. _____
SIGNATURE OF OFFICER/BADGE NUMBER

Jorge Harrison, of 234 Main Street, Apartment B, called police headquarters at 6:10 p.m., Tuesday, May 5, to report that his apartment had been broken into while he was at work. Officers Jane Addison (badge number 567) and Manuel Garza (badge number 290) arrived at the apartment at 6:35 p.m. to investigate the incident. Mr. Harrison reported that he was missing a television set, a laptop computer, and $320 in cash.

3. The incident report can be fully completed based on the information in the paragraph.

   (A) True

   (B) False

   There isn't enough information in the paragraph to fully complete the incident report, so the answer is Choice (B), False. For example, the victim did not provide serial numbers for the stolen items.

4. The incident was reported on May 5.

   (A) True

   (B) False

   The paragraph says that the incident was reported on May 5, so the correct answer is Choice (A), True.

Questions 5 through 9 are based on the following incident report form.

INCIDENT REPORT — POLICE DEPARTMENT

1. ADDRESS OF INCIDENT	2. OFFENSE	3. CODE	4. DATE
584 Benton Drive	Burglary	G9-0974	06/28

5. NAME OF VICTIM: INDIVIDUAL OR BUSINESS	6. ADDRESS PHONE
Isaiah Reynolds	4 Chaplin Drive 555-852-9578

7. ASSIGNED OFFICERS/BADGE NUMBERS	8. AGE OF VICTIM	9. RACE OF VICTIM	10. VICTIM'S DATE OF BIRTH
Sophia Stacey #3459 Kevin Plymouth #9349	42	Black	12/07

11. NAME OF SUSPECT	12. ADDRESS
Charles Richmond	63 Rockaway Drive

13. AGE	14. RACE	15. SEX	16. DATE OF BIRTH	17. HEIGHT	18. WEIGHT
36	Black	Male	05/16	5'11"	180

19. HAIR	20. EYES	21. PHYSICAL DESCRIPTION
Brown	Brown	Wearing blue jeans and black shirt, scar on left wrist

22. CHARGES
Burglary

23. ITEM	24. BRAND	25. SERIAL NUMBER	26. VALUE
40" flat screen television	Sony	H54T3245AY933490	$700

27. ITEM	28. BRAND	29. SERIAL NUMBER	30. VALUE
Cash			$100

31. ITEM	32. BRAND	33. SERIAL NUMBER	34. VALUE

35. *Kevin Plymouth #9349*
SIGNATURE OF OFFICER/BADGE NUMBER

---

5. What distinguishing mark does the suspect have?

   _____

   The suspect has a scar on his left wrist.

6. What is the value of the television taken during the burglary?

   _____

   The value of the television taken during the burglary is $700.

7. What is the birthday of the victim?

   _____

   The victim's date of birth is December 7.

8. Where did the incident take place?

_____

The incident took place at 584 Benton Drive.

9. What is the name of the officer who completed the form?

_____

The name of the officer who completed the form is Kevin Plymouth.

Questions 10 through 14 are based on the following incident report form.

INCIDENT REPORT — POLICE DEPARTMENT

1. ADDRESS OF INCIDENT	2. OFFENSE	3. CODE	4. DATE
194 Willow Boulevard	Larceny	F5416-99	08/28

5. NAME OF VICTIM: INDIVIDUAL OR BUSINESS	6. ADDRESS PHONE
Ashley Cloud	3240 Littman Street

7. ASSIGNED OFFICERS/BADGE NUMBERS	8. AGE OF VICTIM	9. RACE OF VICTIM	10. VICTIM'S DATE OF BIRTH
Alexander Tripp #1598 Kelsey Hampton #6503	65	Native American	04/09

11. NAME OF SUSPECT	12. ADDRESS
Benjamin Torres	734 Thirteenth Avenue

13. AGE	14. RACE	15. SEX	16. DATE OF BIRTH	17. HEIGHT	18. WEIGHT
20	Hispanic	Male	12/18	5'10"	175

19. HAIR	20. EYES	21. PHYSICAL DESCRIPTION
Brown	Brown	Wearing black pants and grey shirt; has tattoo on right forearm

22. CHARGES
Larceny

23. ITEM	24. BRAND	25. SERIAL NUMBER	26. VALUE
Necklace			$300

27. ITEM	28. BRAND	29. SERIAL NUMBER	30. VALUE

31. ITEM	32. BRAND	33. SERIAL NUMBER	34. VALUE

35. _Alexander Tripp #1598_
SIGNATURE OF OFFICER/BADGE NUMBER

---

10. What item did the suspect allegedly take during the incident?

_____

The suspect allegedly took a necklace during the incident.

11. What are the badge numbers of the officers who reported to the incident?

_____

The badge numbers of the reporting officers are 1598 and 6503.

12. When did the incident take place?

_____

The incident took place on August 28.

13. What is the hair color of the suspect?

_____

The suspect's hair color is brown.

14. What is the race of the victim?

_____

The victim's race is Native American.

Practice NYC Incident Report Questions

The following passages and question sets are designed to help you practice answering questions about incident reports as they appear on the NYC exam. Choose the answer that *most correctly* answers the question.

> *Answer Question 1 solely on the basis of the following information.*

While on patrol, Officer Gonzales responded to an armed robbery. The following details were obtained at the scene:

Place of Crime: In front of Judy's Salon

Time of Crime: Between 5:30 p.m. and 6:15 p.m.

Victim: Donna Marks

Crime: Auto theft

Vehicle Stolen: Blue 2007 Hyundai Santa Fe

Suspect: Ralph Samson

1. Officer Gonzales is completing a report of the incident. Which one of the following expresses the preceding information *most clearly, accurately, and completely?*

   (A) Between 5:30 p.m. and 6:15 p.m. Donna Marks or Ralph Samson stole a blue 2007 Hyundai Santa Fe in front of Judy's Salon.

   (B) Between 5:30 p.m. and 6:15 p.m., suspect Ralph Samson stole Donna Marks's blue 2007 Hyundai Santa Fe from in front of Judy's Salon.

   (C) Ralph Samson was in front of Judy's Salon between 5:30 p.m. and 6:15 p.m. Donna Marks owns a blue 2007 Hyundai Santa Fe.

   (D) Donna Marks visited Judy's Salon between 5:30 p.m. and 6:15 p.m. Ralph Samson stole a blue 2007 Hyundai Santa Fe.

Choice (B) is correct because this choice best restates the information. Choice (A) is incorrect because it indicates that Donna Marks may have stolen the vehicle, which isn't true. Choice (C) is incorrect because it doesn't indicate that a crime was committed. Choice (D) is incorrect because it doesn't state that Donna Marks is the owner of the stolen vehicle.

Answer Question 2 solely on the basis of the following information.

While on patrol, Officer Sampsell responded to a traffic accident. The following details were obtained at the scene:

Place of Accident: Intersection of Main and Oak Streets

Time of Accident: 2:40 p.m.

Vehicle Involved: 2008 Audi

Driver: Michael Nyuang

Damage: Vehicle struck a concrete wall causing a damaged front end

2. Officer Sampsell is completing a report of the incident. Which one of the following expresses the preceding information *most clearly, accurately, and completely?*

   (A) A car was involved in an accident at the intersection of Main and Oak Streets at 2:40 p.m., causing a damaged front end.

   (B) At 2:40 p.m. Michael Nyuang was at the intersection of Main and Oak Streets. A 2008 Audi was involved in an accident when it struck a concrete wall causing a damaged front end.

   (C) A 2008 Audi driven by Michael Nyuang struck a concrete wall at the intersection of Main and Oak Streets at 2:40 p.m., causing a damaged front end.

   (D) A 2008 Audi struck Michael Nyuang causing a damaged front end at the intersection of Main and Oak Streets at 2:40 p.m.

Choice (C) is the best answer because it clearly describes the incident using correct grammar. Choice (A) doesn't state that the car was driven by Michael Nyuang. Choice (B) also doesn't make it clear that the car in the accident was Michael Nyuang's. Choice (D) says that the car hit Michael Nyuang, when he was actually driving the car that hit a concrete wall.

Chapter 8

Acing the Law Enforcement Essay Exam

· ·

In This Chapter
▶ Writing responses on the Law Enforcement Essay Exam
▶ Figuring out the exam's scoring system
▶ Practicing essays with sample prompts

· ·

Candidates for police officer jobs have to take a written exam, which contains mostly multiple-choice questions, as well as a physical ability test (PAT). You must also complete psychological and medical evaluations and an oral interview. In addition to these testing components, which I cover in other chapters in this book, some police departments also give the Law Enforcement Essay Exam to ensure that they hire the best candidates for the job.

The *Law Enforcement Essay Exam* consists of a single question, called a *prompt*. To complete this exam, you write several paragraphs in response to the prompt. The prompt isn't about law enforcement — it asks you to recall a specific experience in your life and then reflect upon it. Your essay is graded on a scale of 1 through 6, with 6 being outstanding.

Now, we know what you're thinking: "What does being a good writer have to do with being a good cop?" Well, the ability to write clearly and correctly shows that you're able to communicate effectively when completing written reports, and police officers have to complete a *lot* of written reports.

In this chapter, we arm you with information about the essay exam in case you end up having to take it as a candidate for a police officer job. We start with the steps you should follow to craft a winning essay.

Following the Proper Steps to Craft a Winning Essay

The prompt, or question, on the Law Enforcement Essay Exam asks you to write about a personal experience. It doesn't test your knowledge of police experience. A prompt may look like this:

> Sometimes an event in your life seems negative at first, but it turns out to be good for you in the long run. Recall such an event. Write about what made your perception of this event change from bad to good, and recall what you learned from the experience.

Now, we know what you're thinking: "Huh? Where do I begin?" This section breaks down the steps to follow when you draft your essay in order to craft a clear, thoughtful, and grammatically correct response:

- ✔ Prewriting
- ✔ Writing
- ✔ Revising/proofreading

Prewriting

Prewriting is a fancy word for planning. When you prewrite, you choose a topic, come up with a thesis statement or main idea, and create a rough outline. In other words, you organize your thoughts and get ready to write.

Reread the writing prompt in the preceding section. Brainstorm some negative experiences in your life. Maybe you lost your job, broke your leg before a ski trip, or failed a college course. Choose a negative experience that ultimately resulted in something positive. Maybe losing your job caused you to choose a new, exciting career. Or perhaps you met someone special because your broken leg caused you to stay home from a ski trip. Or maybe failing a college course taught you a valuable lesson: Good study habits lead to success.

Choose a topic you can work with — one that you know you can write a few good paragraphs about. You only have 40 minutes to complete the Law Enforcement Essay Exam, so you don't have time to switch topics and start over.

After you have your topic, come up with a thesis statement or a main idea. Your *thesis statement* is a sentence or two that tells what your essay is about. Here are some decent thesis statements about the topics you just read about:

> "For ten years, I worked as a customer service representative, so I was crushed when the company closed and I was laid off. However, this event turned out to be good for me because it led to my decision to return to school and pursue a new career."

> "Last year I broke my leg and couldn't go on a ski trip to Vermont with my friends. At first I was devastated and in pain, but it turned out to be the best thing that ever happened to me because I met Vicki, my future wife, in the hospital's emergency room."

> "I'll always remember my first college course because I failed it! I was convinced that I wasn't cut out for college, but after this failure, I tried harder and learned to become a good student."

The next step is to create a rough outline. This outline is for your eyes only, so it doesn't have to be formal or grammatically correct. Remember that you only have 40 minutes, so work quickly to make sure you have enough time to write and revise. Here's a rough outline for the losing-your-job topic:

1. Introduction/thesis statement
2. My old job as a customer service rep
    a) What I did/my responsibilities
    b) Why I liked it
3. How I felt when the company closed

4. What I did next

    a) Decided to find a new career

    b) Went back to school to become a police officer

5. Conclusion: Why my job loss turned out to be good for me

Writing

After you finish prewriting, begin writing. Feel free to change your outline a bit as the words start to flow, and don't skimp on details that strengthen your story.

Because most departments give you a booklet to write in, you can't revise as easily as you could if you were drafting your essay on a computer. So be careful and write in complete sentences.

Read this sample essay response to the losing-your-job topic. Notice that each paragraph is about one topic. The organization is logical, and the essay is easy to comprehend.

My New Career

Sometimes, a negative experience turns out to be good for us in the long run. This happened to me. For ten years, I worked as a customer service representative, so I was devastated when the company closed and I was laid off. However, this event turned out to be good for me because it led to my decision to return to school and pursue a new career as a police officer.

I really enjoyed working as a customer service representative at Dalton Industries, a direct-mail company. I spent most of my day answering phones and assisting customers with their orders. Customers depended on my knowledge of the industry and our company to give them accurate estimates regarding completion time and price. I often helped them determine details about their marketing piece. For example, if a customer wanted to send a letter to existing customers about an upcoming sale, I might help the client choose the type of paper, the envelope size, and even the color of the type.

Because I had worked at Dalton for ten years, it felt like home to me. My managers trusted me to work independently. They sometimes allowed me to work flexible hours so I could pick up my children after school. They gave me frequent raises for doing an excellent job. My co-workers at Dalton were like my extended family. We celebrated one another's birthdays and attended special events such as weddings. Even the customers were my friends. Many customers requested that I handle their orders. I was good at my job. I knew that in time I would likely be promoted to management.

Then our country entered a recession. Because of the weak economy, many of our long-term customers went out of business. The number of orders dropped, and Dalton began losing money. Within a year, Dalton's owners held a meeting and explained to the staff that they were shutting down the company. We were all laid off.

At first, I couldn't stop crying. I was losing my paycheck, but I felt as if I was also losing my friends and my future. Then one day, I decided it was time to make a change. I couldn't get my old job back, but I could prepare for a new career in the future.

Because I enjoy helping people, I decided to become a police officer. I enrolled in a criminal justice program at a local university. I went to night school while I worked days as a waitress at a nearby pizza place. My schedule was difficult and I worked very hard, but I did it. In two years, I graduated and was one step closer to obtaining work as a police officer. I was very proud of myself.

Now I'm taking this test as part of the application process to become a police officer. I'm certain that if I am hired, I will do a good job and will find police work rewarding. Losing my job at Dalton turned out to be a good thing. If it didn't happen, I wouldn't have decided to become a police officer.

Proofreading

After you write your essay, proofread it carefully. A good rule of thumb is to read your essay twice: once to make sure your ideas are clear and again, word by word, to make sure your grammar and spelling are correct. Be on the lookout for the errors covered in the following sections.

Sentence fragments

A *sentence fragment* is a group of words that don't express a complete thought. A sentence fragment may lack a subject, a verb, or both. Eliminate sentence fragments in your writing. Use only complete sentences.

> **Sentence fragment:** Because it rained hard this morning.

> **Complete sentence:** Because it rained hard this morning, I couldn't mow the lawn.

> **Sentence fragment:** Although I knew the answer to the sergeant's question.

> **Complete sentence:** Although I knew the answer to the sergeant's question, I didn't say a word.

> **Sentence fragment:** Which is what she said.

> **Complete sentence:** It's important that we work with a partner, which is what she said.

Run-on sentences

A *run-on sentence* is actually two sentences that aren't separated with a period or a coordinating conjunction such as *and, but, yet,* or *or*.

> **Incorrect:** Marshall liked to watch television at night on the weekends he preferred to spend time outdoors.

> **Correct:** Marshall liked to watch television at night. On the weekends, he preferred to spend time outdoors.

> **Also correct:** Marshall liked to watch television at night, but on the weekends, he preferred to spend time outdoors.

> **Incorrect:** Sandra was always a good writer she knew she would be famous someday.

> **Correct:** Sandra was always a good writer. She knew she would be famous someday.

> **Also correct:** Sandra was always a good writer and knew she would be famous someday.

Note the difference between *it's* and *its*. *It's* is a contraction meaning *it is*. If substituting *it is* in a sentence doesn't make sense, the sentence likely requires the possessive pronoun *its*. Also don't confuse *they're, their,* and *there*. *They're* is a contraction for *they are*. (*They're* going to the movies.) *Their* is a pronoun. (*Their* dog is in our yard.) *There* refers to a place. (*There* is our house.)

Comma splices

When two sentences are joined by a comma, it's called a *comma splice*. Eliminate comma splices from your writing by separating sentences with a period or including a coordinating conjunction, such as *and, but, yet,* or *or.* You can also add a subordinate conjunction in front of one of the sentences. Common subordinate conjunctions are *because, although, since,* and *while.*

> **Incorrect:** My boss was upset with me today, I was late for work again.

> **Correct:** My boss was upset with me today because I was late for work again.

> **Incorrect:** Learning to drive is fun, you need to be patient with yourself.

> **Correct:** Learning to drive is fun, but you need to be patient with yourself.

> **Also correct:** Although learning to drive is fun, you need to be patient with yourself.

Subject-verb agreement

The *subject* of a sentence must agree with the *verb*. A singular subject takes a singular verb, and a plural subject takes a plural verb. Read these sentences:

> The children look really happy today. (*Children* is a plural subject; *look* is a plural verb.)

> The child looks really happy today. (*Child* is a singular subject; *looks* is a singular verb.)

> Grandfather enjoys driving his car very fast. (*Grandfather* is a singular subject; *enjoys* is a singular verb.)

> Our three dogs are named Flea, Blubber, and Sausage. (*Dogs* is a plural subject; *are named* is a plural verb.)

> Her cat is named Weezer. (*Cat* is a singular subject; *is named* is a singular verb.)

Be careful not to omit past-tense endings in your writing. Be on the lookout for sentences such as, "Last night, Tanya reach for the peas, but pick a can of corn instead." The sentence should read, "Last night, Tanya reached for the peas, but picked a can of corn instead."

Pronoun-antecedent agreement

A *pronoun* is a noun substitute. An *antecedent* is the noun that the pronoun refers to. Read this sentence:

> Maggie left her jacket on the porch.

In this sentence, *Maggie* is the antecedent and *her* is a pronoun representing Maggie. Pronouns and their antecedents must agree in number. A singular antecedent takes a singular pronoun, and a plural antecedent must have a plural pronoun. Sounds simple, right? The rule is often broken because it creates gender problems. Though people often break this rule when they speak, it's important to follow it in writing. Read these sentences:

> **Incorrect:** A student may pick up their schedule in the office. (*Student* is singular, but the pronoun *their* is plural.)

> **Correct:** A student may pick up his or her schedule in the office. (*Student* is singular, and the pronouns *his* and *her* are also singular.)

> **Also correct:** Students may pick up their schedules in the office. (*Students* is plural, and the pronoun *their* is also plural.)

To brush up on your spelling and to find out more about grammar, turn to Chapter 5.

Understanding How Essays Are Scored

If you take the Law Enforcement Essay Exam, your essay is scored on a scale of 1 to 6, with 6 being the highest grade. Two individuals, called *raters,* read and score your essay. You need a *combined* score *higher* than 6 to pass. So if one rater gives your essay a 5 and the other rater gives your essay a 2, you pass. However, if both raters give your essay a score of 3, you fail the exam.

For a passing score, your essay needs to meet the following criteria:

✔ **It should respond to the prompt.** Sometimes candidates don't respond specifically to the prompt but instead write a more general essay. For example, suppose a prompt asks you to describe a difficult task and the approach you took to complete this task. Instead of writing an essay about a difficult task you performed, you instead write about difficult tasks in general. Your essay may be terrific, but it doesn't respond to the prompt, so you're going to lose points.

✔ **It should include enough details to explain and support your ideas.** If a prompt asks you to describe a difficult task and you choose learning to use a computer, you need to explain what made this task difficult. Perhaps you knew little about computers and had to follow lousy directions. Maybe you had trouble saving the documents you typed — perhaps your computer beeped at you incessantly when you hit the wrong keys. Back up your ideas with enough details to make your point.

✔ **Its meaning should be clear.** The reader must be able to understand your ideas. If you jump from one idea to another without a logical structure, the reader may become confused. How do you make sure your essay is well-organized? By prewriting, which we explain in the earlier "Prewriting" section.

✔ **It should be as error-free as possible.** Neatly correct misspelled words and add missing words. Write in complete sentences. Don't unnecessarily shift from one tense to another. For example, don't write, "I am going on vacation next month. I went to the beach with my children." Write instead, "I am going on vacation next month. I am going to the beach with my children." Or write, "I went on vacation last month. I went to the beach with my children." Carefully proofreading your work helps you correct errors. Though a few errors won't cause you to fail the exam, an essay filled with mistakes won't make the grade.

Raters use this grading scale to score exams:

✔ **An essay receiving a score of 6**

- Responds effectively to the writing task

- Explores the issues thoughtfully and in depth

- Is coherently and logically organized and fully developed

- Has a fluent style marked by sentence variety and language control

- Is generally free from errors in mechanics, usage, and sentence structure

✔ **An essay receiving a score of 5**

- Responds clearly to the writing task

- Explores the issues in some depth

- Is clearly organized and well developed

- Displays some sentence variety and facility in language

- May have a few errors in mechanics, usage, and sentence structure

✔ **An essay receiving a score of 4**

- Responds adequately to the writing task
- May not explore the issues in depth
- Is adequately organized and has sufficient development
- Has basic competence in mechanics, usage, and sentence structure

✔ **An essay receiving a score of 3**

- Does not clearly respond to the writing task
- May not provide adequate development or may lack specificity
- May be poorly organized
- May have an accumulation of errors in mechanics, usage, and sentence structure

✔ **An essay receiving a score of 2**

- May indicate confusion about the topic
- May have weak organization or be seriously underdeveloped
- May lack focus or demonstrate confusion about the writing task
- May be marred by frequent errors in mechanics, usage, and sentence structure

✔ **An essay receiving a score of 1**

- Suggests an inability to comprehend the question
- May be off-topic
- Is unfocused or disorganized
- Is underdeveloped
- May have serious and persistent errors in mechanics, usage, and sentence structure

Warming Up to Sample Essay Prompts

The best way to prepare for the Law Enforcement Essay Exam is to practice writing, especially if you haven't written anything in a while. Set a timer for 40 minutes, the length of time allowed on the actual exam. Choose one of the sample prompts in this section, and write a response to it.

Stop writing after 40 minutes and read your response carefully. Ask yourself whether it makes sense. Note whether your writing is clear and coherent. Look for omitted words, misspelled words, and sentence fragments. Have someone else read your essay and ensure that it meets the criteria outlined in the preceding section. Repeat this exercise until your practice essays meet the scoring criteria and your heart stops racing at the thought of writing an essay.

✔ **Sample Prompt 1:**

Think of a time when you took a stand and stood up for something you believed in. Explain what made you stand up for your beliefs, why you decided to take action, and how your actions resulted in change. Note how you felt afterward.

✔ **Sample Prompt 2:**

We all have people whom we admire. These people are personal heroes who inspire us. Write about someone whom you admire and consider a personal hero. Explain why this person inspires you and how you've modeled your behavior after him or her.

✔ **Sample Prompt 3:**

Most of us have goals that we hope to reach in the future. Write about one of your goals. Explain how and when you plan to reach this goal. Explain why this goal is important to you.

✔ **Sample Prompt 4:**

Think of a time when you did something that you were afraid to do and faced your fear. Recall what made you afraid, what made you take action, and how you felt afterward. Indicate whether you would take this action again in the future.

Practice Law Enforcement Essay Exam Question and Answer

Write a response to the following prompt in 40 minutes. Have about five sheets of paper on hand. Your final essay takes up about two sheets of paper, but you need scrap paper to create a rough outline and jot down your thoughts.

Think of a time when you had trouble learning something new. Describe why you found the task difficult and what you did to master it. Explain how learning this new task helps you in your everyday life.

The following is an example of an essay that would most likely receive a score of 6 from one reviewer on the Law Enforcement Essay Exam. Remember that you need a combined score from two reviewers that's higher than 6 to pass.

Learning to Drive

Two years ago, I received my driver's license. This was a major accomplishment because I'm 30 years old. Driving has always been a difficult task for me. I tried to get my license when I was 16 but didn't have a good experience. However, I recently learned that I can accomplish anything if I work hard at it and believe in myself.

When I was 16, most of my friends applied for a learner's permit, passed the driver's test, and received a driver's license. They did this with such ease that I fooled myself into believing that learning to drive would be easy for me. I, too, applied for my learner's permit and then practiced driving while my mother or father was in the car. I was terri-fied! I had trouble controlling the vehicle and had several near-misses with other cars on the road. I was so scared that when I saw a car in the opposite lane, I veered to the right, nearly hitting parked cars, telephone poles, and curbs. My hands always shook, and I repeatedly hit the brakes too hard. Though my parents continually told me to relax, I let my nerves get the best of me.

I also realized that although I had lived in the same town my entire life, I had no idea how to get around. I wasn't blessed with a good sense of direction. My mother had to explain to me over and over again how to get to my school, the grocery store, and the mall. It was embarrassing. I turned left when I should have turned right. I was nearly always in the wrong lane. Once, I accidentally wound up on a major highway, and my father had to help me pull over to the side of the road so that he could switch places with me and drive us safely home.

After several months, my parents said that they thought I might be "good enough" to take my driver's license test, as long as I promised them I would only drive around our neighborhood. The state trooper who tested me disagreed, however. After he failed me, I decided that I was better off taking the bus and gave up my quest to become a licensed driver.

However, three years ago, my wife and I moved out of the city to an area where buses don't travel everywhere. I didn't want to move, but she was offered a job that was too good to refuse, so we packed up our family and left the city — and I knew that I had to learn to drive.

This time I hired a certified driving instructor, and because I was older, I had more confidence in my abilities. I am a father, after all, and I've held several successful jobs. I told myself that I would learn to do this, one step at a time, and that's just what I did. I took a few driving lessons each week and practiced, but I didn't put a great deal of pressure on myself. In time, I knew I could drive to and from my new job. When I took my driver's test, the state trooper congratulated me, and I received my driver's license.

Being able to drive has changed my life in many ways. I'm able to drive to work and take my children wherever they want to go. It has given me a sense of freedom that I didn't have before. My sense of direction has even improved, and I'm no longer nervous on the road. I learned that you shouldn't give up on reaching goals, even if you're struggling to do so.

Chapter 9

Completing the Personal History Statement

In This Chapter

▶ Finding out about the components of the Personal History Statement

▶ Getting together the information and documentation you need

Stop for a moment and envision the perfect candidate for a job as a police officer. What does this candidate look like? The person you imagine is probably good-looking and in excellent physical condition — with bulging biceps and six-pack abs. Now, think about the perfect candidate's character. He or she is smart, honest, and brave. Can the perfect candidate handle stress? Bring it on! The perfect candidate excels under pressure.

Now, think about the perfect candidate's past. A background investigation wouldn't uncover anything bad because this person is squeaky clean. He or she has never stolen anything, used drugs, or broken the law.

Of course, the perfect police officer candidate doesn't exist. No one is perfect, but law enforcement officials must do everything in their power to ensure that they hire the best candidates for the job. Requiring candidates to complete a Personal History Statement is one way that they do this. Some departments ask you to complete a Personal History Statement immediately after you take your written police officer exam, before you leave the test site. Other departments ask you to complete the Personal History Statement at home and mail it in or deliver it in person, sometimes with a formal job application.

Never lie on the Personal History Statement. Don't omit information, either. In law enforcement, an omission is considered a deceptive answer and a lie. Keep in mind that this statement is the basis for a background investigation. Investigators will verify each detail and look into your background. It's better to be upfront and honest about a past mistake than to give the impression that you're hiding something.

In this chapter, we show you how to complete the Personal History Statement. The statement may vary somewhat from department to department, but if you follow the guidelines in this chapter, you'll have no problem doing a good job.

Becoming Familiar with the Personal History Statement

To complete the Personal History Statement, you must give details about your life and your past. Background investigators then verify each detail to ensure that it's accurate. If they uncover a discrepancy, they either let you know or simply send you a letter saying that you're discontinued from the hiring process. They may also ask you to further explain some of your answers. Be sure to answer every question on the Personal History Statement and be prepared to explain your answers. Even minute details that you think are insignificant may be crucial to the department where you want to work. What you reveal — or don't reveal — on the Personal History Statement affects the department's hiring decision.

While the Personal History Statement may vary from department to department, it usually requests the same information. Most statements request the following:

- A recent photograph
- General information, including your name, address, date of birth, telephone numbers, and driver's license number
- Identifying information, such as your height, weight, hair and eye color, and the presence of scars or tattoos
- Previous interactions with law enforcement, including arrests and notices to appear
- Traffic record information, including accidents and ticket information
- Military service information
- Information about your family members
- Information about your education
- References
- Employment history and work skills
- Residence information, including addresses and names of landlords or neighbors
- Financial obligations
- Club or association memberships
- Awards or accomplishments
- Answers to personal questions
- Answers to theft questions
- Your signature

Refer to Figure 9-1 for sample pages from a Personal History Statement.

APPLICANT IDENTIFICATION

NAME_____ Social Security No. _____-_____-_____
       (Last)   (First)   (Middle)

MAILING ADDRESS (Current)_____( )_____
                (Street)   (City)   (State)   (Zip)   (Daytime Phone)

Date of birth_____ (proof required)   Place of birth_____
                                                 (City)   (State)

List any other names used if different from name given on application._____

We must be able to contact you during the investigation. Please provide the following phone numbers:

Home_____   Work_____   Mobile_____
Pager_____   Other_____
Name of spouse_____   Telephone number (_____)_____

LIST EXACT POSITION FOR WHICH YOU HAVE APPLIED:
_____

Driver's License No._____ State_____ Expiration date_____Class A B C

Height_____ Weight _____ Color of Eyes _____ Color of Hair _____

Scars, tattoos or other distinguishing marks _____

ARRESTS, DETENTIONS AND LAWSUITS

Have you ever been arrested or convicted of an offense?_____

If your answer is "yes," explain in concise detail on a separate sheet of paper, giving the dates and nature of the offense, the name and location of the court, and the disposition of the case. A conviction may not disqualify you, but a false statement will.

Have you ever been on probation or parole? _____ If "yes," explain on separate sheet of paper.

Are you under indictment on charges for a criminal offense? _____ If "yes," explain on separate sheet of paper.

Have you ever been indicted by a grand jury? _____

Have you ever been involved as a party in a lawsuit? _____ If "yes," explain on separate sheet of paper.

Figure 9-1:
An example
of a typical
Personal
History
Statement.

EMPLOYMENT HISTORY

This information will be the official record of your employment history and must accurately reflect all significant duties performed. Summaries of experience should clearly describe your qualifications.

1. Include ALL employment, back to 17 years of age. Begin with your current or last position and work back to your first position.
2. Give a brief summary of the technical and, if appropriate, the managerial responsibilities of each position you have held.
3. For supervisory/managerial positions, indicate the number of employees you supervised.

EMPLOYER'S NAME AND ADDRESS _____

_____ PHONE NO. (_____)_____

DATES EMPLOYED (from) _____ to _____ POSITION HELD _____

DESCRIPTION OF DUTIES PERFORMED_____

_____

_____

STARTING SALARY _____ ENDING SALARY _____

SPECIFIC REASON FOR LEAVING _____

SUPERVISOR'S NAME AND HOME PHONE NUMBER_____(___)_____

CO-WORKER'S NAME AND HOME PHONE NUMBER_____(___)_____

CO-WORKER'S NAME AND HOME PHONE NUMBER_____(___)_____

Are you eligible for rehire? Yes _____ No _____

SUMMARY OF OTHER WORK EXPERIENCE / SPECIAL SKILLS, SPECIAL LICENSES, ETC.
Summarize special skills and qualifications acquired from employment or other experience that may qualify you for work with this organization.

_____

_____

_____

Do you speak, read, or write a language other than English? _____ If "yes," what language(s)? _____

_____ How fluently? Fair _____ Good _____ Excellent _____

Figure 9-1:
An example
of a typical
Personal
History
Statement.

1. Have you ever been arrested for being drunk, public intoxication, DWI, etc? If "yes," give dates and circumstances. _____

2. Have you ever used marijuana or any other drug not prescribed by a physician?_____
   If "yes," indicate substance and frequency, including date last used._____
   _____

3. Have you ever been involved in any way in the manufacturing of an illegal drug?_____ If "yes,"
   explain:_____

4. Have you ever used any of the following: Inhalants, glue, paints, or petroleum products? If "yes," explain:
   _____

5. Have you ever received illegal drugs or narcotics from anyone? _____ If "yes,"
   explain:_____

6. Have you ever completed an application for employment with this or any other law enforcement agency?
   _____
   If "yes," explain status of application, and if applicable, the reason for not being hired.
   _____
   _____
   _____

7. If it became necessary to take a human life in the course of your duties as a police officer, is there anything that
   would prevent you from doing so? _____ If "yes," explain:
   _____
   _____

8. If it became necessary to work weekends, holidays, evenings or nights in the course of your duties as a police
   officer, would your beliefs or any other principles prevent you from doing so? _____ If "yes,"
   explain:_____

THEFT INFORMATION

1. Have you ever stolen anything?   Yes _____   No _____

IF YES, answer the following questions:

2. List everything you can remember stealing during your lifetime.

3. When was the last time you stole anything?

Figure 9-1:
An example
of a typical
Personal
History
Statement.

Getting Ready to Complete the Personal History Statement

While some police departments allow you to complete the Personal History Statement at home, others require you to complete it after you take the written police officer exam. Because the Personal History Statement asks for so much information, you need to prepare for it ahead of time.

Gathering the necessary information

No matter how sharp you think your memory is, you'd be surprised at how much you forget when asked to recall the details of your life, such as your past addresses, employers, volunteer positions, and driving history. To ensure that you don't leave any such information out of your Personal History Statement, follow these steps:

1. **Make a list of every address you've ever lived at up until now, including contact information for landlords, property managers, and/or neighbors.**

    If you can't find or remember all this information, go back as far as you can. Some police departments only require you to list addresses for the past ten years.

2. **Make a list of every job you've ever held, including employer information, addresses, telephone numbers, and anything else you consider relevant to your work history.**

    This includes part-time, full-time, and volunteer positions.

3. **Research your driving history. Some police departments ask you to list every traffic ticket you've ever received, while others ask you to list only the traffic tickets you received in the past five years.**

    Traffic violations include tickets for speeding, failing to stop at a stop sign, and driving with expired license plates. Contact your local department of motor vehicles (DMV) to get a copy of your driving record. You may have to contact DMVs in different states if you have lived and driven in different locations.

    Depending on the state in which you live, getting a copy of your driving record may take several weeks. Keep this in mind when gathering information to complete the Personal History Statement. And don't ask a friend or neighbor who is a law enforcement officer to get you a copy of your driving record because law enforcement officers aren't allowed to do this.

4. **Gather the names of personal references.**

    References are people who will give the investigator unbiased information about you, such as your work history or character. Some departments require as many as six references, while others require fewer. Only provide the names of people you trust. Most departments place restrictions on whom you can list as a reference — you can't list Mom and Dad. Some departments don't accept relatives, employers, or teachers as references. They prefer the names of neighbors and friends. Some departments also put restrictions on the length of time a reference must have known you. For example, you may be asked to only list references who have known you at least three years.

Once you gather this information, keep it together in a safe place.

Collecting the necessary documents

You'll need some documents to complete your Personal History Statement, and you're required to provide them as part of the application process as well. If you're completing the Personal History Statement after the written police officer exam, you're required to bring these documents with you. If the police department asks you to complete the Personal History Statement at home, you must send in or drop off these documents.

If you can't find these documents or are sure that they're lost, apply for new ones as soon as possible. Some documents can take as long as eight weeks to arrive.

Before ordering documents, find out whether the police department wants you to submit originals or copies and how the department would like these documents submitted. Some departments require that documents such as birth certificates and college transcripts be official, certified copies. Others prefer that documents such as college transcripts, credit reports, and driving reports be sent directly from the issuing agency or institution. Others require only copies of these documents. Also ask how current documents such as credit reports or driving reports need to be and whether the documents will be returned to you.

Here's a list of what you need:

- ✔ Birth certificate
- ✔ Social Security card
- ✔ DD 214 (veterans only)
- ✔ Naturalization papers (if applicable)
- ✔ High school diploma or equivalent
- ✔ High school transcripts
- ✔ College transcripts
- ✔ Driver's license (be sure it shows your current address and that it's not expired)
- ✔ Driving record
- ✔ Credit report
- ✔ Selective Service card
- ✔ Marriage certificate, divorce papers, legal separation documents, and name change paperwork

Writing the Personal History Statement

Whether you complete the Personal History Statement when you take the written police officer exam or at home when you complete an application for employment, use the information and documents you've gathered to complete the statement. (See the preceding section for a list of the necessary documents.)

If you need more space than the form provides, attach extra paper. Be sure to number or reference the question(s) you answer on each page.

If you're completing the Personal History Statement after your written police officer test, you're usually allowed only a certain amount of time. Pace yourself so that you have enough time to fill out the form and double-check everything on it.

Understanding that honesty is the best policy

When you complete the Personal History Statement, you give the police department many details about your life and your past. While you may be tempted to omit or lie about negative information, such as a former run-in with the law, doing so may cost you an opportunity to work as a police officer.

The Personal History Statement is used as the basis for a background investigation. If you lie about something, you can bet that investigators will find out about it, and it will hurt your chances of landing a job. It's better to be upfront about a mistake in your past than to try and sweep it under the rug. How you present the details of your life establishes your credibility among your future supervisors and peers. Would you want to work alongside someone you didn't trust?

Consider this example: When Maryann was in high school, she received a few speeding tickets. She paid the fines and never received another traffic ticket. When she was filling out the Personal History Statement, Maryann left out this information about her driving record, thinking it was irrelevant because it happened so many years ago. When the background investigators discovered this information on her driving report and realized that she had left it out of the Personal History Statement, the police department decided not to hire her. The moral of the story: Always tell the truth.

Within the Personal History Statement, you must sign a statement certifying that the information you've provided is truthful. Figure 9-2 shows an example of this type of certification.

PLEASE READ THE FOLLOWING STATEMENTS CAREFULLY AND INDICATE YOUR UNDERSTANDING AND ACCEPTANCE BY SIGNING IN THE SPACE PROVIDED.

1.   I certify that all the information provided by me in connection with my application, whether on this document or not, is true and complete, and I understand that any misstatement, falsification, or omission of information may be grounds for refusal to hire or, if hired, termination.

2.   I understand that as a condition of employment, I may be required to provide legal proof of authorization to work in the United States.

3.   I understand that some agencies will check with the XX Department of Public Safety and/or the Federal Bureau of Investigation for any criminal history in accordance with applicable statutes.

4.   I authorize any of the persons or organizations referenced in this application to give you any and all information concerning my previous employment, education, or any other information they might have, personal or otherwise, with regard to any of the subjects covered by this application, and I release all such parties from all liability from any damages that may result from furnishing such information to you.

THIS APPLICATION WAS COMPLETED BY MYSELF AND NO OTHER PERSON AND IS COMPLETE AND TRUTHFUL.

SIGN HERE: _____   DATE: _____
(Applicant signature)

SUBSCRIBED AND SWORN to before me, by the said _____
this _____ day of _____, 20_____, to certify which witness my hand and seal of office.

_____
Notary Public, State of XX

Figure 9-2: Your signature — and sometimes that of a notary public — certifies the accuracy of your Personal History Statement.

If a police department asks you to complete a Personal History Statement at home and mail it to or drop it off at the police department, you will most likely be required to have it notarized. This means that a notary public gives his or her seal of office to certify that you're the person who completed the document and that you've sworn that the information in the document is accurate.

Following directions and reading questions carefully

Before you begin filling out the Personal History Statement, carefully read all instructions and questions (see Figure 9-3 for sample instructions). If you don't understand a question, don't leave it blank. Ask the person administering the test to clarify it for you.

Be on the lookout for the words *all, any, each, ever, every,* and *excluding.* These words indicate how much and what type of information is required. For example: If you're asked to list *any* and *all* traffic tickets you received in the past ten years, you should include a ticket you received in New York ten years ago.

Here is an example of this type of question:

Have you ever been convicted of a crime? If so, explain.

If you have been convicted of a crime at any time in your life, you should answer "yes" to this question and explain what happened.

INSTRUCTIONS
READ THESE INSTRUCTIONS CAREFULLY BEFORE PROCEEDING

These instructions are provided as a guide to assist you in properly completing the Personal History Statement. It is essential that the information be accurate in all respects. It will be used as the basis for a background investigation that will determine your eligibility for employment.

1. Your Personal History Statement should be printed in ink by you and no other person. Answer all questions to the best of your ability.
2. If a question is not applicable to you, enter N/A in the space provided.
3. Avoid errors by reading the directions carefully before making any entries on the form. Be sure your information is correct and in proper sequence before you begin.
4. You are responsible for obtaining correct names, addresses, and telephone numbers. If you are not sure of an address or telephone number, check it by personal verification. Your local library may have a directory service or copies of area telephone directories. All addresses require zip codes and all telephone numbers require area codes.
5. If there is insufficient space on the form for you to include all information required, attach extra sheets to the Personal History Statement. Be sure to reference the relevant section and question area on the attached sheets.
6. An accurate and complete form will help expedite your investigation. On the other hand, deliberate omissions or falsifications may result in disqualification.
7. Upon completing the form, re-check each section to ensure that all information requested has been provided, or N/A entered if appropriate.
8. The attached Request for Pertaining to Military Records, Employment History Records Release and Authority for Release of Confidential Information and Waiver should be filled out and signed if applicable.
9. The Application for Employment and Personal History Statement may be hand delivered or mailed to City of XX, Human Resource Department, XX.
10. If you are selected for an interview, the Human Resource Department will notify you regarding the time and date.

Figure 9-3: Sample directions for completing a Personal History Statement.

Checking your work

After you've completed the Personal History Statement, check your work by doing the following:

- ✔ Make sure you've answered every question accurately and to the best of your knowledge.

- ✔ Make sure your handwriting is neat and legible.

- ✔ Check your grammar and spelling, paying close attention to names. Use a dictionary or grammar reference book if necessary.

- ✔ Make sure you use complete sentences (see Chapter 5 for coverage of grammar and spelling).

- ✔ Make sure dates, addresses, and phone numbers are correct. Before completing the Personal History Statement, call each number to verify its accuracy.

Part III

After the Written Test: Meeting Other Requirements

The 5th Wave   By Rich Tennant

PREPARING FOR THE POLICE OFFICER
EXAM – PHYSICAL ABILITY PORTION.

@RICHTENNANT

"Wait a minute. Did I say, 'seduce and restrain'?
I meant 'subdue and restrain.'"

In this part . . .

Police officers need to be able to read, write, add, and subtract — but they need other skills, too. A day in the life of a police officer may involve chasing a suspect and scaling a fence. It may require lifting someone who has been injured. Police officers must use good judgment and be able to keep their cool in stressful situations. Because police officers need to be able to do so many things, police departments give tests in addition to the written examination.

Part III prepares you for all the tests that come *after* the written exam. It introduces the exercises you may encounter during the physical ability test (PAT). Part III also supplies tips to succeed on the oral board interview and discusses why medical and psychological exams are necessary. If you have your heart set on becoming a police officer, this part helps round out your preparation.

Chapter 10

Putting Your Physical Ability to the Test

In This Chapter

▶ Understanding why the physical ability test (PAT) is necessary

▶ Exploring the skills tested during the physical ability test

▶ Getting prepared for physical ability test success

▶ Creating an exercise program to get in top shape

▶ Breaking down the events of the physical ability test

The job of a police officer is physically demanding. Sure, police officers spend some time sitting at a desk doing paperwork, but when they're called to active duty, they may have to walk, run, jump, climb, chase, frisk, cuff, squat, kneel, push, pull, and carry. They may have to perform these strenuous tasks in hot sun, pouring rain, sleet, snow — you name it. This is why police departments test your physical abilities as part of the police officer hiring process. They don't test these abilities to see whether you're in good enough shape to perform the job — because you're probably not. They test your physical abilities to see whether you have what it takes to succeed at the police academy, where you'll undergo rigorous physical training. By the time you graduate from the police academy, you'll be in excellent physical condition. In this chapter, we review the physical exam portion of the police officer hiring process.

The physical ability test (PAT) varies depending on the state and police department. Some police departments test traditional fitness skills; they may ask you to sprint and do sit-ups and push-ups. Other departments follow the guidelines of the National Criminal Justice Officer Physical Ability Test (NCJOPAT), which asks applicants to demonstrate skills related to law enforcement, such as the trigger pull and the dummy drag. Some departments use a combination of both types of tests and require candidates to participate in events such as an agility run, a dummy drag, a torso bag carry, and a one-minute sit-up test. The tests can vary, but we've taken care in this chapter to cover the most common events on the physical ability test.

Let's Get Physical: The Whys and Wherefores of the Physical Ability Test

Candidates for police officer jobs face a lengthy, multistep selection process that includes a number of tests. One test in this process is the *physical ability test* (PAT), which is also called the *physical agility test* or *fitness test*. This test typically follows the initial application, the written exam, and, depending on location, the video-based exam. Because the PAT is so strenuous, some departments require you to undergo a medical examination before you take it. Applicants who pass the PAT may continue to the next stage in the hiring process, which is often the oral interview (see Chapter 11 for more on this interview).

The events included in the PAT vary depending on the state and municipality. In other words, individual police departments may test applicants' physical abilities any way they choose. However, expect to face a challenging physical ability test regardless of where you live. Passing this test doesn't prove that you would be a good police officer. Rather, it proves that you may be able to handle the physical demands of a police academy, where the fittest and most successful recruits, or *cadets,* learn to become top-notch police officers.

Understanding why police officers need the physical ability test

Police work is often dangerous. Your ability to stay safe and protect others may depend on your physical fitness. You may have to defend yourself from a criminal, run from a vicious dog, race after a suspect, scale a wall, or carry a crime victim to a safe place. Other not-so-obvious physical strains include everyday tasks such as reaching for items that are far away or standing for a long time regardless of discomfort or pain.

A physical ability test gives those in charge of hiring new police officers a chance to see the candidates — you — in action. The PAT also gives you an opportunity to show that you have what it takes to be a police officer. During the physical ability test, test administrators watch as you perform a number of events that measure not only your speed, strength, endurance, agility, and flexibility, but also your ability to follow directions and efficiently accomplish assignments.

Police departments also give the PAT for financial reasons. Health costs have become an enormous burden for public organizations, such as police departments. If you're not in good shape, you're more likely to suffer health problems that may cause a city's insurance premiums to rise. Being out of work due to health issues also costs police departments money because they have to pay another officer overtime to take your place.

The PAT also narrows down the competition; those who fail the test don't get to continue to the next stage in the hiring process.

Breaking down the skill areas of the typical test

The details of the police officer physical ability test aren't set in stone. The type of tasks you'll be asked to perform are chosen by the department. Most physical ability tests include skills that test at least some of these areas: aerobic power, anaerobic power, strength, endurance, explosive leg power, flexibility, and agility. So what's the difference between the various types of exercise? The following list explains:

- ✔ **Aerobic power exercises** make your heart beat faster and really get your blood pumping through your veins. When you're working out, you breathe harder and your heart beats faster because you're taking in oxygen faster and your heart is pumping it through your body. When you're physically fit, your heart and lungs are able to work hard for a long time. A 1.5-mile run is an example of an aerobic power exercise. Bicycling, swimming, or walking briskly are also types of aerobic exercise.

- ✔ **Anaerobic power exercises** are short-lasting, high-intensity exercises during which your body's demand for oxygen exceeds its supply. A 300-meter sprint is an example of an anaerobic power exercise. Heavy weightlifting can also produce this result.

✔ **Strength exercises** require you to display the force of your muscles. Bench-pressing heavy weights is an example of a strength exercise.

✔ **Endurance exercises** require you to repeatedly use the same group of muscles for an extended time. Push-ups, which pinpoint the muscles in your arms, back, and shoulders, are a type of upper-body muscular endurance exercise. Sit-ups, which target your abdominal muscles, are a type of abdominal muscular endurance exercise.

✔ **Explosive leg power exercises** display leg strength in a quick burst. A vertical jump is a test of explosive leg power.

✔ **Flexibility exercises** test your ability to bend, climb, crawl, or otherwise stretch your muscles.

✔ **Agility exercises** test your coordination by requiring you to change direction quickly. These exercises might require you to hurdle low barriers and negotiate stairs.

Getting the lowdown on the local test

Physical ability tests are usually held in large areas such as in gymnasiums or on sports fields. The location and the time set aside for the test often depend on the number of applicants and the number of events. A little research can help you find out the specific details of your test.

To adequately prepare for the PAT, try to find out exactly what requirements you have to meet to pass this test in your region. Check your municipality's Web site. Contact your city's personnel office or police recruitment office. Find out who gives the test or has information about it. When you get in touch with someone, ask the following questions:

✔ Is a training program to prepare for the physical ability test available? If so, when and where will the training take place, and how can I sign up?

✔ How much does it cost to enroll in the training program?

✔ If a training program is not available, does the department have recommendations for preparing for the test, such as a special workout program?

✔ What events are on the test?

✔ How is the test graded? For example, some tests are pass/fail, while others might be scored on a particular scale.

✔ Is the test timed? If so, how long do I have to complete the test?

✔ Is the test given in a gymnasium or outdoors on a sports field? If it's in a gymnasium, are there any special requirements in terms of attire (for example, black-soled sneakers are not allowed in some gyms)?

✔ Is a diagram of the location of the events in the gymnasium or on the sports field available? Some police departments publish a diagram showing the layout of the course and the order of events.

Before you place the call, make sure you organize all your questions about the test and have a pen and paper ready to record essential information about the test. Getting this information early gives you time to prepare for the test — physically and mentally — and improve your chances of success. After the call, record the date, time, and the name and title of the person you spoke with. This information will help you if you need to speak to the person again in the future.

Getting in Shape before the Test

The police officer physical ability test is very challenging. Passing the test moves you a step closer to a career in law enforcement, a field that requires great physical exertion. Perhaps the best way to prepare yourself for the rigors of the physical exam is to exercise your body and get in the best shape you can. Committing to an exercise program is a great way to do this.

If you like team sports, play games such as baseball, basketball, or football, which increase your stamina, strength, and reaction time. Solo activities, such as running, hiking, or rowing, also help you get and stay in shape. You may also want to join a gym or attend physical education classes. Weight lifting, aerobics, yoga, and martial arts classes help train your body and your mind to meet the tough demands of police work.

Follow these steps when beginning an exercise program:

1. **Check with your doctor before beginning an exercise program to make sure you're healthy enough to handle the strain.**

   Jumping into a fitness program unprepared can lead to injury.

2. **Before each workout, do warm-up exercises and stretches.**

   A warm-up will prepare your body for the activity ahead.

3. **After your workout, do some cool-down exercises.**

   Cool-down exercises such as stretching and walking help you transition back to normal activity.

4. **Remember to keep yourself healthy and fit each day.**

   You can accomplish this by eating a healthy diet, cutting back on snacks, and getting plenty of sleep.

5. **Limit or eliminate unhealthy activities.**

   Smoking or drinking excessively make it more difficult to get into shape.

The following are some tips for a good exercise program:

- ✔ **Be choosy.** Pick exercises that improve your flexibility, strength, and endurance.

- ✔ **Stick to it.** Many experts recommend doing your exercises at least three times per week. Aim for five when preparing for the police officer physical ability test.

- ✔ **Get tired.** When you absolutely can't do one more exercise, you'll know that you've gotten a good workout.

- ✔ **Rest.** Resting is an important part of exercise. When you rest, you give your muscles time to heal and grow.

- ✔ **Repeat and increase.** Do your exercises often, and try to do more each time you work out. That's a sure sign that you're improving.

- ✔ **Don't give up.** Exercises such as running require mental and physical endurance. If you try to run a mile and a half and can't finish, walk the rest of the way. If you give up, you condition your mind and body to quit.

What You Should Know and Do the Day of Your Test

As with many challenges in life, preparation is a key to success in the police officer physical ability test. You want your body and mind to be conditioned for peak performance. Keep a positive attitude and a strong resolve to do your best. In advance of your test, nourish yourself by eating regular, healthy meals and by getting plenty of sleep. In addition, equip yourself with everything you'll need on exam day.

For starters, be sure to dress appropriately. The exam isn't a formal event by any means — expect some sweat and dirt! You may want to wear a T-shirt and gym shorts if the day will be warm. If it's a chilly day, consider a workout suit or a sweat shirt and sweat pants. Layering your clothes is a good idea, so you can take off an outer layer if you become too warm. Make sure your feet are ready for action, too. Sneakers or other durable, comfortable shoes with rubber bottoms are a good bet. If the test is in a gymnasium, you may not be allowed to wear sneakers with black soles.

Choose a plain T-shirt or other simple workout clothes. The examiners won't be impressed if you wear clothing with their agency logo on it. In fact, they may frown upon "wannabe" apparel. Don't wear clothing with offensive or possibly offensive graphics or phrases on it — especially if they relate to law enforcement. Make sure your clothing isn't too tight or revealing, and wear proper undergarments for the tasks at hand.

If the exam is at a location with a locker room and shower facilities, consider taking a towel and a change of clothes, so you don't have to wear your dirty clothes after the test. You should also remember to bring any protective accessories you need, such as kneepads or gloves if these are allowed. (Trust us — you'll want these if the obstacle course requires you to crawl on the ground!)

Applicants are also required to bring paperwork for the PAT. In most cases, you'll need photo identification, such as a driver's license, a passport, or an ID card. You'll also need to bring payment to cover the exam fee. Each department determines its own fee, but it often ranges from $25 to $50; checks and money orders are typically preferred. And don't forget that to qualify for the physical ability test, you may be required to present a note from your doctor. This note should state that you're in good enough shape to take the test. Physical ability tests are rigorous — you need to be in good shape just to participate safely. You may not be allowed to take the exam without it. You may also want to bring some extra paper, in case you want to take notes, and be sure to bring two number-two pencils and black ink pens.

To avoid getting sick, don't eat anything two to three hours before the test, but drink plenty of fluids. After so much physical exertion, you'll probably be famished. We recommend packing a light meal, such as bread, a small sandwich, or fruit. Avoid greasy and fatty foods, because they can upset your stomach in times of stress or heavy activity. Don't forget a good thirst quencher, too, such as water, juice, or a sports drink. You may be allowed to drink between events during the testing process. Staying hydrated is especially important on hot days. Stay away from caffeinated drinks, which can make you jumpy.

Showing Them What You Can Do: Test Events

The events included in the physical ability test may include traditional fitness events, such as sit-ups and push-ups; events related to law enforcement, such as the trigger pull; or a combination of traditional and law enforcement-related events. The events in this section are often included in the police officer PAT.

Some PATs include large events, such as obstacle courses, where you complete one event and then run along the course to the next event. These tests can involve many skills, quick thinking, and a lot of running. Most of these events deal with strength, endurance, agility, and flexibility. Other events test your ability to perform common police-officer tasks. Don't panic! You won't be expected to demonstrate any specialized police skills.

The order in which you complete the events depends on the police department. Some departments have candidates complete the 1.5-mile run in large groups. If the department has an obstacle course, candidates run one at a time. A word of advice: If a department has candidates complete events one at a time, don't go first. Watching those before you gives you a good idea of what the course is like, so aim to be third or fourth in line.

When you arrive at the testing location, you may be allowed to practice some of the events before the test begins. Be sure to do this if you get the opportunity. It helps you get an idea of what to expect. In some cases, instructors may also give applicants a walk-through of the course and explain the events. This is a good time to ask questions and make sure you understand what you need to know. You don't want to be in the middle of the test and realize you don't know what to do next!

One-minute sit-ups

A one-minute sit-up event is included on the fitness tests at the police academy. For this reason, some municipalities also include it in their physical ability test. The minimum number of sit-ups you must be able to do at the police academy depends on your gender and age; Table 10-1 lays out typical requirements.

Table 10-1	One-Minute Sit-Ups: Typical Police Academy Requirements	
Gender	*Age*	*Number of Sit-Ups in One Minute*
Male	20–29 years	35
	30–39 years	32
	40+ years	27
Female	20–29 years	29
	30–39 years	22
	40+ years	17

A sit-up is a measure of the muscular endurance of your abdominal muscles. To do a sit-up properly, follow these steps:

1. **Lie on your back with your knees bent and your heels flat on the floor.**

2. **Lace your fingers behind your head. Have a friend hold down your feet firmly or place your feet beneath a sofa or other heavy object.**

3. **With your hands locked behind your head, sit up and attempt to touch your elbows to your knees.**

   Some departments will disqualify you if you unlace your fingers from behind your head. Keep your hips on the floor at all times — and don't forget to breathe!

4. **Lie back until your shoulder blades touch the floor, returning to the starting position to repeat.**

One-minute push-ups

A one-minute push-up event is included on the fitness tests at the police academy, so don't be surprised if it's included on the local test as well. If this event is included on the local PAT, the minimum number of push-ups you must be able to do in a minute will likely be lower than what the academy requires (see Table 10-2) — you're not expected to be super-human right away! Try to do as many as you can, though, just to be on the safe side.

Table 10-2	One-Minute Push-Ups: Typical Police Academy Requirements	
Gender	*Age*	*Number of Push-Ups in One Minute*
Male	20–29	26
	30–39	20
	40+	15
Female	20–29	13
	30–39	9
	40+	7

A push-up is a measure of muscle endurance in the chest, upper arms, and shoulders. To correctly do a push-up, follow these steps:

1. **Place your hands on the floor, shoulder-width apart with your fingers pointing forward.**

2. **Start from the "up" position with your elbows locked.**

   Keep your back straight — don't let it arch or sway.

3. **Lower your body to the floor until your chest is a few inches off the floor.**

   If you're female, the test administrator might place a 2-inch block under you to denote the targeted distance between the ground and your chest when you lower your body. If you're male, the administrator may use his or her clenched fist.

4. **Return to the "up" position.**

   Only your palms and toes should touch the floor. Some departments allow you to rest in the up position only.

Bench-pressing is a great way to improve muscle strength and increase the number of push-ups you can do in one minute.

Vertical jump

Police officers must scale walls and jump over ditches — tasks that require them to have very strong legs. This type of strength is called explosive leg power, which the vertical jump event is designed to measure. Many departments use a Vertec vertical jump-testing device for this event. This device looks like an adjustable vertical pole with vanes, or lines, on one side. A proctor adjusts the device so that your fingertips just touch the bottom vane when you stand with one arm extended overhead. Follow these steps to complete the event:

1. **Before you jump, stand so that either your left or right foot is no more than 12 inches from the device.**

   This distance will probably be marked with tape. The foot closest to the device must remain stationary before you jump.

2. **Jump as high as you can while reaching upward, and tap the Vertec vanes with one hand to make them move.**

3. **The proctor will ask you to jump three times and will record the highest jump.**

How high should you jump? As high as you possibly can, but 13.5 inches is usually considered acceptable.

1.5-mile run

The 1.5-mile run measures your aerobic power by seeing how fast you can run. Police officers must be able to run fast when they're in pursuit of suspects. A group of applicants usually completes this event together.

Warm up while you're waiting for the event to begin. When the proctor tells you it's time, stand at the starting line. When the proctor shouts "Go!" take off running.

Try not to touch the other runners while you run. Stay within the guidelines of the track; if you run outside of this area, you may be disqualified. Be sure to pace yourself. If you start off running as fast as you can, you may tire within the first half-mile.

Your proctor will call out your time in minutes and seconds when you cross the finish line. Walk for about five minutes after the event to cool down.

How fast is fast enough? A time of 18 minutes, 56 seconds is usually considered acceptable for this distance. Many police departments use the FITNESSGRAM Standards for Healthy Fitness, developed by the Cooper Institute (www.cooperinstitute.org) to determine appropriate times for men and women in different age groups.

440-yard mobility/agility run

The 440-yard (¼-mile) agility run tests your coordination, muscular endurance, and aerobic capacity, as well as your ability to change direction and stride while running. The course for this event looks like a figure eight marked with brightly colored traffic cones. You must run this course six times — but it's not as simple as running six laps around a figure eight. The course also requires you to change direction, hurdle low barriers, and climb stairs. You have to adjust your stride — the size of your steps — during the course. See Figure 10-1 for an example of an agility course.

If you knock down a cone, pick it up and put it back. You won't be allowed to continue until you do this. Always run outside of the cones. Running inside a cone is called a *missed gate*. One missed gate gets you a warning. Do it again, and you have to retrace your steps from the previous cone and correctly complete the course. Also, don't skip more than one step when climbing stairs during this course. If you do this once, you get a warning. If you do it again, your proctor adds three seconds to your time.

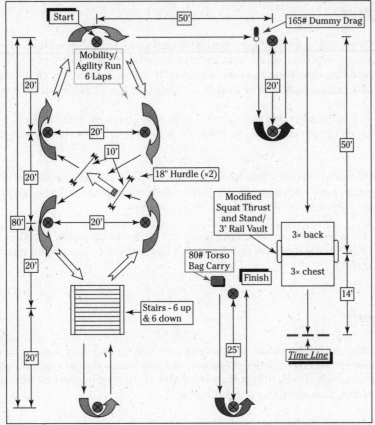

Figure 10-1:
The course for an agility run looks like a figure eight with obstacles such as stairs.

Modified squat thrust

The modified squat thrust event tests your coordination, agility, and stamina — this event is not easy. Here's how it's done:

1. **Begin by lying on your chest on the mat next to the three-foot-high rail vault.**

2. **Stand and vault over the rail vault to the other side. Don't touch the rail or you may be disqualified.**

3. **Once you're on the other side, lie down and touch your back to the mat.**

4. **Stand and vault back over the rail. Lie down and touch your chest to the mat.**

5. **Repeat this process until you have touched your back to the mat three times and your chest to the mat three times.**

Of course, you need to do squat thrusts as quickly as you can because the event is timed. Sixty seconds is usually considered an acceptable time.

Don't grab the rail vault to help you stand. Your proctor will give you a warning if you do this once. If you do it again, your proctor will add three seconds to your time.

Vehicle exit

You may think, "I get out of a vehicle every day! It isn't too hard." Remember, though, that police officers sometimes have to literally spring into action. They may have to race from their cars and perform some physical task within split seconds. That's a lot harder than it looks! And it's why exiting a squad car may be an event on the physical ability test.

For this event, you begin seated in the driver's seat with your seat belt buckled. The door is usually open. The challenge is for you to unfasten your belt and exit the car as quickly as possible.

Some police departments require you to complete another task after you exit the vehicle, such as opening the trunk with a key that's in the glove compartment. Other departments have you complete this task while wearing a 10-pound vest.

Events such as the vehicle exit, stair climb, fence obstacles, trigger pull, and dummy drag are usually not individually timed. A proctor keeps track of your time as you complete an entire course, or test.

Stair climb

Climbing stairs, like exiting a vehicle, may sound very simple and easy, but it can be a real challenge in law-enforcement situations. Imagine being a police officer responding to a crime at the top of a high-rise building. Now imagine carrying an injured victim back down! In situations like this, stair climbing is a difficult feat.

If this task is part of the physical ability test, you may be required to climb two flights of stairs in a building. You need to get up the steps as fast as possible and put your feet on a designated spot on the top. Then you have to run down again. You're judged on your over-all time. The technique you use to move on the steps — for instance, whether you use the handrails — is up to you. You can skip steps if this improves your speed. Just be careful not to trip!

Fence obstacles

The residential areas in which many police officers work are full of unexpected obstacles. Imagine chasing a suspect through some residential yards. You may find yourself facing some tall fences, and there's only one fast way to get past them — over the top! Climbing over fences and other walls is a necessary ability for a well-rounded police officer, so many physical ability tests include this event. In a standard fence-obstacle event, you're required to scale a 6-foot fence. This fence usually has footholds to help you climb, but it's still a tough test, and every second counts because you're judged by how quickly you climb over the fence.

Trigger pull

In the movies, police officers often take part in some fancy gunplay. They make it look so easy! In reality, though, the gun is a tool, and using it properly takes practice, discipline, and physical ability. For example, an officer may have to hold his or her weapon ready for extended periods. This may sound easy, but it can take a toll on the arms and shoulders and end up being very painful. During the physical ability test, you may be required to hold a realistic model gun in your hands and extend your arms together in front of you for one minute. Keep your arms straight — you're not allowed to hold them at an angle. This test is harder than it sounds, and you're not allowed to rest or lower your weapon. If you do, you risk disqualification.

Your hands and arms must be strong to succeed at the trigger pull. Purchase an inexpensive pair of grips from an athletic store and squeeze them while you're driving in your car. You can also squeeze a tennis ball to ramp up your hand strength.

Dummy drag

Go ahead and make "dummy" jokes all you want, but a dummy might give you a real challenge during your physical ability test. Prospective police officers are often made to move full-size dummies. Some tests require applicants to pull a 165-pound dummy out of a car and then drag it 25 feet along the ground. This task not only shows your strength and endurance, but it also simulates events that might happen in the line of duty, such as rescuing an injured person or subduing a criminal. Use your legs and not your back to avoid injury.

Chapter 11

Presenting Yourself Well in the Oral Board Interview

....

In This Chapter

▶ Exhibiting professionalism in the oral board interview

▶ Knowing what to expect from the interview

▶ Practicing with sample interview scenarios

....

*H*ave you ever watched a cop show on television? In nearly every episode, the cops drag a suspect into the interrogation room and grill the suspect about a crime he or she allegedly committed. Eventually, the suspect erupts into a fit of tears and confesses all. It's melodrama at its best.

We have some good news for you: The oral interview portion of the police officer exam isn't as intense as those TV scenes. Keep in mind, however, that some of the same officers who interrogate suspects day in and day out likely hold positions on the oral interview board, and the interview is their chance to grill you. Our point: Prepare yourself to field some difficult questions during the interview.

The oral board interview for police officers is quite different from a standard job interview. The questions dig deeper, and the interview panel's members arrive armed with detailed information about your background and personal history. Their goal is to find the diamonds in the rough — those candidates who've consistently demonstrated maturity, good judgment, honesty, and integrity throughout their lives and who would probably make good police officers.

In this chapter, we explain everything you need to know about the oral board interview, from your manner of dress and speaking to the types of questions you can expect from the interviewers. If you're nervous about the oral board interview, stick with us — we have you covered.

Comporting Yourself Well

As a police officer, you're expected to act and dress professionally and speak clearly and confidently. It should come as no surprise, therefore, that you need to demonstrate these qualities in every step of the hiring process, including the oral board interview. This interview is your chance to demonstrate that you have the essential skills and motivation to become an excellent police officer. It's an opportunity to explain any questionable matters that arise from your background investigation and to clarify information from your Personal History Statement (see Chapter 9). In general, you want to prove that you have nothing to hide and leave no doubt in the interviewers' minds that you're a top-notch candidate.

During the oral interview, honesty is the best policy. Answer questions truthfully, and don't try to hide information from the interviewers. The purpose of the background investigation is to turn up any details that you omit from your Personal History Statement.

Dressing professionally

People always say, "You can't judge a book by its cover," but that doesn't keep people from making snap decisions about you based on your appearance. Police departments are paramilitary organizations, which means they have a military-like structure. They're sticklers for uniformity and precision, and dress is no exception. Perhaps you've noticed that members of military and paramilitary organizations always have a neat and orderly appearance — clean, well-groomed hair; crisp, pressed uniforms; and precisely placed pins and badges. Therefore, it's important to dress appropriately for the oral interview.

What does this mean for you? On interview day, consider wearing a business suit (men may want to add a tie) or, at the very least, dress pants or a skirt with a dress shirt. And make sure you shine your shoes and comb your hair. Clothing and grooming may seem like trivial concerns, but they show that you put forth effort to look presentable, which makes interviewers take you more seriously. If you show up in a ripped T-shirt and jeans that look like Swiss cheese, interviewers will think that you don't care, and you'll have to work a lot harder to impress them.

Acting professionally

Perhaps more important than dressing professionally is acting professionally, and acting professionally begins long before you ever set foot in the interview room. Prior to the oral interview — often when you submit your application to a police department (see Chapter 1) — you have to complete a Personal History Statement, which includes information such as a photograph, contact information, education, job history, former run-ins with the law, and so on. Background investigators use this statement as a jumping-off point for a thorough investigation into your past. They make sure you didn't lie or omit information on the statement, and if they find something suspicious, you can expect the interviewers to ask about it in the oral interview.

You can avoid raising red flags through honesty and a conscious effort to show respect for the law at all times. As a future police officer, you have to act professionally, even in your personal life. If you have too much to drink, call a cab; don't drive under the influence. Obey traffic laws and speed limits when you drive. You know the old saying, "You're only as good as the company you keep"? Choose your friends carefully because spending time with troublemakers only leads to trouble. Everyone makes mistakes, but sound decision-making can help you avoid errors that have the potential to ruin your chances of becoming a police officer.

Also be aware of your presence on social networks, such as Facebook and MySpace. It's a good idea to stop posting information on these sites or significantly modify what you post, because law enforcement officers may discover this information. They can also discover the circle of individuals you're connected to as "friends," so be sure these people are respectable. If you have a goofy e-mail address, get a professional one to include on applications.

A few days before the interview, make sure you know the exact date, time, and place of the interview. Consider doing a practice drive to the interview site so you know how long it takes to get there, where to park, and where to find the interviewers. Arrive 10 to 15 minutes before your scheduled interview time; arriving late to an interview is very unprofessional. And on the day of the interview, make sure you look neat and clean (we cover dressing professionally in the preceding section). Be professional to receptionists and anyone else you come into contact with when entering the parking lot of the building. These folks often offer their opinions to members of the oral board.

From the moment you set foot in the interview room, the interviewers observe you. First, they'll notice nonverbal cues — are you making eye contact or staring at the floor? Are you standing up straight or walking with slumped shoulders? These cues send certain signals about your professionalism, personality, and attitude. For example, interviewers may interpret slumped shoulders and a downward gaze as, "I'm not confident in myself." This isn't the message you want to convey. Stand up straight, greet the interviewers with a smile, and firmly shake their hands. These actions send the message that you're friendly, well-mannered, self-assured, and not easily intimidated — all good qualities for a poised, professional police officer to possess.

Of course, interviewers also listen to what you say, so when you answer questions, speak clearly and be polite. Say "Yes, sir" instead of "Yeah"; "No, ma'am" instead of "Nope"; and "I'm not sure I understand the question. Could you please repeat it?" instead of "Huh?" As the interview continues, remain aware of your body language and avoid yawning or slouching. Rather, make eye contact and sit up straight.

At the end of the interview, interviewers may ask you whether you have anything to add. This is your last chance to stress the qualities that you possess that would make you a good police officer. Choose two or three qualities and say something like, "I enjoy working with people and solving problems." Remember to thank the interviewers for taking the time to meet with you.

A well-groomed appearance, a prompt arrival, and good manners during the interview demonstrate that you're a true professional.

Speaking in front of others

The typical panel of interviewers for the oral board interview includes at least two — and usually more — members, and may include civilians, business professionals, high-ranking police officers, and psychologists. Therefore, if you're one of the many people with a fear of public speaking, you may want to consider practicing before the interview.

Unless you can predict the future, you have no way of knowing what the interviewers may ask, but you can still practice by having friends or family members ask you common interview questions. As you respond, have them take notes about what you say, how you say it, and how you act as you give your answer. For example, you may not realize that you begin each sentence with "Um," speak too quickly, or nervously shake your foot for the duration of your response. After you identify these problem areas, you can work on correcting them before the interview.

The following are a few other things to consider when you speak in front of others:

✔ **Listen carefully.** This is a job interview, after all — it's not the time for daydreams! Listen intently to what the interviewers have to say and respond appropriately. Be sure to provide complete responses to the questions, but avoid rambling or volunteering unnecessary information. Nerves often take their toll on interview candidates, and candidates often misinterpret questions, answer questions they haven't been asked, or repeat the same response for nearly every question. If you don't understand a question, don't be afraid to ask for clarification.

✔ **Remember to breathe.** Before you respond, take a deep breath and collect your thoughts. By taking just a few seconds to think about what you want to say, you can compose an organized, thoughtful response.

✔ **Speak clearly.** Mumbling, speaking quietly, or talking too fast can lead interviewers to misinterpret your responses. If you notice yourself speaking too quietly, speak up. If you're speaking too fast, gradually slow yourself down.

Honing Your Question and Answer Skills

Think back to the last time you went on a job interview. What kind of questions were you asked? Your interviewer most likely asked questions to determine whether you had the skills to do the job. During the oral board interview, several interviewers ask you questions — and not just to see whether you have the skills necessary to work as a cop. They try to determine whether you have the moral character to be a good cop. Read this section carefully, and then practice answering questions so you present yourself in the best possible light during the oral board interview.

Expecting the right types of questions

During the oral board interview, the interviewers ask a variety of questions based on documents such as your résumé and Personal History Statement, as well as on the background investigation. Be sure to review these documents before the interview, because interviewers compare your interview answers to the information you supply on the documents. If discrepancies exist, you can expect to answer questions about them.

The following are a few more types of questions you can expect the interviewers to ask:

✔ **Icebreaker questions:** Interviewers use icebreaker questions to get you talking and get the interview train on track. These questions generally arise from information you supply in your résumé or Personal History Statement. Such questions may ask about a specific job you held, a hobby you mentioned, and so on. They may also include common interview questions such as, "Why have you decided to pursue a career as a police officer?"

✔ **Open-ended questions:** Open-ended questions require more than a simple "yes" or "no" answer. These questions allow you to give the board a taste of your personality. As you respond, the interviewers consider both what you say (your response) and how you say it (the way you communicate your thoughts). Open-ended questions can range from the interview favorite, "Tell us about yourself," to more specific questions drawn from information you supply, such as, "What is it that you enjoy most about your annual rock-climbing expedition?"

✔ **Probing questions:** Probing questions are designed to dig deeper into your background, and it may not always be clear why interviewers are asking them. For example, say that in your Personal History Statement, you say that you've never had a brush with the law. The background investigation, however, reveals two speeding tickets. The interviewers may pointedly ask whether you've ever received a ticket. They already know the answer, but they want to see how you respond.

Do you say "no" and stick to your original story? If you do, the interviewers are sure to push further: "Really? No tickets? It says here that you received two speeding tickets shortly after receiving your driver's license." It's better to confess to the tickets and offer a plausible explanation: "I did, in fact, receive two speeding tickets just after I turned 16 and got my license. It was so long ago that I forgot about them. I quickly realized that exceeding the speed limit is dangerous for both myself and others, and since then, I've become more careful about watching my speed."

✔ **Situational or scenario-based questions:** These questions typically put you in the driver's seat. The interviewers set up a situation or scenario and ask you to explain how you'd handle it. For example, the interviewers may ask how you'd handle an unruly citizen at a demonstration. In some cases, they may ask you to *role-play,* or act out, your response. Many police academies rely on role-playing as a tool for training new officers, and these questions are becoming more common in interview settings.

✔ **Ethics questions:** Similar to situational or scenario-based questions, ethics questions test your honesty and integrity. Interviewers present situations that put your morals and values to the test. For example, what would you do if you saw a fellow officer steal drugs from an evidence locker? Report him? Pull him aside and talk to him privately? When answering ethics questions, honesty is always the best policy.

✔ **Personal questions:** During most job interviews, interviewers are prohibited from asking potential employees personal questions, such as age, marital status, and so on. But in the oral board interview to become a police officer, all details of your life are fair game.

Some police departments conduct *structured* interviews, which means the interviewers ask all candidates the same questions in the same order. They also have scoring guidelines, or "best responses," which they use to analyze candidates' responses to the questions.

Knowing what the interviewers want to hear from you

The preceding section tells you what interviewers ask during the oral board interview. But what do they expect to hear when you answer? In one word: truth. We've said it before and we'll say it again: Honesty is the best policy.

Interviewers want to hear what *you* have to say: What do *you* think? How do *you* feel? What is *your* opinion? How would *you* act? You should answer these questions concisely and completely. Don't be afraid to share your opinions or explain how you think you'd react in certain situations. And remember that the manner in which you answer questions — calm and collected or flustered and defensive — is just as important as what you say.

Never answer a question with what you *think* the interviewers want to hear. They interview people every day, and they'll see right through your answers if you aren't sincere and truthful.

If the oral board interview has you stressed, consider the following tips to practice and prepare to answer questions:

✔ **Understand what police officers do.** Talk to police officers to find out what's involved in the job's day-to-day duties. You can expect questions that put you in an officer's shoes, so you should know what officers are expected to do.

✔ **Familiarize yourself with the town.** Find out as much as you can about the area in which you'd be working if the department hired you. You'll impress interviewers if you show that you have a good understanding of the place and the people you'd be serving.

✔ **Review common interview questions.** Consider how you'd respond to these questions:

   • "Would you please tell us about yourself?" Keep in mind that they don't want to know about your favorite TV show. Tell them about your education and experience. Show that you have determination and that you're reliable.

   • "What is your greatest strength?" This is not the time to be modest. Are you smart? Hardworking? Exceptionally honest? Say it!

- "What is your greatest weakness?" Be careful with this one. Say something that's true but that's not severe enough to knock you out of the race. Perhaps you're impatient. Maybe you overanalyze things. Perhaps you tend to take on more work than you can handle instead of delegating it. Whatever you say, mention how you're trying to address this weakness. And never try to turn a strength into a weakness. Don't say, "I work too hard," or, "I care too much about people." Interviewers see right through these responses and may even ask you to state a real weakness.

✔ **Stick to your guns during situational questions.** Always take the high road — and stay there, even if the interviewers badger you. You may be asked a question like, "Suppose you pull over a speeding car and discover that the driver is a relative or a friend. What do you do?" You give the driver a ticket — even if she's your mother.

✔ **Review your job application, résumé, and Personal History Statement.** Know these documents like the back of your hand. Try to pinpoint a few areas that may pique the interviewers' interest. The more you prepare, the more comfortable you'll feel in the interview setting.

✔ **Practice interviewing with friends, family, or a fellow candidate.** Remember that the oral board interview typically includes two or more interviewers, so practice answering questions in front of friends or family, or find a fellow candidate and practice interviewing each other. At the very least, practice answering questions in front of a mirror so that you can identify bad habits, such as twirling your hair or drumming your fingers as you speak.

✔ **Know your ethical and moral standards.** You can expect the interviewers to present some sticky situations in which ethics and morals play an important role. Know where you stand, and don't compromise your beliefs, even if you *think* the interviewers won't like your response. They're looking for honesty and integrity.

Sample Scenarios

At this point, you should have a good understanding of the oral board interview from the perspective of a candidate, so let's switch it up and put you in the interviewer's chair. Consider the following interview scenarios and see whether you can pinpoint the mistakes these candidates make.

Interview 1

Marcus Johnson, 25, arrives ten minutes early, wearing a navy-blue suit, a dress shirt, and a tie. He's clean-shaven, and his hair looks neat. Upon entering the interview room, he shakes hands with the interviewers and introduces himself with a smile. During the interview, the following exchange takes place:

Interviewer: Mr. Johnson, you say in your Personal History Statement that you've never had a run-in with the law, but it says here that police brought you in for questioning in connection with a fight when you were a junior in college. Would you care to explain what happened?

Johnson: I was at a football game when I noticed two guys who had had too much to drink arguing loudly. Before I knew it, they started throwing punches. I stepped in to break it up, and one of them clocked me in the eye. When the police arrived, they took the three of us and a few witnesses to the station. I gave a statement, which the witnesses confirmed, and they released me. I figured that since I wasn't charged with a crime that it wasn't important to include that information, but I apologize for my oversight.

Interview 2

Teresa Ramirez, 24, arrives ten minutes early, wearing dress pants and a blouse. Her hair is neatly pinned back. Upon entering the interview room, she gives the interviewers a smile and takes her seat. During the interview, she speaks quietly and avoids looking directly at the interviewers. The following exchange takes place:

Interviewer: Ms. Ramirez, tell us why you want to become a police officer.

Ramirez: My dad was a police officer for 25 years.

Interviewer: Really? Well, what is it about police work that interests you?

Ramirez: My dad seemed to enjoy his job. He always said that it made him feel good to make the streets safer for everyone.

Interviewer: And why do you want to follow in his footsteps and become a police officer?

Ramirez: I look up to my dad. He's one of my heroes.

Interview 3

Jon Woo, 23, arrives right on time. He's wearing dress pants, but he hasn't tucked in his shirt. His hair is uncombed, and he looks like he may have overslept. Upon entering the room, he shakes hands with the interviewers, makes eye contact, and introduces himself. During the interview, the following exchange takes place:

Interviewer: Tell us about your volunteer work, Mr. Woo.

Woo: Oh, sure. I've been volunteering at the soup kitchen for five years now. I go there each Saturday and help prepare and serve meals.

Interviewer: So you enjoy volunteering there?

Woo: Yeah. It's a great way to give back to the community and help those who are less fortunate, and I've met some really interesting people over the years.

Assessing the sample scenarios

So, which candidate got it right? In our opinion, Marcus Johnson gets it all right. He dresses and acts professionally and composes a calm, collected, and plausible response to the interviewer's question. His run-in with the law was actually an effort to prevent others from harm, and interviewers aren't likely to hold that against him.

Teresa Ramirez dresses professionally. She acts professionally by arriving on time, but she seems timid and nervous. She provides short, clipped responses to the interviewer's questions, which don't really allow the interview panel to see her true colors. Everything she says is about her father — the interviewers want to know about her, not about her dad. A better response may have been something like the following: "My father was a police officer for 25 years, and he made the streets a safer place. I truly respect the work that he did, and I want to follow in his footsteps and make the streets safer for my own family and friends." See the difference?

Jon Woo seems like a nice guy who really cares about people and wants to help, but his professionalism could use a little work. If he polished up his appearance, interviewers could pay more attention to the friendly attitude and self-confidence he displays when entering the room. In answering questions, he uses the slang "Yeah" instead of the more professional "Yes" or "Yes, sir/ma'am." This detracts from the genuine interest he has in bettering the community and helping those in need.

If you chose Marcus Johnson, then you know just what the interviewers expect from you in the oral board interview. Keep these qualities in mind as you prepare for your own interview.

Chapter 12

Preparing for Medical and Psychological Evaluations

In This Chapter

▶ Understanding what the medical exam entails

▶ Knowing what to expect during the psychological evaluation

Have you ever watched Olympic athletes run the hurdles? To reach the finish line, they have to successfully clear a number of obstacles in their path. The process of becoming a police officer is like running the hurdles. To receive a conditional offer of employment, you first have to clear the written exam, followed by the physical ability test, and then the oral interview. After you receive a conditional offer of employment, you have two more hurdles before you: a medical evaluation and a psychological evaluation.

Police work is both physically and mentally demanding. As a police officer, you have to make people abide by the law and punish those who don't. You have to serve and protect others, while sometimes putting yourself in the face of danger. You have to prevent crime, perform traffic stops, collect evidence, direct traffic, testify in court, and so on. Therefore, before departments hire you, they want to make sure that you don't have any medical conditions or disabilities that may prevent you from performing these duties. They also want to ensure that you're mentally prepared for the stress that's a natural part of the job. The good news is that you're closing in on the finish line. If you make it over these last two hurdles, most departments consider you to be a good candidate to enter a police training academy.

In this chapter, we provide information about the medical and psychological evaluations. Unlike the written exam, you can't study for the medical evaluation. You have little control over how well you see and hear or if high blood pressure runs in your family. You also can't prepare for the psychological evaluation; after all, it's hard to study for a test that evaluates your personality. With the information in this chapter, however, you can know what to expect during each of these evaluations.

The results of medical and psychological evaluations in part determine whether you become a police officer or any other type of law enforcement officer. These evaluations are intimidating for sure. To ease your nerves, do some research. Find out as much as you can about these tests. The more you know, the better you'll feel during the actual evaluations.

Getting Tested, Poked, and Prodded in the Medical Evaluation

The medical evaluation is similar to other physical exams your physician has likely performed in the past — it's just more detailed. You start by providing your medical history to the physician administering the evaluation.

Before the exam, write down details about your known health issues, such as past surgeries, immunizations, vaccinations, daily medications, and allergies. That way you won't forget to mention them when you're trying to recall years' worth of medical history.

During the exam, the physician usually inquires about your family's health history, which she uses to determine whether you're at risk for certain disorders or diseases that can affect your overall health and performance as a police officer. This should go without saying, but don't lie or purposely omit anything about your health. Just like the background investigation can reveal red flags on your record, the medical exam can reveal important health information you've withheld, and it could be held against you.

After taking your history, the doctor measures your weight and height, takes your temperature, and checks your blood pressure. Many departments have height, weight, and body-fat-percentage standards that candidates must meet to be eligible to continue in the hiring process. In general, your weight shouldn't interfere with your ability to perform essential functions of the job, such as chasing a suspect. The physician also checks your eyes, ears, nose, and mouth and listens to your heart and lungs to check for any potential problems. After covering the basics, the physician conducts a more detailed exam to ensure that you're healthy enough to protect and serve others.

Don't worry about this portion of the evaluation. Though you can take steps to control your weight and prevent certain medical conditions and disorders, some conditions are simply hereditary; they're in your genes, and you can't really control them. The medical evaluation is designed to uncover certain medical conditions that *may* eliminate you from the running. Some of these conditions aren't severe enough to hinder your performance as a police officer, but others are. In addition, some conditions that would disqualify you in one department don't matter to others. It's up to the physician and the police department to decide whether you're healthy enough to perform the job, both for your own safety and the safety of others. If you come back with a clean bill of health, you move on to the final stage of the hiring process — the psychological evaluation (which we cover later in this chapter).

The Americans with Disabilities Act makes it illegal for departments to conduct medical exams or ask questions that may reveal a disability before making a conditional offer of employment. However, a department can revoke a conditional offer of employment if a certain medical condition or disability can affect your ability to perform your job as a police officer. If this occurs, medical records from your own physician may serve as proof enough that you're able to work as a police officer.

In the following sections, we review some of the specific tests and checks that a physician may perform during the medical exam.

What can you see? Testing your vision

Trips to the eye doctor are almost always the same: You look at a chart full of letters and numbers from a distance and tell the eye doctor which ones you can see. Then she makes it a little tougher and places lenses over your eyes to see which one makes your vision clearer. The vision part of the police officer medical exam is similar to this. A physician conducts a standard vision exam to determine how well you can see with or without the aid of contacts or glasses. You may also be checked for the following conditions:

- **Color-blindness:** The inability to distinguish between certain colors

- **Eye diseases:** Any conditions that affect the health of the eye

- **Peripheral vision:** The ability to see from the outer part of the field of vision (what you can see from the corners of your eyes when you're staring straight ahead)

Police officers must have good vision. They have to read street signs and license plate numbers while driving, determine whether suspects have weapons, and identify suspects. Certain eye conditions only temporarily disqualify candidates. For example, with treatment, pink eye lasts only a short while. Other conditions such as a myopic eye may be corrected with surgery. The evaluating physician bases her determination on the condition's severity. Color-blindness, however, usually automatically disqualifies candidates because police officers need to be able to tell the difference among colors when identifying specific car colors or a suspect's clothing or hair color.

Each police department has its own set of medical standards. Contact the department for more information about these requirements.

Can you hear me now? Testing your hearing

In addition to seeing well, police officers must have good hearing. For example, as a police officer, you need to be able to hear gunshots, sirens, and communications in person or by radio contact.

During the medical exam, the physician looks into your ears to check for signs of infection. You'll likely know if you have an ear infection because it can cause an ache or pain in the ear. The physician also looks for signs of other conditions that may disqualify you from employment, such as an ear deformity or an ear injury that has resulted in permanent damage to your ear.

In addition to checking for physical signs of infection and other ear conditions, the physician conducts a hearing test using an *audiometer* to measure how well you hear a series of tones. During the test, you wear headphones through which you hear various tones, ranging from very high-pitched sounds to very low-pitched sounds. You hold a feedback button in your hand, which you press each time you hear a sound. Based on your feedback, the physician can tell how well you hear.

Having some hearing loss may not automatically disqualify you from becoming a police officer. Physicians base their decision on the severity of the hearing loss and whether a hearing aid can correct hearing so that it falls within an acceptable range. These standards may vary from department to department.

Although you can't really practice for the medical evaluation, you can prepare your body to undergo the tests you'll most likely have to complete. The night before your medical evaluation, go to bed early and plan to get at least eight full hours of sleep. On the day of your examination, wake up with enough time to shower and dress so you're not rushed or stressed on your way to the evaluation. Also, be sure to eat something before you go to your evaluation so you will feel your best.

Not for the squeamish: Blood and urine tests

Blood tests and urinalyses can help doctors learn a lot about your overall health. We hope you're not afraid of needles or shy about providing a urine sample, because these tests are required as part of the medical evaluation. Blood tests, for example, may reveal an iron deficiency, an indicator of *anemia*, which is a low amount of healthy red blood cells that can result in fatigue. Though not necessarily disqualifying, anemia can cause you to feel tired and run-down. Taking an iron supplement or eating iron-rich foods can put the pep back in your step.

Doctors use urinalyses to check for a number of conditions and to make sure kidneys are functioning properly. For example, a urinalysis may reveal kidney dysfunction related to high blood pressure, which is an indicator of heart disease. Candidates with uncontrolled high blood pressure may be immediately disqualified from their pursuit of becoming a police officer. (See the next section for more on blood pressure.)

Laboratory tests can help doctors detect other diseases and conditions, too, such as diabetes, cancer, HIV/AIDS, and hepatitis. Physicians also may use these tests to screen for illicit drug use.

The presence of illicit drugs in a blood test or urinalysis almost certainly results in the termination of your conditional offer of employment. Illicit drugs affect both body and mind and threaten the safety of both police officers and the public they've sworn to protect. In sum: Don't do drugs if you want to be a police officer.

Breathe in, breathe out: Checking your heart and lungs

During the medical exam, the doctor checks your pulse (how fast your heart beats) and your blood pressure. A higher than average blood pressure is an indicator of hypertension (chronic high blood pressure), which is a symptom of heart disease. A lower than average blood pressure is an indicator of hypotension, which can result in the heart and brain not getting enough blood. These conditions, depending on their severity, can disqualify you from becoming a police officer.

The physician also uses a stethoscope to listen to your heart and lungs to detect unusual rhythms. The physician may send you for a chest X-ray, an electrocardiogram, or a cardiac stress test, which she uses to determine the health of your heart and lungs.

- ✔ A *chest X-ray* is used to evaluate your lungs, airway, heart, and chest wall. During a chest X-ray, you either stand with your chest pressed up against an image plate or lie on a table. Radiation passes through your body and takes a picture of your lungs and heart. The doctor uses this image to determine whether you have any lung or heart problems.

- ✔ An *electrocardiogram* (ECG) determines your heart health by recording your heart's electrical activity. During the test, you usually lie flat while the person performing the test attaches small electrodes to your skin in several locations, including your arms, legs, and chest. The electrodes detect heartbeats and transmit information about your heart's electrical activity to a recorder. The recorder generates wavy lines either on a screen or on paper, which the physician evaluates to diagnose heart conditions and discover more about your cardiac health.

- ✔ A *cardiac stress test* evaluates blood flow to the heart during exercise. For this test, the physician attaches electrodes to your skin to record information on an ECG machine. Then, she instructs you to walk on a treadmill, gradually increasing your speed to increase the intensity of your exercise. The physician frequently checks your pulse and blood pressure during the test.

  After the test, you cool down for a while and then lie still until your heart rate and blood pressure return to normal. At this point, the physician removes the electrodes and permits you to leave. Using the results of the cardiac stress test, doctors can diagnose heart conditions that may pose a threat to you on the job.

How low can you go? Monitoring muscular and skeletal disorders

During the medical exam, the physician looks for disorders of your muscular and skeletal systems (often called the *musculoskeletal system*). In general, physicians want to make sure that you have full use of your arms, hands, legs, and feet. For some departments, using a brace or a prosthesis doesn't automatically disqualify a candidate, but the candidate must be able to demonstrate that he can complete all police officer duties without posing a security risk.

During this part of the medical exam, doctors may also check your back, neck, skull, and spine to evaluate your range of motion and reflexes and to look for any signs of deformity. They may have you move or stretch to make sure that you have full range of motion along your spine and in your extremities and to ensure that your reflexes work the way they should. After all, police officers sometimes find themselves running long distances, crawling through tight spaces, or climbing fences in pursuit of a suspect, so it's essential to be able to bend, stretch, and move without hurting yourself.

Other conditions

Physicians may also look for a few other conditions during the medical exam. The following problems, depending on their severity, may or may not disqualify candidates:

- **Hernias:** *Hernias* occur when the membrane, muscle, or tissue surrounding an organ weakens or breaks open, usually as a result of muscle strain, and part of the organ pushes through the hole. Hernias usually are only temporarily disqualifying because they can be fixed through surgery; if they're small, doctors may simply monitor them.

- **Gastrointestinal disorders:** *Gastrointestinal disorders* are conditions that affect the digestive system, which is responsible for breaking down food and absorbing nutrients into the body. Depending on the severity of the condition, gastrointestinal disorders may disqualify candidates.

- **Genitourinary disorders:** *Genitourinary disorders* are conditions that affect the reproductive organs and the urinary system. During the medical exam, physicians determine whether genitourinary disorders are severe enough to result in disqualification.

- **Glandular disorders:** *Glandular disorders* are medical conditions that affect your glands, which are part of the endocrine system. The *endocrine system* regulates your body through the release of hormones. Again, doctors determine whether glandular disorders are severe enough to warrant disqualification.

Researching different job opportunities

If you find out that you have a medical condition that bars you from getting a job with a municipal or state police organization, research whether the same medical condition may be acceptable for jobs in other organizations. Remember, many different organizations hire people who investigate crimes and enforce laws and policies. Consider researching positions such as park ranger, campus security officer, housing police officer, railroad police officer, and sheriff.

Even if you're perfectly healthy, you may consider employment in an organization other than a municipal or state police force. Many organizations and agencies require the help of talented, eager law enforcement officers, so do some research to find the perfect position for you.

Understanding What Happens during the Psychological Evaluation

The thought of undergoing a psychological evaluation is enough to make anyone go mad. It's a nerve-racking ordeal, but many police departments require a psychological evaluation before admitting you into a training academy. Other departments may require a psychological evaluation only if something raises a red flag (such as a prior arrest that turns up during the background investigation).

Psychological exams are designed to test your mental stability and evaluate how you handle stressful situations. Police departments use them to make sure they're choosing the right person for the job. The evaluation also reveals important personality traits such as honesty, leadership skills, and the ability to work in a team environment.

The psychological evaluation usually consists of a personality test that may or may not be accompanied by a session with a professional psychologist or psychiatrist. The following sections outline what you can expect from the psychological evaluation.

Honesty is always the best policy. Be truthful on the personality test and during questioning with the psychologist. Don't try to hide your true feelings or give answers that you think the psychologist wants to hear. The psychologist isn't there to deceive or trick you; he's there to evaluate the *way* you answer his questions.

Taking the personality test

Some police departments may require you to complete a personality questionnaire, which is a list of questions designed to evaluate different aspects of your personality, such as your attitude, interests, and motivation for wanting to become a police officer. The questions ask you to rank how you'd feel or act in certain situations. These tests can be rather lengthy, involving hundreds of questions and taking several hours to complete. In most cases, the department or hiring agency responsible for administering the test lets you know how much time to allot for the personality test.

Don't spend too much time analyzing any one question on the personality test. Go with your gut feeling. Personality tests have no right or wrong answers.

You can't prepare for a personality test. The best advice is to stay calm and answer the questions honestly. The following are a few samples of the types of statements you may encounter on the personality test:

I am more conservative than risk-taking.

I like to follow schedules.

I find it hard to keep my mind on a task or job.

I am liked by most people who know me.

I think it's acceptable to bend the rules to complete a task on time.

The questionnaire may ask for true-false responses to these questions, or it may ask you to rank your opinions of these statements on a scale such as the following:

1. Strongly Agree

2. Agree

3. Neither Agree nor Disagree

4. Disagree

5. Strongly Disagree

If you have to use the ranking system, don't be afraid to state how you truly feel. If you strongly agree or strongly disagree with a particular statement, select 1 or 5. The questions aren't designed to trick you. They're designed to compare your responses to the responses of other successful police officers to see whether you have the right personality traits to become a police officer. In addition, the same question may be asked in different ways to test for consistency in your answers.

Interviewing with a psychologist

Some departments may require candidates to meet with a professional psychologist or psychiatrist. Don't worry about meeting with a psychologist. He isn't going to expose your deepest, darkest secrets or bring up painful childhood memories. His job is to ask you questions about your school and work experiences, family and friend relationships, and hobbies and interests.

The psychologist may also inquire about problems in your past that may have been revealed through your background check. The best way to deal with such questions is to accept full responsibility for an incident and be honest about it. Let's face it — at one time or another, almost everyone has done something he regrets. Whatever happened, don't make excuses or claim that the records are false. Rather, take responsibility for the mistake and explain that you've remedied your ways. Departments will appreciate your honesty, and you won't necessarily be disqualified.

He's (or she's) got personality

The following are some personality traits that police departments consider a good fit for officers:

✔ Accepts criticism

✔ Accepts extra responsibility without compensation

✔ Accepts responsibility for self and others

✔ Compromises for greater good

✔ Displays honesty

✔ Displays trustworthiness

✔ Exudes a positive attitude

✔ Exudes confidence

✔ Handles stress and controls emotions

✔ Lends assistance

✔ Shows leadership skills

✔ Shows teamwork skills

The psychologist may ask you questions that further explain information listed on your application or personal history, or he may ask what you'd do in hypothetical scenarios. These questions aren't meant to test your knowledge of certain procedures; they're designed to test your behavior in these types of situations. The following are a few sample questions the psychologist may ask:

Why did you change your major in college?

How do you react to criticism?

How do you spend your free time?

What types of things scare you?

How would you react to a situation that left you permanently injured?

The psychologist may also open the floor to you with the following dreaded statement: "Tell me about yourself." This commonly asked question often throws people off guard. If you think about how you're going to answer beforehand, however, you should have no problem explaining what interests you about police work and why you're qualified for the job.

Remember, the psychological evaluation is for your benefit. It's your chance to put your best foot forward and be honest and open about yourself.

In some cases, the psychologist may review your responses to the personality questionnaire and ask you to further expand upon your answers. For example, if you answered (1) Strongly Agree to the statement, "I find it hard to keep my mind on a task or job," the psychologist may delve further into why you feel like this. He may ask you additional questions, such as, "Why can't you concentrate?" "What keeps you from focusing?" or "What helps you concentrate?" The way in which you respond to these questions helps the psychologist learn more about your personality and your ability to handle the stress that many police officers experience on the job. Police departments use the results of the psychological evaluation to determine whether you have the mental and emotional stability to become a police officer.

You can't study for an interview with the psychologist, because you have no idea what he may ask. The following tips, however, can help you during the evaluation:

✔ **Relax.** Breathe deeply to help calm your nerves. If you act jumpy and anxious during something as simple as an interview, the psychologist may question your ability to handle a stressful emergency, which, as a police officer, you'll encounter quite often.

✔ **Be honest.** The old adage holds true: Honesty is the best policy. Answer questions truthfully, and don't be afraid to say how you feel. If you have a strong opinion about something, voice it, but don't be unreasonable or come off as arrogant.

✔ **Follow your first instinct.** Don't read too much into the questions. They aren't meant to trick or confuse you. The questions are direct, so answer them directly.

✔ **Answer only the questions you're asked.** Think before you speak. If you're unsure about what's being asked, ask the psychologist for clarification. Don't volunteer information, however, and avoid rambling on and on when you respond.

Near the end of the evaluation, the psychologist may ask whether you have any questions. If you do, that's the time to ask them. In addition, don't be concerned if the psychologist sends you on your way without asking any questions. If everything on the questionnaire and the background investigation checks out, the psychologist may not have any questions for you. See, you did all that worrying for nothing.

Part IV
Practice Police Officer Exams

The 5th Wave
By Rich Tennant

In this part . . .

You've heard it a thousand times: Practice makes perfect. What better way to prepare for a real police officer test than to take some practice tests? The practice exams in Part IV can help you identify areas where you could use some extra study time, as well as strengthen your skill and boost your confidence in areas where you're already proficient.

The first three practice exams in this part are similar to the National Police Officer Selection Test (POST), a test many police departments use. The fourth is based on New York City's written exam, which is a civil service exam. Take one or take them all — each includes plenty of practice questions in a wide variety of subject areas, which can help you get into the test-taking mind-set.

Chapter 13

Practice Test 1: The National Police Officer Selection Test (POST)

Practice Test 1 is modeled after the National Police Officer Selection Test (POST). Many police departments use the POST to screen job candidates. The POST has four sections, and each section is timed separately. Time yourself as you complete each section of this practice test or have someone else tell you when to begin and when your time is up. While it's fine to take a break between sections, try to complete the entire test in one day, as you would on the actual test.

Section	Test	Number of Items	Time
1	Mathematics	20	20 minutes
2	Reading Comprehension	25	25 minutes
3	Grammar	20	15 minutes
4	Incident Report Writing	10	15 minutes

Sections 1, 2, and 3 of Practice Test 1 contain multiple-choice and true-and-false questions. Section 4, Incident Report Writing, contains open-ended questions for which you write out your answers in grammatically correct sentences.

Use a number-two pencil and mark your answers for Sections 1, 2, and 3 on the following answer sheet. Make sure your marks are heavy and completely fill in the oval. Completely erase any marks that you wish to change. Be sure to blacken only one oval for each question, and be sure that you're blackening the oval for the correct question. It's easy to skip a question and become confused when marking your answers on the answer sheet. While this answer sheet won't be computer scored like the answer sheet on the actual POST, pretending that it will be helps you better prepare for the exam. For Section 4, write your answers on the lines underneath each question.

Pace yourself as you work through the questions on Practice Test 1 so that you have enough time to complete all the questions. Don't spend too much time on one question. Try to answer every question on this test. If a question really stumps you, take a good guess and move on. Your score is based on the number of questions you answer correctly, so there is no penalty for guessing.

You won't be allowed to use a calculator on the actual POST, but you will be given scratch paper. Use scratch paper to work your way through the problems on this practice test.

After you complete the entire sample test, check your answers against the answers and explanations in Chapter 14. Be sure to read the answer explanations even for questions that you've answered correctly. Doing so helps you learn more about the test and gives you an extra edge on the actual POST. Note that on the actual POST, you need an overall score of 70 to pass and move on to the next stage in the hiring process. To determine your overall score, figure out your score on each section: Questions in the Reading Comprehension section (25 questions) are worth 4 points each, questions in the Mathematics and Grammar sections (40 questions) are worth 5 points each, and questions in the Incident Report Writing section (10 questions) are worth 10 points each. Add your scores together and divide by 4 to determine your overall score.

Answer Sheet for Practice Test 1

1 Ⓐ Ⓑ Ⓒ Ⓓ Ⓔ	21 Ⓐ Ⓑ Ⓒ Ⓓ Ⓔ	41 Ⓐ Ⓑ Ⓒ Ⓓ Ⓔ	61 Ⓐ Ⓑ Ⓒ Ⓓ Ⓔ
2 Ⓐ Ⓑ Ⓒ Ⓓ Ⓔ	22 Ⓐ Ⓑ Ⓒ Ⓓ Ⓔ	42 Ⓐ Ⓑ Ⓒ Ⓓ Ⓔ	62 Ⓐ Ⓑ Ⓒ Ⓓ Ⓔ
3 Ⓐ Ⓑ Ⓒ Ⓓ Ⓔ	23 Ⓐ Ⓑ Ⓒ Ⓓ Ⓔ	43 Ⓐ Ⓑ Ⓒ Ⓓ Ⓔ	63 Ⓐ Ⓑ Ⓒ Ⓓ Ⓔ
4 Ⓐ Ⓑ Ⓒ Ⓓ Ⓔ	24 Ⓐ Ⓑ Ⓒ Ⓓ Ⓔ	44 Ⓐ Ⓑ Ⓒ Ⓓ Ⓔ	64 Ⓐ Ⓑ Ⓒ Ⓓ Ⓔ
5 Ⓐ Ⓑ Ⓒ Ⓓ Ⓔ	25 Ⓐ Ⓑ Ⓒ Ⓓ Ⓔ	45 Ⓐ Ⓑ Ⓒ Ⓓ Ⓔ	65 Ⓐ Ⓑ Ⓒ Ⓓ Ⓔ
6 Ⓐ Ⓑ Ⓒ Ⓓ Ⓔ	26 Ⓐ Ⓑ Ⓒ Ⓓ Ⓔ	46 Ⓐ Ⓑ Ⓒ Ⓓ Ⓔ	
7 Ⓐ Ⓑ Ⓒ Ⓓ Ⓔ	27 Ⓐ Ⓑ Ⓒ Ⓓ Ⓔ	47 Ⓐ Ⓑ Ⓒ Ⓓ Ⓔ	
8 Ⓐ Ⓑ Ⓒ Ⓓ Ⓔ	28 Ⓐ Ⓑ Ⓒ Ⓓ Ⓔ	48 Ⓐ Ⓑ Ⓒ Ⓓ Ⓔ	
9 Ⓐ Ⓑ Ⓒ Ⓓ Ⓔ	29 Ⓐ Ⓑ Ⓒ Ⓓ Ⓔ	49 Ⓐ Ⓑ Ⓒ Ⓓ Ⓔ	
10 Ⓐ Ⓑ Ⓒ Ⓓ Ⓔ	30 Ⓐ Ⓑ Ⓒ Ⓓ Ⓔ	50 Ⓐ Ⓑ Ⓒ Ⓓ Ⓔ	
11 Ⓐ Ⓑ Ⓒ Ⓓ Ⓔ	31 Ⓐ Ⓑ Ⓒ Ⓓ Ⓔ	51 Ⓐ Ⓑ Ⓒ Ⓓ Ⓔ	
12 Ⓐ Ⓑ Ⓒ Ⓓ Ⓔ	32 Ⓐ Ⓑ Ⓒ Ⓓ Ⓔ	52 Ⓐ Ⓑ Ⓒ Ⓓ Ⓔ	
13 Ⓐ Ⓑ Ⓒ Ⓓ Ⓔ	33 Ⓐ Ⓑ Ⓒ Ⓓ Ⓔ	53 Ⓐ Ⓑ Ⓒ Ⓓ Ⓔ	
14 Ⓐ Ⓑ Ⓒ Ⓓ Ⓔ	34 Ⓐ Ⓑ Ⓒ Ⓓ Ⓔ	54 Ⓐ Ⓑ Ⓒ Ⓓ Ⓔ	
15 Ⓐ Ⓑ Ⓒ Ⓓ Ⓔ	35 Ⓐ Ⓑ Ⓒ Ⓓ Ⓔ	55 Ⓐ Ⓑ Ⓒ Ⓓ Ⓔ	
16 Ⓐ Ⓑ Ⓒ Ⓓ Ⓔ	36 Ⓐ Ⓑ Ⓒ Ⓓ Ⓔ	56 Ⓐ Ⓑ Ⓒ Ⓓ Ⓔ	
17 Ⓐ Ⓑ Ⓒ Ⓓ Ⓔ	37 Ⓐ Ⓑ Ⓒ Ⓓ Ⓔ	57 Ⓐ Ⓑ Ⓒ Ⓓ Ⓔ	
18 Ⓐ Ⓑ Ⓒ Ⓓ Ⓔ	38 Ⓐ Ⓑ Ⓒ Ⓓ Ⓔ	58 Ⓐ Ⓑ Ⓒ Ⓓ Ⓔ	
19 Ⓐ Ⓑ Ⓒ Ⓓ Ⓔ	39 Ⓐ Ⓑ Ⓒ Ⓓ Ⓔ	59 Ⓐ Ⓑ Ⓒ Ⓓ Ⓔ	
20 Ⓐ Ⓑ Ⓒ Ⓓ Ⓔ	40 Ⓐ Ⓑ Ⓒ Ⓓ Ⓔ	60 Ⓐ Ⓑ Ⓒ Ⓓ Ⓔ	

Section 1

Mathematics

Time: 20 minutes

Directions: In this section of the exam, you are provided with situations that require the use of basic arithmetic. Read each situation and solve the problem. You may not use a calculator in this section, but you may use scratch paper.

1. Officer Harrison visits schools as part of a drug-use prevention program. If Officer Harrison visits four schools every week, except for 12 weeks during the summer, how many schools does she visit?

    (A) 48

    (B) 150

    (C) 152

    (D) 160

    (E) 208

2. Officer Lepore received a drunk and disorderly call at 1:20 a.m. and arrived at the scene at 1:32 a.m. He took a man into custody and left the scene at 1:48 a.m. He arrived at the station at 2:01 a.m. How much time elapsed from the time of the call until Officer Lepore returned to the station?

    (A) 12 minutes

    (B) 28 minutes

    (C) 39 minutes

    (D) 41 minutes

    (E) 44 minutes

Questions 3 and 4 are based on the following information.

In preparing a report on a burglary at a dry cleaners, Officer Ramirez lists the following stolen items and their values:

Desktop computer	$1,250
Printer	$380
Cash register	$509
Paper shredder	$210

3. What is the total value of all the stolen goods?

    (A) $2,039

    (B) $2,249

    (C) $2,300

    (D) $2,349

    (E) $2,359

4. What is the value of all the stolen goods *except* the cash register?

    (A) $1,240

    (B) $1,840

    (C) $1,940

    (D) $1,969

    (E) $2,039

5. During a five-day period, Officer Washington drove her patrol motorcycle 308 miles. If she drove 60 miles one day, how many miles did she average on each of the other days?

    (A) 50 miles

    (B) 60 miles

    (C) 62 miles

    (D) 64 miles

    (E) 124 miles

Go on to next page

6. Officer Lee typically works the 11 p.m. to 7 a.m. shift, but Sergeant Beck asks him to stay until 9:15 a.m. to help another officer with a special assignment. Assuming he works his entire shift, how much overtime can Officer Lee report for that day?

   (A) 15 minutes

   (B) 1 hour and 15 minutes

   (C) 1 hour and 45 minutes

   (D) 2 hours

   (E) 2 hours and 15 minutes

7. Burglars broke into an electronics store and stole eight laptop computers with a total retail value of $9,200. What is the average value of each laptop computer?

   (A) $1,100

   (B) $1,125

   (C) $1,150

   (D) $1,250

   (E) $2,150

8. Employees of a 24-person police force are given a uniform allowance of $350 each. If half of the employees use the allowance in one year, how much money did the department spend on uniforms?

   (A) $3,000

   (B) $4,200

   (C) $4,250

   (D) $5,200

   (E) $8,400

9. A police officer apprehends a thief carrying three gold rings, two watches, two cellphones, and four wallets. According to the information below, what is the total value of the recovered items?

Item	Value
1 wallet	$50
1 ring	$100
1 watch	$150
1 cellphone	$125

   (A) $425

   (B) $850

   (C) $900

   (D) $1,050

   (E) $1,150

10. Officer Sanchez visits local businesses as part of a theft prevention program. If Officer Sanchez visits one business every two weeks, how many businesses does she visit in one year?

    (A) 26

    (B) 28

    (C) 50

    (D) 52

    (E) 104

11. During a ten-day period, two officers drove their patrol car 1,065 miles. If they drove 75 miles one day, how many miles did they average on each of the other days?

    (A) 75 miles

    (B) 100 miles

    (C) 110 miles

    (D) 118 miles

    (E) 120 miles

Go on to next page

Questions 12 and 13 are based on the following information.

In preparing a report for a burglary in a home, Officer Kramer lists the following stolen items and their values:

Item	Value
Jewelry	$1,800
Television	$850
Laptop computer	$900
Cellphone	$100
Cash	$320

12. What is the total value of all the stolen goods?

    (A) $2,970

    (B) $3,830

    (C) $3,930

    (D) $3,970

    (E) $4,870

13. What is the value of all the stolen goods *except* the cellphone and the cash?

    (A) $220

    (B) $420

    (C) $3,550

    (D) $3,650

    (E) $3,900

14. Burglars broke into a gun store and left with 20 pistols with a total retail value of $13,900. What is the average retail value of each pistol?

    (A) $595

    (B) $685

    (C) $690

    (D) $695

    (E) $1,390

15. If a patrol car averages 20 miles per gallon of gasoline and is driven 80 miles per day, how many gallons of gasoline does it need for a five-day workweek?

    (A) 4 gallons

    (B) 16 gallons

    (C) 20 gallons

    (D) 40 gallons

    (E) 160 gallons

16. Officer Sampson received a domestic disturbance call at 5:32 p.m. and arrived at the scene at 5:41 p.m. After resolving the situation, he left the scene at 5:51 p.m. How much time elapsed from the time of the call and the time when he left the scene?

    (A) 9 minutes

    (B) 10 minutes

    (C) 19 minutes

    (D) 20 minutes

    (E) 21 minutes

17. Burglars broke into a school and stole 25 computers. Each computer was worth $650. What is the total retail value of the computers?

    (A) $16,250

    (B) $16,500

    (C) $16,575

    (D) $17,250

    (E) $17,500

18. Officer Jones typically works the 7 a.m. to 3 p.m. shift but Sergeant Kibler asked her to stay until 4:25 p.m. for a training class. Assuming she works her entire shift, how much overtime can Officer Jones report for that day?

    (A) 25 minutes

    (B) 1 hour and 10 minutes

    (C) 1 hour and 15 minutes

    (D) 1 hour and 20 minutes

    (E) 1 hour and 25 minutes

Go on to next page

19. Employees on a 32-person police force are asked to complete four hours of community service per month for six months. Half of the employees on this police force meet this requirement. How many hours of community service were completed by this police force?

    (A) 128 hours

    (B) 130 hours

    (C) 384 hours

    (D) 386 hours

    (E) 768 hours

20. A police officer apprehends the driver of a car containing stolen goods. Upon investigation the arresting officer finds that the car contains 10 cellphones, 15 gold watches, and 3 pairs of diamond earrings. According to the chart below, what is the total value of the recovered items?

Item	Value
1 cellphone	$200
1 gold watch	$300
1 pair earrings	$200

    (A) $700

    (B) $710

    (C) $6,100

    (D) $7,100

    (E) $8,100

STOP DO NOT TURN THE PAGE UNTIL TOLD TO DO SO.
DO NOT RETURN TO A PREVIOUS TEST.

Section 11

Reading Comprehension

Time: 25 minutes

Directions: This section measures reading comprehension. Read the passages relating to police duty and then answer the questions that follow. No prior knowledge of law or law enforcement is needed to answer these questions.

The passages in this section are not intended to represent actual laws in any particular state. They present potential rules and laws relating to police work.

Three types of questions appear in this section:

- ✔ True/False questions that ask you to determine a statement's accuracy based on the information presented in the passage or sample report form

- ✔ Questions that ask you to choose the correct answer according to the information presented in the passage or sample report form

- ✔ Questions that ask you to choose the alternative that best completes the sentence, based on the information in the passage or on the report form

---

Questions 21 through 25 are based on the following passage.

In an effort to protect the health and safety of young people, police in Lincoln City are enforcing a new curfew. The curfew states that persons under the age of 17 cannot remain on a street, in a park, in a vehicle, or on any property in Lincoln City during curfew hours. The curfew applies to all persons under the age of 17 regardless of whether they are residents of Lincoln City.

For the months of September through June, curfew from Sunday through Thursday begins at 11:00 p.m. and continues until 6:00 a.m. the next morning. Curfew on Friday begins at 12:00 a.m. Saturday morning and continues until 6:00 a.m. Saturday morning. Curfew on Saturday begins at 12:00 a.m. Sunday morning and continues until 6:00 a.m. Sunday morning. During July and August, curfew begins at 12:00 a.m. and lasts until 6:00 a.m. seven days a week.

Persons under the age of 17 (minors) are exempt from the curfew if they are accompanied by a parent or guardian, passing through Lincoln City during interstate travel, traveling to or from work, involved in an emergency situation, attending a school activity, or running an errand under the direction of a parent or guardian if they do not stop or detour. Minors are also exempt if they are participating in a recreational activity sponsored by Lincoln City.

A minor who violates curfew may be ordered to perform up to 20 hours of community service. The parent of a minor violating curfew breaks the law if the parent knowingly permits the minor to violate curfew. Such parents are subject to a fine of $500 and community service. Parents who neglect to monitor the whereabouts of minor children may also be subject to a fine or community service.

Lincoln City has a variety of programs and centers that serve young people. Participating in these programs is a viable alternative to being on the streets after curfew. These programs include dances, socials, sporting events, and educational programs. For more information, contact Lincoln City Town Hall Monday through Friday between the hours of 8:00 a.m. and 5:00 p.m.

Go on to next page

21. According to the passage, a 16-year-old resident of Lincoln City who is out on Friday night must be home by

    (A) 6:00 a.m. on Saturday.

    (B) 8:00 a.m. on Saturday.

    (C) 11:00 p.m. on Friday.

    (D) 12:00 a.m. on Saturday.

    (E) 12:30 a.m. on Saturday.

22. Mitch, a 17-year-old, is out with his father on a Monday night. According to the passage, Mitch's curfew

    (A) does not apply.

    (B) is 11:00 p.m. on Monday.

    (C) is 12:00 a.m. on Tuesday.

    (D) is between 11:00 p.m. and 12:00 a.m.

    (E) is 6:00 a.m. on Tuesday.

23. According to the passage, what is the penalty for Mrs. Jackson, a mother who lets her teenagers stay out after curfew?

    (A) She receives only a fine.

    (B) She receives a fine or community service.

    (C) She has to complete 20 hours of community service.

    (D) She receives a fine of $500 and community service.

    (E) She has to participate in an alternative program.

24. True or false: According to the passage, persons under the age of 17 who are in Lincoln City but who do not reside there must obey the curfew.

    (A) True

    (B) False

25. According to the passage, which of the following statements is accurate?

    (A) In July and August the curfew is later on weeknights.

    (B) Persons who are under 17 are allowed out at 5:00 a.m. on most days.

    (C) Persons who are under 17 must obey the curfew if they are traveling to or from work.

    (D) Persons who are under 17 are often involved in emergency situations.

    (E) From September to June, the curfew only applies on school nights.

Go on to next page

> Question 26 is based on the following passage. Do not assume anything to be true that is not stated in the passage or in the question.

Murder is the unlawful killing of one person by another person.

First-degree murder is a deliberate, intentional killing that is premeditated. It may be in conjunction with another felony, such as arson or kidnapping, and may involve a weapon, such as a gun or knife.

Second-degree murder is a death resulting from an assault. Unlike first-degree murder, second-degree murder lacks premeditation and the death is a consequence of the assault.

Third-degree murder is often called involuntary manslaughter. It is an unintentional killing that may result from dangerous conduct, such as reckless driving.

26. Which of the following best describes second-degree murder?

    (A) Juanita drove drunk and hit another car head-on, killing the driver of the car.

    (B) Sam robbed a convenience store and shot and killed the clerk when the clerk refused to hand over the money in the cash register.

    (C) Roberta argued with a woman in a bar and shot the woman in the knee. The woman later bled to death.

    (D) A man killed Matthew's teenage daughter. Matthew stalked the man and then shot and killed him.

    (E) Kendrick lost control of his car and hit a tree. A passenger in his car was killed.

Go on to next page

Questions 27 and 28 are based on the following incident report and incident description.

INCIDENT REPORT — POLICE DEPARTMENT

1. ADDRESS OF INCIDENT	2. OFFENSE	3. CODE	4. DATE

5. NAME OF VICTIM: INDIVIDUAL OR BUSINESS	6. ADDRESS PHONE

7. ASSIGNED OFFICERS/BADGE NUMBERS	8. AGE OF VICTIM	9. RACE OF VICTIM	10. VICTIM'S DATE OF BIRTH

11. NAME OF SUSPECT	12. ADDRESS

13. AGE	14. RACE	15. SEX	16. DATE OF BIRTH	17. HEIGHT	18. WEIGHT

19. HAIR	20. EYES	21. PHYSICAL DESCRIPTION

22. CHARGES

23. ITEM	24. BRAND	25. SERIAL NUMBER	26. VALUE
27. ITEM	28. BRAND	29. SERIAL NUMBER	30. VALUE
31. ITEM	32. BRAND	33. SERIAL NUMBER	34. VALUE

35. _____
SIGNATURE OF OFFICER/BADGE NUMBER

Sandra Cason, who works as a paralegal at 2217 Main Avenue, Miami, was walking from her office building to her car when a man stole her purse. She went back into the office building and called police at 6:10 p.m., Tuesday, May 4, to report the incident. Officers Kelly James and Tony Falto arrived at the scene at 6:15 p.m. to investigate. Ms. Cason was able to identify the man as a white male in his 20s with brown hair. He was wearing a hooded jacket and jeans.

27. True or false: The incident report can be fully completed based on the information in the paragraph.

(A) True

(B) False

28. True or false: Police arrived at the scene at 6:15 p.m.

(A) True

(B) False

Go on to next page

> *Questions 29 through 33 are based on the following passage.*

In an effort to keep the community clean and its residents healthy, police in Washington Town are enforcing new garbage and recycling regulations. Residents should pick up a collection schedule at Washington Town City Hall. This schedule indicates which day is their garbage collection day.

Monday and Thursday are garbage collection days. When a holiday falls on a Monday, pickup for that week will be Tuesday and Friday. When a holiday falls on a Thursday, pickup for that week will be on Monday and Friday.

Residents must place garbage containers curbside before 6:30 a.m. on their collection day. Containers may be placed curbside no earlier than 6:00 p.m. on the day before the scheduled pickup day. Containers must be placed in an area that does not cause an obstruction for pickup. Garbage placed in an obstructed area will not be collected. Residents must remove empty garbage containers by the end of their collection day. Only garbage containers supplied by Washington Town are acceptable. Plastic, paper, or plywood containers will be collected and disposed of as trash and residents will be fined. Plastic bags inside garbage containers must weigh no more than 50 pounds.

Only household waste may be placed curbside on garbage collection days. The following will not be picked up on regular collection days: rugs, building materials, hazardous materials, leaves, lawn clippings, brush or tree limbs, aluminum cans, and plastic bottles and jars.

Recyclables will be collected on Wednesdays. When a holiday falls on Monday, pickup for that week will be on Thursday. Recyclables must be placed in a container supplied by Washington Town or in a clear plastic bag. If possible, flatten plastic containers. Containers and paper may not be mixed together in one container or bag. Cardboard may be flattened and tied together. It is not necessary to put cardboard in a container or plastic bag. Acceptable items to be recycled include aluminum cans, plastic, glass, paper, and cardboard.

Washington Town police are authorized to ticket residents who repeatedly violate garbage and recycling regulations. The objective of these regulations is to keep the city clean. For more information about garbage collection and recycling, contact Washington Town City Hall.

29. True or false: According to the passage, residents may put recyclables in a clear plastic bag instead of in a container supplied by the city.

    (A) True

    (B) False

30. According to the passage, when a holiday falls on a Monday, garbage collection for that week will be on

    (A) Monday and Friday.

    (B) Thursday.

    (C) Wednesday.

    (D) Tuesday and Friday.

    (E) Saturday.

31. Rob Keenan puts his garbage containers behind a parked car. This is an obstruction for pickup. According to the passage, what will happen?

    (A) Rob's garbage will not be collected.

    (B) Rob's containers will be taken away.

    (C) Rob will receive a ticket and pay a fine.

    (D) Rob's garbage will be collected the next day.

    (E) Rob will have to visit Washington Town City Hall.

Go on to next page

32. Becca Kelly is putting out plastic containers for recycling. According to the passage, what should she do to the containers?

    (A) Mix them with paper

    (B) Tie them together

    (C) Flatten them

    (D) Take off the caps

    (E) Weigh them

33. According to the passage, which of the following statements is accurate?

    (A) Plastic bottles and jars are considered household waste.

    (B) All residents have their recyclables picked up on Wednesdays.

    (C) Aluminum cans are considered household waste.

    (D) All residents have their garbage picked up on Tuesdays.

    (E) Leaves and lawn clippings are considered recyclables.

Question 34 is based on the following passage. Do not assume anything to be true that is not stated in the passage or in the question.

The **Fifteenth Amendment** prohibits the government from denying a citizen the right to vote based on that citizen's race, color, or previous condition of servitude.

The **Nineteenth Amendment** gives all U.S. citizens the right to vote regardless of sex.

The **Twenty-Fourth Amendment** prohibits the restriction of voting rights due to the nonpayment of poll taxes.

The **Twenty-Eighth Amendment** established the voting age as 18.

34. Which of the following best describes the Twenty-Fourth Amendment?

    (A) A woman in 1922 is allowed to vote for president for the first time.

    (B) An 18-year-old male may vote even though he does not yet pay property taxes.

    (C) An African American male in 1895 no longer has to pay to vote.

    (D) An African American is told he may not vote until after he pays property taxes.

    (E) Slaves on a plantation are now free to do as they choose.

Go on to next page

Questions 35 through 39 are based on the following passage.

In an effort to ensure the safety of its citizens, police in Union City are enforcing new ordinances applying to buyers and sellers at the town's Giant Sunday Flea Market. These ordinances pertain to the safety of buyers and sellers. For flea market rates, rules, and regulations, contact Mark Harris at 555-444-3333.

Sellers may be fined for discarding items, including empty boxes, next to trash cans or in the Giant Sunday Flea Market dumpster. The new ordinance states that if you bring it in, you must take it out.

Sellers and buyers are now allowed to bring prepared foods and drinks with them to the flea market. Prepared foods include, but are not limited to, sandwiches, chicken, pizza, baked goods, and snack foods. Bottled and canned drinks are permitted as well as insulated beverage containers of coffee, tea, or hot chocolate. Alcoholic beverages are strictly prohibited and smoking is not allowed inside facilities or near stands.

Sellers are now restricted from selling certain legal items. They may no longer sell live animals such as pets and livestock. They may not sell legal fireworks, weapons, or ammunition. Weapons include BB and pellet guns and knives. They may not sell tattoos or tattoo supplies. Sellers may not sell counterfeit merchandise of any kind. This includes bootlegged CDs and DVDs and imitation designer purses, clothes, watches, and shoes.

Sellers and buyers must behave in a way that is appropriate in a family atmosphere. They should expect to be fined for using profane language or fighting. The objective of these changes is to ensure that the Giant Sunday Flea Market is a pleasurable, safe place to both buyers and sellers.

35. According to the passage, a seller may be fined for

(A) selling designer items.

(B) bringing in prepared foods.

(C) leaving behind discarded items.

(D) selling stuffed animals.

(E) bringing in cardboard boxes.

36. According to the passage, sellers are restricted from selling

(A) tools.

(B) tattoos.

(C) watches.

(D) shoes.

(E) food.

37. True or false: According to the passage, a seller who uses profane language will be fined.

(A) True

(B) False

38. Mrs. Hendrickson would like to sell crafts at a stand at the Giant Sunday Flea Market. According to the passage, to find out the rates she should contact

(A) other sellers.

(B) Mark Harris.

(C) Union City Police.

(D) Union City Town Hall.

(E) the flea market office.

39. According to the passage, which of the following statements is accurate?

(A) The new ordinances apply only to buyers at the Giant Sunday Flea Market.

(B) Sellers at the Giant Sunday Flea Market may not sell weapons of any kind.

(C) The new ordinances apply only to sellers at the Giant Sunday Flea Market.

(D) Sellers at the Giant Sunday Flea Market may only sell animals as pets.

(E) Sellers at the Giant Sunday Flea Market may use the dumpster.

Go on to next page

Questions 40 and 41 are based on the following incident report and incident description.

INCIDENT REPORT — POLICE DEPARTMENT

1. ADDRESS OF INCIDENT	2. OFFENSE	3. CODE	4. DATE

5. NAME OF VICTIM:	INDIVIDUAL OR BUSINESS	6. ADDRESS	PHONE

7. ASSIGNED OFFICERS/BADGE NUMBERS	8. AGE OF VICTIM	9. RACE OF VICTIM	10. VICTIM'S DATE OF BIRTH

11. NAME OF SUSPECT	12. ADDRESS

13. AGE	14. RACE	15. SEX	16. DATE OF BIRTH	17. HEIGHT	18. WEIGHT

19. HAIR	20. EYES	21. PHYSICAL DESCRIPTION

22. CHARGES

23. ITEM	24. BRAND	25. SERIAL NUMBER	26. VALUE
27. ITEM	28. BRAND	29. SERIAL NUMBER	30. VALUE
31. ITEM	32. BRAND	33. SERIAL NUMBER	34. VALUE

35. _____
SIGNATURE OF OFFICER/BADGE NUMBER

Brett Millard, owner of Brett's Tavern at 256 S. Main Street, called police headquarters at 10:20 a.m., June 20, to report that his tavern had been broken into during the night. Officers Juana Torres (badge #456) and Lenny Michaels (badge #129) arrived at the scene at 10:36 a.m. to investigate. Mr. Millard said that a safe containing $1,368 in cash was taken. Its serial number is AE976540 and it is made by First Alert. Mr. Millard said he suspects a man named Ronald Halpern. Halpern is about 5'7" tall and weighs about 200 pounds. He has brown hair and brown eyes. Mr. Millard said he saw Halpern near the bar when it closed and that Halpern has served time in prison for burglary. He did not know Halpern's address. Mr. Millard is 46 years old and his date of birth is May 19, 1964.

40. True or false: The incident report can be fully completed based on the information in the paragraph.

(A) True

(B) False

41. True or false: The suspect has brown hair and green eyes.

(A) True

(B) False

Go on to next page

Questions 42 through 45 are based on the following passage.

In an effort to ensure good health for young persons, police in Bartlett Town are enforcing new ordinances regarding the sale of tobacco to minors. These laws will be strictly enforced and apply to both residents and nonresidents in Bartlett Town.

Persons under 18 years of age are considered minors. Minors who buy, accept, or have in their possession tobacco products will be charged with a misdemeanor. Tobacco products include cigarettes, cigars, or tobacco in any other form. Tobacco products also include cigarette papers or wrappers intended to wrap tobacco into a cigarette. Persons who give tobacco products to minors may also be charged with a misdemeanor.

Minors may not enter, remain in, or loiter around a retail tobacco business. Owners of such establishments may not permit minors to enter, remain in, or loiter around their business. Retail businesses that sell tobacco must employ a person to sit or stand at each entrance and examine photo identification from each person entering the establishment to ensure that persons under 18 do not enter the establishment alone. Failure to do this is considered a misdemeanor. Furthermore, minors using false photo identification to obtain tobacco products will be charged with a misdemeanor.

Minors may enter a tobacco retailer with a parent or guardian so that the parent or guardian may purchase tobacco products for himself or herself. Minors may also possess, but not sell or distribute, tobacco products in the course of employment for duties such as stocking shelves or carrying tobacco products to a customer's vehicle.

Bartlett Town police are authorized to arrest and take into custody individuals violating these new ordinances. The objective of these ordinances is to keep minors in Bartlett Town safe and healthy.

42. According to the passage, minors may only enter a tobacco retailer if they

(A) have photo identification.

(B) are with a parent or guardian.

(C) are buying for another person.

(D) are assisting a customer.

(E) remain inside the business.

43. According to the passage, tobacco products include

(A) cigarette cartons.

(B) cigarette wrappers.

(C) cigar holders.

(D) cigarette advertisements.

(E) cigar boxes.

44. True or false: A minor who works for a store may carry tobacco products to a customer's car.

(A) True

(B) False

45. True or false: According to the passage, a person who gives cigarettes to a minor will be issued a written warning.

(A) True

(B) False

STOP DO NOT TURN THE PAGE UNTIL TOLD TO DO SO.
DO NOT RETURN TO A PREVIOUS TEST.

Section III

Grammar

Time: 15 minutes

Directions: This section of the exam tests your knowledge of grammar, punctuation, and spelling. Choose the best answer for each question, following the specific instructions for each subsection.

For questions 46 through 55, choose the alternative that correctly fills in the blank. Be sure to read carefully any text appearing before or after the blank, because the right answer may be dependent on it.

46. The suspect knew Officer Barrow and
_____.

    (A) I

    (B) me

47. Traffic violations near the intersection
_____ decreased this year.

    (A) is

    (B) was

    (C) have

    (D) has

48. _____ a police officer's responsibility to
stop criminal activity.

    (A) It's

    (B) Its

    (C) Its'

49. Officers Vargas and Ramsay understood
that _____ presence at the training seminar
was required.

    (A) there

    (B) their

    (C) they're

50. The _____ names were engraved on a
plaque on the wall.

    (A) officer

    (B) officer's

    (C) officers'

    (D) officers's

51. As a safety precaution, Officer Medina
planned _____ wear a vest.

    (A) two

    (B) to

    (C) too

52. When it comes to the law, you should know
_____ rights.

    (A) you're

    (B) your

53. The _____ witnessed the robbery.

    (A) boys

    (B) boys'

    (C) boy's

54. The officer wanted to determine _____ car
was blocking the alley.

    (A) who's

    (B) whose

55. The sergeant used her equipment allowance to _____ new cuffs.

    (A) by

    (B) bye

    (C) buy

*For Questions 56 through 65, choose the answer
that identifies the misspelled word in each
sentence.*

Go on to next page

56. On Wednesday, October 5, Officer Sterne investigated a disorderly conduct complaint about a man outside of a grocery store.

    (A) Wedesday

    (B) investigated

    (C) disorderly

    (D) complaint

    (E) grocery

57. The teenagers were apprehended after drinking alcohol in the cemetary.

    (A) teenagers

    (B) apprehended

    (C) alcohol

    (D) cemetary

    (E) None of the above

58. The woman who heard the rumor about the suspects found it difficult to seperate fact from fiction.

    (A) heard

    (B) rumor

    (C) suspects

    (D) seperate

    (E) fiction

59. The police officers used specially trained dogs to search the school for illegal drugs.

    (A) officers

    (B) specially

    (C) school

    (D) illegal

    (E) None of the above

60. The driver of the vehical was embarrassed that he did not see the traffic signal.

    (A) driver

    (B) vehical

    (C) embarrassed

    (D) traffic

    (E) signal

61. The personnal at the quaint hotel where the disturbance occurred were very cooperative.

    (A) personnal

    (B) quaint

    (C) occurred

    (D) cooperative

    (E) None of the above

62. Officer Simonson and her fellow officers were asked to complete a questionaire about which supplies they need to better perform their jobs.

    (A) fellow

    (B) complete

    (C) questionaire

    (D) supplies

    (E) perform

63. Sergeant Casey believed that most of the evidence was not relevant in determining who broke the office windowpane.

    (A) believed

    (B) evidence

    (C) relevant

    (D) determining

    (E) windowpane

64. Most of the workers the officers suspected as being illegal aliens were born in foriegn countries in northern South America.

    (A) suspected

    (B) illegal

    (C) aliens

    (D) foriegn

    (E) None of the above

65. An informent reported to Officer Darling that he had witnessed suspicious activity taking place behind the library.

    (A) informent

    (B) witnessed

    (C) suspicious

    (D) activity

    (E) library

STOP DO NOT TURN THE PAGE UNTIL TOLD TO DO SO.
DO NOT RETURN TO A PREVIOUS TEST.

Section IV

Incident Report Writing

Time: 15 minutes

Directions: This section tests your writing skills. On this page is a completed sample incident report form. Use the information contained on the form to answer the questions that follow and write your answers in the spaces provided. All your answers must contain the correct information and be written in complete sentences. The sentences must be grammatically correct, and all words should be correctly spelled.

Questions 66 through 70 are based on the following incident report form.

INCIDENT REPORT — POLICE DEPARTMENT

1. ADDRESS OF INCIDENT	2. OFFENSE	3. CODE	4. DATE
123 Delaney Street	Burglary	A6-250	September 21

5. NAME OF VICTIM: INDIVIDUAL OR BUSINESS	6. ADDRESS	PHONE
Craig Fulton	210 Gedding Street	234-5678

7. ASSIGNED OFFICERS/BADGE NUMBERS	8. AGE OF VICTIM	9. RACE OF VICTIM	10. VICTIM'S DATE OF BIRTH
Charles Dziak #304 Mike Bishop #153	44	White	03/30/66

11. NAME OF SUSPECT	12. ADDRESS
Jim Dobrowski	Unknown

13. AGE	14. RACE	15. SEX	16. DATE OF BIRTH	17. HEIGHT	18. WEIGHT
21	White	Male	Unknown	5'8"	about 140

19. HAIR	20. EYES	21. PHYSICAL DESCRIPTION
Blonde	Green	has a tattoo of an eagle on right arm

22. CHARGES
Burglary

23. ITEM	24. BRAND	25. SERIAL NUMBER	26. VALUE
Cash	N/A	N/A	$280

27. ITEM	28. BRAND	29. SERIAL NUMBER	30. VALUE
Television	Sony	EF18MN2341986	$1,200

31. ITEM	32. BRAND	33. SERIAL NUMBER	34. VALUE
Laptop Computer	Dell	390645DK223390	$2,000

35. ___Charles Dziak #304___
SIGNATURE OF OFFICER/BADGE NUMBER

Go on to next page

66. Where does the victim reside?

   _____

67. What items were stolen from the victim?

   _____

68. Where did the incident take place?

   _____

69. What is the name of the suspect?

   _____

70. What color is the suspect's hair?

   _____

Questions 71 through 75 are based on the following incident report form.

INCIDENT REPORT — POLICE DEPARTMENT

1. ADDRESS OF INCIDENT	2. OFFENSE	3. CODE	4. DATE
56 Center Street	Armed Robbery	AF-100	October 10

5. NAME OF VICTIM: INDIVIDUAL OR BUSINESS	6. ADDRESS PHONE
Alfonzo Cortes	10 Curtis Street

7. ASSIGNED OFFICERS/BADGE NUMBERS	8. AGE OF VICTIM	9. RACE OF VICTIM	10. VICTIM'S DATE OF BIRTH
Renee Templeton #251 Ken Ritz #110	24	Hispanic	04/15/86

11. NAME OF SUSPECT	12. ADDRESS
Unknown	Unknown

13. AGE	14. RACE	15. SEX	16. DATE OF BIRTH	17. HEIGHT	18. WEIGHT
20	White	Male	Unknown	5'5"	150

19. HAIR	20. EYES	21. PHYSICAL DESCRIPTION
Brown	Brown	Wearing jeans, black t-shirt

22. CHARGES
Robbery

23. ITEM	24. BRAND	25. SERIAL NUMBER	26. VALUE
Cash	N/A	N/A	$76

27. ITEM	28. BRAND	29. SERIAL NUMBER	30. VALUE
Watch			$150

31. ITEM	32. BRAND	33. SERIAL NUMBER	34. VALUE

35. _Renee Templeton #251_
   SIGNATURE OF OFFICER/BADGE NUMBER

Go on to next page

71. What is the victim's name?

_____

72. What was the suspect wearing?

_____

73. What items were stolen?

_____

74. What is the victim's date of birth?

_____

75. What is the suspect's height and weight?

_____

STOP DO NOT TURN THE PAGE UNTIL TOLD TO DO SO.
DO NOT RETURN TO A PREVIOUS TEST.

Chapter 14

Answers and Explanations for Practice Test 1

• •

After you take the practice National Police Officer Selection Test (POST) in Chapter 13, use this chapter to check your answers. If you aren't sure why an answer is incorrect, use this chapter to get explanations of the answers. If you correctly answered a question, you may still want to read the explanations to get a better understanding of the thought process that helped you choose the correct answer. If you're short on time, turn to the end of this chapter to find an abbreviated answer key.

Section 1: Mathematics

1. **D.** There are 52 weeks in one year. She visits schools 40 weeks per year, because she doesn't visit schools 12 weeks during the summer. She visits four schools per week, so $4 \times 40 = 160$.

2. **D.** Officer Lepore received the call at 1:20 a.m. and he returned to the station at 2:01 a.m. This is a difference of 41 minutes.

3. **D.** To find the total value of all the goods, add $1,250, $380, $509, and $210. The answer is $2,349.

4. **B.** To find the value of the stolen goods except for the cash register, add $1,250, $380, and $210. The answer is $1,840.

5. **C.** To answer this question, subtract 60 from 308 to get the total number of miles Officer Washington drove on the four other days. This number is 248. Divide 248 by 4 to find the average number of miles on these days. The answer is 62 miles.

6. **E.** If Officer Lee's 8-hour shift ends at 7 a.m. but he stays until 9:15 a.m., that's an additional 2 hours and 15 minutes of work. He can report that amount as overtime.

7. **C.** To find the average value of each laptop computer, divide $9,200 by 8. The answer is $1,150.

8. **B.** Only half of the 24-person police force used the allowance, so 12 people used it. The allowance per year is $350. To find the total amount the department spent on uniforms, multiply 12 by $350. The answer is $4,200.

9. **D.** The thief stole three gold rings, which are worth $100 each, so the value of the rings is $300. The thief stole two watches, which are worth $150 each, so the value of the watches is also $300. The thief stole two cellphones valued at $125 each, so the cellphones are worth $250. Lastly, the thief was carrying four wallets valued at $50 each, so the wallets are worth $200. To find the answer, add $300, $300, $250, and $200. The answer is $1,050.

10. **A.** One year has 52 weeks, and Officer Sanchez visits one school every other week. She visits 26 schools per year.

11. **C.** The question says the officers drove 75 miles on one day and 1,065 miles during a ten-day period, so subtract 75 from 1,065 to get 990, the number of miles they drove on the other nine days. To find the average number of miles the officers drove on the remaining nine days, divide 990 by 9. The answer is 110 miles.

12. **D.** To find the value of all the stolen goods, add the numbers in the list: $1,800, $850, $900, $100, and $320. The answer is $3,970.

13. **C.** To find the value of all the items except the cellphone and the cash, add $1,800, $850, and $900. The answer is $3,550.

14. **D.** To find the average retail value of each pistol, divide $13,900, the total value, by 20, the number of pistols. The answer is $695.

15. **C.** If the patrol car averages 20 miles per gallon of gasoline and it's driven 80 miles per day, you find the average gallons of gas per day by dividing: 80 ÷ 20 = 4. The question asks you to find the number of gallons in a five-day workweek, so multiply 4 by 5. The answer is 20.

16. **C.** Officer Sampson received the call at 5:32 p.m. and left the scene at 5:51 p.m. The difference between these times is 19 minutes.

17. **A.** To find the total retail value of the computers, multiply 25, the number of computers, by $650, the value of each computer. The answer is $16,250.

18. **E.** If Officer Jones's shift usually ends at 3 p.m. and she stays until 4:25 p.m., she has worked 1 hour and 25 minutes of overtime.

19. **C.** To find the number of hours of community service completed by this police force in six months, multiply 16, the number of officers who participated in the program, by 4, the number of hours required per month. This equals 64 hours, the number of hours completed in one month. The question asks for the number of hours in six months, so multiply 64 by 6. The answer is 384 hours.

20. **D.** The car contained 10 cellphones, valued at $200 each. The total value of the cellphones is $2,000. The car contained 15 gold watches, valued at $300 each. The total value of the watches is $4,500. The car also contained 3 pairs of earrings, which are worth $200 each. The value of all the earrings is $600. To find the total value of the recovered items, add $2,000, $4,500, and $600. The answer is $7,100.

Section 11: Reading Comprehension

21. **D.** The curfew on Friday night begins at 12:00 a.m. the next day. A 16-year-old resident of Lincoln must be home by this time.

22. **A.** The third paragraph of this passage says that persons under the age of 17 are exempt from curfew if they are accompanied by a parent or guardian. Therefore, the curfew would not apply to Mitch.

23. **D.** The fourth paragraph of the passage says that a parent who knowingly permits the minor to violate curfew is subject to a fine of $500 and community service. This is the penalty Mrs. Jackson would receive.

24. **A.** The first paragraph of the passage says that the curfew applies to persons under the age of 17 regardless of whether they are residents of Lincoln City.

25. **A.** From September through June, the curfew begins at 11:00 p.m. Sunday through Thursday. In July and August, it begins later, at 12:00 a.m. the next morning.

26. **C.** Answer Choice (C) best describes second-degree murder. While Roberta did not intend to kill the woman, she did assault her, and the woman died as a result of that assault. Choices (A) and (E) describe third-degree murder, and Choices (B) and (D) describe first-degree murder.

27. **B.** The incident report cannot be fully completed based on the information in the paragraph. For example, it does not give the victim's race or date of birth.

28. **A.** According to the incident report, the police arrived at the scene at 6:15 p.m.

29. **A.** The passage says that recyclables must be put in a container supplied by the city or in a clear, plastic bag. Therefore, the statement is true.

30. **D.** The passage says that when a holiday falls on a Monday, garbage collection for that week will be on Tuesday and Friday.

31. **A.** The third paragraph of the passage says that garbage placed in an obstructed area will not be collected. Rob would only receive a ticket if he repeatedly violated garbage and recycling regulations.

32. **C.** The fifth paragraph says that plastic containers should be flattened, if possible. Therefore, Becca Kelly should try to flatten her plastic containers.

33. **B.** The passage says that recyclables are collected on Wednesdays. It does not indicate that there is a collection schedule for recyclables, so this must be true for all residents.

34. **C.** Choice (C) best describes the Twenty-Fourth Amendment. If an African American male in 1895 was told he had to pay to vote, this was considered a poll tax. This amendment made such taxes illegal.

35. **C.** The passage says that sellers may be fined for discarding items next to trash cans or in the Giant Sunday Flea Market dumpster.

36. **B.** The fourth paragraph of the passage says that sellers may not sell tattoos or tattoo supplies.

37. **A.** The last paragraph of the passage says that sellers who use profane language will be fined.

38. **B.** The first paragraph of the passage says that people should contact Mark Harris for information about flea market rates, rules, and regulations.

39. **B.** The fourth paragraph says that sellers may not sell weapons or ammunition. The ordinances apply to both sellers and buyers, so Choices (A) and (C) are not correct. Sellers may not sell animals as pets or use the dumpster.

40. **B.** This statement is false. While a lot of information is presented in this paragraph, some sections of the incident report would still be blank.

41. **B.** The paragraph says the suspect has brown hair and brown eyes.

42. **B.** The fourth paragraph of this passage says that minors may enter a tobacco business with a parent or guardian.

43. **B.** Wrappers used to wrap tobacco are considered a tobacco product.

44. **A.** The fourth paragraph states that a minor may possess tobacco products in the course of employment and may carry them to a customer's vehicle.

45. **B.** The passage says that a person who gives tobacco products to a minor may be charged with a misdemeanor.

Section III: Grammar

46. **B.** You and Officer Barrow together are the object of the sentence, but to decide which word is correct, you can remove Office Barrow from the sentence without changing anything. You would say "The suspect knew me," not "The suspect knew I." So the correct object pronoun in this sentence is *me*.

47. **C.** The subject of this sentence, *traffic violations,* is plural. Therefore, the plural auxiliary word (or helping verb) *have* is used.

48. **A.** The contraction *it's* means *it is.* This contraction makes sense in this sentence.

49. **B.** A pronoun is needed in this sentence, so the answer is *their.* Remember that the contraction *they're* means *they are,* and *there* typically refers to a place.

50. **C.** Because the subject of this sentence, *names,* is plural, *officers* must also be plural. In this sentence, *officers* should also be possessive. Because the noun *officers* is plural, you only have to add an apostrophe to make it possessive. *Officers' names* is correct.

51. **B.** The preposition *to* is correct in this sentence. *Two* refers to the number, and *too* means *also* or *in addition to.*

52. **B.** The pronoun *your* is correct in this sentence. The contraction *you're* means *you are.*

53. **A.** The plural noun *boys* is correct in this sentence. There is no need to make *boys* possessive.

54. **B.** The pronoun *whose* is correct in this sentence. The contraction *who's* means *who is.*

55. **C.** The verb *buy* is correct in this sentence. *By* is a preposition meaning *near,* and *bye* is short for *goodbye.*

56. **A.** The correct spelling is *Wednesday.*

57. **D.** The correct spelling is *cemetery.*

58. **D.** The correct spelling is *separate.*

59. **E.** All words in this sentence are spelled correctly.

60. **B.** The correct spelling is *vehicle.*

61. **A.** The correct spelling is *personnel.*

62. **C.** The correct spelling is *questionnaire.*

63. **B.** The correct spelling is *evidence.*

64. **D.** The correct spelling is *foreign.*

65. **A.** The correct spelling is *informant.*

Section IV: Incident Report Writing

66. The victim resides at 210 Gedding Street.

67. The items stolen from the victim were cash, a television, and a laptop computer.

68. The incident took place at 123 Delaney Street.

69. The name of the suspect is Jim Dobrowski.

70. The suspect's hair is blonde.

71. The victim's name is Alfonzo Cortes.

72. The suspect was wearing jeans and a black T-shirt.

73. The items stolen were cash and a watch.

74. The victim's date of birth is April 15, 1986.

75. The suspect's height is 5 feet 5 inches and his weight is 150 pounds.

Answer Key for Practice Test 1

Section 1

1. D	8. B	15. C
2. D	9. D	16. C
3. D	10. A	17. A
4. B	11. C	18. E
5. C	12. D	19. C
6. E	13. C	20. D
7. C	14. D	

Section II

21. D	30. D	39. B
22. A	31. A	40. B
23. D	32. C	41. B
24. A	33. B	42. B
25. A	34. C	43. B
26. C	35. C	44. A
27. B	36. B	45. B
28. A	37. A	
29. A	38. B	

Section III

46. B	53. A	60. B
47. C	54. B	61. A
48. A	55. C	62. C
49. B	56. A	63. B
50. C	57. D	64. D
51. B	58. D	65. A
52. B	59. E	

Chapter 15

Practice Test 2: The National Police Officer Selection Test (POST)

●●

*P*ractice Test 2 is modeled after the National Police Officer Selection Test (POST). Many police departments use the POST to screen job candidates. The POST has four sections, and each section is timed separately. Time yourself as you complete each section of this practice test, or have someone else tell you when to begin and when your time is up. Although you may want to take a break between sections while you're practicing, we recommend that you try to complete the entire test in one day, as you would on the actual test.

Section	Test	Number of Items	Time
1	Mathematics	20	20 minutes
2	Reading Comprehension	25	25 minutes
3	Grammar	20	15 minutes
4	Incident Report Writing	10	15 minutes

Sections 1, 2, and 3 of Practice Test 2 contain multiple-choice and true-and-false questions. Section 4, Incident Report Writing, contains open-ended questions for which you write out your answers in grammatically correct sentences.

Use a number-two pencil and mark your answers for Sections 1, 2, and 3 on the following answer sheet. Make sure your marks are heavy and completely fill in the ovals. Completely erase any marks that you wish to change. Be sure to blacken only one oval for each question, and be sure that you're blackening the oval for the correct question. It's easy to skip a question and become confused when marking your answers on the answer sheet. While this answer sheet won't be computer scored like the answer sheet on the actual POST, pretending that it will be helps you better prepare for the exam. For Section 4, write your answers on the lines underneath each question.

Pace yourself as you work through the questions on Practice Test 2 so that you have enough time to complete all the questions. Don't spend too much time on one question. Try to answer every question on this test. If a question really stumps you, take a good guess and move on. Your score is based on the number of questions you answer correctly, so there's no penalty for guessing.

You won't be allowed to use a calculator on the actual POST, but you will be given scratch paper, so use scratch paper to work your way through the problems on this practice test.

After you complete the entire sample test, check your answers against the answers and explanations in Chapter 16. Be sure to read the answer explanations for all questions — even those that you've answered correctly. Doing so helps you learn more about the test and gives you an extra edge on the actual POST. Note that on the actual POST, you need an overall score of 70 to pass and move on to the next stage in the hiring process.

To determine your overall score, figure out your score on each section: Questions in the Reading Comprehension section (25 questions) are worth 4 points each, questions in the Mathematics and Grammar sections (40 questions) are worth 5 points each, and questions in the Incident Report Writing section (10 questions) are worth 10 points each. Add your scores together and divide by 4 to determine your overall score.

Answer Sheet for Practice Test 2

1 Ⓐ Ⓑ Ⓒ Ⓓ Ⓔ	21 Ⓐ Ⓑ Ⓒ Ⓓ Ⓔ	41 Ⓐ Ⓑ Ⓒ Ⓓ Ⓔ	61 Ⓐ Ⓑ Ⓒ Ⓓ Ⓔ
2 Ⓐ Ⓑ Ⓒ Ⓓ Ⓔ	22 Ⓐ Ⓑ Ⓒ Ⓓ Ⓔ	42 Ⓐ Ⓑ Ⓒ Ⓓ Ⓔ	62 Ⓐ Ⓑ Ⓒ Ⓓ Ⓔ
3 Ⓐ Ⓑ Ⓒ Ⓓ Ⓔ	23 Ⓐ Ⓑ Ⓒ Ⓓ Ⓔ	43 Ⓐ Ⓑ Ⓒ Ⓓ Ⓔ	63 Ⓐ Ⓑ Ⓒ Ⓓ Ⓔ
4 Ⓐ Ⓑ Ⓒ Ⓓ Ⓔ	24 Ⓐ Ⓑ Ⓒ Ⓓ Ⓔ	44 Ⓐ Ⓑ Ⓒ Ⓓ Ⓔ	64 Ⓐ Ⓑ Ⓒ Ⓓ Ⓔ
5 Ⓐ Ⓑ Ⓒ Ⓓ Ⓔ	25 Ⓐ Ⓑ Ⓒ Ⓓ Ⓔ	45 Ⓐ Ⓑ Ⓒ Ⓓ Ⓔ	65 Ⓐ Ⓑ Ⓒ Ⓓ Ⓔ
6 Ⓐ Ⓑ Ⓒ Ⓓ Ⓔ	26 Ⓐ Ⓑ Ⓒ Ⓓ Ⓔ	46 Ⓐ Ⓑ Ⓒ Ⓓ Ⓔ	
7 Ⓐ Ⓑ Ⓒ Ⓓ Ⓔ	27 Ⓐ Ⓑ Ⓒ Ⓓ Ⓔ	47 Ⓐ Ⓑ Ⓒ Ⓓ Ⓔ	
8 Ⓐ Ⓑ Ⓒ Ⓓ Ⓔ	28 Ⓐ Ⓑ Ⓒ Ⓓ Ⓔ	48 Ⓐ Ⓑ Ⓒ Ⓓ Ⓔ	
9 Ⓐ Ⓑ Ⓒ Ⓓ Ⓔ	29 Ⓐ Ⓑ Ⓒ Ⓓ Ⓔ	49 Ⓐ Ⓑ Ⓒ Ⓓ Ⓔ	
10 Ⓐ Ⓑ Ⓒ Ⓓ Ⓔ	30 Ⓐ Ⓑ Ⓒ Ⓓ Ⓔ	50 Ⓐ Ⓑ Ⓒ Ⓓ Ⓔ	
11 Ⓐ Ⓑ Ⓒ Ⓓ Ⓔ	31 Ⓐ Ⓑ Ⓒ Ⓓ Ⓔ	51 Ⓐ Ⓑ Ⓒ Ⓓ Ⓔ	
12 Ⓐ Ⓑ Ⓒ Ⓓ Ⓔ	32 Ⓐ Ⓑ Ⓒ Ⓓ Ⓔ	52 Ⓐ Ⓑ Ⓒ Ⓓ Ⓔ	
13 Ⓐ Ⓑ Ⓒ Ⓓ Ⓔ	33 Ⓐ Ⓑ Ⓒ Ⓓ Ⓔ	53 Ⓐ Ⓑ Ⓒ Ⓓ Ⓔ	
14 Ⓐ Ⓑ Ⓒ Ⓓ Ⓔ	34 Ⓐ Ⓑ Ⓒ Ⓓ Ⓔ	54 Ⓐ Ⓑ Ⓒ Ⓓ Ⓔ	
15 Ⓐ Ⓑ Ⓒ Ⓓ Ⓔ	35 Ⓐ Ⓑ Ⓒ Ⓓ Ⓔ	55 Ⓐ Ⓑ Ⓒ Ⓓ Ⓔ	
16 Ⓐ Ⓑ Ⓒ Ⓓ Ⓔ	36 Ⓐ Ⓑ Ⓒ Ⓓ Ⓔ	56 Ⓐ Ⓑ Ⓒ Ⓓ Ⓔ	
17 Ⓐ Ⓑ Ⓒ Ⓓ Ⓔ	37 Ⓐ Ⓑ Ⓒ Ⓓ Ⓔ	57 Ⓐ Ⓑ Ⓒ Ⓓ Ⓔ	
18 Ⓐ Ⓑ Ⓒ Ⓓ Ⓔ	38 Ⓐ Ⓑ Ⓒ Ⓓ Ⓔ	58 Ⓐ Ⓑ Ⓒ Ⓓ Ⓔ	
19 Ⓐ Ⓑ Ⓒ Ⓓ Ⓔ	39 Ⓐ Ⓑ Ⓒ Ⓓ Ⓔ	59 Ⓐ Ⓑ Ⓒ Ⓓ Ⓔ	
20 Ⓐ Ⓑ Ⓒ Ⓓ Ⓔ	40 Ⓐ Ⓑ Ⓒ Ⓓ Ⓔ	60 Ⓐ Ⓑ Ⓒ Ⓓ Ⓔ	

Section 1

Mathematics

Time: 20 minutes

Directions: In this section of the exam, you are provided with situations that require the use of basic arithmetic. Read each situation and solve the problem. You may not use a calculator in this section, but you may use scratch paper.

Questions 1 and 2 are based on the following information.

In preparing a report on a burglary in an office, Sergeant Miller listed the following stolen items and their values:

Item	Value
Photocopy machine	$1,000
Telephones	$400
Computers	$2,500
Printers	$500

1. What is the total value of all the stolen goods?

   (A) $4,000

   (B) $4,200

   (C) $4,400

   (D) $5,100

   (E) $5,200

2. What is the total value of all the stolen goods *except* the computers?

   (A) $700

   (B) $1,400

   (C) $1,500

   (D) $1,900

   (E) $4,200

3. Burglars broke into an electronics store and took 20 stereos with a total retail value of $11,000. What is the average retail value of each stereo?

   (A) $550

   (B) $575

   (C) $600

   (D) $625

   (E) $650

4. During a five-day period, Officer Marion drove his patrol motorcycle 410 miles. If he drove 70 miles one day, how many miles did he average on each of the other days?

   (A) 70 miles

   (B) 75 miles

   (C) 80 miles

   (D) 85 miles

   (E) 90 miles

5. The average paycheck for a police officer in a certain town is $680 per week before taxes. What is the annual salary for a police officer in this town?

   (A) $34,000

   (B) $35,360

   (C) $35,460

   (D) $36,360

   (E) $38,460

Go on to next page

6. Officer Ostrowski visits banks as part of a theft-prevention program. If Officer Ostrowski visits two banks every week, except during her two-week vacation, how many banks does she visit in one year?

   (A) 50

   (B) 100

   (C) 104

   (D) 200

   (E) 204

Questions 7 and 8 are based on the following information.

A police officer apprehends a thief trying to steal a purse. Upon investigation, the arresting officer finds that the thief is carrying two wallets, three cellphones, five gold chains, and one watch.

Item	Value
1 wallet	$30
1 cellphone	$150
1 gold chain	$100
1 watch	$150

---

7. What is the total value of all the stolen goods?

   (A) $1,100

   (B) $1,160

   (C) $2,100

   (D) $2,160

   (E) $2,200

8. What is the value of all the stolen goods *except* the gold chains?

   (A) $500

   (B) $560

   (C) $660

   (D) $700

   (E) $760

9. If a gas tank in a patrol car holds 18 gallons, and premium-grade gasoline costs $1.92 per gallon, how much will it cost to fill the tank (assuming that the tank is two-thirds empty)?

   (A) $11.52

   (B) $11.51

   (C) $23.04

   (D) $24.04

   (E) $34.56

10. Officer McKinley earns $12 an hour before taxes for his first 40 hours of work per week. After this, he earns time-and-a-half pay. He worked 46 hours this week. What is his pay before taxes?

    (A) $480

    (B) $552

    (C) $588

    (D) $720

    (E) $960

11. Burglars broke into a motorcycle store and stole three ATVs with a total retail value of $20,400. What is the average retail value of each ATV?

    (A) $5,100

    (B) $5,700

    (C) $6,700

    (D) $6,800

    (E) $10,200

12. During a five-day period, Officer Cane drove 720 miles. If Officer Cane drove 120 miles one day, how many miles did he average on each of the other days?

    (A) 100 miles

    (B) 144 miles

    (C) 148 miles

    (D) 150 miles

    (E) 155 miles

Go on to next page

Questions 13 and 14 are based on the following information.

In preparing a report on a burglary in a doctor's office, Officer Lopez listed the following stolen items and their values:

Item	Value
Petty cash box	$50
Medical equipment	$350
Office furniture	$500
Coffee machine	$40

13. What is the total value of all the stolen goods?

    (A) $940

    (B) $950

    (C) $1,040

    (D) $1,050

    (E) $1,075

14. What is the value of all the stolen goods _except_ the coffee machine and the petty cash box?

    (A) $500

    (B) $750

    (C) $850

    (D) $890

    (E) $900

15. Officer Balchune typically works the 3:00 p.m. to 11:00 p.m. shift, but her sergeant asks her to stay until 1:05 a.m. to fill in for another officer. Assuming she works her entire shift, how much overtime can Officer Balchune report for that day?

    (A) 55 minutes

    (B) 60 minutes

    (C) 1 hour and 5 minutes

    (D) 1 hour and 55 minutes

    (E) 2 hours and 5 minutes

16. Officer Knowles visits local schools with his K-9 dog three times a month as part of a responsible animal care program. If Officer Knowles visits schools all months of the year except June, July, and August, how many schools does he visit in one year?

    (A) 9

    (B) 12

    (C) 18

    (D) 27

    (E) 36

17. Employees of a 30-person police force are given an equipment allowance of $400 each. If two-thirds of the employees use this allowance in one year, how much money did the department spend on equipment for its officers?

    (A) $6,000

    (B) $7,000

    (C) $8,000

    (D) $10,000

    (E) $12,000

18. If a patrol car averages 23 miles per gallon of gasoline and is driven 69 miles per day, how many gallons of gasoline does it need for ten work days?

    (A) 10 gallons

    (B) 15 gallons

    (C) 25 gallons

    (D) 30 gallons

    (E) 35 gallons

Go on to next page

19. Burglars broke into a gun store and took 35 rifles with a total retail value of $29,750. What is the average retail value of each rifle?

    (A) $850

    (B) $855

    (C) $875

    (D) $950

    (E) $975

20. Officer Roland received a traffic accident call at 12:02 a.m. and arrived at the scene at 12:07 a.m. After observing that the occupants of both cars involved in the accident were not injured, Officer Roland completed a police report and left the scene at 1:05 a.m. How much time elapsed from the time of the call and the time when she left the scene?

    (A) 35 minutes

    (B) 45 minutes

    (C) 1 hour and 2 minutes

    (D) 1 hour and 3 minutes

    (E) 1 hour and 15 minutes

STOP DO NOT TURN THE PAGE UNTIL TOLD TO DO SO.
DO NOT RETURN TO A PREVIOUS TEST.

Section 11

Reading Comprehension

Time: 25 minutes

Directions: This section measures reading comprehension. Read the passages relating to police duty and then answer the questions that follow. No prior knowledge of law or law enforcement is needed to answer these questions.

The passages in this section are not intended to represent actual laws in any particular state. They present potential rules and laws relating to police work.

Three types of questions appear in this section:

✔ True/False questions that ask you to determine a statement's accuracy based on the information presented in the passage or sample report form.

✔ Questions that ask you to choose the correct answer according to the information presented in the passage or sample report form.

✔ Questions that ask you to choose the alternative that best completes the sentence, based on the information in the passage or the report form.

Questions 21 through 25 are based on the following passage.

The Seaside City Police Department has new regulations for units (groups) participating in the town's annual Fourth of July parade. These regulations differ from those of past years, so units must ensure that they follow this year's regulations to avoid being ticketed and fined. The objective of these new regulations is to ensure the safety and enjoyment of the more than 10,000 parade spectators.

Unlike last year, each unit will not receive a unit number until the morning of the parade. Units must check-in at their specific check-in location. Parade maps and check-in locations will be mailed to participants at least two weeks before the parade. All units must arrive at their check-in location no later than 8:45 a.m. on Saturday, July 4th. The parade will begin at 10:00 a.m. regardless of the weather. The route is 2.5 miles long.

To control the crowd, only those participating in the parade will be allowed in check-in areas. Police will escort others out of check-in areas. Food is allowed at the check-in area, but please do not litter. Dispose of waste appropriately in trash and recycling receptacles. We strongly recommend bringing water bottles to stay hydrated in warm weather.

Only persons, floats, and vehicles registered as part of a unit may participate in the parade. Police will ticket other vehicles and walkers. Members of units should not approach spectators along the route. Participants may *not* throw candy, treats, toys, balloons, pamphlets, or any other objects to spectators. Persons violating this rule will be fined $250 and may be asked to refrain from participating in future parades. Vehicles may not display political signs. Doing so will result in a fine of $200.

Go on to next page ➡

Units should be aware that this year the route includes Center Street, which narrows at two locations. The three-lane street narrows to two lanes just before its intersection with Jackson Street, and immediately after its intersection with Broad Street. Your unit must be able to travel the entire route without having to stop at these locations.

For more information about the parade, contact this year's parade coordinator, Dale Evans, at 444-444-4444.

21. Sarah Snow drives a vehicle in a unit in the parade with a sign on the side showing her support for a man running for mayor. According to the passage, Sarah should expect to be

 (A) taken out of the parade.

 (B) fined $200.

 (C) fined $250.

 (D) arrested.

 (E) asked to go to check-in.

22. Mike Koslowski is part of a unit registered for the parade. According to the passage, on the morning of the parade Mike and his unit will receive

 (A) a unit number.

 (B) bottles of water.

 (C) snack food.

 (D) a parade map.

 (E) a check-in location.

23. According to the passage, where should Lucy, a spectator and friend of some members of a unit, wait for the parade to start?

 (A) In the unit's check-in area

 (B) On Center Street

 (C) On the unit's float

 (D) Outside of the check-in area

 (E) On Broad Street

24. True or false: According to the passage, a unit with a small float may have trouble driving on Center Street near the intersections of Jackson Street and Broad Street.

 (A) True

 (B) False

25. According to the passage, which of the following statements is true?

 (A) Fewer spectators than last year are expected to attend the parade.

 (B) People in parades often travel along Center Street.

 (C) It is acceptable to arrive at your check-in area after the parade begins.

 (D) A few units will ride bicycles in this year's parade.

 (E) People in parades sometimes throw candy, treats, and toys to spectators.

Go on to next page

> Question 26 is based on the statements below. Do not assume anything to be true that is not stated in the passage or in the question.

A felony is a serious crime punishable by more than one year in prison or by death. Rape, murder, grand theft, and some drug crimes are felonies. States typically divide felonies into classes, with a Class A Felony being the most serious.

Class A Felony: These crimes involve the unlawful use of a nuclear, biological, or chemical weapon of mass destruction; murder in the first degree (premeditated) and in the second degree (not premeditated but resulting from an assault); arson in the first degree; conspiracy in the first degree; kidnapping in the first degree; and criminal sale of a controlled substance in the first degree.

Class B Felonies are often divided into two classes:

Class B Violent Felony: These crimes include aggravated assault upon a police officer, sexual abuse in the first degree, arson in the second degree, burglary in the first degree, sexual misconduct against a child in the first degree, gang assault in the first degree, intimidating a victim or witness in the first degree, rape in the first degree, robbery in the first degree, and criminal sale of a firearm in the first degree.

Class B Nonviolent Felony: These crimes include aggravated insurance fraud, receiving a bribe, bribery, criminal mischief, criminal sale of a controlled substance in the third degree, criminal sale of a controlled substance in or near a school ground, welfare fraud, insurance fraud, and tampering with a witness in the first degree.

26. Which of the following best describes a Class B Nonviolent Felony?

(A) Ron, who has little money, receives welfare checks even though he has unreported income.

(B) Jorge is a member of a gang who seriously injured a teenage boy from a different gang.

(C) Rachel sells heroin out of her apartment and intimidates a witness to her activities.

(D) Susan illegally sells her pistol to a neighbor because Susan needs money to support a drug addiction.

(E) Jamie, a serial arsonist, burns down a neighbor's home while they are on vacation.

Go on to next page

Questions 27 and 28 are based on the following incident report and incident description.

INCIDENT REPORT — POLICE DEPARTMENT

1. ADDRESS OF INCIDENT	2. OFFENSE	3. CODE	4. DATE

5. NAME OF VICTIM: INDIVIDUAL OR BUSINESS	6. ADDRESS PHONE

7. ASSIGNED OFFICERS/BADGE NUMBERS	8. AGE OF VICTIM	9. RACE OF VICTIM	10. VICTIM'S DATE OF BIRTH

11. NAME OF SUSPECT	12. ADDRESS

13. AGE	14. RACE	15. SEX	16. DATE OF BIRTH	17. HEIGHT	18. WEIGHT

19. HAIR	20. EYES	21. PHYSICAL DESCRIPTION

22. CHARGES

23. ITEM	24. BRAND	25. SERIAL NUMBER	26. VALUE
27. ITEM	28. BRAND	29. SERIAL NUMBER	30. VALUE
31. ITEM	32. BRAND	33. SERIAL NUMBER	34. VALUE

35. _____
SIGNATURE OF OFFICER/BADGE NUMBER

Gene Galli, who lives at 325 Shoemaker Avenue in Dalton, was walking from his home to the local convenience store when he was attacked by a man and thrown to the ground. Mr. Galli said the man kicked and hit him several times and then stole his wallet. The man escaped on foot. Mr. Galli went back into his home and called police at 8:20 p.m., Friday, January 22, to report the incident. Officers Ray Stanton and Angela Martinez arrived at the scene at 8:25 p.m. to investigate. Mr. Galli was unable to describe his attacker.

27. True or false: Mr. Galli called police at 8:25 p.m.

(A) True

(B) False

28. True or false: The incident report can be fully completed based on the information in the passage.

(A) True

(B) False

Go on to next page

Questions 29 through 33 are based on the following passage.

The town of Peterson tabulated its accident reports for the past five years to determine the cause of a significant rise in vehicle accidents in recent years and to identify measures to lower this disturbing trend.

It was noted that 58 percent of all accidents in Peterson involved a teen driver, and of these accidents, 40 percent involved a teen driver who was talking or texting on a cellphone. In traffic accidents involving a driver older than 19, 10 percent had a driver who was using a cellphone. Approximately 80 percent of all traffic accidents occurred between 3:00 p.m. and 1:00 a.m. Reports show that during the last five years, 8 percent of all traffic accidents resulted in a death.

Inattentive driving due to cellphone usage was the primary reason for all traffic accidents involving teen drivers. Fellow passengers were another reason (10 percent). For traffic accidents involving teen fatalities, 30 percent involved the use of a cellphone while driving and 15 percent occurred in bad weather.

Studies of other towns in the state found that those that had banned the use of cellphones while driving saw a significant decrease in the number of accidents, especially among teen drivers. The Peterson Police Department supports such a ban in Peterson. Peterson is considering banning talking, dialing, reading text, sending text, and browsing the Web on a cellphone when a car is not parked and in a stationary position. The ban would also apply to those on a bicycle or a skateboard. The ban would allow police in Peterson to ticket drivers caught using a cellphone. Fines would range from $75 for a first offense to $150 for subsequent offenses. Continued offenses would result in the suspension of the driver's license.

29. According to the passage, what percentage of traffic accidents in Peterson resulted in death over the past five years?

(A) 80 percent

(B) 58 percent

(C) 25 percent

(D) 10 percent

(E) 8 percent

30. True or false: The Peterson Police Department would like to ban the use of cellphones while driving.

(A) True

(B) False

31. Assume that Peterson passes the proposed ban described in the passage. Kim Conner is caught using a cellphone while driving. It is her first offense, so

(A) Kim's license will be suspended.

(B) Kim will receive a fine of $50.

(C) Kim will receive a fine of $75.

(D) Kim will receive a fine of $150.

(E) Kim will receive only a warning.

32. True or false: The ban on cellphone use would apply to persons riding bicycles.

(A) True

(B) False

33. According to the passage, which of the following statements is accurate?

(A) The majority of accidents in Peterson involving a teen fatality occurred in bad weather.

(B) The majority of accidents in Peterson involved a teen driver.

(C) Fellow passengers were the main cause of inattentive driving for teens.

(D) More teens involved in accidents were texting than talking on cellphones.

(E) The majority of accidents in Peterson occurred after 1:00 a.m. on weekends.

Go on to next page

> *Question 34 is based on the following statements. Do not assume anything to be true that is not stated in the passage or in the question.*

Involuntary manslaughter is the unintentional killing of a human being. Many states recognize two types of involuntary manslaughter:

Criminally Negligent Manslaughter: A death resulting from a high degree of negligence or an omission or failure to perform a duty. The person must have a responsibility to perform an act and fail to uphold this responsibility.

Unlawful Act Manslaughter: A death caused while someone is attempting to commit an unlawful act, which is usually a misdemeanor. A death resulting from an assault may be considered Unlawful Act Manslaughter.

34. Which of the following best describes Criminally Negligent Manslaughter?

    (A) Martha drives drunk and hits another car, killing the driver of the car.

    (B) Dave punches a man in a bar; the man falls, injures his head, and later dies.

    (C) Ryan works as a lifeguard but does not attempt to save a woman who drowns in the pool.

    (D) Stephen is involved in a drug deal and shoots and kills someone who has shot at him.

    (E) While trying to shoplift an item, Celia bumps into an elderly woman, who falls and later dies from her injury.

> *Questions 35 through 39 are based on the following passage.*

While certain noise levels must be tolerated by all citizens of Wesley, police are enforcing new ordinances concerning excessive noise levels. These restrictions apply to both businesses and residents of Wesley as well as to persons visiting the city.

Construction noise: Construction workers may not engage in repair or excavation work without a Police Commission permit. They must not operate equipment between the hours of 9:00 p.m. and 7:00 a.m. They may not operate equipment in a residential zone or within 500 feet of a residential zone before 8:00 a.m. or after 6:00 p.m. on Saturday or any time on Sunday.

Music, radio, and television noise: Persons may not operate any music- or sound-producing device in such a way that it can be heard by the human ear at 150 feet from the noise source. They may not operate such devices in a way that disturbs the peace, quiet, or comfort of neighboring residents. Owners of businesses that play music may not play music between the hours of 2:00 a.m. and 5:00 a.m.

Go on to next page

Noise from garbage collection: Commercial garbage collectors may not collect garbage in residential areas between the hours of 9:00 p.m. and 6:00 a.m. They may not collect garbage on Saturday or Sunday.

Noise from vehicles: Persons may not unreasonably operate a motor vehicle, accelerate the engine, or sound the horn so that it disturbs the peace and comfort of persons in residential areas. Noise from vehicles should not be audible to the human ear at a distance in excess of 150 feet from the noise source. Persons engaged in vehicle repair may not do so between the hours of 8:00 p.m. and 8:00 a.m. Vehicle repairs should not be audible to the human ear at a distance in excess of 150 feet from the noise source.

Police will enforce these noise ordinances 24 hours a day. Violators will be subject to a $50 fine for a first violation, a $100 fine for a second violation, and $500 for a third or subsequent violation. Repeated violations may result in the violator being arrested and charged with a misdemeanor. The objective of these changes is to better maintain the comfort and peace of persons living in and visiting Wesley.

35. According to the passage, a commercial garbage collector may collect garbage in a residential area

    (A) on weekdays only.

    (B) on weekends only.

    (C) between the hours of 8:00 p.m. and 8:00 a.m.

    (D) between the hours of 9:00 p.m. and 6:00 a.m.

    (E) between the hours of 2:00 a.m. and 5:00 a.m.

36. According to the passage, which of the following is allowed under the new noise ordinances?

    (A) A business playing music at 3:00 a.m. on Friday

    (B) A person fixing a vehicle at 9:00 p.m. on a weeknight

    (C) Construction workers operating equipment at 5:00 p.m. on Saturday

    (D) Garbage collectors collecting garbage at 7:00 a.m. on Saturday

    (E) A person playing music so that it can be heard 200 feet from the noise source

37. True or false: According to the passage, someone violating the new noise ordinances for the second time may receive a $500 fine.

    (A) True

    (B) False

38. According to the passage, which of the following statements is accurate?

    (A) Construction workers cannot work without a Police Commission permit.

    (B) The new noise ordinances apply only to residents of Wesley.

    (C) Repeated violations might result in the violator being charged with a felony.

    (D) The new noise ordinances apply only to businesses in Wesley.

    (E) Garbage collectors cannot work without a Police Commission permit.

39. Police in Wesley say that Mr. Perez has violated the noise ordinances by playing his stereo very loudly. According to the passage, because it is his first offense, he

    (A) receives only a warning.

    (B) is fined $50.

    (C) is fined $100.

    (D) is fined $500.

    (E) is charged with a misdemeanor.

Go on to next page

Questions 40 and 41 are based on the following incident report and incident description.

INCIDENT REPORT — POLICE DEPARTMENT

1. ADDRESS OF INCIDENT	2. OFFENSE	3. CODE	4. DATE

5. NAME OF VICTIM: INDIVIDUAL OR BUSINESS	6. ADDRESS PHONE

7. ASSIGNED OFFICERS/BADGE NUMBERS	8. AGE OF VICTIM	9. RACE OF VICTIM	10. VICTIM'S DATE OF BIRTH

11. NAME OF SUSPECT	12. ADDRESS

13. AGE	14. RACE	15. SEX	16. DATE OF BIRTH	17. HEIGHT	18. WEIGHT

19. HAIR	20. EYES	21. PHYSICAL DESCRIPTION

22. CHARGES

23. ITEM	24. BRAND	25. SERIAL NUMBER	26. VALUE
27. ITEM	28. BRAND	29. SERIAL NUMBER	30. VALUE
31. ITEM	32. BRAND	33. SERIAL NUMBER	34. VALUE

35. _____
SIGNATURE OF OFFICER/BADGE NUMBER

Sarah Baron, who works as an attorney at 159 Main Street, called police headquarters at 9:46 a.m. to report that her office had been broken into during the night. Officers Karen Dominick and Jacob Cane arrived at the scene to investigate at 10:02 a.m. Ms. Baron reported that her computer had been stolen as well as her paper shredder and an expensive vase. She suspects a temporary maintenance man named Roy White. When she last saw White, he was wearing dark jeans and a light blue T-shirt. He has light brown hair and is about 6 feet tall.

40. True or false: There is enough information in the paragraph to fill in parts 23, 27, and 31 of the incident form.

(A) True

(B) False

41. True or false: The maintenance man's name is Jacob Cane.

(A) True

(B) False

Go on to next page

> *Questions 42 through 45 are based on the following passage.*

In an effort to protect the health, safety, and welfare of the citizens of Alberta, police are prohibiting the operation of motorized scooters and motorized skateboards on public property.

A motorized scooter is a low-powered device with a long footboard between end wheels. It is controlled by an upright steering handle attached to the front wheel. A motorized scooter is propelled with fuel or an electric motor. A motorized skateboard is also a low-powered device with a single platform mounted on wheels. A motorized skateboard may also be propelled by fuel or an electric motor.

Public property is an area or a structure that is owned or operated by the town of Alberta. It includes, but isn't limited to, public parks, streets, parking lots, sidewalks, and alleys. These areas are not designed for motorized scooters and skateboards, which can damage roadways and vehicles and injure pedestrians.

This ordinance makes it illegal for persons over the age of 17 to operate a motorized scooter or a motorized skateboard on public property. It is also illegal for a parent to allow a minor (under the age of 18) child to operate one of these vehicles on public property within the city.

While residents of Alberta may operate such low-powered devices on private property such as driveways, they must be aware of the following restrictions. It is illegal to operate these devices at speeds higher than 35 miles per hour. Minors must wear a helmet when operating or riding on a motorized scooter or motorized skateboard. They must also have adult supervision while driving or riding on motorized vehicles.

First-time offenders will be fined $50. This includes children who are caught operating a motorized vehicle on private property without a helmet or adult supervision. Second and subsequent violators will be fined $100.

42. According to the passage, a person over 17 may operate a motorized scooter

    (A) in a park.

    (B) on a driveway.

    (C) in a parking lot.

    (D) on a sidewalk.

    (E) in an alley.

43. True or false: An 18-year-old boy does not have to wear a helmet when operating a motorized skateboard on private property.

    (A) True

    (B) False

44. According to the passage, a person operating a motorized vehicle on private property must not drive faster than

    (A) 10 miles per hour.

    (B) 15 miles per hour.

    (C) 25 miles per hour.

    (D) 35 miles per hour.

    (E) 40 miles per hour.

45. According to the passage, a motorized scooter is controlled by

    (A) a single platform.

    (B) two side handles.

    (C) an upright steering handle.

    (D) a driver's movements.

    (E) an electric motor.

STOP DO NOT TURN THE PAGE UNTIL TOLD TO DO SO. DO NOT RETURN TO A PREVIOUS TEST.

Section III

Grammar

Time: 15 minutes

Directions: This section of the exam tests your knowledge of grammar, punctuation, and spelling. Choose the best answer for each question, following the specific instructions for each subsection.

For Questions 46 through 55, choose the alternative that correctly fills in the blank. Be sure to read carefully any text appearing before or after the blank, because the right answer may be dependent on it.

46. The reduction in staff did not _____ the officers' positive attitude about working hard to keep their community safe.

    (A) effect

    (B) affect

47. Sergeant Cosgrove told Officer Castillo to interview the witness _____.

    (A) two

    (B) to

    (C) too

48. Each of the officers _____ planning to attend the reception at city hall.

    (A) is

    (B) are

49. Sergeant Green and _____ responded to the call.

    (A) me

    (B) I

50. The officers gave a presentation at the _____ school.

    (A) childrens

    (B) children's

    (C) childrens'

51. After faking an injury, the suspect broke _____ from the officer's grasp.

    (A) lose

    (B) loose

52. The officers _____ decided to throw the sergeant a surprise party.

    (A) have

    (B) has

    (C) is

    (D) are

53. A good police dog listens to _____ police handler.

    (A) it's

    (B) its

    (C) its'

54. Officer Smith returned to the construction _____ where the crime occurred.

    (A) sight

    (B) cite

    (C) site

55. Three _____ had to move from their homes because of the city ordinance.

    (A) family's

    (B) families

    (C) families'

    (D) familys

For Questions 56 through 65, choose the answer that identifies the misspelled word in each sentence.

Go on to next page

56. The impoverished city did not have enough officers to accomodate the needs of its citizens.

    (A) impoverished

    (B) enough

    (C) officers

    (D) accomodate

    (E) citizens

57. Officer Reese was certain that the suspect commited a serious crime but was denying it.

    (A) suspect

    (B) commited

    (C) serious

    (D) denying

    (E) None of the above

58. The victim was not consious, so Officer Alfano called another squad car and an ambulance to assist with the situation.

    (A) victim

    (B) consious

    (C) squad

    (D) ambulance

    (E) situation

59. Sergeant Medina thought it was apparant that a burglar had broken into the enormous apartment complex.

    (A) apparant

    (B) enormous

    (C) apartment

    (D) complex

    (E) None of the above

60. Trying to maneuver a police criuser through a roadway blocked by traffic is no easy feat.

    (A) maneuver

    (B) criuser

    (C) through

    (D) traffic

    (E) feat

61. The officer completed an incident report about a disturbance at a popular restaurant.

    (A) completed

    (B) incident

    (C) disturbance

    (D) restaurant

    (E) None of the above

62. The sergeant took immediete action and sent several officers to question the frightened grandmother.

    (A) immediete

    (B) several

    (C) question

    (D) frightened

    (E) grandmother

63. Officer Lopez used good jugement when he considered safety before entering the abandoned building.

    (A) jugement

    (B) considered

    (C) safety

    (D) abandoned

    (E) None of the above

64. The group of boys continued to harrass the storeowner even after several officers arrived at the crowded scene.

    (A) continued

    (B) harrass

    (C) arrived

    (D) crowded

    (E) scene

65. The officers apprehend the thieves, who had both illegal drugs and weapons in their posession.

    (A) apprehended

    (B) thieves

    (C) weapons

    (D) posession

    (E) None of the above

STOP DO NOT TURN THE PAGE UNTIL TOLD TO DO SO.
DO NOT RETURN TO A PREVIOUS TEST.

Section IV

Incident Report Writing

Time: 15 minutes

Directions: This section tests your writing skills. The following is a completed sample incident report form. Use the information contained on the form to answer the questions that follow and write your answers in the spaces provided. All your answers must contain the correct information and be written in complete sentences. The sentences must be grammatically correct, and all words should be spelled correctly.

Questions 66 through 70 are based on the following incident report form.

INCIDENT REPORT — POLICE DEPARTMENT

1. ADDRESS OF INCIDENT	2. OFFENSE	3. CODE	4. DATE
118 Root Street	Assault	A6-130	March 30

5. NAME OF VICTIM: INDIVIDUAL OR BUSINESS	6. ADDRESS	PHONE
Sandy Myers	1 May Street	510-343-2222

7. ASSIGNED OFFICERS/BADGE NUMBERS	8. AGE OF VICTIM	9. RACE OF VICTIM	10. VICTIM'S DATE OF BIRTH
Cindy Ryder #450 Joseph Falzone #908	25	African American	09/14/85

11. NAME OF SUSPECT	12. ADDRESS
Ian Ketron	56 Main Street

13. AGE	14. RACE	15. SEX	16. DATE OF BIRTH	17. HEIGHT	18. WEIGHT
25	African American	Male	04/30/85	5'10"	about 160

19. HAIR	20. EYES	21. PHYSICAL DESCRIPTION
Black	Brown	He was wearing a black jacket and black slacks

22. CHARGES
Assault

23. ITEM	24. BRAND	25. SERIAL NUMBER	26. VALUE
Cash			$120

27. ITEM	28. BRAND	29. SERIAL NUMBER	30. VALUE

31. ITEM	32. BRAND	33. SERIAL NUMBER	34. VALUE

35. *Cindy Ryder Badge #450*
SIGNATURE OF OFFICER/BADGE NUMBER

Go on to next page

66. Where does the victim reside?

_____

67. What items were stolen from the victim?

_____

68. What is the victim's date of birth?

_____

69. What is the name of the suspect?

_____

70. What was the suspect wearing?

_____

> *Questions 71 through 75 are based on the following incident report.*

INCIDENT REPORT — POLICE DEPARTMENT

1. ADDRESS OF INCIDENT	2. OFFENSE	3. CODE	4. DATE
Valley Mall parking lot	Armed Robbery	AF-100	June 5

5. NAME OF VICTIM: INDIVIDUAL OR BUSINESS	6. ADDRESS	PHONE
Christina Dalecki	123 Skytop Drive	450-234-9065

7. ASSIGNED OFFICERS/BADGE NUMBERS	8. AGE OF VICTIM	9. RACE OF VICTIM	10. VICTIM'S DATE OF BIRTH
Jamie Harris #314 Fred Layton #610	34	White	03/10/16

11. NAME OF SUSPECT	12. ADDRESS
Unknown	Unknown

13. AGE	14. RACE	15. SEX	16. DATE OF BIRTH	17. HEIGHT	18. WEIGHT
25	White	Male	Unknown	6'	200

19. HAIR	20. EYES	21. PHYSICAL DESCRIPTION
	Green	Wearing a black hoodie, jeans, face mask

22. CHARGES
Robbery

23. ITEM	24. BRAND	25. SERIAL NUMBER	26. VALUE
Cash	N/A	N/A	$90

27. ITEM	28. BRAND	29. SERIAL NUMBER	30. VALUE
Watch			$200

31. ITEM	32. BRAND	33. SERIAL NUMBER	34. VALUE
Ring			$1,500

35. _Jamie Harris #314_
SIGNATURE OF OFFICER/BADGE NUMBER

Go on to next page ⇨

71. What is the victim's name?

_____

72. What was the suspect wearing?

_____

73. What items were stolen?

_____

74. Where did the incident take place?

_____

75. How old is the victim?

_____

STOP DO NOT TURN THE PAGE UNTIL TOLD TO DO SO.
DO NOT RETURN TO A PREVIOUS TEST.

Chapter 16

Answers and Explanations for Practice Test 2

● ●

After you take the practice National Police Officer Selection Test (POST) in Chapter 15, use this chapter to check your answers. If you aren't sure why an answer was incorrect, use this chapter to get explanations of the answers. If you correctly answered a question, you may still want to read the explanations to get a better understanding of the thought process that helped you choose the correct answer. If you're short on time, turn to the end of this chapter to find an abbreviated answer key.

Section 1: Mathematics

1. **C.** To find the total value of all the goods, add $1,000, $400, $2,500, and $500. The answer is $4,400.

2. **D.** To find the total value of all the goods except the computers, add $1,000, $400, and $500. The answer is $1,900.

3. **A.** Divide $11,000, the total retail value, by 20, the number of stereos. The answer is $550.

4. **D.** Subtract 70 from 410, the number of miles Officer Marion drove his patrol motorcycle in five days. Then divide this number, 340, by 4, to find the average number of miles on the remaining days. The answer is 85 miles.

5. **B.** Multiply $680, the average paycheck for a police officer in this town, by 52, the number of weeks in a year. The answer is $35,360.

6. **B.** There are 52 weeks in a year, and Officer Ostrowski is on vacation for 2 weeks, so she visits banks 50 weeks per year. If she visits two banks per week, she visits 100 banks per year.

7. **B.** To find the total value of all the stolen goods, determine the value of each good stolen. The value of two wallets is $60, the value of three cellphones is $450, the value of five gold chains is $500, and the value of one watch is $150. Add these amounts. The answer is $1,160.

8. **C.** To find the value of all the stolen goods except the gold chains, add $60 (the value of the wallets), $450 (the value of the cellphones), and $150 (the value of the watch). The answer is $660.

9. **C.** The gas tank is two-thirds empty, and two-thirds of 18 is 12. Multiply 12 by $1.92, the cost per gallon of gas. The answer is $23.04.

10. **C.** To find Officer McKinley's regular salary per week, multiply $12, his hourly wage, by 40, the number of hours he works. His regular salary is $480. His overtime rate is $18 per hour ($12 × 1½) and he worked 6 hours of overtime. His overtime pay is $108. Add $480 and $108. The answer is $588.

11. **D.** Divide $20,400, the retail value of the ATVs, by 3, the number of ATVs. The retail value of each ATV is $6,800.

12. **D.** When you subtract 120 miles (driven one of the five days) from 720 miles (the total amount driven), you get 600 miles driven in the remaining four days. Divide 600 miles by 4 to get 150, the average number of miles driven on these days.

13. **A.** To find the total value of all the stolen goods, add $50, $350, $500, and $40. The answer is $940.

14. **C.** To find the value of all the stolen goods except the coffee machine and the petty cash box, add $350 and $500. The answer is $850.

15. **E.** Officer Balchune's shift ends at 11 p.m. If she stays until 1:05 a.m., she will have worked 2 hours and 5 minutes of overtime.

16. **D.** Officer Knowles visits schools three times a month for nine months a year. Multiply 3 by 9 to find that he visits schools 27 times a year.

17. **C.** Two-thirds of 30 employees, or 20 employees, use the allowance. The amount of the allowance is $400. Multiply 20 by $400. The answer is $8,000.

18. **D.** To find how many gallons are used each day, divide 69 by 23. The patrol car uses 3 gallons of gas per day. To find out how many gallons it uses in ten days, multiply 3 by 10. The answer is 30.

19. **A.** The total value of the rifles is $29,750. Divide this number by 35, the number of rifles stolen. The answer is $850.

20. **D.** Officer Roland arrived on the scene at 12:02 a.m. She left the scene at 1:05 a.m. The difference between these times is 1 hour and 3 minutes.

Section 11: Reading Comprehension

21. **B.** The fourth paragraph of the passage says that displaying a political sign on a vehicle will result in a $200 fine.

22. **A.** The second paragraph explains that each unit will receive a unit number on the morning of the parade.

23. **D.** The passage does not state that the parade starts on Center or Broad Streets, so Choices (B) and (E) are out. Lucy is not a member of a unit, and the passage says that only those participating in the parade are allowed in the check-in area, so Choices (A) and (C) are also out. The passage says nothing about waiting outside the check-in area, so you can assume that Lucy may wait in an area outside of the check-in area.

24. **B.** Center Street narrows to two lanes near the intersections of Jackson Street and Broad Street, so a large float may have trouble. A small float would not, so the answer is False.

25. **E.** Based on the information in the passage, you can conclude that people in parades sometimes throw candy, treats, and toys to spectators since people in this parade are not allowed to do this.

26. **A.** Welfare fraud is a Class B Nonviolent Felony. The crimes in the other answer choices — gang violence, intimidating a witness, the criminal sale of a firearm, and arson — are Class B Violent Felonies.

27. **B.** This statement is false. Mr. Galli called police at 8:20 p.m., and police arrived at the scene at 8:25 p.m.

28. **B.** There is not enough information in the paragraph to fully complete the incident report.

29. **E.** The second paragraph of the passage reports that 8 percent of all traffic accidents resulted in death.

30. **A.** The last paragraph of the passage states that the Peterson Police Department supports a cellphone ban in Peterson.

31. **C.** The last paragraph says that the fine for a first-time offense would be $75.

32. **A.** According to the last paragraph, a ban on cellphone use would also apply to those on a bicycle or a skateboard.

33. **B.** The only conclusion you can draw is that the majority of accidents in Peterson involved a teen driver. The second paragraph says that 58 percent of all accidents in Peterson involved a teen driver.

34. **C.** Criminally Negligent Manslaughter is a death resulting from a high degree of negligence. A lifeguard's job is to prevent drowning, so not helping a person who is drowning fits this description.

35. **A.** The fourth paragraph of this passage says that commercial garbage collectors may not collect garbage on Saturday and Sunday.

36. **C.** Construction workers are allowed to work between 8:00 a.m. and 6:00 p.m. on Saturday.

37. **B.** A person who violates the noise ordinance for a second time will receive a fine of $100.

38. **A.** The second paragraph says that construction workers cannot work without a Police Commission permit.

39. **B.** The fine for a first offense is $50.

40. **A.** These sections list the items stolen, and this information is given in the paragraph.

41. **B.** The maintenance man's name is Roy White. Jacob Cane is one of the officers investigating the scene.

42. **B.** A person may only operate a motorized scooter on private property. A driveway is private property.

43. **A.** Only minors must wear a helmet.

44. **D.** The fifth paragraph of the passage says that operating low-power devices at speeds higher than 35 miles per hour is illegal.

45. **C.** The second paragraph says that a motorized scooter is controlled by an upright steering handle attached to the front wheel.

Section III: Grammar

46. **B.** *Affect* is a verb and is correct because the blank needs to tell you what the reduction in staff did not *do*. *Effect* is a noun.

47. **C.** *Too* means *in addition to* or *also*. It is correct in this sentence; Sergeant Cosgrove told Officer Castillo to also interview the witness.

48. **A.** *Each,* the subject of the sentence, is singular and requires a singular noun. *Is* is the correct verb in this sentence.

49. **B.** This sentence has a compound subject, but you can leave Sergeant Green out of it to see whether *me* or *I* is correct. You would say "I responded to the call," so *I* is correct in this sentence.

50. **B.** *Children* is plural. To make it possessive, add *'s.*

51. **B.** *Loose* is an adverb that describes how the subject breaks away, and it's correct in this sentence. *Lose* is a verb.

52. **A.** Because the subject of the sentence, *officers,* is plural, a plural auxiliary word (also called a helping verb) is needed. *Have* is the correct answer.

53. **B.** The possessive pronoun *its* is correct in this sentence. *It's* is a contraction meaning *it is.* *Its'* is not a word, because you cannot have a plural *it.*

54. **C.** *Site* is the correct noun here. *Sight* refers to vision, and *cite* is a verb that means *to make a notation.*

55. **B.** The plural of *family* is *families.* There is no need to make it possessive.

56. **D.** The correct spelling is *accommodate.*

57. **B.** The correct spelling is *committed.*

58. **B.** The correct spelling is *conscious.*

59. **A.** The correct spelling is *apparent.*

60. **B.** The correct spelling is *cruiser.*

61. **E.** All words in this sentence are spelled correctly.

62. **A.** The correct spelling is *immediate.*

63. **A.** The correct spelling is *judgment.*

64. **B.** The correct spelling is *harass.*

65. **D.** The correct spelling is *possession.*

Section IV: Incident Report Writing

66. The victim resides at 1 May Street.

67. Cash in the amount of $120 was stolen from the victim.

68. The victim's date of birth is September 14, 1985.

69. The suspect's name is Ian Ketron.

70. The suspect was wearing a black jacket and black slacks.

71. The victim's name is Christina Dalecki.

72. The suspect was wearing a black hooded jacket, jeans, and a face mask.

73. The items stolen were cash, a watch, and a ring.

74. The incident took place in the parking lot of Valley Mall.

75. The victim is 34 years old.

Answer Key for Practice Test 2

Section 1

1. C	8. C	15. E
2. D	9. C	16. D
3. A	10. C	17. C
4. D	11. D	18. D
5. B	12. D	19. A
6. B	13. A	20. D
7. B	14. C	

Section II

21. B	30. A	39. B
22. A	31. C	40. A
23. D	32. A	41. B
24. B	33. B	42. B
25. E	34. C	43. A
26. A	35. A	44. D
27. B	36. C	45. C
28. B	37. B	
29. E	38. A	

Section III

46. B	53. B	60. B
47. C	54. C	61. E
48. A	55. B	62. A
49. B	56. D	63. A
50. B	57. B	64. B
51. B	58. B	65. D
52. A	59. A	

Chapter 17

Practice Test 3: The National Police Officer Selection Test (POST)

• •

*P*ractice Test 3 is modeled after the National Police Officer Selection Test (POST). Many police departments use the POST to screen job candidates. The POST has four sections, and each section is separately timed. Time yourself as you complete each section of this practice test or have someone else tell you when to begin and when your time is up. While it's fine to take a break between sections, try to complete the entire test in one day, as you would the actual test.

Section	Test	Number of Items	Time
1	Mathematics	20	20 minutes
2	Reading Comprehension	25	25 minutes
3	Grammar	20	15 minutes
4	Incident Report Writing	10	15 minutes

Sections 1, 2, and 3 of Practice Test 3 contain multiple-choice and true-and-false questions. Section 4, Incident Report Writing, contains open-ended questions for which you write out your answers in grammatically correct sentences.

Use a number-two pencil and mark your answers for Sections 1, 2, and 3 on the following answer sheet. Make sure your marks are heavy and completely fill in the oval. Completely erase any marks that you wish to change. Be sure to blacken only one oval for each question, and be sure that you're blackening the oval for the correct question. It's easy to skip a question and become confused when marking your answers on the answer sheet. While this answer sheet won't be computer scored like the answer sheet on the actual POST, pretending that it will be helps you better prepare for the exam. For Section 4, write your answers on the lines underneath each question.

Pace yourself as you work through the questions on Practice Test 3 so that you have enough time to complete all the questions. Don't spend too much time on one question. Try to answer every question on this test. If a question really stumps you, take a good guess and move on. Your score is based on the number of questions you answer correctly, so there is no penalty for guessing.

You won't be allowed to use a calculator on the actual POST, but you will be given scratch paper. Use scratch paper to work your way through the problems on this practice test.

After you complete the entire sample test, check your answers against the answers and explanations in Chapter 18. Be sure to read the answer explanations for all questions — even those that you've answered correctly. Doing so helps you learn more about the test and gives you an extra edge on the actual POST. Note that on the actual POST, you need an overall score of 70 to pass and move on to the next stage in the hiring process.

To determine your overall score, figure out your score on each section: Questions in the Reading Comprehension section (25 questions) are worth 4 points each, questions in the Mathematics and Grammar sections (40 questions) are worth 5 points each, and questions in the Incident Report Writing section (10 questions) are worth 10 points each. Add your scores together and divide by 4 to determine your overall score.

Answer Sheet for Practice Test 3

1 Ⓐ Ⓑ Ⓒ Ⓓ Ⓔ	21 Ⓐ Ⓑ Ⓒ Ⓓ Ⓔ	41 Ⓐ Ⓑ Ⓒ Ⓓ Ⓔ	61 Ⓐ Ⓑ Ⓒ Ⓓ Ⓔ
2 Ⓐ Ⓑ Ⓒ Ⓓ Ⓔ	22 Ⓐ Ⓑ Ⓒ Ⓓ Ⓔ	42 Ⓐ Ⓑ Ⓒ Ⓓ Ⓔ	62 Ⓐ Ⓑ Ⓒ Ⓓ Ⓔ
3 Ⓐ Ⓑ Ⓒ Ⓓ Ⓔ	23 Ⓐ Ⓑ Ⓒ Ⓓ Ⓔ	43 Ⓐ Ⓑ Ⓒ Ⓓ Ⓔ	63 Ⓐ Ⓑ Ⓒ Ⓓ Ⓔ
4 Ⓐ Ⓑ Ⓒ Ⓓ Ⓔ	24 Ⓐ Ⓑ Ⓒ Ⓓ Ⓔ	44 Ⓐ Ⓑ Ⓒ Ⓓ Ⓔ	64 Ⓐ Ⓑ Ⓒ Ⓓ Ⓔ
5 Ⓐ Ⓑ Ⓒ Ⓓ Ⓔ	25 Ⓐ Ⓑ Ⓒ Ⓓ Ⓔ	45 Ⓐ Ⓑ Ⓒ Ⓓ Ⓔ	65 Ⓐ Ⓑ Ⓒ Ⓓ Ⓔ
6 Ⓐ Ⓑ Ⓒ Ⓓ Ⓔ	26 Ⓐ Ⓑ Ⓒ Ⓓ Ⓔ	46 Ⓐ Ⓑ Ⓒ Ⓓ Ⓔ	
7 Ⓐ Ⓑ Ⓒ Ⓓ Ⓔ	27 Ⓐ Ⓑ Ⓒ Ⓓ Ⓔ	47 Ⓐ Ⓑ Ⓒ Ⓓ Ⓔ	
8 Ⓐ Ⓑ Ⓒ Ⓓ Ⓔ	28 Ⓐ Ⓑ Ⓒ Ⓓ Ⓔ	48 Ⓐ Ⓑ Ⓒ Ⓓ Ⓔ	
9 Ⓐ Ⓑ Ⓒ Ⓓ Ⓔ	29 Ⓐ Ⓑ Ⓒ Ⓓ Ⓔ	49 Ⓐ Ⓑ Ⓒ Ⓓ Ⓔ	
10 Ⓐ Ⓑ Ⓒ Ⓓ Ⓔ	30 Ⓐ Ⓑ Ⓒ Ⓓ Ⓔ	50 Ⓐ Ⓑ Ⓒ Ⓓ Ⓔ	
11 Ⓐ Ⓑ Ⓒ Ⓓ Ⓔ	31 Ⓐ Ⓑ Ⓒ Ⓓ Ⓔ	51 Ⓐ Ⓑ Ⓒ Ⓓ Ⓔ	
12 Ⓐ Ⓑ Ⓒ Ⓓ Ⓔ	32 Ⓐ Ⓑ Ⓒ Ⓓ Ⓔ	52 Ⓐ Ⓑ Ⓒ Ⓓ Ⓔ	
13 Ⓐ Ⓑ Ⓒ Ⓓ Ⓔ	33 Ⓐ Ⓑ Ⓒ Ⓓ Ⓔ	53 Ⓐ Ⓑ Ⓒ Ⓓ Ⓔ	
14 Ⓐ Ⓑ Ⓒ Ⓓ Ⓔ	34 Ⓐ Ⓑ Ⓒ Ⓓ Ⓔ	54 Ⓐ Ⓑ Ⓒ Ⓓ Ⓔ	
15 Ⓐ Ⓑ Ⓒ Ⓓ Ⓔ	35 Ⓐ Ⓑ Ⓒ Ⓓ Ⓔ	55 Ⓐ Ⓑ Ⓒ Ⓓ Ⓔ	
16 Ⓐ Ⓑ Ⓒ Ⓓ Ⓔ	36 Ⓐ Ⓑ Ⓒ Ⓓ Ⓔ	56 Ⓐ Ⓑ Ⓒ Ⓓ Ⓔ	
17 Ⓐ Ⓑ Ⓒ Ⓓ Ⓔ	37 Ⓐ Ⓑ Ⓒ Ⓓ Ⓔ	57 Ⓐ Ⓑ Ⓒ Ⓓ Ⓔ	
18 Ⓐ Ⓑ Ⓒ Ⓓ Ⓔ	38 Ⓐ Ⓑ Ⓒ Ⓓ Ⓔ	58 Ⓐ Ⓑ Ⓒ Ⓓ Ⓔ	
19 Ⓐ Ⓑ Ⓒ Ⓓ Ⓔ	39 Ⓐ Ⓑ Ⓒ Ⓓ Ⓔ	59 Ⓐ Ⓑ Ⓒ Ⓓ Ⓔ	
20 Ⓐ Ⓑ Ⓒ Ⓓ Ⓔ	40 Ⓐ Ⓑ Ⓒ Ⓓ Ⓔ	60 Ⓐ Ⓑ Ⓒ Ⓓ Ⓔ	

Section 1

Mathematics

Time: 20 minutes

Directions: In this section of the exam, you are provided with situations that require the use of basic arithmetic. Read each situation and solve the problem. You may not use a calculator in this section, but you may use scratch paper.

1. Burglars broke into an electronics store and left with four flat-screen televisions with a total retail value of $8,400. What is the average retail value of each flat-screen television?

   (A) $2,100

   (B) $2,200

   (C) $2,300

   (D) $2,800

   (E) $4,200

2. The average paycheck for a police officer in a certain town is $740 per week before taxes. What is the six-month salary for a police officer in this town?

   (A) $4,440

   (B) $17,760

   (C) $18,240

   (D) $19,240

   (E) $38,480

3. During one three-day period, Officer White drove his patrol motorcycle 200 miles. If he drove 50 miles on one day, how many miles did he average on each of the other two days?

   (A) 50 miles

   (B) 75 miles

   (C) 100 miles

   (D) 150 miles

   (E) 200 miles

Questions 4 and 5 are based on the following information.

In preparing a report on a burglary in a home, Sergeant Mosby lists the following stolen items and their values:

Televisions	$1,500
Cash	$250
Computer	$800
China	$300

4. What is the value of the televisions and the computer?

   (A) $1,300

   (B) $1,400

   (C) $2,300

   (D) $2,400

   (E) $2,600

5. What is the total value of all the stolen goods?

   (A) $1,450

   (B) $1,650

   (C) $2,450

   (D) $2,650

   (E) $2,850

Go on to next page

6. Officer Grimes visits local businesses as part of a workplace security program. If Officer Grimes visits 4 area businesses every week except for her two-week vacation, how many businesses does she visit in one year?

   (A) 50

   (B) 75

   (C) 100

   (D) 200

   (E) 250

7. Officer Malone typically works the 3 p.m. to 11 p.m. shift but must work until 2:30 a.m. because of a special training program. Assuming he works his entire shift, how much overtime can Officer Malone report for that day?

   (A) 2 hours and 30 minutes

   (B) 3 hours

   (C) 3 hours and 30 minutes

   (D) 4 hours

   (E) 4 hours and 30 minutes

8. If a gas tank in a patrol car holds 17 gallons, and premium-grade gasoline costs $2.10 per gallon, how much will it cost to fill the tank (assuming that the tank is ½ empty)?

   (A) $17.00

   (B) $17.75

   (C) $17.85

   (D) $17.95

   (E) $35.70

9. Officer Rawlings earns $14 an hour before taxes for the first 40 hours he works each week. After this, he earns time-and-a-half pay. He worked 43 hours this week. What is his pay before taxes?

   (A) $560

   (B) $623

   (C) $624

   (D) $633

   (E) $634

10. A 40-member police force reported that 5 percent of its officers were injured on the job last year. How many officers were injured?

    (A) 1

    (B) 2

    (C) 3

    (D) 4

    (E) 5

Questions 11 and 12 are based on the following information.

In preparing a report on a burglary at a restaurant, an officer lists the following stolen items and their values:

Cash register	$750
Sculpture	$250
Drink mixers	$100
Television	$400

11. What is the total value of the stolen goods?

    (A) $1,500

    (B) $1,550

    (C) $1,600

    (D) $1,650

    (E) $1,675

12. What is the value of all the stolen goods *except* the cash register?

    (A) $500

    (B) $600

    (C) $650

    (D) $700

    (E) $750

13. Burglars broke into a sporting goods store and stole six kayaks with a total retail value of $2,544. What is the average retail price of each kayak?

    (A) $423

    (B) $424

    (C) $426

    (D) $433

    (E) $434

Go on to next page

14. Officer Taylor received a domestic disturbance call at 2:45 p.m. and arrived at the scene at 2:52 p.m. Believing the incident to be fabricated, Officer Taylor left the scene at 3:10 p.m. How much time elapsed from the time of the call and the time when she left the scene?

    (A) 10 minutes

    (B) 15 minutes

    (C) 20 minutes

    (D) 25 minutes

    (E) 30 minutes

15. A 45-person police department will provide safety vests for any officer who requests one. Each safety vest costs the department $725. If 38 officers request the vests, how much will this cost the department?

    (A) $26,450

    (B) $26,550

    (C) $27,550

    (D) $27,650

    (E) $32,625

16. If a patrol car averages 25 miles per gallon of gasoline and is driven 75 miles per day, how many gallons of gasoline does it need for 20 work days?

    (A) 40

    (B) 45

    (C) 50

    (D) 60

    (E) 65

17. Employees on a 60-person police force are asked to complete five hours of training per month for one year. Two-thirds of the employees on this police force meet this requirement. How many hours of training were completed by this police force?

    (A) 2,000

    (B) 2,200

    (C) 2,400

    (D) 3,400

    (E) 3,600

18. During a 15-day period, two officers drove their patrol car 1,215 miles. If they drove 90 miles on one day, how many miles did they average on each of the other days?

    (A) 75

    (B) 80

    (C) 85

    (D) 90

    (E) 100

19. Burglars broke into a home and stole six diamond rings with a total retail value of $6,600. What is the average retail value of each ring?

    (A) $660

    (B) $1,000

    (C) $1,010

    (D) $1,100

    (E) $2,010

20. A police officer apprehends a thief trying to steal a backpack. Upon investigation, the arresting officer finds that the thief is carrying five stolen lobster tails, two pounds of frozen shrimp, and three pounds of crab legs. According to the chart below, what is the total cost of the recovered items?

Item	Value
1 lobster tail	$15.00
1 pound shrimp	$8.00
1 pound crab legs	$10.00

    (A) $120.00

    (B) $121.00

    (C) $131.00

    (D) $132.00

    (E) $133.00

STOP DO NOT TURN THE PAGE UNTIL TOLD TO DO SO.
DO NOT RETURN TO A PREVIOUS TEST.

Section 11

Reading Comprehension

Time: 25 minutes

Directions: This section measures reading comprehension. Read the passages relating to police duty, and then answer the questions that follow. No prior knowledge of law or law enforcement is needed to answer these questions.

The passages in this section are not intended to represent the actual laws of any particular state. The passages present potential rules and laws relating to police work.

Three types of questions appear in this section:

✔ True/False questions that ask you to determine a statement's accuracy based on the information presented in the passage or sample report form

✔ Questions that ask you to choose the correct answer according to the information presented in the passage or sample report form

✔ Questions that ask you to choose the alternative that best completes the sentence, based on the information in the passage or on the report form

Questions 21 through 25 are based on the following passage.

The Mayberry Town Council has unanimously approved a new recycling ordinance. This ordinance will reduce the amount of waste the city currently sends to Sanders Landfill. Recycling ordinances like this one have been implemented in other cities and towns throughout the state with great success.

The following schedule shows when the new recycling ordinance will take effect:

January 1: All single-family residences

January 15: Multifamily residential facilities with up to 49 residential units

January 30: Multifamily residential facilities with at least 50 but not more than 99 residential units

March 30: Multifamily residential facilities with 100 or more residential units

All residences must pick up a blue recycling container at City Hall. Containers will be available two weeks before your recycling implementation date (see schedule above). Residents may choose a 96-gallon container, a 64-gallon container, or a 32-gallon container. Please do not take containers with you if you move to another city. Recycling containers are the property of Mayberry. Residents will place filled containers curbside on their regular garbage collection day.

Go on to next page

The following items may be put into recycling containers: glass and plastic bottles and jars, empty aerosol cans, cardboard, aluminum cans, aluminum foil, foil trays, paper bags, metal cans, phone books, paper or frozen food boxes, mail, magazines, paper, and catalogs.

These items may NOT be put into recycling containers: glassware, milk cartons, juice boxes, clothing, textiles, shoes, plastic pots, ceramics, plastic grocery bags, batteries, plastic cups and utensils, Styrofoam, and hazardous product containers.

The Mayberry Police Department would like to remind residents that the new recycling program is not optional — it is mandatory. Those who do not participate may be fined as much as $500 per year. Records will be kept of households not participating in the recycling program.

21. According to the passage, a resident who lives in an apartment complex with 75 units will begin the recycling program on

    (A) January 1

    (B) January 15

    (C) January 30

    (D) March 15

    (E) March 30

22. According to the passage, which of the following items may be put in a recycling container?

    (A) A plastic pot

    (B) A catalog

    (C) A milk carton

    (D) A juice box

    (E) A plastic cup

23. If you move to another city, you should take your blue recycling container with you.

    (A) True

    (B) False

24. All households in Mayberry must participate in the recycling program, or they risk being fined.

    (A) True

    (B) False

25. According to the passage, which of the following statements is true?

    (A) Only single-family residents must participate in the recycling program.

    (B) Residents of Mayberry may recycle old clothing.

    (C) Most residential facilities in Mayberry are multifamily.

    (D) Few residents of Mayberry recycled in the past.

    (E) Residents of Mayberry may choose the size of their recycling container.

Go on to next page

> Question 26 is based on the following passage. Do not assume anything to be true that is not stated in the passage or in the question.

Many states have specific laws dealing with drunk driving offenses. These laws often result in additional penalties to the person who is convicted of a drunk driving offense. The following are some of these laws:

Child endangerment: An individual who has driven under the influence with a minor in the car is subject to a separate offense or a harsher DUI/DWI penalty.

Felony DUI: An individual who has a number of previous convictions may be charged with a felony, which has a mandatory prison sentence of a year or more.

Dram shop: Under this law, owners of establishments who sell alcohol to obviously intoxicated persons who cause death or injury to third parties in alcohol-related crashes are held liable.

High blood alcohol content laws: An individual is subject to increased penalties for driving with a blood alcohol concentration of .15 or higher at the time of arrest.

Social host: An individual who serves alcohol to persons who are obviously intoxicated and are involved in third-party crashes is held liable.

26. Which of the following best describes a *social host?*

(A) Hailey's friend Rich gives her beer even though she is drunk, and Hailey is later involved in an automobile accident.

(B) Jason is served drinks at a bar after hours and is later involved in an accident resulting in a fatality.

(C) A waitress serves Juanita wine even though the waitress can see that Juanita is intoxicated.

(D) A bartender serves Eliot alcohol even though Eliot is obviously intoxicated and driving home with a minor in the car.

(E) Enrico is involved in a fatal automobile crash and his blood alcohol content is higher than .15.

Go on to next page

Questions 27 and 28 are based on the following incident report form and incident description.

INCIDENT REPORT — POLICE DEPARTMENT

1. ADDRESS OF INCIDENT	2. OFFENSE	3. CODE	4. DATE

5. NAME OF VICTIM: INDIVIDUAL OR BUSINESS	6. ADDRESS	PHONE

7. ASSIGNED OFFICERS/BADGE NUMBERS	8. AGE OF VICTIM	9. RACE OF VICTIM	10. VICTIM'S DATE OF BIRTH

11. NAME OF SUSPECT	12. ADDRESS

13. AGE	14. RACE	15. SEX	16. DATE OF BIRTH	17. HEIGHT	18. WEIGHT

19. HAIR	20. EYES	21. PHYSICAL DESCRIPTION

22. CHARGES

23. ITEM	24. BRAND	25. SERIAL NUMBER	26. VALUE
27. ITEM	28. BRAND	29. SERIAL NUMBER	30. VALUE
31. ITEM	32. BRAND	33. SERIAL NUMBER	34. VALUE

35. _____
SIGNATURE OF OFFICER/BADGE NUMBER

Jim Martin, a teacher who lives at 567 Broad Street, was unlocking his car in the Madison High School parking lot when he was approached by a man with a knife. The man stole his wallet, his watch, his cellphone, and his wedding ring. Mr. Martin went back inside the school and called police at 5:35 p.m., on Friday, November 12, to report the incident. Officers Pat Conahan and Joseph DeSanto arrived at the scene at 5:42 p.m. to investigate. Mr. Martin identified the suspect as Thom Fischer. Fischer is 23 years old, and about 5 feet 6 inches tall. He was wearing a brown leather jacket.

27. Sections 19 and 20 on the incident report can be completed based on the information in the paragraph.

(A) True

(B) False

28. The victim's name was Thom Fischer.

(A) True

(B) False

Go on to next page

Questions 29 through 33 are based on the following passage.

Lakeland Township officials are planning to reexamine the township's open burning policy at a special meeting this month, which is open to the public. Officials are considering passing a new ordinance that would eliminate virtually all open burning.

Open burning is the burning of unwanted waste, such as garbage, paper, trees, leaves, grass, and other debris. The Environmental Protection Agency (EPA) reports that such burning emits a large amount of toxic chemicals into the air. Smoke from 5 pounds of leaves contains about 1 pound of air pollution.

Open burning can cause health problems such as eye, nose, and throat irritation. Other problems caused by open burning include shortness of breath and coughing, stomach or intestinal upset, headaches and memory loss, skin burns and irritations, and eye damage.

Open burning in Lakeland Township is presently permitted on Wednesdays and Saturdays from noon until 8 p.m. from Memorial Day through Labor Day.

The ordinance would make it illegal for Lakeland Township residents to burn solid waste in metal drums, incinerators, and in outdoor fireplaces and fire pits. The ordinance would allow campfires under 30 inches in diameter and fires started to cook food while camping. Supervised fires would be permitted such as those started to train fire personnel or to clear fields. Officials contend that open burning threatens residents' health, safety, and security. They also note that several forest fires over the past few years have started from open burning.

If the ordinance is passed, violators could face both civil and criminal penalties. A violator should expect a fine of not less than $100, but not more than $2,500. Those who cannot pay the fine will serve 90 days of imprisonment for each offense.

Persons wanting to attend the meeting should contact City Hall for more information.

29. According to the passage, what type of fires will be allowed under the new ordinance?

(A) Fires to burn leaves

(B) Fires to burn paper

(C) Fires in fire pits

(D) Small campfires

(E) Incinerator fires

30. According to the passage, until the ordinance is passed, what would happen to a resident of Lakeland Township who burns garbage in a backyard drum on a Wednesday afternoon in the summer?

(A) The resident would receive a fine of at least $100.

(B) The resident would face both civil and criminal penalties.

(C) The resident would be allowed to burn the garbage.

(D) The resident would receive a fine of less than $2,500.

(E) The resident would go to prison for 90 days.

Go on to next page

31. Smoke from 10 pounds of leaves contains about 2 pounds of air pollution.

    (A) True

    (B) False

32. Under the new ordinance, a person who is caught burning leaves would receive

    (A) a fine of $100.

    (B) a fine that is between $100 and $2,500.

    (C) a mandatory prison sentence of 90 days.

    (D) no punishment.

    (E) a fine of $2,500.

33. According to the passage, which of the following is accurate?

    (A) Open burning is now allowed in Lakeland Township during the winter.

    (B) Open burning can cause breathing problems.

    (C) Burning to clear fields does not cause health problems.

    (D) The new ordinance does not allow fires to cook food.

    (E) The EPA supports open burning in some instances.

Question 34 is based on the following passage. Do not assume anything to be true that is not stated in the passage or in the question.

Simple assault: To knowingly or recklessly cause or attempt to cause physical harm to someone without the use of a weapon

Aggravated assault: To attack a person with the intention of causing severe bodily injury, often with the use of a weapon

Weapons law violations: To unlawfully manufacture, sell, or possess a deadly weapon; to carry a deadly weapon; to furnish such weapons to minors

Larceny–theft: To unlawfully take property from another through pocket picking, purse snatching, and shoplifting; also includes thefts of motor vehicles, motor vehicle parts, and bicycles

34. Which of the following best describes *simple assault?*

    (A) A man injures several co-workers when he hits them with a baseball bat.

    (B) A man points a gun at the driver of a car and steals the car.

    (C) A high school girl punches another girl in the face several times.

    (D) A woman enters a mall armed with an illegal pistol.

    (E) A man with a gun opens fire in a crowded restaurant.

Go on to next page

Questions 35 through 39 are based on the following passage.

With summer quickly approaching, the Seaside Beach Police Department would like to remind residents and visitors of the following ordinances. These ordinances apply to the public beach, which is the area between the Atlantic Ocean and the closest property line of properties owned by private individuals or corporations.

It is illegal to drive any type of vehicle on Seaside Beach. The only exceptions are city police and emergency vehicles. To launch and load boats, vehicles may access the public beach at Second Street. Vehicles may remain in this area only temporarily for the limited purpose of launching or loading a boat. Parking is prohibited. This area is closed from sunset to sunrise April 1 through September 15.

Visitors of Seaside Beach are expected to behave responsibly. It is illegal to sleep on the beach between the hours of 9 p.m. and sunrise. All persons are responsible for removing their own trash. Glass containers are not allowed on the beach. No alcoholic beverages, controlled substances, or persons under the influence are allowed on the beach. Animals are not allowed on the beach from April 1 through September 15. No fires are allowed on the beach. Smoking is also prohibited. While guests may play music on the beach, it should be played at a low volume so as not to disturb those nearby. Profanity is prohibited. Fishing is allowed on the beach before 9:30 a.m. and after 6:30 p.m.

Parking is not allowed on the roads leading up to Seaside Beach. The speed limit on these roads is 15 miles per hour. Roadways must not be blocked at any time.

Swimming is only allowed when lifeguards are on duty. Weather permitting, lifeguards will be stationed at the beach from 9 a.m. to 6 p.m. seven days a week.

Any violator of these ordinances is subject to a fine of $25 for each offense, payable to the town of Seaside Beach. Frequent violations may lead to suspension of beach privileges.

35. According to the passage, which is a violation of the beach ordinances?

(A) Fishing at 8:30 a.m.

(B) Swimming at 8 a.m.

(C) Playing music at a low volume

(D) Launching a boat at Second Street

(E) Sleeping on the beach at 11 a.m.

36. According to the passage, which person on the beach is in violation of the new ordinances?

(A) A man walking his dog in March

(B) A woman launching her boat at noon in April

(C) A woman drinking a soda from a glass container

(D) A child eating an ice-cream cone

(E) A man eating a cheeseburger on a plastic plate

37. According to the passage, which of the following statements is accurate?

(A) Smoking is never allowed on the beach.

(B) Swimming is always allowed on the beach.

(C) Fishing is always allowed on the beach.

(D) Sleeping is never allowed on the beach.

(E) Fires are sometimes allowed on the beach.

38. A woman who parks on a road leading up to the beach will receive a fine of $25.

(A) True

(B) False

39. Those wanting to launch a boat should access the beach at Second Street.

(A) True

(B) False

Go on to next page

> *Questions 40 and 41 are based on the following incident report form and incident description.*

INCIDENT REPORT — POLICE DEPARTMENT

1. ADDRESS OF INCIDENT	2. OFFENSE	3. CODE	4. DATE

| 5. NAME OF VICTIM: INDIVIDUAL OR BUSINESS | 6. ADDRESS   PHONE | | |

7. ASSIGNED OFFICERS/BADGE NUMBERS	8. AGE OF VICTIM	9. RACE OF VICTIM	10. VICTIM'S DATE OF BIRTH

11. NAME OF SUSPECT	12. ADDRESS

13. AGE	14. RACE	15. SEX	16. DATE OF BIRTH	17. HEIGHT	18. WEIGHT

19. HAIR	20. EYES	21. PHYSICAL DESCRIPTION

22. CHARGES

23. ITEM	24. BRAND	25. SERIAL NUMBER	26. VALUE
27. ITEM	28. BRAND	29. SERIAL NUMBER	30. VALUE
31. ITEM	32. BRAND	33. SERIAL NUMBER	34. VALUE

35. _____
SIGNATURE OF OFFICER/BADGE NUMBER

Latisha DeYan, who owns the deli at the corner of Market and North Streets, called police headquarters at 11:10 a.m. to report that an angry customer had thrown a rock through the front window of the deli. Officers Garrett Gad and Courtney Soltis arrived at the scene to investigate at 11:16 a.m. Ms. DeYan identified the man as Gene Samsell. Samsell was wearing a green jacket and tan pants. He is about 65 years old, has gray hair, and blue eyes. Ms. DeYan does not know where he lives.

40. The incident report can be fully completed based on the information in the paragraph.

(A) True

(B) False

41. Ms. DeYan called police at 11:16 a.m.

(A) True

(B) False

Go on to next page

Questions 42 through 45 are based on the following passage.

Police in Sheraton are enforcing a new sign ordinance. The ordinance was passed to eliminate unattractive signs in the city because such signs deter businesses from relocating to the city.

The new ordinance bans portable signs, including those with arrows and lights. It also bans signs that include the words "stop" and "danger" to attract the attention of passersby. Other signs prohibited under the ban include those that interfere with traffic, make noise, have movable parts, or project light beams. Signs with reflectors and those that revolve, rotate, or swing are not allowed under the new ordinance.

Other signs prohibited by the new ordinance include those that extend higher than the roof of a building. Signs comprised of manmade materials and displayed on the surface of the ground are now banned. Signs containing profanity are strictly prohibited, and signs on vehicles are not allowed.

Signs allowed under the new ordinance include those mounted to the front of businesses identifying the business and/or its street address. Historical markers are permitted. Businesses may display a corporate flag showing a company logo if they also display the U.S. flag. The business flag should be no larger than the U.S. flag.

Sheraton city officials recommend that signs be rectangular and only as large as they need to be to contain their message. However, larger signs are not prohibited.

When police determine that a business is in violation of the new sign ordinance, police will notify the business in writing that it has ten days to remove the sign. They will also fine the business $100. If the business does not remove the sign after ten days, business owners will face court charges. They will also be fined $100 for each additional day the sign remains.

42. According to the passage, which of the following signs is allowed under the new sign ordinance?

(A) A sign higher than a roof

(B) A sign on a vehicle

(C) A sign that rotates

(D) A rectangular sign on a building

(E) A ground sign made of manmade materials

43. A business may display a flag with a company logo as long as the business also displays the U.S. flag.

(A) True

(B) False

44. According to the passage, which of the following signs is a violation of the new ordinance?

(A) A historical marker

(B) A rectangular sign

(C) A sign with a street address

(D) A sign with the name of a business

(E) A sign using the word "stop"

45. According to the passage, which of the following statements is accurate?

(A) A business violating the sign ordinance must face court charges.

(B) A business violating the sign ordinance for the first time must pay $100.

(C) Signs on the ground containing manmade materials are allowed.

(D) Signs with reflectors and lights are permitted.

(E) Most businesses in the city use portable signs.

STOP DO NOT TURN THE PAGE UNTIL TOLD TO DO SO.
DO NOT RETURN TO A PREVIOUS TEST.

Section III

Grammar

Time: 15 minutes

Directions: This section of the exam tests your knowledge of grammar, punctuation, and spelling. Choose the best answer for each question, following the specific instructions for each subsection.

For Questions 46 through 55, choose the alternative that correctly fills in the blank. Be sure to read carefully any text appearing before or after the blank, because the right answer may be dependent on it.

46. The children _____ always liked Officer Murphy.

    (A) has

    (B) have

    (C) is

    (D) are

47. Once the car was in the lieutenant's _____, he knew it had been reported stolen.

    (A) sight

    (B) cite

    (C) site

48. _____ citizens respect our town's police force.

    (A) Us

    (B) We

49. Officer Gale said she will attend the _____ meeting.

    (A) women

    (B) womens'

    (C) women's

50. Officer Perez said that those who were arrested know _____ rights.

    (A) there

    (B) their

    (C) they're

51. If you are part of a community, you need to obey _____ laws.

    (A) its

    (B) it's

    (C) its'

52. The man _____ wearing a blue jacket is the lieutenant.

    (A) who's

    (B) whose

53. There _____ two sides to every story.

    (A) is

    (B) are

54. Sergeant Blake told Harry and _____ to carefully follow his directions.

    (A) I

    (B) me

55. The riot had a devastating _____ on the town.

    (A) effect

    (B) affect

Go on to next page

> For Questions 56 through 65, choose the answer that identifies the misspelled word in each sentence.

56. The principal of the school said she considered it an honor and a priveledge to have worked in such a wonderful community for so many years.

    (A) principal

    (B) considered

    (C) honor

    (D) priveledge

    (E) community

57. The mischeivous adolescents had spray painted graffiti on the front and side of the newly constructed garage.

    (A) mischeivous

    (B) adolescents

    (C) graffiti

    (D) constructed

    (E) None of the above

58. Officer Santos found it difficult to arrive at her scheduled time because the name of the avenue was mispelled on her directions.

    (A) difficult

    (B) scheduled

    (C) avenue

    (D) mispelled

    (E) directions

59. Sergeant Farrell questioned the building's maintenence manager as well as several tenants who overheard the commotion.

    (A) questioned

    (B) maintenence

    (C) tenants

    (D) commotion

    (E) None of the above

60. Three officers who had been in the vicinity quickly responded to the call about a firey crash on the interstate involving an overturned trailer.

    (A) vicinity

    (B) responded

    (C) firey

    (D) interstate

    (E) trailer

61. Officer Garrett found it humourous that the criminal had managed to become caught in the fence when he was trying to escape.

    (A) humourous

    (B) managed

    (C) caught

    (D) escape

    (E) None of the above

62. In her leizure time, Officer Wudarski enjoys bicycling to new places and vacationing in the mountains near her community.

    (A) leizure

    (B) bicycling

    (C) vacationing

    (D) mountains

    (E) community

63. The members of the police department appreciated the new patrol cars and were especially gratefull for the police dog.

    (A) department

    (B) appreciated

    (C) especially

    (D) gratefull

    (E) None of the above

Go on to next page

64. Sergeant Freeman ocasionally liked to patrol the town's square on motorcycle, particularly when a special event was taking place.

    (A) ocasionally

    (B) motorcycle

    (C) particularly

    (D) special

    (E) event

65. Officer Lang did not see an immediatte need to take the disheveled man into custody even though he admitted to being at the scene of the crime.

    (A) immediatte

    (B) disheveled

    (C) admitted

    (D) scene

    (E) None of the above

STOP DO NOT TURN THE PAGE UNTIL TOLD TO DO SO.
DO NOT RETURN TO A PREVIOUS TEST.

Section IV

Incident Report Writing

Time: 15 minutes

Directions: This section tests your writing skills. The following is a completed sample incident report form. Use the information contained on the form to answer the questions that follow. You should write your answers in the spaces provided. All your answers must contain the correct information and be written in complete sentences. The sentences must be grammatically correct, and all words should be spelled correctly.

Questions 66 through 70 are based on the following incident report form.

INCIDENT REPORT — POLICE DEPARTMENT

1. ADDRESS OF INCIDENT	2. OFFENSE	3. CODE	4. DATE
9 Beverly Avenue	Burglary	A6-120	July 10

5. NAME OF VICTIM: INDIVIDUAL OR BUSINESS	6. ADDRESS PHONE
Nick Carver	9 Beverly Avenue

7. ASSIGNED OFFICERS/BADGE NUMBERS	8. AGE OF VICTIM	9. RACE OF VICTIM	10. VICTIM'S DATE OF BIRTH
Dick Wilson #900 Karen Stella #610	61	White	02/20/43

11. NAME OF SUSPECT	12. ADDRESS
Suzanne Angelone	15 Beverly Avenue

13. AGE	14. RACE	15. SEX	16. DATE OF BIRTH	17. HEIGHT	18. WEIGHT
35	White	F		5'10"	200

19. HAIR	20. EYES	21. PHYSICAL DESCRIPTION
Black	Blue	She was wearing black sweatpants and a green sweatshirt

22. CHARGES
Burglary

23. ITEM	24. BRAND	25. SERIAL NUMBER	26. VALUE
Television	Sharp	XNT900551654	$800

27. ITEM	28. BRAND	29. SERIAL NUMBER	30. VALUE
Microwave	Kitchen Aid		$400

31. ITEM	32. BRAND	33. SERIAL NUMBER	34. VALUE
Silver			$500

35. _Dick Wilson Badge #900_
SIGNATURE OF OFFICER/BADGE NUMBER

Go on to next page

66. Where does the victim reside?

_____

67. Where does the suspect reside?

_____

68. What was the suspect wearing?

_____

69. What is the name of the suspect?

_____

70. What is the victim's date of birth?

_____

Questions 71 through 75 are based on the following incident report form.

INCIDENT REPORT — POLICE DEPARTMENT

1. ADDRESS OF INCIDENT	2. OFFENSE	3. CODE	4. DATE
900 Main Street	Armed Robbery	AF-100	May 11, 2010

5. NAME OF VICTIM: INDIVIDUAL OR BUSINESS	6. ADDRESS PHONE
Sam's Convenient Store Jake Hassey	31 Lackawanna Ave

7. ASSIGNED OFFICERS/BADGE NUMBERS	8. AGE OF VICTIM	9. RACE OF VICTIM	10. VICTIM'S DATE OF BIRTH
Mike Kennedy #180 Roberta Black #450	17	African American	11/12/93

11. NAME OF SUSPECT	12. ADDRESS
Unknown	Unknown

13. AGE	14. RACE	15. SEX	16. DATE OF BIRTH	17. HEIGHT	18. WEIGHT
25	African American	Male	Unknown	5'8"	180

19. HAIR	20. EYES	21. PHYSICAL DESCRIPTION
Brown	Brown	Wearing a black coat and a blue baseball cap

22. CHARGES

Robbery

23. ITEM	24. BRAND	25. SERIAL NUMBER	26. VALUE
Cash	N/A	N/A	$230

27. ITEM	28. BRAND	29. SERIAL NUMBER	30. VALUE

31. ITEM	32. BRAND	33. SERIAL NUMBER	34. VALUE

35. _____Mike Kennedy Badge #180_____
SIGNATURE OF OFFICER/BADGE NUMBER

Go on to next page →

71. Where did the incident take place?

   _____

72. What is the victim's name?

   _____

73. What is the victim's address?

   _____

74. How much money did the suspect steal?

   _____

75. What was the suspect wearing?

   _____

STOP DO NOT TURN THE PAGE UNTIL TOLD TO DO SO.
DO NOT RETURN TO A PREVIOUS TEST.

Chapter 18

Answers and Explanations for Practice Test 3

After you take the practice National Police Officer Selection Test in Chapter 17, use this chapter to check your answers. If you aren't sure why an answer was incorrect, use this chapter to get explanations of the answers. If you correctly answered a question, you may still want to read the explanation to get a better understanding of the thought process that helped you choose the correct answer. If you're short on time, turn to the end of this chapter to find an abbreviated answer key.

Section 1: Mathematics

1. **A.** To find the average retail value of each flat-screen television, divide $8,400, the total retail value, by 4, the number of flat-screen televisions stolen. The correct answer is $2,100.

2. **D.** This question asks you to find the six-month salary for a police officer who earns $740 per week before taxes. There are 52 weeks in a year, so there are 26 weeks in six months. Multiply $740 by 26. The answer is $19,240.

3. **B.** Begin by subtracting 50 from 200, the number of miles Officer White drove his patrol motorcycle in three days. Then divide 150, the number of remaining miles, by 2. The answer is 75 miles.

4. **C.** The value of the televisions is $1,500, and the value of the computer is $800. When you add $1,500 and $800, the answer is $2,300.

5. **E.** To find the value of all the stolen goods, add $1,500, $250, $800, and $300. The answer is $2,850.

6. **D.** Subtract 2, the number of weeks Officer Grimes is on vacation, from 52 weeks, the number of weeks in a year. Multiply this number, 50, by 4, the number of businesses she visits each week. The answer is 200.

7. **C.** If Officer Malone works until 11 p.m., any hours he works after this are considered overtime. If he worked until 2:30 a.m., he worked 3 hours and 30 minutes of overtime.

8. **C.** Because the gas tank holds 17 gallons and it's half full, divide 17 by 2, which is 8.5. Multiply this number by $2.10, the cost per gallon of gasoline. The answer is $17.85.

9. **B.** If Officer Rawlings is paid $14 an hour for 40 hours, he earns $560 of regular pay. If he's paid time-and-a-half for overtime, he's paid $21 per hour of overtime. He worked 3 hours of overtime, for which he was paid $63. Add $560 and $63. The correct answer is $623.

10. **B.** To answer this question, you need to find 5 percent of 40. Multiply .05 by 40. The answer is 2.

11. **A.** To find the total value of the stolen goods, add $750, $250, $100, and $400. The answer is $1,500.

12. **E.** To find the value of the stolen goods except the cash register, add $250, $100, and $400. The answer is $750.

13. **B.** To find the average retail price of each kayak, divide $2,544, the total retail value, by 6, the number of kayaks. The answer is $424.

14. **D.** Officer Taylor received the call at 2:45 p.m. and left the scene at 3:10 p.m. Twenty-five minutes elapsed during this time.

15. **C.** Multiply 38, the number of officers requesting a safety vest, by $725, the cost per vest. The answer is $27,550.

16. **D.** Divide 75, the number of miles the patrol car is driven each day, by 25, the number of miles per gallon it averages. The patrol car uses 3 gallons of gas each day. Multiply 3 by 20, the number of work days. The answer is 60.

17. **C.** There are 60 employees on the police force and two-thirds met the training requirement, so 40 employees met the training requirement. They had to complete 5 hours of training per month for 12 months. This is 60 hours of training per year. Multiply 60 by 40. The answer is 2,400.

18. **B.** Subtract 90 from 1,215. Then divide this number, 1,125, by 14 to find the average number of miles. The answer is about 80.

19. **D.** Divide the total value of the rings, $6,600, by 6, the number of rings. The answer is $1,100.

20. **B.** To find the cost of the lobster tails, multiply 5 by $15, the cost of one tail. Lobster tails cost $75. To find the cost of the shrimp, multiply 2 by $8, the cost of one pound of shrimp. To find the cost of the crab legs, multiply 3 by $10, the cost of one pound of crab legs. Add $75, $16, and $30. The answer is $121.

Section 11: Reading Comprehension

21. **C.** The passage says that residents who live in multifamily residential facilities with at least 50 but not more than 99 residential units will begin the recycling program on January 30.

22. **B.** A catalog is included in the list of items that may be placed in a recycling container. According to the passage, the items in the other answer choices cannot be recycled.

23. **B.** The passage says that you should not take your recycling container with you if you move. Containers are the property of Mayberry.

24. **A.** The last paragraph of the passage says that the recycling program is mandatory. If residents do not participate, they will be fined.

25. **E.** The only answer option that is true based on the information in the passage is Choice (E). According to the passage, residents of Mayberry may choose a 96-gallon container, a 64-gallon container, or a 32-gallon container.

26. **A.** The passage says that a social host serves alcohol to persons who are obviously intoxicated. A social host is not a business.

27. **B.** Sections 19 and 20 on the incident report ask for the suspect's hair and eye color. This information is not given in the paragraph, so the statement is false.

28. **B.** The victim's name is Jim Martin; Thom Fischer is the suspect. The statement is false.

29. **D.** The passage says that campfires under 30 inches in diameter will be allowed under the new ordinance. Fires to burn leaves and paper are not allowed. Fires in fire pits and incinerators are also banned.

30. **C.** The fourth paragraph of the passage says that open burning is permitted on Wednesdays and Saturdays from noon until 8 p.m. from Memorial Day through Labor Day. Therefore, the resident would be allowed to burn garbage.

31. **A.** The passage says smoke from 5 pounds of leaves contains about 1 pound of air pollution; therefore, smoke from 10 pounds of leaves contains about 2 pounds of air pollution.

32. **B.** Under the new ordinance, a person caught burning leaves would receive a fine of not less than $100 and not more than $2,500.

33. **B.** The third paragraph of the passage lists the health problems associated with open burning; some of these problems are breathing problems.

34. **C.** In simple assault, the attacker does not use a weapon to harm someone. A girl punching another girl is simple assault.

35. **B.** The passage says that swimming is only allowed at the beach when lifeguards are on duty. They are on duty from 9 a.m. to 6 p.m., so swimming at 8 a.m. is a violation of the ordinance.

36. **C.** Glass containers are not allowed on the beach.

37. **A.** The passage says that smoking is prohibited.

38. **A.** Violators will receive a fine of $25 for each offense, and people are not allowed to park on the roads leading up to the beach, so this statement is true.

39. **A.** The second paragraph of the passage says that persons launching and loading boats should access the beach at Second Street.

40. **B.** The incident report cannot be fully completed based on the information in the paragraph. For example, the age and race of the victim are not provided.

41. **B.** Ms. DeYan called police at 11:10 a.m., so this statement is false.

42. **D.** According to the fifth paragraph in the passage, a rectangular sign on a business is permitted.

43. **A.** The fourth paragraph explains that a flag with a company logo is permitted as long as the business also displays the U.S. flag.

44. **E.** The passage says that signs containing the words "stop" and "danger" are banned.

45. **B.** The last paragraph of the passage says that a business will be fined $100 when it receives notice to remove the sign.

Section III: Grammar

46. **B.** The subject of this sentence, *children,* requires a plural auxiliary word (also called a helping verb). *Have* is the correct answer.

47. **A.** *Sight* refers to vision and is correct here. *Site* refers to a place, such as a construction site. *Cite* means to make a notation about something.

48. **B.** *We* is a subjective pronoun and is correct here because it is the subject of the sentence.

49. **C.** *Women* is plural. To make it possessive, add *'s.*

50. **B.** The pronoun *their* is correct in this sentence. It refers to the persons who were arrested.

51. **A.** The pronoun *its* is correct in this sentence. *It's* is the contraction for *it is. Its'* is not a word.

52. **A.** The contraction *who's* is correct here. It means *who is.*

53. **B.** The verb *are* is correct. The words *two sides* require a plural verb.

54. **B.** The objective pronoun *me* is needed in this sentence because it is part of the object in the sentence.

55. **A.** The noun *effect* is correct in this sentence. *Affect* is a verb.

56. **D.** The correct spelling is *privilege*.

57. **A.** The correct spelling is *mischievous*.

58. **D.** The correct spelling is *misspelled*.

59. **B.** The correct spelling is *maintenance*.

60. **C.** The correct spelling is *fiery*.

61. **A.** The correct spelling is *humorous*.

62. **A.** The correct spelling is *leisure*.

63. **D.** The correct spelling is *grateful*.

64. **A.** The correct spelling is *occasionally*.

65. **A.** The correct spelling is *immediate*.

Section IV: Incident Report Writing

66. The victim resides at 9 Beverly Avenue.

67. The suspect resides at 15 Beverly Avenue.

68. The suspect was wearing black sweat pants and a green sweat shirt.

69. The suspect's name is Suzanne Angelone.

70. The victim's date of birth is February 20, 1943.

71. The incident took place at Sam's Convenient Store at 900 Main Street.

72. The victim's name is Jake Hassey.

73. The victim's address is 31 Lackawanna Avenue.

74. The suspect stole $230.

75. The suspect was wearing a black coat and a blue baseball cap.

Answer Key for Practice Test 3

Section 1

1. A	8. C	15. C
2. D	9. B	16. D
3. B	10. B	17. C
4. C	11. A	18. B
5. E	12. E	19. D
6. D	13. B	20. B
7. C	14. D	

Section 11

21. C	30. C	39. A
22. B	31. A	40. B
23. B	32. B	41. B
24. A	33. B	42. D
25. E	34. C	43. A
26. A	35. B	44. E
27. B	36. C	45. B
28. B	37. A	
29. D	38. A	

Section 111

46. B	53. B	60. C
47. A	54. B	61. A
48. B	55. A	62. A
49. C	56. D	63. D
50. B	57. A	64. A
51. A	58. D	65. A
52. A	59. B	

Chapter 19

Practice Test 4: The New York City Police Department Police Officer Candidate Test

• •

*P*ractice Test 4 is modeled after the New York City (NYC) Police Department Police Officer Candidate Test. This test is a civil service test used in New York City, but some other police departments give tests that are similar to this. Unlike the POST, the NYC test isn't broken into sections that are individually timed.

This test contains 85 multiple-choice items, and you have about 2½ hours to complete the test. The questions on the NYC test assess these skills:

- ✔ **Memorization:** The ability to remember information; candidates are given a picture to study for ten minutes. Then they're told to turn a page and can no longer see the picture as they answer questions about its content.

- ✔ **Spatial orientation:** The ability to determine where you are in relation to an object or where the object is in relation to you; candidates may be given a map with one-way streets or streets that are obstructed. Candidates are asked to determine the most efficient route from one place to another while obeying all traffic regulations.

- ✔ **Written comprehension:** The ability to understand written sentences and paragraphs; candidates read a paragraph or paragraphs and answer questions about what they have read.

- ✔ **Visualization:** The ability to imagine how something would look when it is moved or its parts are rearranged; candidates predict how an object, a set of objects, or patterns appear after changes are made.

- ✔ **Deductive reasoning:** The ability to apply general rules to specific problems; candidates are given a definition and have to choose an example that fits this definition.

- ✔ **Inductive reasoning:** The ability to combine separate pieces of information to form general rules or conclusions; candidates read information and choose a conclusion based on this information.

- ✔ **Problem sensitivity:** The ability to tell when something is likely to go wrong; candidates must use common sense to identify problematic situations.

- ✔ **Number facility:** The ability to add, subtract, multiply, and divide correctly; candidates must solve real-world problems involving math.

Use a number-two pencil and mark your answers on the following answer sheet. Make sure your marks are heavy and completely fill in the oval. Completely erase any marks that you wish to change. Be sure to blacken only one oval for each question, and be sure that you're blackening the oval for the correct question. It's easy to skip a question and become confused when marking your answers on the answer sheet. While this answer sheet won't be computer scored like the answer sheet on the actual test, pretending that it will be helps you better prepare for the exam.

Pace yourself as you work through the questions on Practice Test 4 so that you have enough time to complete all the questions. Don't spend too much time on one question. Try to answer every question on this test. If a question really stumps you, take a good guess and move on. Your score is based on the number of questions you answer correctly, so there is no penalty for guessing.

After you complete the entire practice test, check your answers against the answers and explanations in Chapter 20.

Answer Sheet for Practice Test 4

1 Ⓐ Ⓑ Ⓒ Ⓓ Ⓔ	21 Ⓐ Ⓑ Ⓒ Ⓓ Ⓔ	41 Ⓐ Ⓑ Ⓒ Ⓓ Ⓔ	61 Ⓐ Ⓑ Ⓒ Ⓓ Ⓔ
2 Ⓐ Ⓑ Ⓒ Ⓓ Ⓔ	22 Ⓐ Ⓑ Ⓒ Ⓓ Ⓔ	42 Ⓐ Ⓑ Ⓒ Ⓓ Ⓔ	62 Ⓐ Ⓑ Ⓒ Ⓓ Ⓔ
3 Ⓐ Ⓑ Ⓒ Ⓓ Ⓔ	23 Ⓐ Ⓑ Ⓒ Ⓓ Ⓔ	43 Ⓐ Ⓑ Ⓒ Ⓓ Ⓔ	63 Ⓐ Ⓑ Ⓒ Ⓓ Ⓔ
4 Ⓐ Ⓑ Ⓒ Ⓓ Ⓔ	24 Ⓐ Ⓑ Ⓒ Ⓓ Ⓔ	44 Ⓐ Ⓑ Ⓒ Ⓓ Ⓔ	64 Ⓐ Ⓑ Ⓒ Ⓓ Ⓔ
5 Ⓐ Ⓑ Ⓒ Ⓓ Ⓔ	25 Ⓐ Ⓑ Ⓒ Ⓓ Ⓔ	45 Ⓐ Ⓑ Ⓒ Ⓓ Ⓔ	65 Ⓐ Ⓑ Ⓒ Ⓓ Ⓔ
6 Ⓐ Ⓑ Ⓒ Ⓓ Ⓔ	26 Ⓐ Ⓑ Ⓒ Ⓓ Ⓔ	46 Ⓐ Ⓑ Ⓒ Ⓓ Ⓔ	66 Ⓐ Ⓑ Ⓒ Ⓓ Ⓔ
7 Ⓐ Ⓑ Ⓒ Ⓓ Ⓔ	27 Ⓐ Ⓑ Ⓒ Ⓓ Ⓔ	47 Ⓐ Ⓑ Ⓒ Ⓓ Ⓔ	67 Ⓐ Ⓑ Ⓒ Ⓓ Ⓔ
8 Ⓐ Ⓑ Ⓒ Ⓓ Ⓔ	28 Ⓐ Ⓑ Ⓒ Ⓓ Ⓔ	48 Ⓐ Ⓑ Ⓒ Ⓓ Ⓔ	68 Ⓐ Ⓑ Ⓒ Ⓓ Ⓔ
9 Ⓐ Ⓑ Ⓒ Ⓓ Ⓔ	29 Ⓐ Ⓑ Ⓒ Ⓓ Ⓔ	49 Ⓐ Ⓑ Ⓒ Ⓓ Ⓔ	69 Ⓐ Ⓑ Ⓒ Ⓓ Ⓔ
10 Ⓐ Ⓑ Ⓒ Ⓓ Ⓔ	30 Ⓐ Ⓑ Ⓒ Ⓓ Ⓔ	50 Ⓐ Ⓑ Ⓒ Ⓓ Ⓔ	70 Ⓐ Ⓑ Ⓒ Ⓓ Ⓔ
11 Ⓐ Ⓑ Ⓒ Ⓓ Ⓔ	31 Ⓐ Ⓑ Ⓒ Ⓓ Ⓔ	51 Ⓐ Ⓑ Ⓒ Ⓓ Ⓔ	71 Ⓐ Ⓑ Ⓒ Ⓓ Ⓔ
12 Ⓐ Ⓑ Ⓒ Ⓓ Ⓔ	32 Ⓐ Ⓑ Ⓒ Ⓓ Ⓔ	52 Ⓐ Ⓑ Ⓒ Ⓓ Ⓔ	72 Ⓐ Ⓑ Ⓒ Ⓓ Ⓔ
13 Ⓐ Ⓑ Ⓒ Ⓓ Ⓔ	33 Ⓐ Ⓑ Ⓒ Ⓓ Ⓔ	53 Ⓐ Ⓑ Ⓒ Ⓓ Ⓔ	73 Ⓐ Ⓑ Ⓒ Ⓓ Ⓔ
14 Ⓐ Ⓑ Ⓒ Ⓓ Ⓔ	34 Ⓐ Ⓑ Ⓒ Ⓓ Ⓔ	54 Ⓐ Ⓑ Ⓒ Ⓓ Ⓔ	74 Ⓐ Ⓑ Ⓒ Ⓓ Ⓔ
15 Ⓐ Ⓑ Ⓒ Ⓓ Ⓔ	35 Ⓐ Ⓑ Ⓒ Ⓓ Ⓔ	55 Ⓐ Ⓑ Ⓒ Ⓓ Ⓔ	75 Ⓐ Ⓑ Ⓒ Ⓓ Ⓔ
16 Ⓐ Ⓑ Ⓒ Ⓓ Ⓔ	36 Ⓐ Ⓑ Ⓒ Ⓓ Ⓔ	56 Ⓐ Ⓑ Ⓒ Ⓓ Ⓔ	76 Ⓐ Ⓑ Ⓒ Ⓓ Ⓔ
17 Ⓐ Ⓑ Ⓒ Ⓓ Ⓔ	37 Ⓐ Ⓑ Ⓒ Ⓓ Ⓔ	57 Ⓐ Ⓑ Ⓒ Ⓓ Ⓔ	77 Ⓐ Ⓑ Ⓒ Ⓓ Ⓔ
18 Ⓐ Ⓑ Ⓒ Ⓓ Ⓔ	38 Ⓐ Ⓑ Ⓒ Ⓓ Ⓔ	58 Ⓐ Ⓑ Ⓒ Ⓓ Ⓔ	78 Ⓐ Ⓑ Ⓒ Ⓓ Ⓔ
19 Ⓐ Ⓑ Ⓒ Ⓓ Ⓔ	39 Ⓐ Ⓑ Ⓒ Ⓓ Ⓔ	59 Ⓐ Ⓑ Ⓒ Ⓓ Ⓔ	79 Ⓐ Ⓑ Ⓒ Ⓓ Ⓔ
20 Ⓐ Ⓑ Ⓒ Ⓓ Ⓔ	40 Ⓐ Ⓑ Ⓒ Ⓓ Ⓔ	60 Ⓐ Ⓑ Ⓒ Ⓓ Ⓔ	80 Ⓐ Ⓑ Ⓒ Ⓓ Ⓔ
			81 Ⓐ Ⓑ Ⓒ Ⓓ Ⓔ
			82 Ⓐ Ⓑ Ⓒ Ⓓ Ⓔ
			83 Ⓐ Ⓑ Ⓒ Ⓓ Ⓔ
			84 Ⓐ Ⓑ Ⓒ Ⓓ Ⓔ
			85 Ⓐ Ⓑ Ⓒ Ⓓ Ⓔ

Directions: Study the following photograph for ten minutes and try to remember as many details as you can. You may not write or make any notes during this time. After these ten minutes are up, cover up the photograph and answer Questions 1 through 10 about the image; you may not review the photo until you have completed the exam.

Photo courtesy Detroit Publishing Company Photograph Collection (Library of Congress)

Answer Questions 1 through 10 on the basis of the photograph.

1. Two people are standing in front of a building. What name is on the sign on the front of the building?

   (A) Coach Lamps

   (B) Carey & Co.

   (C) Birthplace of Old Glory

   (D) Berger Bros.

2. The name of a printer is on one sign on a building. What is this printer's name?

   (A) Samuel L. Drake

   (B) Laurence R. Roth

   (C) David J. Kimball

   (D) Matthew C. Smith

Go on to next page ⟶

3. Which animal is in the picture?

   (A) Dog

   (B) Horse

   (C) Cat

   (D) Donkey

4. Which building has a flag and a ladder in front of it?

   (A) The printers

   (B) Carey & Co.

   (C) Birthplace of Old Glory

   (D) Berger Bros.

5. Which of these best describes the street in front of the buildings?

   (A) Dirt

   (B) Gravel

   (C) Brick

   (D) Pavement

6. What does Carey & Co. sell?

   (A) Bloomer buttons

   (B) Coach lamps

   (C) Paper products

   (D) Dry goods

7. A utility pole is in the picture. Which building is it in front of?

   (A) The printers

   (B) Carey & Co.

   (C) Birthplace of Old Glory

   (D) Berger Bros.

8. How many windows are shown on the second floor of the Berger Bros. building?

   (A) 0

   (B) 1

   (C) 2

   (D) 3

9. Which of these buildings says it is open to the public?

   (A) The printers

   (B) Carey & Co.

   (C) Birthplace of Old Glory

   (D) Berger Bros.

10. Which building has pictures in the front window?

    (A) Carey & Co.

    (B) Samuel L. Drake

    (C) Berger Bros.

    (D) Birthplace of Old Glory

Directions: Complete Questions 11 through 53. Be sure to read each question carefully.

Answer Question 11 solely on the basis of the following passage.

While questioning a witness of a purse snatching, you are told that the suspect shoved the victim to the ground and took off down the street, heading south. He dashed across a busy intersection, ran one more block, and then turned left, disappearing around the corner of a brick office building.

11. According to the information you received, you would be most correct if you reported that the suspect was last seen traveling

    (A) north.

    (B) south.

    (C) east.

    (D) west.

Go on to next page

Answer Questions 12 through 14 solely on the basis of the following passage.

On May 24, 2010, Officers Keller and Gerard responded to a call at 58 Main Street, Apt. 4C, at 6:32 p.m., in response to a burglary reported by Mr. Schmidt. They arrived at the apartment at 6:37 p.m., rang the doorbell, and were greeted by Mr. and Mrs. Schmidt. Mr. Schmidt told the officers that he left for his teaching job at the local elementary school at 7:15 a.m., and that his wife left for her job as a journalist at the town's newspaper at 8:00 a.m. Because Mrs. Schmidt walks to work, Mr. Schmidt picked her up when school let out. They went out for dinner and returned to their apartment around 6:15 p.m. When Mrs. Schmidt entered the bedroom, she noticed that her jewelry box was on the floor, face down and empty. The safe in the closet was open and empty as well. Her husband called the police while she checked the rest of the apartment. While waiting for the police, they discovered that Mrs. Schmidt's collection of antique porcelain dolls that she displays in a glass case in the living room was also missing.

While Officer Keller interviewed the Schmidts and took notes, Officer Gerard visited the four other apartments on the floor. Her goal was to interview the neighbors to see whether anyone heard or saw anything that might be useful for their investigation.

Mrs. Brown, age 39, who runs a private daycare from home, lives in Apt. 4D, located across the hall from the elevator and emergency stairwell. Mrs. Brown told Officer Gerard that she heard unfamiliar voices in the hallway outside her apartment door at 2:30 p.m. The voices, quiet at first, soon escalated, and she peered out the peephole in her door to try to figure out what was happening. She saw two young men standing by the door to the stairwell. One was slightly taller than the other. The taller male was white, about 18 or 19 years old, 6 feet tall, and 180 pounds, with curly brown hair. He was wearing glasses and carrying a black backpack. The other male appeared younger, approximately 16 years old, 5 feet 10 inches tall, and 165 pounds, with blond hair cut close to his head. When he turned around, she noticed a tribal tattoo around his arm, near his elbow. He was also carrying a black bag, but Mrs. Brown noticed red hair or fur sticking out of an open section of the bag. Both males wore khaki pants and polo shirts. The taller one's shirt was dark blue, while the other's shirt was orange.

Officer Gerard then tried to talk to the residents who live in Apts. 4A, 4B, and 4E. The person who lives in Apt. 4A was not home, and those who spoke to Officer Gerard from Apts. 4B and 4E said that they did not hear anything in the hall. Officer Gerard went back to the Schmidts' apartment to tell Officer Keller what she had learned. In the meantime, Mrs. Schmidt had told Officer Keller that she thought that the most expensive doll in her collection had red hair and painted freckles on its porcelain face.

Officers Keller and Gerard returned to the station to complete their crime report at 7:45 p.m.

12. The taller male outside of Mrs. Brown's door had what color hair?

(A) Orange

(B) Brown

(C) Blond

(D) Black

13. What time did Officers Keller and Gerard arrive at the Schmidts' apartment?

(A) 6:15 p.m.

(B) 6:32 p.m.

(C) 6:37 p.m.

(D) 7:15 p.m.

14. Which apartment does Mrs. Brown live in?

(A) 4A

(B) 4B

(C) 4C

(D) 4D

Go on to next page

Answer Question 15 solely on the basis of the following information.

While on patrol, Officer Portas responds to a traffic accident. He records the following details when he arrives at the scene:

Location of Accident: Scott Street

Time of Accident: 2:20 p.m.

Vehicle Involved: 2006 Ford

Driver: Jacob Carillo

Damage: Vehicle hit a utility pole, resulting in a broken headlight and crushed front bumper.

15. Officer Portas must write a report about the incident. Which of the following expresses the above information *most clearly, accurately, and completely?*

(A) At 2:20 p.m., Jacob Carillo was driving on Scott Street. A 2006 Ford was involved in an accident when it struck a utility pole resulting in a broken headlight and crushed front bumper.

(B) A 2006 Ford driven by Jacob Carillo struck a utility pole on Scott Street at 2:20 p.m., resulting in a broken headlight and a crushed front bumper.

(C) A car was involved in an accident on Scott Street at 2:30 p.m. It struck a utility pole, resulting in a broken headlight and crushed front bumper. Jacob Carillo has a 2006 Ford.

(D) A 2006 Ford struck Jacob Carillo, causing a broken headlight and crushing the front bumper on Scott Street at 2:20 p.m.

Go on to next page

> *Answer Question 16 solely on the basis of the following information.*

A recruit officer is preparing an announcement about upcoming street closings within New York City. She reviews the rough draft of her announcement, which contains the following two sentences:

1. Third Avenue on June 12 will be closed between May Place and 14th Street also between St. Rita's Place and 7th Street will be closed.

2. For the New York City Police Museum Car Show on June 12, Front and Water Streets will be closed from 12:00 p.m. until 5:00 p.m.

16. Which of the following best describes the preceding sentences?

(A) Only Sentence 1 is grammatically correct.

(B) Only Sentence 2 is grammatically correct.

(C) Neither Sentence 1 nor Sentence 2 is grammatically correct.

(D) Both Sentence 1 and Sentence 2 are grammatically correct.

> *Answer Question 17 solely on the basis of the following passage.*

Officers responding to an in-progress bank robbery should follow these guidelines:

1. Drive quickly but cautiously to the scene of the alleged robbery. Officers may use their lights and sirens to get to the scene more quickly, but they should use caution as they get closer to the scene. Lights and sirens could alert the perpetrator or perpetrators and ruin the element of surprise.

2. Stay alert for any additional information from dispatch and any signs of a getaway vehicle on the road. As officers approach the scene, they should also keep watch for any perpetrators located near the scene.

3. Do *not* approach the bank alone. Instead, officers should radio dispatch to give location information and to request backup. Then, officers should take a safe position outside the bank and watch bank exits for fleeing perpetrators. Officers should also stop citizens from entering the bank.

4. Backup officers arriving on the scene should assume similar safe positions around the bank's exterior. These officers should also monitor bank exits and windows to watch for fleeing perpetrators. No officers should enter the bank unless they are instructed to do so by a superior officer.

5. Allow perpetrators leaving the bank to move far enough away from the bank's entrance so that they cannot reenter as officers approach. Then, officers should make every effort to apprehend the perpetrators with the least amount of danger to the officers and the perpetrators.

Go on to next page

17. Officer Riley receives a call from dispatch reporting a bank robbery in progress at the Chester Bank on 103rd Street. Riley is only two blocks from the bank, and he reports back to dispatch that he is responding. As Officer Riley travels toward the scene of the crime, he stays alert for additional information. Officer Riley arrives on the scene and radios dispatch. What should Officer Riley do when he radios dispatch?

(A) Tell dispatch the number of exits to the building.

(B) Describe the perpetrators and tell dispatch he is going inside.

(C) Request backup and tell dispatch his location.

(D) Ask if he can go inside the bank to apprehend perpetrators.

Answer Question 18 solely on the basis of the following passage.

Officers arriving at the scene of an officer-involved shooting should follow these guidelines:

1. Make sure no officers, suspects, or civilians are at risk of harm.

2. Secure and separate all suspects.

3. Inform dispatch of any information about other possible suspects who may have fled the scene, and request backup or emergency services (such as emergency medical assistance) if necessary.

4. If necessary, perform first aid procedures on yourself or on others at the scene.

5. Holster, secure, or put into evidence any guns at the scene. Do not attempt to open, unload, or otherwise tamper with the weapons.

6. Observe the scene and take notes about individuals involved, the time, and other important facts.

7. Secure the area by putting up crime-scene tape, and ensure that no evidence is lost or damaged.

8. Talk to all possible witnesses and take notes of their names and contact information. Ask witnesses to stay so that they can write down a statement.

Go on to next page

18. Officer Torres arrives on the scene of an officer-involved shooting. Officer Johnson discharged his weapon and shot an allegedly armed crime suspect. Officer Johnson is wounded in the left arm, but he's coherent and alert. The crime suspect is lying on the ground, motionless. Officer Torres observes that no other suspects are at the scene and no one else is in danger. What should Officer Torres do next?

    (A) Secure the scene by putting up crime-scene tape.

    (B) Perform first aid on the suspect and on Officer Johnson.

    (C) Holster, secure, or put into evidence the guns at the scene.

    (D) Request emergency medical assistance from dispatch.

Answer Question 19 solely on the basis of the following passage.

Today, a class of recruit officers received a visit from Officer Jamie Fuhler, a member of the local police department's bomb squad. Officer Fuhler discussed the types of bombs that squads across the United States have dealt with throughout history, such as pipe bombs and soda-bottle bombs. He then went on to explain threats that are currently growing in our country, such as suicide bombers, and radio-controlled and vehicle-borne improvised explosive devices. According to Fuhler, due to the emergence of new bombs, the National Bomb Squad Commanders Advisory Board updated equipment requirements for bomb squads across the nation in 2009. The new requirements included the following:

1. Participation of the InterAgency Board

2. Robots

3. Updated bomb suit standards

4. Updated X-ray standards

5. Updated categorizations of department resources

19. Based on this information, it would be most correct for the recruits to assume that the primary purpose of bomb squads possessing robots is

    (A) to learn how to make more powerful bombs for use during war times.

    (B) to deactivate bombs without threatening the lives of human officers.

    (C) to build updated bomb suits and X-rays according to new standards.

    (D) to act as representatives of humans when testing the effects of a blast.

Go on to next page

Answer Question 20 based solely on the following information.

Officers studying the law are learning about working with police dogs. To understand which breed is best for specific tasks, the class receives a handout containing the following information.

BREED	TASK	DESCRIPTION OF TASK
Akita Inu	Public order enforcement	Chase after suspect and detain.
Basset Hound	Illicit substance detection	Sniff airplane passengers/luggage for drugs, bombs, and food items.
Beagle	Cadaver-sniffing; illicit substance detection	Detect scent of decomposing bodies; substance detection
Blood Hound	Cadaver-sniffing; tracking	Detect scent of decomposing bodies; sniff trails to find missing persons.
Foxhound	Illicit substance detection	Sniff airplane passengers/luggage for drugs, bombs, and food items.
German Shepherd	Public order enforcement; chase after suspect and detain; tracking	Tracking; sniff trails to find missing persons.
Rottweiler	Public order enforcement	Chase after suspect and detain.
Schnauzer	Illicit substance detection	Sniff airplane passengers/luggage for drugs, bombs, and food items.

20. After reviewing the preceding table, it would be most correct for an officer to conclude that

(A) police dogs, regardless of breed, can perform most tasks.

(B) police dogs use their sense of smell to perform most tasks.

(C) police dogs spend most of their time looking for cadavers.

(D) police dogs are all members of commonly feared breeds.

Answer Question 21 based solely on the following passage.

Officer Johns reported to the scene of a bank robbery. The witnesses in the bank gave varying accounts of the incident:

1. "A white male, about 25 years old, 6 feet 5 inches tall, wearing a blue leather jacket and a baseball cap, approached a female teller at the counter, demanded money, and indicated he had a gun in his pocket. The teller put the money from her drawer into a plastic bag, and the man grabbed the money and ran from the bank. He got into a red sedan and drove southbound on Lenox Street."

Go on to next page

2. "A white male, about 25 years old, 6 feet tall, wearing a black leather jacket and a baseball cap, approached a female teller at the counter, demanded money, and indicated he had a gun in his pocket. The teller put the money from her drawer into a plastic bag, and the man grabbed the money and ran from the bank. He got into a red sedan and drove northbound on Lenox Street."

3. "A white male, about 25 years old, 6 feet tall, wearing a black leather jacket and a baseball cap, approached a female teller at the counter, demanded money, and indicated he had a gun in his pocket. The teller put the money from her drawer into a plastic bag, and the man grabbed the money and ran from the bank. He got into a red sedan and drove southbound on Lenox Street."

4. "A white male, about 25 years old, 6 feet tall, wearing a black leather jacket and a baseball cap, approached a female teller at the counter, demanded money, and indicated he had a gun in his pocket. The teller put the money from her drawer into a paper bag, and the man grabbed the money and ran from the bank. He got into a black sedan and drove southbound on Lenox Street."

21. Which one of the preceding accounts is most likely to be correct?

(A) Account 1

(B) Account 2

(C) Account 3

(D Account 4

Answer Question 22 based solely on the following passage.

Four witnesses give different accounts of the license plate of a vehicle involved in a hit-and-run accident.

22. Which one of the following is most likely to be correct?

(A) 952T4P

(B) 954T5P

(C) 592T5P

(D) 952T5P

Go on to next page

> *Answer Question 23 based solely on the following information.*

Officer Davis issued the following citations during a four-week period.

Week Number	Traffic Violation Citation	Disorderly Conduct Citation
1	20	7
2	12	10
3	14	5
4	19	9

23. Officer Davis is required to enter the total number of citations in his Activity-Log at the end of the four-week period. Which one of the following formulas will provide an accurate amount of citations issued?

(A) $(1 + 2 + 3 + 4) \times (20 + 12 + 14 + 19)$

(B) $20 + 12 + 14 + 19 + 7 + 10 + 5 + 9$

(C) $1 + 2 + 3 + 4 + 7 + 10 + 5 + 9$

(D) $(20 + 12 + 14 + 19) \times (7 + 10 + 5 + 9)$

Go on to next page

> *Answer Question 24 solely on the basis of the following information.*

As Officer Fisher patrols the area, he takes note of the types and sizes of the buildings he passes. These are shown in the following figure.

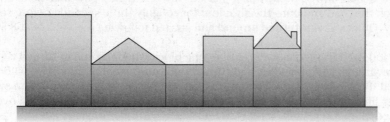

24. Officer Fisher is always sure to check the back of the buildings he patrols, as well. Which one of the following would look most like the view Officer Fisher would have from the rear of this set of buildings?

(A)

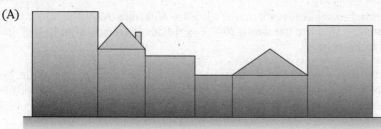

(B)

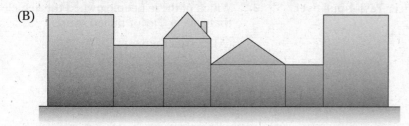

(C)

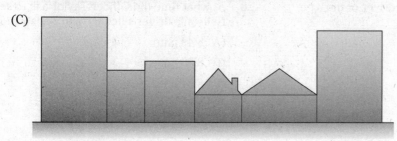

(D)

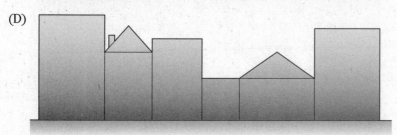

Go on to next page

Answer Questions 25 through 28 solely on the basis of the following passage.

Officer Taylor was patrolling her usual area and driving along Fifth Avenue on May 2, 2009. At 8:49 p.m., Office Taylor turned left onto Fordham Street and observed a tan sedan driving toward her. The sedan slowed rapidly as it passed Officer Taylor's patrol vehicle. Then, the sedan veered off the road and onto the shoulder for roughly three seconds before returning to the roadway. Officer Taylor turned around and started following the vehicle at 8:50 p.m.

Officer Taylor followed the sedan for less than one block when the sedan turned right onto Kennedy Boulevard, picked up speed, and turned right onto Washington Drive. Officer Taylor followed the sedan for another three blocks when she observed the sedan swerve over the center line. Officer Taylor put on her signaling lights at 8:53 p.m. to pull over the driver of the sedan.

At 8:54 p.m. Officer Taylor approached the vehicle and noticed the strong smell of an alcoholic beverage. The driver of the sedan, who identified himself as Nathan Neilson (age 22), was accompanied by three other occupants: Stacy Ramirez (age 24), Richard King (age 23), and Laurence Thomas (age 21).

Officer Taylor requested to see Neilson's driver's license and registration at 8:55 p.m. Officer Taylor determined that the car was a 2006 Toyota Corolla, registered to the suspect's mother, Lauren Danvers.

Officer Taylor gave Neilson a field sobriety test, which he failed. Taylor arrested Mr. Neilson on the charge of driving under the influence. Officer Taylor took Neilson into custody without incident and traveled to the precinct at 9:10 p.m.

25. On which street did Officer Taylor pull over the sedan?

   (A) Fordham Street

   (B) Kennedy Boulevard

   (C) Fifth Avenue

   (D) Washington Drive

26. What was the age of the driver of the vehicle?

   (A) 21

   (B) 22

   (C) 23

   (D) 24

27. Which of these people owned the vehicle that Officer Taylor pulled over?

   (A) Lauren Danvers

   (B) Nathan Neilson

   (C) Laurence Thomas

   (D) Stacy White

28. At what time did Officer Taylor ask to see Neilson's driver's license and registration?

   (A) 8:49 p.m.

   (B) 8:50 p.m.

   (C) 8:54 p.m.

   (D) 8:55 p.m.

Go on to next page

Answer Question 29 solely on the basis of the following information.

While patrolling the area, Officer Matthews was called to a nearby traffic accident. He recorded the following details when he arrived at the scene:

Location of Accident: Intersection of Second Street and Main Street

Time of Accident: 8:45 p.m.

Vehicle(s) Involved: 2008 Toyota (Vehicle 1) and 2007 Ford (Vehicle 2)

Drivers: Richard Saxton (Vehicle 1) and Lila Benner (Vehicle 2)

Damage: Vehicle 1 rear-ended Vehicle 2 at a stop light, resulting in a broken tail light for Vehicle 2 and damage to Vehicle 1's front bumper.

29. Officer Matthews must write a report about the incident. Which of the following expresses the preceding information *most clearly, accurately, and completely?*

(A) At 8:45 p.m., Richard Saxton and Lila Benner were driving on Second Street and Main Street. A 2008 Toyota and a 2007 Ford were involved in an accident when the two vehicles struck each other, resulting in a broken tail light and damaged front bumper.

(B) Two cars were involved in an accident at the intersection of Second Street and Main Street at 8:45 p.m. They struck each other resulting in a broken tail light for Vehicle 2 and damage to Vehicle 1's front bumper. Richard Saxton has a 2008 Toyota and Lila Benner has a 2007 Ford.

(C) A 2008 Toyota driven by Richard Saxton (Vehicle 1) struck a 2007 Ford driven by Lila Benner (Vehicle 2) at the intersection of Second Street and Main Street at 8:45 p.m., resulting in a broken tail light for Vehicle 2 and damage to Vehicle 1's front bumper.

(D) A 2008 Toyota struck Lila Benner causing a broken tail light and damaged front bumper at the intersection of Second Street and Main Street at 8:45 p.m.

Go on to next page

Answer Question 30 solely on the basis of the following passage.

Officer Mendez responds to the scene of a motor vehicle accident at Orchard Lane and River Street. The man driving Vehicle 2 tells the officer that he was traveling south on Orchard Lane when Vehicle 1, traveling west on River Street, failed to stop at a stop sign and continued straight through the intersection. Vehicle 2 hit Vehicle 1 in the intersection and was then struck from behind by Vehicle 3.

30. Which diagram is most consistent with the driver's statement?

(A)

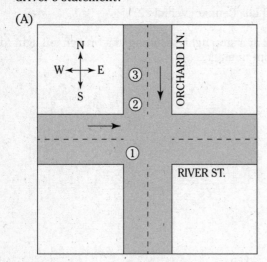

(C)

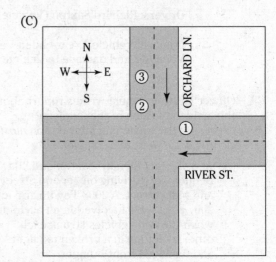

(B)

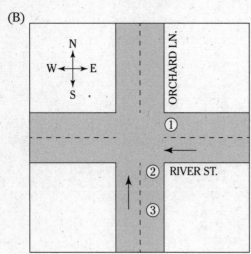

(D)

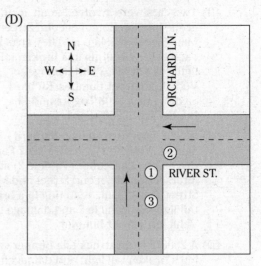

Go on to next page

> *Answer Question 31 solely on the basis of the following information.*

While on patrol, Officer Lang is called to the scene of a stabbing. He makes note of the following details once he is on the scene:

Place of Crime: 85 Northampton St.

Time of Crime: 11:15 p.m.

Victim: Marcus Russel

Crime: Assault with a deadly weapon

Suspect: Unidentified

31. When Officer Lang gets back to the police station, he must write a report of the incident. Which of the following expresses the preceding information *most clearly, accurately, and completely?*

(A) At 11:15 p.m., Marcus Russel was at 85 Northampton St. Someone was stabbed by an unidentified person.

(B) Someone was stabbed at 85 Northampton St. at 11:15 p.m. by an unidentified person.

(C) An unidentified person at 85 Northampton St. stabbed another person at 11:15 p.m. Marcus Russel is a person.

(D) An unidentified person stabbed Marcus Russel at 85 Northampton St. at 11:15 p.m.

Go on to next page

Answer Question 32 solely on the basis of the following information.

While on patrol, Officer Williams responds to a report of grand larceny. She makes note of the following details once she is on the scene:

Place of Crime: In front of 112 Seaside Blvd.

Time of Crime: Between 2:00 a.m. and 10:30 a.m.

Victim: Ronda McMicken

Crime: Car theft

Vehicle Stolen: 2006 Chevy

Suspect: Unidentified

32. When Officer Williams gets back to the police station, she must write a report of the incident. Which of the following expresses the preceding information *most clearly, accurately, and completely?*

(A) An unidentified person in front of 112 Seaside Blvd. stole a car between 2:00 a.m. and 10:30 a.m. Ronda McMicken has a 2006 Chevy.

(B) An unidentified person stole Ronda McMicken's 2006 Chevy in front of 112 Seaside Blvd. between 2:00 a.m. and 10:30 a.m.

(C) Between 2:00 a.m. and 10:30 a.m., Ronda McMicken was in front of 112 Seaside Blvd. A 2006 Chevy was stolen by an unidentified person.

(D) A 2006 Chevy was stolen in front of Ronda McMicken at 112 Seaside Blvd. between 2:00 a.m. and 10:30 a.m.

Go on to next page

> *Answer Question 33 solely on the basis of the following information.*

When police officers have obtained a warrant to conduct a search of a person's property, they are required to knock and announce their presence at the entrance. This policy allows the residents of the home time to open their doors and cooperate with the police before officers decide to instead knock down their door. The knock-and-announce rule falls under the Fourth Amendment and varies by state. However, in 1997 the Supreme Court ruled in *Richards v. Wisconsin* that there are times when law enforcement officials do not have to knock and can instead enter the premises without warning. These exceptions to the rule include the following:

1. When the situation may involve physical violence or a threat to a person's life.

2. When crucial evidence may be destroyed if the resident receives warning.

3. When knocking would not produce results that differ from not knocking.

Note: It is important to remember that the knock-and-announce rule does not protect officials who choose to destroy any property while entering a residence.

33. Police Officer Heinz and his team tracked a murder suspect to his apartment. Believing that the suspect might grab a weapon or would run from them using the fire escape outside his window, Heinz chose not to knock and identify himself. Instead, his team kicked in the door and caught the suspect off-guard while he was preparing dinner in his kitchen. Officer Heinz's choice not to knock was

(A) illegal, because the suspect was not armed and there was no threat of violence.

(B) illegal, because Heinz's team damaged property while entering the suspect's residence.

(C) legal, because Heinz's team believed the suspect may have had a deadly weapon inside.

(D) legal, because police do not have to obtain warrants for searches and arrests when tracking murder suspects.

Go on to next page

> *Answer Questions 34 through 36 solely on the basis of the definitions given before each question.*

Aggravated assault: The law typically defines assault as committing a violent act against another person. In most states, aggravated assault differs from assault, as the consequences of committing the crime are greater. A person may be charged with or convicted of aggravated assault when the crime they committed involves

1. An intentional attempt to cause serious physical harm or injuries.

2. An intentional attempt to force sexual activity upon a person 14 years old or younger.

3. An intentional attempt to injure someone with a deadly weapon.

34. According to the definition given, which one of the following is the best example of aggravated assault?

(A) Mary, a young woman, stabs her co-worker with a pair of scissors for going through her desk drawers.

(B) Ben, an older man, attempts to coerce an 18-year-old female into having sex with him.

(C) Shirley, an older woman, pinches her grandchildren's cheeks when they visit her.

(D) Mark, a young man, accidentally punches someone near him while dancing at a rock concert.

Criminal trespass: If a police officer discovers a person on private property that has been clearly marked by signs, gates, or locked doors, then he or she may be charged with criminal trespass. A person may be convicted of criminal trespass if

1. The owner of the property would not want, or would not recognize, the person in question on their property.

2. The person in question stays on the property after hours, when the property is closed to the public, or if the property is a private space and the person has been asked to leave.

3. The person in question originally intended to rob, vandalize, or illegally use technology or machinery on the premises.

Go on to next page

35. According to the preceding information, which of the following should not be charged with criminal trespass?

    (A) Amanda, a 20-year-old college student, has been given permission to use the library's computers even though it is after hours.

    (B) Nicholas, a 40-year-old man, snuck back into his company's building at night to use the printer in his office to print his child's research report.

    (C) Gerard, a 15-year-old teenager, occasionally jumps his neighbors' fence with his friends to swim in their pool when they are not home.

    (D) Alicia, a 55-year-old woman, hid in the dressing room of a local department store and tried on clothes after the employees had left for the night.

    Self-defense: Although what is categorized as self-defense differs between jurisdictions and states, self-defense is typically defined as acting in physical ways to

    1. Defend yourself against physical harm.

    2. Defend your property against physical harm.

    3. Defend someone else against physical harm.

36. According to this definition, which of the following should not be classified as self-defense?

    (A) Margaret, a housewife, pushed her abusive husband down the stairs after he hit their toddler and turned on her.

    (B) Billy, a junior high school student, was cornered in an alley by the school bully and hit repeatedly before he kicked the other teenager in the ribs.

    (C) Raphael, an unemployed bartender, stabbed a woman who tried to shove him away after he attempted to steal her purse.

    (D) Caprice, a college student, sprayed an ex-boyfriend with mace and kicked him in the stomach when she found him attempting to slash her car's tires.

Go on to next page

Answer Question 37 on the basis of the following illustration.

37. Examine the following boot print.

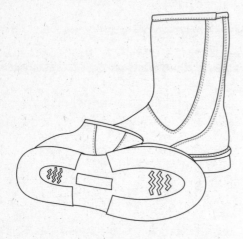

Which of the following boot prints best matches the preceding print?

(A)

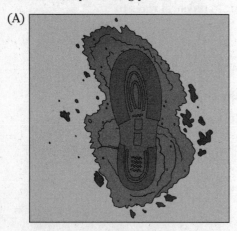

(B)

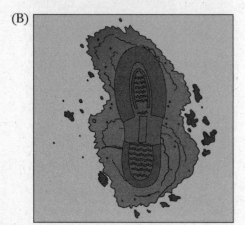

(C)

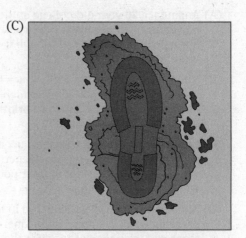

(D)

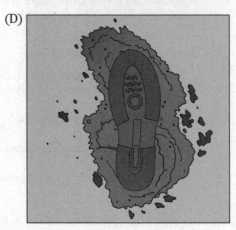

Go on to next page

> *Answer Questions 38 and 39 solely on the basis of the following information.*

In an attempt to prevent detainee suicide, officers should do the following:

1. Observe the suspect's actions, moods, behaviors, and statements at the scene of the incident and during the suspect's transportation. Also, consider previous interactions with the suspect in question.

2. After transportation, ask the suspect questions about his or her physical, emotional, and psychological states. For example, ask:

   - Are you tired?

   - Have you been drinking or using drugs?

   - Are you dependant on drugs or alcohol?

   - Have you ever considered suicide before?

   - Are you currently considering suicide?

3. Observe any physical signs (for example, wringing of hands, overall look of despondence) that could indicate the suspect is agitated.

4. Rate the suspect's overall likelihood of attempting suicide based on observations, conversations, and other factors.

5. Ensure that the suspect does not have items that could be used in a suicide attempt, such as ties, belts, chains, drawstrings, lighters, or matches.

6. Take the suspect into custody. Put suspects at a very high risk of a suicide attempt closer to the dispatch office.

7. Monitor suspects at least every 30 minutes. Monitor suspects at a very high risk of suicide at all times.

8. If the prisoner must be transferred, inform the agency taking the prisoner about any suicidal behaviors or actions.

Go on to next page

38. Officer Davis apprehends a robbery suspect and transports him to the precinct. At the scene of the apprehension and during transportation, Officer Davis observes the suspect's actions, moods, behaviors, and statements. Officer Davis has had no previous interactions with the suspect. After transportation, Officer Davis asks the suspect a list of questions regarding his physical, emotional, and psychological states. He then looks for physical signs that might indicate that the subject is agitated. What should Officer Davis do next?

   (A) Rate the suspect's overall likelihood of attempting suicide.

   (B) Ensure the suspect does not have items that could aid a suicide attempt.

   (C) Put the suspect into custody close to the dispatch office.

   (D) Inform another agency about any suicidal behaviors or actions.

39. Officer Huang apprehends an aggravated assault suspect who appears to be under the influence of drugs. She transports him to the precinct. At the scene of the apprehension and during transportation, the suspect says repeatedly that his life is over and he does not want to live anymore. She rates him as being at a high risk of suicide and makes sure that he does not have items that could be used in a suicide attempt. Now that he is in custody, what should Officer Huang do next?

   (A) Monitor him every 30 minutes.

   (B) Monitor him at all times.

   (C) Ask him questions about his emotional state.

   (D) Observe physical signs that could indicate he is agitated.

Answer Questions 40 through 43 solely on the basis of the following map. The flow of traffic is indicated by the arrows.

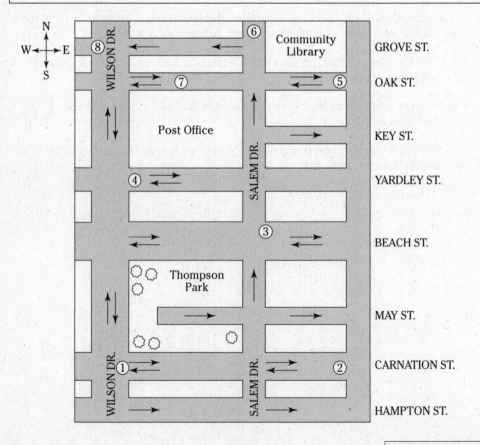

Go on to next page

40. If you are located at Carnation Street and Wilson Drive and you drive east on Carnation Street to Salem Drive, then turn north on Salem Drive, and turn west on Oak Street you will be closest to Point

    (A) 2.

    (B) 3.

    (C) 7.

    (D) 8.

41. If you are located at Point 5 and travel west on Oak Street to Wilson Drive, then drive south on Wilson Drive to Beach Street, you will be closest to Point

    (A) 1.

    (B) 4.

    (C) 6.

    (D) 8.

42. You are located at Grove Street and Wilson Drive. You receive a call of a crime in progress at the intersection of May Street and Salem Drive. Which one of the following is the most direct route for you to take in your patrol car, making sure to obey all traffic regulations?

    (A) Travel south on Wilson Drive to Beach Street, then east on Beach Street to Salem Drive, and then south on Salem Drive to May Street.

    (B) Travel south on Wilson Drive to Carnation Street, then east on Carnation Street to Salem Drive, then north on Salem Drive to May Street.

    (C) Travel south on Wilson Drive to Yardley Street, then east on Yardley Street to Salem Drive, then south on Salem Drive to May Street.

    (D) Travel south on Wilson Drive to Beach Street, then east on Beach Street to Monarch Drive, then south to May Street, then west on May Street to Salem Drive.

43. You are located at Yardley Street and Wilson Drive and must respond to a burglary at Hampton Street and Monarch Drive. Which one of the following is the most direct route for you to take in your patrol car, making sure to obey all traffic regulations?

    (A) Travel south on Wilson Drive to Beach Street, then take Beach Street east to Salem Drive, then take Salem Drive south to Carnation Street, then take Carnation Street to Monarch Drive, then take Monarch Drive south to Hampton Street.

    (B) Travel north on Wilson Drive to Hampton Street, then drive east on Hampton Street to Monarch Drive.

    (C) Travel east on Yardley Street to Salem Drive, then South on Salem Drive to Beach Street, then east on Beach Street to Monarch Drive, then south on Monarch Drive to Hampton Street.

    (D) Travel east on Yardley Street to Monarch Drive, then drive south on Monarch Drive to Hampton Street.

Go on to next page

Answer Question 44 solely on the basis of the following passage.

Between January 25 and January 27 four bank robberies occurred in a 10-mile radius. Based on the eyewitness accounts and video surveillance, officers believe the same suspect committed all four robberies. The suspect is being described as a white male with gray hair and a prosthetic leg, weighing approximately 180 pounds and wearing a dark hat.

44. Officer Reynolds has stopped four white males for questioning. Which one of these items of information provided by the witness should Officer Reynolds consider the most helpful in identifying the suspect?

(A) The suspect has a prosthetic leg.

(B) The suspect is approximately 180 pounds.

(C) The suspect is wearing a dark hat.

(D) The suspect has gray hair.

Answer Question 45 solely on the basis of the following passage.

On April 23, a woman reported her purse being stolen in front of the library on West Hampton Drive. The woman and a number of other witnesses gave police a description of the suspect. According to police reports, the suspect is a Hispanic male, approximately 25 years old, wearing a jean jacket, with a glass eye and a beard.

45. Which of the following pieces of information provided by the victim is most helpful in identifying the suspect?

(A) The suspect has a beard.

(B) The suspect is wearing a jean jacket.

(C) The suspect has a glass eye.

(D) The suspect is approximately 25 years old.

Go on to next page

Answer Questions 46 and 47 solely on the basis of the following passage.

Officer Landon is assigned to Miracle Farms Housing Development on North 87th Street and Meade Street. Landon took time to familiarize himself with the crime rates and statistics of four of the buildings in the development for April. He found that any robberies that occurred took place at 14 N. 87th St. Any assaults or cases of domestic violence took place at 8 Meade St. Tool sheds were broken into at 4 Meade St. and any report of rapes from April came from 19 N. 87th St. The robberies that were reported occurred between 5:00 p.m. and 6:00 p.m. Assaults or domestic violence disputes happened between 12:00 p.m. and 2:00 p.m. The tool sheds were discovered between 5:00 p.m. and 5:30 p.m. and suspected to have been broken into between 3:00 p.m. and 5:00 p.m. Rapes appeared to have taken place between 2:00 p.m. and 3:30 p.m.

When Landon is working a 10:00 a.m. to 6:00 p.m. shift, he has no choice but to divide his time amongst the four buildings in the development if he is to prevent these crimes from occurring.

46. To reduce the number of robberies, he should patrol

(A) 19 N. 87th St. between 5 p.m. and 6 p.m.

(B) 8 Meade St. between 3 p.m. and 5 p.m.

(C) 14 N. 87th St. between 5 p.m. and 6 p.m.

(D) 14 N. 87th St. between 12 p.m. and 2 p.m.

47. To reduce the number of rapes, he should patrol

(A) 4 Meade St. between 2 p.m. and 4 p.m.

(B) 14 N. 87th St. between 12 p.m. and 2 p.m.

(C) 19 N. 87th St. between 5 p.m. and 6 p.m.

(D) 19 N. 87th St. between 2 p.m. and 4 p.m.

Answer Questions 48 through 51 solely on the basis of the following passage.

Occasionally, a police officer may have to watch an area for suspicious activity, including the presence of suspicious vehicles.

48. For which of the following should an officer consider a vehicle suspicious in most states?

(A) If it has a broken rearview mirror

(B) If its lights are not on at night while it is moving

(C) If it is playing loud, unfamiliar music

(D) If it has multiple decals on its trunk or bumper

49. For which of the following should an officer consider a vehicle not suspicious in most states?

(A) If it has been in the same parking spot for days

(B) If it has a thick film over its license plate

(C) If it has passed by the area multiple times within minutes

(D) If it has multiple antennae or neon lighting

Go on to next page

50. A police officer may have to escort a convoy from one place to another. In which of the following situations would a police escort be unnecessary?

    (A) If a high-profile celebrity is making an appearance downtown

    (B) If a person is injured and an ambulance is not immediately available

    (C) If a person is lost and cannot find his or her way back home

    (D) If a government official needs to catch an important flight

51. Police officers often are assigned to patrol specific areas of the city. Which of the following areas should police officers *not* patrol on a regular basis?

    (A) A city block containing a suspected meth lab

    (B) A park where teenagers often gather after school

    (C) A block containing two families who do not get along

    (D) A quiet, upper-class development with low crime rates

---

Answer Question 52 solely on the basis of the following passage.

Officer Orlando has been told by his sergeant to distribute 63 training manuals equally among the nine different squads assigned to the precinct.

52. Which one of the following choices correctly states the number of training manuals that are to be assigned to each squad?

    (A) 5

    (B) 6

    (C) 7

    (D) 9

Answer Question 53 solely on the basis of the following information.

Officer Orlando arrested Timothy Lyons, who had the following stolen electronic items in his possession:

    4 cellphones each valued at $125

    2 stereos each valued at $375

    1 television set valued at $1,200

    4 speakers each valued at $75

53. Which one of the following is the total value of the stolen property?

    (A) $1,775

    (B) $2,750

    (C) $3,950

    (D) $4,575

Go on to next page

Directions: Study the following photograph for ten minutes and try to remember as many details as you can. You may not write or make any notes during this time. After these ten minutes are up, cover the photograph and answer Questions 54 through 63 about the image; you may not turn back to review the photo until you have completed the exam.

Photo courtesy www.public-domain-image.com

Answer Questions 54 through 63 on the basis of the photograph.

54. How many pieces of baseball equipment are in the picture?

(A) 1

(B) 2

(C) 3

(D) 4

55. What type of baseball bat is in the picture?

(A) Old Hickory

(B) Wilson

(C) Louisville Slugger

(D) Easton

56. Where is the American flag in the picture?

(A) Underneath all the other items in the picture

(B) To the left of the apples and behind the rest of the items

(C) To the right of all the other items in the picture

(D) Over the top of the items in the picture

57. How many apples are in the picture?

(A) 2

(B) 3

(C) 4

(D) 5

Go on to next page

58. What color or colors are the apples in the picture?

    (A) Yellow

    (B) Yellow and green

    (C) Red

    (D) Red and green

59. Which of these is located on the left side of the picture?

    (A) A cake

    (B) A pie

    (C) A cookie

    (D) A doughnut

60. Which of these is *not* in the picture?

    (A) A baseball glove

    (B) A flag

    (C) An apple

    (D) A baseball cap

61. Where is the baseball located in the picture?

    (A) Next to the baseball bat

    (B) Under the baseball bat

    (C) Next to the apples

    (D) Mixed in with the apples

62. What is above the dessert in the picture?

    (A) An apple

    (B) A star

    (C) A stripe

    (D) A plate

63. A dessert is included in the picture. Which of the following is correct?

    (A) It is cut in half.

    (B) It is cut into four pieces.

    (C) One piece has been cut out of it.

    (D) It is whole.

Directions: Complete Questions 64 through 85. Be sure to read each question carefully.

Answer Question 64 solely on the basis of the following passage.

While questioning a crime victim, you are told that Suspect 1 held a knife to the victim while Suspect 2 took his wallet, cellphone, and MP3 player. Both suspects, white males in their late 20s, ran north up the street. The crime victim chased them for three blocks and then they split up. Suspect 1 turned left and Suspect 2 went right. Suspect 1 ran directly into a crowded park.

64. According to the information you received, you would be most correct if you reported that Suspect 1 was last seen entering a park located in which direction from the location of the incident?

    (A) Northeast

    (B) Southeast

    (C) Northwest

    (D) Southwest

Go on to next page

> *Answer Questions 65 through 68 solely on the basis of the following passage.*

Officer Wilson patrolled his usual area and drove south on Oak Avenue. At 11:58 p.m., Officer Wilson received a call from dispatch about a possible disturbance of the peace at a residence on Maple Lane. Officer Wilson was three blocks away from the residence, so he radioed dispatch to say that he would take the call. Officer Wilson made a left turn onto Front Street at 11:59 p.m. and proceeded toward the residence in question.

At 12:01 a.m., Officer Wilson turned right onto Parnell Street and turned left onto Maple Lane, arriving at address 108, the residence that reported the disturbance of the peace. When Officer Wilson exited his car, he heard loud music coming from a residence across the street. Officer Wilson was approached by a man and a woman who identified themselves as Edward Thomas, age 50, and Debbie Thomas, age 52. Mr. Thomas told Officer Wilson that the residence at 105 Maple Lane had been blaring loud music since approximately 9:00 p.m. Mr. Thomas also said that he asked his neighbors to turn down the music at 11:15 p.m., but they refused.

Officer Wilson determined that the noise level coming from 105 Maple Lane was both excessive and unreasonable. At 12:07 a.m., Officer Wilson walked to 105 Maple Lane and knocked on the door. A man who identified himself as Rodger Whitney, age 25, opened the door. Officer Wilson identified himself and explained that the noise coming from the house was excessive and unreasonable. The officer asked to see the owner of the residence. Then, Officer Wilson gave the owner of the residence, Madeline Ray, age 26, a citation for disturbing the peace. The officer left the residence at 12:17 p.m. without incident.

65. On which street was Officer Wilson patrolling when he got the call from dispatch?

(A) Front Street

(B) Maple Lane

(C) Parnell Street

(D) Oak Avenue

66. At what time did Officer Wilson arrive on Maple Lane?

(A) 11:15 p.m.

(B) 11:58 p.m.

(C) 12:01 a.m.

(D) 12:15 p.m.

67. Who received a citation for the disturbance of the peace?

(A) Madeline Ray

(B) Edward Thomas

(C) Rodger Whitney

(D) Debbie Thomas

68. Who reported the disturbance of the peace?

(A) Rodger Whitney

(B) Officer Wilson

(C) Madeline Ray

(D) Edward Thomas

Go on to next page

Answer Question 69 solely on the basis of the following information.

While patrolling the area with his horse, Officer Diaz responded to a traffic accident. He recorded the following details when he arrived at the scene:

Location of Accident: Willow Avenue

Time of Accident: 6:45 a.m.

Vehicle Involved: 2007 Subaru

Driver: Natasha Maloney

Damage: Vehicle struck a fire hydrant, resulting in minor body damage and a broken tail light.

69. Officer Diaz must write a report about the incident. Which of the following expresses the preceding information *most clearly, accurately, and completely?*

(A) At 6:45 p.m., Natasha Maloney was parking on Willow Avenue. A 2007 Subaru was involved in an accident when it struck a fire hydrant resulting in minor body damage and a broken tail light.

(B) A car was involved in an accident on Willow Avenue at 6:45 p.m. It struck a fire hydrant resulting in a broken tail light and minor body damage. Natasha Maloney is the owner of a 2007 Subaru.

(C) A 2007 Subaru struck Natasha Maloney causing a broken tail light and minor body damage on Willow Avenue at 6:45 a.m.

(D) A 2007 Subaru driven by Natasha Maloney struck a fire hydrant on Willow Avenue at 6:45 a.m., resulting in minor body damage to the car and a broken tail light.

Answer Question 70 solely on the basis of the following information.

An officer is preparing the first-person narrative portion of her preliminary report on an incident of domestic violence that occurred earlier in the afternoon. She reviews the first draft of her report and pauses when she gets to the following sentences:

1. On April 16, 2010, at 1:52 p.m., I, Officer Linda Marx, received a call to respond to 222 N. Carvington St. for a report of a domestic dispute.

2. The victim said that her husband, who had left the house after the dispute took place and was wearing black athletic shorts, a blue T-shirt with the sleeves cut off, and had a red baseball hat on.

Go on to next page

70. Which of the following best describes the preceding sentences?

(A) Sentence 1 does not contain grammatical errors.

(B) Sentence 2 does not contain grammatical errors.

(C) Sentence 1 and Sentence 2 contain grammatical errors.

(D) Neither Sentence 1 nor Sentence 2 contains grammatical errors.

Answer Questions 71 and 72 solely on the basis of the following information.

Officers responding to a car accident should

1. Determine whether any injuries were sustained in the crash.

2. Request emergency medical services, the fire department, and/or a supervisor if the crash includes serious injuries or other unusual circumstances.

3. Secure the crash scene and ensure no one leaves or enters the scene.

4. Determine whether the driver or drivers are capable of moving vehicles from the road. Drivers should not move vehicles off the road if:

   a. Injuries could become worse from moving the vehicles.

   b. Someone was fatally injured in the crash.

   c. The vehicle is carrying hazardous material.

   d. A driver is suspected to be under the influence of drugs or alcohol.

5. Ask capable drivers to move vehicles off the road.

6. Collect names, license plate numbers, and insurance information from all drivers involved in the crash.

7. Take photographs of the crash scene and damaged vehicles.

8. Determine the need for any specialized department or agency, including gas companies, electric companies, hazmat teams, and so forth. Request any required specialized services and/or tow trucks and wreckers.

Go on to next page

71. Officer Lopez is called to the scene of a car crash on a local highway. After Lopez arrives on the scene, he determines no one has sustained life-threatening injuries but calls emergency medical services for a minor injury sustained by a passenger. Officer Lopez secures the crash scene, determines that the drivers are capable of moving their vehicles, and asks them to move their vehicles off the road. What should Officer Lopez do next?

    (A) Determine whether any of the vehicles are carrying hazardous material.

    (B) Take photographs of the crash scene and damaged vehicles.

    (C) Collect names, license plate numbers, and insurance information.

    (D) Determine the need for any specialized department or agency.

72. Officer Miller is called to the scene of a vehicle crash along the back road. After Miller arrives on the scene, he determines that the driver of the car may have sustained life-threatening injuries and the passenger in the car is also injured. He calls emergency medical services. What should he do next?

    (A) Move the vehicle off the road.

    (B) Take photographs of the crash scene.

    (C) Try to find the insurance information.

    (D) Secure the crash scene.

Answer Questions 73 through 75 solely on the basis of the following map. The arrows indicate one- and two-way streets: One arrow represents a one-way street, while two arrows represent a two-way street.

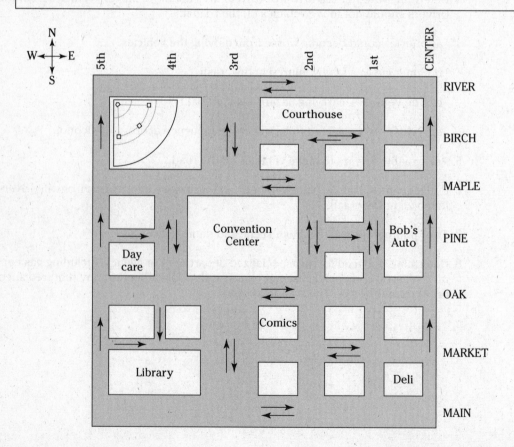

73. If you are located at the Courthouse on River Street, travel south on 3rd Street, and then turn east onto Maple Street and stop, you will be closest to which of the following?

    (A) A day care

    (B) A convention center

    (C) Bob's Auto

    (D) A comics shop

74. You are located at Bob's Auto on Center Street and receive a call about a crime in progress in front of the library. Which one of the following is the most direct route for you to take in your patrol car, making sure to obey all traffic regulations?

    (A) Travel north on Center Street to Maple Street, then west on Maple Street to 1st Street, then south on 1st Street until Oak Street, then west onto Oak Street until 3rd Street, and then south on 3rd Street to the library.

    (B) Travel south on Center Street to Oak Street, then west on Oak Street until 3rd Street, and then south on 3rd Street to the library.

    (C) Travel south on Center Street to Market Street, and then west on Market Street to the library.

    (D) Travel north on Center Street to Maple Street, then west on Maple Street to 2nd Street, then south on 2nd Street until Oak Street, then east on Oak Street until 1st Street, then south on 1st Street until Market Street, and then west on Market Street to the library.

75. You are located at the day care on 4th Street and must respond to a disturbance at the deli on Market Street. Which one of the following is the most direct route for you to take in your patrol car, making sure to obey all traffic regulations?

    (A) Travel south on 4th Street until Market Street, and then west on Market Street to the deli.

    (B) Travel south on 4th Street to Oak Street, then east on Oak Street until 1st Street, and then south on 1st Street until Market Street. Travel east on Market Street to the deli.

    (C) Travel south on 4th Street until Oak Street, then east on Oak Street until 2nd Street, then south on 2nd Street until Market Street, then east on Market Street until 1st Street, then north on 1st Street until Oak Street, then east on Pine Street until Market Street, and then south on Market Street to the deli.

    (D) Travel north on 4th Street until Pine Street, west on Pine street until 5th Street, south on 5th Street until Main Street, east on Main Street to Market Street, and then north on Market Street to the deli.

Go on to next page

Answer Question 76 solely on the basis of the following information.

Police Officer Kendell is on foot in pursuit of a man who just snatched a purse from and assaulted a woman who was walking in the downtown area. Officer Kendell follows the suspect to the street pictured in the following illustration, and the suspect runs into the fourth house from the left. Officer Kendell notes the shape of the building and runs to the back to try to stop the suspect from running out of the back of the building.

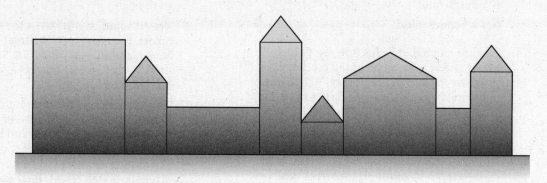

76. When Officer Kendell reaches the alley behind this set of buildings he is too close to count which building he should enter, but he is able to determine the shapes of the buildings as he passes them. Which building should Officer Kendell watch for the suspect?

(A)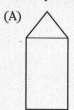

(B)

(C)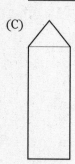

(D)

Go on to next page

> *Answer Questions 77 through 80 solely on the basis of the following passage.*

Officers James Gilford and Alex Smith were driving southbound on Samson Lane on July 14. At 4:45 p.m. the officers were dispatched to a commercial building located at 202 South Street for complaints of criminal trespass. Officers arrived at the address at 4:50 p.m.

The officers entered the abandoned building, a four-story warehouse belonging to the Foster Furniture Company, and began investigating. At approximately 4:57 p.m. officers Gilford and Smith had investigated the first and second floors of the building and had not located any suspects. As the officers approached the third floor of the building, they heard voices. When the officers reached the third floor, they found Anthony Miller (of 478 Fordham Rd.), age 23; Joseph Robinson (of 684 Jackson Ave.), age 25; and Garrett Henderson (of 104 First Ave.), age 20.

The men told the officers they did not know they had been trespassing. Mr. Robinson had an open container of beer, and Mr. Henderson had an open container of vodka. The officers also saw empty containers of malt liquor and whiskey on the floor near the men. Officers Gilford and Smith cited Mr. Henderson for underage drinking, and all three men were cited for criminal trespassing. At 5:25 p.m., the officers escorted the men out of the building and left the premises without incident.

77. On which street is the Foster Furniture Company warehouse located?

(A) Samson Lane

(B) Fordham Road

(C) Jackson Avenue

(D) South Street

78. On which floor of the building did the officers locate the suspects?

(A) First

(B) Second

(C) Third

(D) Fourth

79. Which of these people was cited for underage drinking?

(A) Garrett Henderson

(B) Alex Smith

(C) Joseph Robinson

(D) Anthony Miller

80. At what time did officers Gilford and Smith arrive at the warehouse?

(A) 4:45 p.m.

(B) 4:50 p.m.

(C) 4:57 p.m.

(D) 5:25 p.m.

Go on to next page

> *Answer Question 81 solely on the basis of the following information.*

While at a training camp, recruit officers learn that they may one day be called to a scene only to find that it has become a hostage situation. Once they arrive on scene, many officers will have specific tasks that they must complete to secure the area, ensure the safety of bystanders, and gather information about the situation. One or more officers may be asked to gather the following information and more about the hostage taker:

1. Name, age, sex, and race

2. Marital status and history

3. History of or involvement in criminal activities

4. History of physical or mental health conditions

5. Style of personality (for example, aggressive, narcissistic, dependent, compulsive)

6. Employment history and socioeconomic status

7. History of substance abuse (for example, alcohol, drugs)

8. History of military training or participation

9. Level of education (for example, high school, some college, college graduate, trade school)

10. Daily activity

81. Based on the preceding information, it would be most correct for recruits to assume that the main reason officers collect these details about the hostage-taker is

(A) to determine how many officers are needed to overtake the subject.

(B) to have accurate information for the report they must write.

(C) to determine whether the subject might be willing to negotiate and cooperate.

(D) to release to the media when they ask for the identity of the subject.

Go on to next page

Answer Question 82 solely on the basis of the following information.

Officers studying juvenile law are learning about the curfew ordinances in several different boroughs and towns in their state.

JURISDICTION	AGE	WEEKDAY TIMES	PARENTAL FINES
Ashville (town)	Under 17	11 P.M. to 5 A.M.	Up to $75
	Under 15	11 P.M. to 5 A.M.	Up to $175
Madison (borough)	15 and under	10 P.M. to 6 A.M.	Up to $300
Smithville (borough)	16 and under	10 P.M. to 5 A.M.	$100–$200
Johnstown (town)	Under 16	11 P.M. to 6 A.M.	Up to $100
Collegeville (town)	Under 17	12 A.M. to 5 A.M.	None
	Under 15	11 P.M. to 5 A.M.	$50
South Pines (borough)	16 and under	11 P.M. to 6 A.M.	Up to $200
Franklin (town)	Under 17	12 A.M. to 6 A.M.	$50–$100
	15 and under	11 P.M. to 6 A.M.	$100
Clinton (borough)	15 and under	11 P.M. to 5 A.M.	$200 or 60 hours of service

82. After reviewing the preceding table, it would be most correct for an officer to conclude that

(A) boroughs generally set earlier juvenile curfew times than towns do.

(B) most boroughs and towns have two different age ranges for juveniles.

(C) towns are stricter than boroughs about juveniles violating their curfews.

(D) towns and boroughs generally give harsher curfew fines to younger juveniles.

Answer Question 83 solely on the basis of the following information.

Juvenile proceedings are similar to adult proceedings in many ways. Juveniles must be notified of all charges, they have the right to an attorney and can receive one for no cost if their family cannot pay, and they can invoke their Fifth Amendment rights. They can also confront their accuser, cross-examine witnesses, and they must be found guilty beyond reasonable doubt. The following are a few ways juvenile proceedings differ from adult proceedings:

1. Juvenile offenders do not commit "crimes." Instead, they commit "delinquent acts."

2. Juveniles do not have a constitutional right to a bail, to a public trial, or to a jury. Instead of a jury, one judge hears juvenile cases.

3. Juveniles attend "adjudication hearings," not "trials."

4. Juveniles are not to be "punished" if they are found delinquent. Instead, they are "rehabilitated" so that they can return to society as soon as possible.

Go on to next page

83. Officer White arrests a 13-year-old boy he finds spray-painting anti-Semitic symbols on the back of an office building downtown. Greatly offended by the symbols that the juvenile was painting, Officer White is disappointed when the boy, a first-time offender, only receives mandatory community service and probation as his punishment for breaking the law. The sentence the juvenile offender received did not include jail time because

    (A) juveniles only appear in court before a judge, not a full jury.

    (B) juveniles are rehabilitated, not punished for their delinquent acts.

    (C) juveniles attend an adjudication hearing, which is not as serious as a trial.

    (D) juveniles have the right to better attorneys who make them appear innocent.

Answer Question 84 solely on the basis of the following information.

One of the most important, yet overlooked, jobs that police officers perform on a daily basis is the writing of preliminary reports. Many officers believe preliminary reports should be brief, but a longer report that requires more time at the desk and contains specific and accurate details may serve as a better tool. Many times, officers place "none," "N/A," or "NFD" (no further description) in fields where critical information is needed. If specific details are not available to officers at first, they should do whatever they can to obtain them. Although each department formats its preliminary report differently, the following informational fields appear on all regardless of department:

1. Date and time of incident or offense

2. Location

3. Description of suspect(s)

4. First-person narrative of officer's observations

Note: If preliminary reports are not typed on computers, handwriting should be clear and legible.

Go on to next page

84. After responding to a call about a home invasion, Officer Jefferies sits down at her desk to write her preliminary report. It is past 11 p.m., and as soon as she finishes the report, her shift is over. As she fills in the blank fields, she remembers that her victim said her cellphone was stolen in the robbery and she no longer has a landline. Because she does not have a phone number for the victim, she writes "none" in the corresponding field. She turns in the report at 11:30 p.m. and heads home. Officer Jefferies's report may be criticized by those who read it because

    (A) she submitted it at the end of the workday.

    (B) she wrote it in sloppy, unreadable handwriting.

    (C) she did not supply a way to contact the victim.

    (D) she forgot to record the suspect's description.

Answer Question 85 solely on the basis of the following information.

Officer Lang arrested Shirley Washington, who had the following stolen items in her possession:

   2 gold rings each valued at $250

   3 gold chains each valued at $130

   4 watches each valued at $800

85. Which one of the following is the total value of the stolen property?

    (A) $1,180

    (B) $3,700

    (C) $4,090

    (D) $4,900

STOP DO NOT TURN THE PAGE UNTIL TOLD TO DO SO. DO NOT RETURN TO A PREVIOUS TEST.

Chapter 20

Answers and Explanations for Practice Test 4

● ●

After you take the practice New York City Police Department Police Officer Candidate Test in Chapter 19, use this chapter to check your answers. If you aren't sure why an answer was incorrect, use this chapter to get explanations of the answers. If you correctly answered a question, you may still want to read the explanations to get a better understanding of the thought process that helped you choose the correct answer. If you're short on time, turn to the end of this chapter to find an abbreviated answer key.

1. **D.** Two people are standing in the doorway of the building with a sign on it that reads Berger Bros. These are the only people shown in the photograph.

2. **A.** The printer's name is on a sign on the second story of a building on the left side of the photograph. The printer's name is Samuel L. Drake.

3. **B.** A horse is shown on the left side of the photograph. It looks as if the horse is pulling a carriage.

4. **C.** The building in the center of the photograph has a flag and a ladder in front of it. The sign on this building says Birthplace of Old Glory.

5. **C.** The street in front of the buildings is brick.

6. **B.** The sign on the first story of the building on the left side of the photograph says Carey & Co. on top and Coach Lamps underneath. This means that Carey & Co. sells coach lamps.

7. **D.** The utility pole is on the right side of the photograph. It is in front of Berger Bros.

8. **D.** Three windows are shown on the second story of the Berger Bros. building.

9. **C.** The building in the center says that it is open to the public. This building has a sign on it that says Birthplace of Old Glory.

10. **D.** The building in the center has several pictures in the front window along with flags. This building is Birthplace of Old Glory.

11. **D.** If the suspect was running south and then turned left, he would be traveling west.

12. **B.** The passage says that the taller male had curly, brown hair while the other male, who appeared younger, had blond hair cut close to his head.

13. **C.** According to the first paragraph of the passage, the officers arrived at the apartment at 6:37 p.m.

14. **D.** The third paragraph of the passage says that Mrs. Brown lives in Apt. 4D.

15. **B.** The most clearly written sentence is in Choice (B). Choices (A) and (C) are ambiguous; it isn't clear in either sentence that the 2006 Ford was driven by Carillo. Choice (D) makes it sound as if the Ford was not driven by Carillo.

16. **B.** Only the second sentence is grammatically correct. A better way to write Sentence 1 is: On June 12, Third Avenue will be closed between May Place and 14th Street and between St. Rita's Place and 7th Street.

17. **C.** Officer Riley should request backup and tell dispatch his location. This is the proper procedure to follow according to the third step in the passage.

18. **D.** According to the third step in the passage, Officer Torres should request emergency medical assistance.

19. **B.** The passage mentions that new, growing threats in our country include suicide bombers and radio-controlled and vehicle-borne explosives. Therefore, the most likely reason to use robots is to deactivate bombs without putting people in jeopardy.

20. **B.** The best conclusion based on the information in the table is that police dogs use their sense of smell to perform most tasks, such as detecting illicit substances, detecting cadavers, and tracking suspects.

21. **C.** Choice (C) is the best answer because all the information in this description is corroborated by the other three descriptions. Choices (A), (B), and (D) are incorrect because they all include pieces of information that are not corroborated by any other description.

22. **D.** Choice (D) is the best answer because all the numbers and letters in this plate number are corroborated by other descriptions. Choices (A), (B), and (C) are incorrect because they all include numbers or letters that are not corroborated by other descriptions.

23. **B.** Choice (B) is the best answer because Officer Davis needs the total number of citations he issued during the four-week period, and Choice (D) adds together all the citations.

24. **D.** The back of the building should look exactly like the front of the building but in reverse. Choice (D) is correct.

25. **D.** According to the second paragraph of the passage, Officer Taylor was on Washington Drive when she pulled over the sedan.

26. **B.** The driver of the sedan identified himself as Nathan Neilson, age 22.

27. **A.** The fourth paragraph of the passage says that the car was registered to the suspect's mother, Lauren Danvers.

28. **D.** The fourth paragraph says that Officer Taylor asked to see Neilson's driver's license and registration at 8:55 p.m.

29. **C.** The meaning of the sentence in Choice (C) is clear, and the sentence is grammatically correct. In Choices (A) and (B), it is not clear which cars or drivers were involved in the accident. Choice (D) does not include all available information.

30. **C.** Answer Choice (C) correctly shows the directions in which the vehicles were traveling. While Choice (A) may look as if it's correct, Vehicle 1 is traveling east in this diagram, instead of west as it says in the description.

31. **D.** The meaning of the sentence in Choice (D) is clear, and the sentence is grammatically correct. Choice (A) does not make it clear that Marcus Russel was the person who was stabbed. Choice (B) does not mention Marcus Russel, and Choice (C) is awkward.

32. **B.** The sentence in Choice (B) clearly states the meaning and is grammatically correct. Choices (A), (C), and (D) don't make it clear that it was Ronda McMicken's car that was stolen.

33. **C.** Officer Heinz's choice not to knock was legal because he believed that the suspect may have had a weapon. The passage says officers do not have to knock when the situation may involve physical violence or a threat to a person's life.

34. **A.** Choice (A) best matches the definition of aggravated assault. Mary's actions were intentional and she planned to harm her victim. Scissors can also be considered a deadly weapon.

35. **A.** This question asks you to choose the answer option that is not an example of criminal trespass. Choice (A) is correct because Amanda has permission to be in the library after hours.

36. **C.** This question asks you to choose the answer option that is not an example of self-defense. Choice (C) is correct because Rafael stabbed a woman who only shoved him — and she only did this because he was trying to steal her purse.

37. **C.** To answer this question, you need to look carefully at the design on the bottom of the boot. There is a vertical line in the center and three wavy lines on the top and bottom. Choice (C) shows this pattern.

38. **A.** According to the information in the passage, the next thing Officer Davis should do is rate the suspect's overall likelihood of attempting suicide. Then Officer Davis should make sure the suspect does not have items that could be used to attempt suicide.

39. **B.** Because Officer Huang has rated the suspect as being at a high risk of suicide, she should monitor him at all times.

40. **C.** To answer this question, you must first find Carnation Street on the map and use the key to determine which direction is east. Then go north on Salem Drive and turn west onto Oak Street. At this location, you are close to point 7.

41. **B.** To answer this question, find point 5 on the map. Then look at the key to determine which direction is west. Travel on Oak Street, and then turn onto Wilson Drive and drive to Beach Street. Point 3 is on Beach Street, but you're closer to point 4.

42. **B.** To answer this question, you have to find the intersection of Grove Street and Wilson Drive. Then find the intersection of May Street and Salem Drive. Then select the answer option that gives a direct route from the first place to the second. Choice (B) is correct.

43. **D.** Begin by finding the intersection of Yardley Street and Wilson Drive. Then find the intersection of Hampton Street and Monarch Drive. Using the directional key, choose the direct route from one location to the other. Choice (D) is correct.

44. **A.** To answer this question, choose the answer option that gives the suspect's most outstanding trait. Choice (A), the suspect has a prosthetic leg, is correct.

45. **C.** To answer this question, choose the answer option that gives the suspect's most outstanding trait. Choice (C), the suspect has a glass eye, is correct.

46. **C.** The passage says that any report of robberies came from 14 N. 87th St. and that they took place between 5 p.m. and 6 p.m. Therefore, Choice (C) is correct.

47. **D.** The passage says that any report of rapes came from 19 N. 87th St. and that they took place between 2 p.m. and 3:30 p.m. Therefore, to reduce the number of rapes, he should patrol this area between 2 p.m. and 4 p.m.

48. **B.** Choice (B) is the best answer; in most states, a vehicle moving at night without its lights on is suspicious.

49. **D.** Choice (D) is the correct answer; a vehicle with multiple antennae or neon lighting is probably not suspicious.

50. **C.** Choice (C) is correct because the police officer could simply give the person directions.

51. **D.** Police officers should patrol areas where people are likely to be in danger. Choice (D) describes an area where people are rarely in danger.

52. **C.** To find the number of training manuals that should be distributed equally among nine squads, divide 63, the number of training manuals, by the number of squads, 9. The answer is 7.

53. **B.** To find the answer to this question, begin by finding the total value of each type of item. The total value of the cellphones is $500; the total value of the stereos is $750; the value of the television set is $1,200; and the value of the speakers is $300. When you add together these amounts, the answer is $2,750.

54. **C.** Three pieces of baseball equipment are shown in the picture: a bat, a baseball, and a glove.

55. **C.** The baseball bat has the words "Louisville Slugger" on it.

56. **A.** All the items in the picture are placed on top of the American flag.

57. **B.** Three apples are shown in the picture.

58. **D.** Two apples in the picture are red and one is green.

59. **B.** A pie is located on the left side of the photograph.

60. **D.** A baseball cap is not shown in the photograph.

61. **A.** The baseball is touching the bat in the photograph.

62. **B.** A star on the American flag is shown directly above the pie in the photograph.

63. **D.** The dessert in the picture is a pie and it's whole, meaning it does not have any slices cut or removed.

64. **C.** To answer this question, you need to determine in which direction Suspect 1 was traveling. The information tells you that he ran north up the street and away from the incident. Then, Suspect 1 turned left and ran into a park. The direction Suspect 1 traveled is northwest from the incident.

65. **D.** The first paragraph of the passage says that Officer Wilson was patrolling Oak Avenue when he received the call from dispatch.

66. **C.** The second paragraph of the passage says that Officer Wilson turned right onto Parnell Street and turned left onto Maple Lane at 12:01 a.m.

67. **A.** The last paragraph of the passage says that the owner of the residence, Madeline Ray, received a citation for disturbing the peace.

68. **D.** The second paragraph of the passage says that the residence that reported the disturbance was 108 Maple Lane. When Officer Wilson exited his car, he was approached by Edward and Debbie Thomas, the residents of this address who reported the disturbance.

69. **D.** The sentence in Choice (D) includes all the information and is grammatically correct. Choices (A) and (B) do not make it clear that Natasha Maloney was driving the 2007 Subaru. Choice (C) says that the Subaru hit Maloney, which is not correct.

70. **A.** Sentence 1 is free from grammatical errors. Sentence 2, on the other hand, is not a complete thought. It should be revised like this: "The victim said that her husband, who had left the house after the dispute and was wearing black athletic shorts, a blue T-shirt with the sleeves cut off, and a red baseball cap, was probably going to his mother's house."

71. **C.** The passage states that Officer Lopez followed these steps: He determined that no one had life-threatening injuries; he called emergency medical services; he secured the scene; and he had the drivers move their vehicles off the road. According to the listed steps, Officer Lopez should next collect names, license plate numbers, and insurance information.

72. **D.** Officer Miller should secure the crash scene and make sure no one enters the scene. Up to this point, Miller followed these steps: He determined that the driver had life-threatening injuries and called emergency medical services.

73. **B.** To answer this question correctly, begin at the Courthouse on River Street, then, using the directional key, move south on 3rd Street, and then turn east onto Maple Street. This path takes you to the convention center.

74. **A.** To answer this question, begin at Bob's Auto on Center Street — and note that Center Street is a one-way. To get to the library, you need to travel north on Center Street. Then travel west on Maple Street until 1st Street, then south on 1st Street until Oak Street. Then turn west onto Oak Street until 3rd Street. Travel south on 3rd Street and proceed to the library. This is the most direct path from Bob's Auto to the library without violating any traffic regulations.

75. **B.** To answer this question, begin at the day care on 4th Street. Travel south on 4th Street, a two-way street, until Oak Street. Travel east on Oak Street until 1st Street. Travel south on 1st Street until Market Street and east on Market Street until you reach the deli.

76. **C.** The fourth house from the left is the same shape and size as the house in Choice (C), so Choice (C) is the right answer.

77. **D.** This question asks you to identify the street on which the warehouse was located. The officers responded to a warehouse at 202 South Street, so Choice (D) is correct.

78. **C.** The officers searched the first and second floors and found no suspects, and the officers did not enter the fourth floor. The officers found the suspects on the third floor, Choice (C).

79. **A.** Suspect Garret Henderson is the only suspect under the legal drinking age and was the only suspect cited for underage drinking.

80. **B.** At 4:57 p.m. the officers finished searching the first and second floors.

81. **C.** The main reason police would want to obtain as much information about a hostage-taker as possible is to determine whether they have a chance at getting the hostage-taker to negotiate. This is the reason they want to determine the hostage-taker's personality style and history of involvement in crimes.

82. **D.** You can use inductive reasoning to conclude from the information in the table that towns and boroughs give harsher curfew fines to younger juveniles. For example, in Franklin, juveniles under 17 receive a fine of $50 to $100, but juveniles 15 and under automatically receive a fine of $100.

83. **B.** According to the fourth rule, the juvenile offender did not receive jail time because the juvenile was delinquent and therefore needs rehabilitation.

84. **C.** Officer Jefferies did not supply a telephone number because the victim's cellphone was stolen in the robbery and the victim does not have a landline. She should have included an alternate way to contact the victim.

85. **C.** To correctly answer this question, you need to first determine the total value of each type of item. The total value of the two gold rings is $500, the total value of the three gold chains is $390, and the total value of the four watches is $3,200. Therefore, the total value of the stolen goods is $4,090.

Answer Key for Practice Test 4

1. D	23. B	45. C	67. A
2. A	24. D	46. C	68. D
3. B	25. D	47. D	69. D
4. C	26. B	48. B	70. A
5. C	27. A	49. D	71. C
6. B	28. D	50. C	72. D
7. D	29. C	51. D	73. B
8. D	30. C	52. C	74. A
9. C	31. D	53. B	75. B
10. D	32. B	54. C	76. C
11. D	33. C	55. C	77. D
12. B	34. A	56. A	78. C
13. C	35. A	57. B	79. A
14. D	36. C	58. D	80. B
15. B	37. C	59. B	81. C
16. B	38. A	60. D	82. D
17. C	39. B	61. A	83. B
18. D	40. C	62. B	84. C
19. B	41. B	63. D	85. C
20. B	42. B	64. C	
21. C	43. D	65. D	
22. D	44. A	66. C	

Part V
The Part of Tens

The 5th Wave   By Rich Tennant

"Your buddy says the two of you were peripheral to the incident in question. You just said you were superficial to the incident. Now which is it, peripheral or superficial?!"

In this part . . .

No *For Dummies* book is complete without the Part of Tens. This part includes our police officer exam top-ten lists. The first list gives you tips to help you succeed on the written police officer exam. The second list covers some basics that every police officer candidate should know about the police academy. The chapters in this part are short and cut right to the chase, so give 'em a quick read and get on your way.

Chapter 21

Ten Tips to Help You Succeed on the Exam

• •

In This Chapter

▶ Preparing your mind, body, and schedule for the police officer tests

▶ Following directions, pacing yourself, and making sure your answers count

• •

T aking a test isn't fun — at least we don't think so. Think of some tests you've taken in the past — in high school or college, or even your driver's test. How did you feel beforehand? If you're like most people, you felt nervous and uncomfortable. Maybe you even had trouble sleeping the night before these tests.

You're likely to feel nervous before the written police officer test, the physical ability test (PAT), the oral board review, and the medical and psychological evaluations. We can't go with you, hold your hand, and tell you to relax, but in this chapter we give you some tips to help you feel good about taking the police officer tests. Remember, too, that the worst that can happen is you fail a test. You can always apply for another police officer job and retake the tests. Try to think of the police officer tests as a learning experience — if you don't succeed the first time, learn from the experience and try again.

Prepare Yourself

You know that old question: "How do you get to Carnegie Hall?" "Practice." This tip may seem like a no-brainer, but you need to prepare yourself for each police officer test before you take it. The name of the game is practice, practice, practice.

Before you take the written test, call the police department or view its Web site to find out whether the test is the National Police Officer Selection Test (POST) or a civil service test, such as the New York City (NYC) Police Department Police Officer Candidate Test. Then study the information in Chapter 2, which covers both of these tests. Speak to the police department again (or check its Web site) before you take the physical ability test (PAT). Find out where the test is held and what you have to do during the test. Practice these exercises ahead of time. Knowing what to expect is a great way to relieve anxiety.

Gather everything you need to take each test the night before. Before the written test, collect pencils (No. 2), pens, and a watch. Also grab your admission notice and a photo ID, such as your driver's license. Getting your clothes ready the night before each test is also a good idea so that you don't rush in the morning and forget something.

Be aware that you aren't allowed to bring cellphones, beepers, or any other electronic communications devices into the testing area. You could be disqualified if you're caught using a cellphone in a hallway or restroom.

Get Plenty of ZZZs

Your body needs sleep to function properly. If you're tired, you won't be able to concentrate on the written exam. The same is true of the physical ability test (PAT): How many push-ups can you do in a minute if you're wiped out? And dozing during the oral interview is definitely frowned upon. Get a good night's sleep before the tests, and every night if you can. Your mind and body will perform better if you do.

Eat Healthfully

Eat something before each exam, but stay away from junk foods and highly caffeinated beverages that provide a quick burst of energy but that can leave you feeling drained and sleepy a short time later. Eating something healthful and light a few hours before the exam helps you feel well enough to do your best. This is especially important when you're preparing for the physical ability test (PAT). Never drink alcohol the night before any test.

Arrive Early

Go to the testing site before the day of the test. Make sure you know where it is and where you should park. On the big day, arrive at least ten minutes early so you can choose a comfortable seat — you may not like a seat by the window or in a corner, for example. Refrain from chatting with other test-takers about how difficult the test may be — their anxiety may be contagious. Also, don't share any information about the test with any other applicant — this is considered cheating. Remember that your friends who may also be testing are competing against you. If you happen to test before them, don't tell them what questions are on the test.

Relax!

If you discover that your hands are trembling and your heart is beating rapidly, close your eyes and take several deep breaths to relax. Keep a positive attitude, and remind yourself that you're going to do well.

Carefully Read or Listen to Directions

Carefully read all directions on the written test. Remember that police officer tests can vary. Don't assume that you know what to do. The same holds true for the physical ability test (PAT). Listen carefully to what you're told to do. If you can't clearly hear the directions, say, "Excuse me. Would you please repeat that?" Otherwise, you may make a mistake that can cost you points.

Read the Questions First

When answering questions about reading passages on the written test, don't be afraid to read the questions before you read the passage. It's not cheating! If you read the questions first, you'll know what to look for as you read.

However, if you do this, be sure to read the entire passage. Don't just scan it looking for the correct answer. Some incorrect answer choices contain information that's in the passage but that doesn't answer the question. For example, a passage may say that police officers arrived at an accident scene at 10:30 a.m. and that they called for assistance at 10:35 a.m. It may also say that they left the scene at 10:55 a.m. A test question may ask what time the officers called for assistance, and 10:30 a.m. and 10:55 a.m. may also be choices along with the correct answer, 10:35 a.m. Read carefully and pay attention to details.

Pace Yourself

When you take the practice tests in this book, time yourself. Know where you should be one-quarter of the way through test time, one-half of the way through test time, and so forth. Answer the easy questions first. If a question really stumps you, skip it. Pace yourself so that you have time to go back and make a good guess at questions you skipped. Always check your answers. Don't leave the room as soon as you finish. Make good use of extra time.

Mark the Right Spot!

When you check your answers, check to make sure you didn't blacken more than one oval for any question. Written police officer tests are scanned by a computer. If you mark more than one oval, the computer scores your answer as incorrect — even if one of your ovals is the correct answer. Be aware that most written police officer tests use ovals A through E, not A through D.

Stop every so often and make sure you didn't accidentally skip a question on the answer sheet. Check to make sure you've blackened the correct oval. If you skip a question, make sure you skip that question on the answer sheet.

Completely fill each oval and make sure you don't have stray marks in the test booklet. Completely erase any answer you want to change.

Take a Guess

Most written police officer tests only count correct answers, which means that you aren't penalized for guessing. Don't leave questions blank. Eliminate answer choices that you know are incorrect and make a good guess. Guessing correctly will improve your score.

Avoid changing your answer again and again. Your first instinct is usually correct.

Chapter 22

Ten Things to Expect at the Police Academy

In This Chapter

▶ Following the rules, training your mind and body, and learning new skills

▶ Working well with other officers and the public

A t the turn of the 20th century, new police officers mainly learned through firsthand experience on the streets. Training programs and specialized classes didn't exist — police officers simply showed up for their shifts and took it from there. The process was clearly trial and error — it either worked or it didn't.

Over the past few decades, however, things have changed drastically for new recruits. Today, there's no such thing as an unprepared police officer. After candidates have passed the written, physical, medical, psychological, and oral exams, they attend a police academy, where they receive focused training and in-depth knowledge of police work.

Because every state sets its own rules and regulations pertaining to its police forces, every police academy differs in what it teaches or requires of cadets. For example, Iowa's police academies may last only five months, while New York's may last eight months. Vermont may require cadets to perform 29 push-ups in a minute, while Arkansas may require a few more reps.

For the most part, however, all police officers receive similar training. In general, you can expect the following experience at your police academy.

Rigorous Rule Enforcement

Police academies have been compared to military training programs in regards to rule enforcement and high standards. Most police academies last six to eight months and require recruits to live on campus, sometimes in dormitories. All recruits conduct their days in a similar manner and according to a specific schedule. They train together, study together, and learn to trust one another. Some academies operate during the evening hours and on weekends to accommodate recruits who have regular jobs.

Academies schedule recruits' days to the minute. Most require recruits to be awake and ready for training at 5 a.m. After completing course work and physical training for the day, they eat dinner and are allowed some time to study before lights out at 10 p.m.

Restrictions apply on just about everything at the police academy. From the clothing you wear to the actions you perform, you're first and foremost a recruit, and you must remember that your behavior reflects upon the entire academy. All academies hold their cadets to high standards in both behavior and appearance.

Many academies don't allow men or women to wear jewelry or cosmetics of any kind. Women specifically can't wear anything in their hair that distinguishes them from fellow recruits. Men keep their hair cropped short, while women pull their hair back from their face. Both men and women wear the basic training camp uniform, which resembles military fatigues, and their shoes must always be shined.

Physical Challenges

Upon entrance into the police academy, you have to take a physical fitness test similar to the one you must later pass at the end of your training stint. This test is essentially a pretest; it allows academy instructors to see what you're able to do at the beginning of the program before you receive proper training.

Many recruits are unable to pass this initial test. In fact, estimates suggest that nearly two-thirds of the recruits at police academies in New York can't pass this test when they enter the academy. Academy instructors expect this, however, so don't beat yourself up if you're one of the many who can't complete the test.

Don't get discouraged, but you can expect to struggle through the first week or two of training. Push as hard as you can and always make an effort to complete every activity, especially those that offer the toughest challenges.

Before you complete your training at the police academy, you have to complete your final fitness test. Instructors compare your times and scores from the pretest to your final exam to measure the improvements you made throughout the course of your training.

Strength Training

Academy instructors love to make recruits run. Through running, weight-training exercises, and the proper diet, your body quickly changes and you grow stronger. You learn to be aware of your environment at all times; sounds and smells take on new meanings. You become faster, stronger, and more flexible — at times, you'll surely surprise yourself and your instructors.

You may want to show off your new abilities, but you have to learn to control your new-found strength. Though being able to chase down suspects is important, knowing what to do when you catch them is equally important. Academy instructors demonstrate how to avoid seriously injuring anyone, even someone suspected of committing a crime.

The academy teaches you how to use your strength and speed properly. Instructors explain how to use just enough force to disarm and apprehend criminals. You also learn how to apply handcuffs and use tools such as batons, Tasers, and pepper spray. You learn self-defense techniques and tactics that prepare you to protect yourself and those around you in the event that you have to subdue a suspect and take control of a dangerous situation.

Firearms Training

Firearms training is a necessity at all police academies. In Los Angeles, for example, recruits spend 113 of their 828 academy hours handling guns. The only areas on which they spend more time are academics and physical training.

Instructors teach you the ins and outs of using multiple types of guns during training. Though handling the kickback and working with the safety are important parts of firearms training, instructors put the most emphasis on precision. You must have excellent aim to pass police academy marksman tests — lives depend on it. If you face a suspect who's armed, you may have only one or two shots to take him down. You don't want to waste bullets or risk hurting someone in the crossfire.

To hit the required marks, especially on a moving target, recruits must pay close attention to their firearm trainers. They have to practice to improve their speed and precision. To graduate from the academy, recruits often have to score 80 percent or higher on multiple marksman tests using different firearms such as handguns, pistols, and shotguns.

EVOC Training

Although high-speed police chases don't happen every day, they occur frequently enough that every recruit in the nation is trained using the *Emergency Vehicle Operations Course,* or *EVOC.*

Imagine the driving test you took when you were a teenager. Now imagine it on steroids — that's the EVOC. The course trains you to pursue vehicles on all terrains and, depending on your location, in all weather conditions. You learn to control your squad car as you skid around tight turns at high speeds. You learn to multitask safely, using your two-way radio to update dispatch while tailing a suspect's vehicle. You even learn to avoid crashes as you move throughout neighborhoods with one-way streets and four-lane highways during rush hour.

Like hostage situations and bomb threats, high-speed car chases are something you may never encounter during your entire career in law enforcement. However, that doesn't mean that you shouldn't be prepared. It's better to know what to do if the situation does occur than to feel panicked and clueless if you find yourself in the middle of it.

Academic Integrity

Cadets spend much of their time at the police academy in the classroom, learning about the law's intricacies. You already know that you can't be a police officer without having knowledge of the law. Think about it — how would you ever make arrests if you didn't know that someone was committing a crime? How would you know when you had enough evidence to request a warrant? How would you even know that you had to request a warrant before bursting into somebody's home and haphazardly searching for illicit drugs?

The classes at the police academy familiarize you with the U.S. Constitution and all its amendments, the criminal and juvenile justice systems, victimology and crisis intervention, and statutory and case law. They explain the ins and outs of property crimes and criminal intent, the difference between larceny in the second degree and larceny in the third degree, and the distinction between murder and manslaughter. You leave the classroom prepared to deal with difficult cases involving abused and neglected children, sexual abuse, and missing persons.

Many of the lessons you learn during physical training are reiterated in an academic setting. These lessons, however, provide more detail and teach you the "why" instead of the "what." You already know that it's important for police officers to stay in shape, but perhaps you don't know the common health issues that pose problems for officers every year. These lessons teach you about cardiovascular health, nutrition, and even stress management. You also relearn the steps for making an arrest, but this time you cover the history of Miranda rights ("You have the right to remain silent . . .") and what happens if you arrest someone without proof that he committed a crime or without a warrant stating that the arrest is legal.

Language Training

Many police academies in the United States have started offering training in foreign languages. For example, the Los Angeles Police Department Academy offers Spanish-language training because of the high (and growing) number of Spanish-speaking residents in the city.

Since the 1990s, many police departments in other countries have embraced the idea of teaching multiple languages at their academies. The Cyprus Ministry of Education and Culture, for example, developed an entire school dedicated to training its recruits to speak Arabic, French, German, Italian, Russian, Spanish, and Turkish. U.S. departments are finally catching on, offering courses at a variety of police academies in languages suitable for their region.

Ethics Training

Similar to language training, ethics training has become a part of many police academies in the past decade or so. Research has drawn numerous connections between ethics and successful police departments and has provided new ways to teach ethics in the classroom. At one time, many believed that people learned ethics only by experiencing dilemmas that forced them to question their moral code. Today's research, however, shows that teaching ethics in a classroom setting has a positive impact on students or recruits.

Ethics training is a major part of the academic training cadets receive today. In a 1997 poll, approximately 80 percent of departments said that they dedicated numerous lessons to ethical practices in the law enforcement field. Today, that number continues to rise as academies develop more ways to teach ethics, including video simulation, in-class lectures, and role-play scenarios in which recruits must express their own moral code and listen to the perspectives of other recruits from different backgrounds and cultures.

One of the main reasons academies now offer ethics training is to cut back on civil lawsuits against departments. During the 20th century, police departments across the United States struggled to fight off claims of racial discrimination and profiling, excessive use of force, and even civil rights violations. Ethics training gives cadets practice in dealing with situations where these issues may arise and teaches them how to respond ethically, professionally, and respectfully.

Academy instructors want to instill a sense of patience in recruits during ethics training. Their main goal is to get cadets to think before they act. As a police officer, you may find yourself in the heat of the moment, struggling to make the right decision. At times like this, you have to stop and reflect upon the decision you need to make. You should always attempt to avoid any type of harassment or violence, even when facing a belligerent suspect.

Human Relations

As you've probably noticed while studying for the written police officer exam, the ways in which you treat your fellow recruits and officers, your superiors, and the public at large heavily affect the success you experience in the law enforcement field. Interpersonal relations and public relations are important every day, whether you're on or off duty. The academy teaches you the correct way to communicate with people.

While at the academy you spend nearly every day with the same group of men and women. You room together, eat together, train together, and study together. Everything you learn, they learn. Though you want to let your skills shine and show others what you can do, it's important that you're able to work with a team. Competition is healthy but not when lives are on the line. At the academy, you learn how to work with your fellow recruits under stressful circumstances. You learn to trust your partner with your life while simultaneously learning how to let others know that they can trust you, too. Brotherhood is important in police work; the members of your squad, specifically your partner, become like members of your own family. Being open and honest with them is key to having a successful career.

Honesty and humility are important in law enforcement work. The ability to take orders and perform duties, whether you agree with them or want to do them, is vital. You must always follow your superior's orders, whether that superior is a detective of a slightly higher rank or the chief of police. If you want to question the order, do so respectfully and privately. As you associate with your instructors at the training academy, you quickly discover how to speak to your superiors and show them that you respect them and that you deserve respect in return.

Finally, when you wear your uniform in public, you represent your entire squad or department. The way you act reflects upon the rest of the men and women on your team; therefore, it's important to always mind your behavior. When you speak to the media, be polite, but firm. When people approach you on the street with a concern, show interest and give advice, if appropriate. Never take your position of authority for granted. Your job is to protect and serve the public, so keep the safety and feelings of others in mind at all times.

Field Training Program

After graduating from the police academy, you're one step away from becoming a police officer. Graduating from the academy means that you're certified, but it doesn't mean that you're ready to jump in and play ball. Instead, you spend a few months with a senior officer — a mentor, if you will.

Because the situations you faced at the academy took place within a controlled environment, you don't have real-life experience in the field until you complete your time with a senior officer. Until this moment, all your training was scenario-based. The suspects weren't really guilty of heinous crimes, the victims went home at night and slept soundly, and your life wasn't in any real danger.

During this probationary period, you finally experience real police work. You complete real patrols, respond to real calls, and arrest real suspects. You sit in on interviews with distraught victims, and you may deal with real ethical dilemmas. This on-the-job training allows you to gain true experience in the field and helps you decide whether you want to specialize in a particular field after your training is complete.

Depending on the size of your department and the services it offers, you may choose to work in homicide, narcotics, missing persons, bike patrol, or even with juvenile offenders. As time passes, you may choose to become certified in a number of areas, improving your chances for promotions and working with special teams or forces.

Part VI
Appendixes

The 5th Wave   By Rich Tennant

"This was definitely the work of organized crime.
Very organized. Look how neatly everything's
labeled. And we're pretty sure they vacuumed
the carpet before leaving."

In this part . . .

Police officers and other law enforcement personnel often use codes and special terminology when they speak. You'll learn this special "cop lingo" at the police academy, but we thought you might like to get a head start, so we include it in Appendix A in this part.

While working as a cop may be your dream, after a few years, you may decide you'd like a higher position in law enforcement. The police officer chain of command is similar to that of the armed services. In Appendix B, we tell you about the law enforcement hierarchy and how and when you can climb the law enforcement ladder.

Appendix A

Law Enforcement Terminology and Resources

• •

*1*magine that you're patrolling when a call comes in over the police scanner. The dispatcher says, "We have a 10-50 on Main and Parkway with a DOA and a possible 10-55. BOLO for a male juvenile last seen traveling on foot north on Main."

If you're not familiar with the terminology that police officers use to converse with one another or other emergency personnel, you may not understand the message you just read, which translates to, "We have a vehicle accident on Main and Parkway with one dead on arrival and the driver is a possible DUI (driving under the influence). Officers should be on the lookout for a young male who was last seen running north on Main."

When you go to the police academy, you learn all you need to know about the terminology and codes police officers use to communicate. Before you know it, this communication will be second nature to you. Until then, use this appendix to brush up on terminology, codes, and resources.

Law Enforcement Terminology

Police officers use terminology every day that the average person may not be familiar with. Study the following list of frequently used terms, and refer back to it as you prepare for your exams.

abuse: A physical maltreatment

accomplice: A person who aids another person in committing a crime

aggravated assault: To attack a person with the intent to cause severe bodily injury

arrest: To take or keep in custody by authority of law

arson: The unlawful damage of personal property by means of fire or explosives

assault: A physical or verbal attack

burglary: The act of illegally entering a dwelling with intent to commit a felony or theft

chain of command: The hierarchy of police personnel

chain of custody: The process of tracking individuals who've had contact with evidence until it's presented in court

confiscate: To seize something legally

crime: A violation of law

evidence: The physical proof of a crime

felony: A serious crime in which the punishment may be death or imprisonment

first-degree murder: Taking an individual's life intentionally

fraud: Intentional perversion of truth to induce an individual to part with something of value

harassment: Verbal or physical conduct that's uninvited and unwelcome

homicide: A planned killing of an individual; includes all degrees of murder and manslaughter

incident report: A form filled out by a police officer after he or she responds to an incident

intent: The design or purpose to commit a wrongful or criminal act

investigate: To observe or closely examine

involuntary manslaughter: Taking an individual's life unintentionally while behaving carelessly or not paying attention to the situation at hand

juvenile: A youth or young person not yet of adult age. The age of a juvenile varies by state, but in many states, a person is a juvenile until the age of 18.

larceny: The unlawful taking of personal property with intent to deprive the rightful owner of it permanently

manslaughter: An unplanned killing of an individual

motive: Something that causes a person to act

murder: The unlawful killing of an individual, especially with malice aforethought

narcotics: Addictive drugs

perpetrator: A person who commits a crime

prosecute: To bring legal action against someone who may have committed a crime

robbery: The act of removing or attempting to remove a piece of property from its owner's possession by use of force, intimidation, or threat of violence

second-degree murder: The intentional but not premeditated taking of an individual's life

seize: To take possession of something legally

suspect: An individual suspected of a crime

theft: The unlawful taking of personal property

undercover: Acting or executing in secret

victim: An individual who is acted on and usually adversely affected by another individual

voluntary manslaughter: Taking an individual's life unintentionally during a fit of rage or passion or in the process of committing another, less serious crime

warrant: A writ that authorizes an officer to make an arrest or seizure or conduct a search

Law Enforcement Codes

Police officers use codes to represent different crimes and commonly used phrases to save time when exchanging information. These codes vary by department and can contain letters or numbers. Ten-codes are an example of numeric codes. These codes begin with the number 10 and are used to denote common crimes. Some jurisdictions are phasing out the use of codes and ten-codes in favor of plain language, but many officers still use codes, so you'll learn them at the police academy. The following are some of the codes commonly used by police officers:

- **AC:** Animal control
- **ADW:** Assault with a deadly weapon
- **APB:** All points bulletin
- **ATL:** Attempt to locate
- **BKG:** Booking
- **BOLO:** Be on the lookout
- **DB:** Dead body
- **DOA:** Dead on arrival
- **DUI:** Driving under the influence
- **DWI:** Driving while intoxicated
- **EDP:** Emotionally disturbed person
- **ETA:** Estimated time of arrival
- **FTA:** Failure to appear
- **GOA:** Gone on arrival
- **GTA:** Grand theft auto
- **LKA:** Last known address
- **LNU:** Last name unknown
- **PC:** Probable cause
- **PI:** Personal injury
- **POSS:** Possession
- **ROF:** Report on file
- **UTL:** Unable to locate
- **10-0:** Caution
- **10-1:** Unable to copy
- **10-3:** Stop transmitting
- **10-9:** Repeat message

- 10-12: Stand by
- 10-15: Prisoner in custody
- 10-16: Domestic disturbance
- 10-20: Location
- 10-22: Disregard last assignment
- 10-31: Crime in progress
- 10-32: Drowning
- 10-50: Accident
- 10-53: Man down
- 10-55: Suspected DUI
- 10-57: Missing person
- 10-63: Prepare to copy
- 10-71: Shooting
- 10-72: Gun involved
- 10-79: Bomb threat
- 10-80: Chase in progress
- 10-91: Animal
- 10-97: Arrived at scene

Additional Resources

The Internet has a wealth of information on the police officer exam and police work around the country. Access these Web sites for additional information about the field:

- **Commission on POST:** www.post.ca.gov
- **CopCareer.com:** www.copcareer.com
- **Fire & Police Selection, Inc.:** www.fpsi.com
- **LawEnforcement.com:** www.lawenforcement.com
- **LawOfficer.com:** www.lawofficer.com
- **NYPD:** www.nyc.gov/nypd
- **New York State Police:** www.troopers.state.ny.us
- **Officer.com:** www.officer.com
- **PoliceEmployment.com:** www.policeemployment.com
- **PoliceLink.com:** www.policelink.com
- **PoliceOne.com:** www.policeone.com
- **U.S. Capitol Police:** www.uscapitolpolice.gov
- **U.S. Department of Justice:** www.justice.gov
- **USA Cops:** www.usacops.com

Appendix B
Climbing the Law Enforcement Ladder

• •

*1*f you plan to pursue a career as a police officer — and we assume that you do because you're reading this book — you may one day want to climb the law enforcement ladder.

In the United States, police officers are grouped into three ranks, which are identifiable by the presence or lack of bars and stars on their uniform. You may pursue several different positions within each rank. As you work your way to the top of the ladder, we guarantee that you'll have plenty to keep you busy.

Keep in mind that depending on your location and the way in which your specific department is organized, your salary and benefits package may be different from a counterpart positioned across the country, or even in the next town. Your responsibilities also vary depending on the number of people in your department and the size of the jurisdiction your department covers.

Starting on the Bottom Rung: Unranked

If you have your sights set on the position of top dog — police chief — you have to prove yourself in various ways over the course of a very long career in law enforcement. Similar to your peers, your career begins at the bottom rung as an officer. Those men and women at the bottom of the ladder are considered unranked, so they don't wear any distinguishing bars or stars on their uniform to signify a ranking. Beyond officer, available positions are detective/investigator and sergeant.

Officer

Officers are responsible for preserving public peace, preventing crimes, arresting offenders, preserving order at public events, preventing and removing nuisances in public areas, enforcing laws and ordinances, and protecting the general rights of all persons and their property. Officers aren't typically in charge of their own cases or investigations and frequently patrol with a partner. Some departments may refer to officers as *deputies* or *corporals*.

Detective/Investigator

You may become a *detective,* also called an *investigator,* after completing approximately two to three years as a uniformed officer. Although the position of detective doesn't necessarily outrank that of an officer, detectives typically carry their own caseload and are in charge of performing thorough investigations that include collecting facts and evidence. Detectives often work in street clothes and are referred to as *plainclothes officers.*

Sergeant

In larger departments, the *sergeant* is the first managerial position available to many unranked men and women. Officers and detectives may be promoted to this position based on written test scores and on-the-job performance. Sergeants are responsible for supervising all officers and detectives during an assigned shift. Although they don't wear bars or stars, they're often distinguished by a patch of three inverted chevrons.

Moving to Middle Management: Bars

Officers, detectives, and sergeants who want to be promoted to middle management often take exams that show their growing knowledge of the field. They may have to demonstrate that they can work within a budget, speak to the public and media, and keep their cool in stressful or demanding situations. Some departments require middle management to have a bachelor's degree in business administration, political science, social science, or criminal justice.

Lieutenant

Law enforcement officials typically complete at least five years on the job before applying for the position of *lieutenant*. Lieutenants may supervise two or three sergeants per shift, in addition to supervising entire investigative squads such as narcotics or homicide. They may develop new department policies and budget projections and play a part in hiring new recruits. Lieutenants perform more administrative duties and less field work than sergeants. They wear a silver or gold bar on both collars or on both shoulder epaulets.

Captain

In small departments, *captains* may be in charge of entire divisions or precincts. In large departments, like the New York City Police Department, captains may only be responsible for portions of precincts or divisions. Captains develop staffing plans or schedules, study crime locally and nationally to identify growing trends, and often speak to the media in representation of their department. They wear two silver or gold bars on both collars or on both shoulder epaulets.

Major/Deputy inspector

In most departments, *major/deputy inspectors* are responsible for leading investigative teams in complicated or high-profile cases. Candidates for this position often need to take a specific written test demonstrating their investigative and interview skills and their knowledge of the law. If a deputy inspector isn't active in a case, she may be training new recruits or recently promoted detectives to work investigations. Depending on the department, major/deputy inspectors wear a gold or silver oak leaf on their uniform.

Becoming the Top Dog: Stars

A police officer's drive often determines whether he achieves a starred ranking within a department. Law enforcement officials who show they're motivated and ready to learn new skills each day often make it to the highest rungs of the proverbial ladder. If you have the determination and motivation to acquire the skills necessary to become a top dog, there's no reason you can't earn a star or two within your career.

Inspector/Commander

The responsibilities of an *inspector* or *commander* differ depending on the department. For example, an inspector in San Francisco has an entirely different list of duties than an inspector in New York City. But typically, an inspector supervises one or more divisions or a group of precincts. In times of emergencies, such as fires or riots, inspectors may take control of the force and assign responsibilities and duties as they see fit. Inspectors may represent their department at community meetings or may sit on community boards. A single star on their uniform identifies their position in the department.

Assistant chief

Depending on the size of the department and the demand for the position, the *assistant chief* may share responsibilities or duties with the deputy chief. In some departments, assistant chiefs are called *assistant commissioners*. They may wear up to two stars on their uniform. Some departments opt to eliminate this position altogether.

Deputy chief

In the absence of an assistant chief, the *deputy chief* reports directly to the chief of police. She is recognized as second in command and is responsible for creating a direct link between the chief and his inspectors and lieutenants. The deputy chief, also known as the *deputy commissioner, deputy superintendent,* or *undersheriff,* oversees the workings of the entire department in the field and on paper. A deputy chief's uniform may have up to three stars.

Chief of police

Many departments require that their candidates for chief of police hold at least five years of major command experience. Police chiefs call all the shots — everyone in the department reports to them and follows their orders and commands. They're responsible for representing and speaking on behalf of the entire department in the media and at social functions. They maintain discipline and set long- and short-term goals for the department as a whole. They play a part in scheduling shifts, hiring new recruits, and promoting officials to higher ranks.

Additional jobs in law enforcement

In addition to the positions covered in this appendix, which are part of the hierarchy in most police departments, other jobs within the law enforcement industry include automobile patrol, foot patrol, traffic officer, bicycle patrol, motorcycle patrol, horse patrol, marine patrol, aircraft patrol, juvenile officer, canine officer, crime scene investigator, crime prevention officer, community policing officer, hostage negotiations team, bomb squad officer, warrant officer, airport police, housing police, port authority police, and transit police. Officials may also become state troopers.

You may also be interested in federal law-enforcement careers, such as the following: the Federal Bureau of Investigation (FBI); the Federal Drug Enforcement Administration (DEA); the U.S. Marshals Service; the Federal Bureau of Prisons; the Bureau of Alcohol, Tobacco, Firearms, and Explosives (ATF); the Department of Homeland Security (DHS); the U.S. Immigration and Customs Enforcement (ICE); the Transportation Security Administration (TSA); the U.S. Secret Service; and the Special Agents for the Fish and Wildlife Service.

Index

• Numerics •

1.5-mile run, 176
10-0 (caution), 349
10-1 (unable to copy), 349
10-3 (stop transmitting), 349
10-9 (repeat message), 349
10-12 (stand by), 350
10-15 (prisoner in custody), 350
10-16 (domestic disturbance), 350
10-20 (location), 350
10-22 (disregard last assignment), 350
10-31 (crime in progress), 350
10-32 (drowning), 350
10-50 (accident), 350
10-53 (man down), 350
10-55 (suspected DUI), 350
10-57 (missing person), 350
10-63 (prepare to copy), 350
10-71 (shooting), 350
10-72 (gun involved), 350
10-79 (bomb threat), 350
10-80 (chase in progress), 350
10-91 (animal), 350
10-97 (arrived at scene), 350
440-yard mobility/agility run, 176–177

• A •

abuse, 347
AC (animal control), 349
academic integrity, at police academy, 341–342
academy (police)
  academic integrity, 341–342
  ethics training, 342
  EVOC training, 341
  field training program, 343
  firearms training, 341
  human relations, 343
  language training, 342
  physical challenges, 340
  rule enforcement, 339–340
  strength training, 340
accident (10-50), 350
accomplice, 347

ADA (Americans with Disabilities Act), 190
addends, 34
addition questions (POST)
  overview, 34–36
  practice questions, 47–53
adjectives, 86–87
ADW (assault with a deadly weapon), 349
aerobic power exercises, 170
aggravated assault, 347
agility exercises, 171
all points bulletin (APB), 349
Americans with Disabilities Act (ADA), 190
anaerobic power exercises, 170
anemia, 191
animal (10-91), 350
animal control (AC), 349
answers and explanations
  practice test 1 (POST)
    grammar, 223–224
    incident report writing, 224
    mathematics, 221–222
    reading comprehension, 222–223
  practice test 2 (POST)
    grammar, 251–252
    incident report writing, 252
    mathematics, 249–250
    reading comprehension, 250–251
  practice test 3 (POST)
    grammar, 279–280
    incident report writing, 280
    mathematics, 277–278
    reading comprehension, 278–279
  practice test 4 (NYC test), 327–332
APB (all points bulletin), 349
applications (job)
  acting professionally, 14
  disqualifications, 14
  overview, 10–11
  reviewing, 186
  sample, 12–13
  screening process. See also specific tests
    elimination during, 20

Law Enforcement Essay Exam, 18, 147–155
medical exam, 19–20, 28–29, 189–193
Notice of Examination (NOE), 9–10
oral interview, 19, 20, 27–28, 181–188
PAT (physical ability test), 18–20, 27, 169–179
Personal History Statement, 17–18
psychological exam, 19–20, 28, 194–196
written test, 2, 15–17, 20, 23, 24–27
arrest, 347
arrived at scene (10-97), 350
arriving early for tests, 336
assault, 347
assault with a deadly weapon (ADW), 349
assessing sample oral interview scenarios, 187–188
assistant chief, role of, 353
assistant commissioners, role of, 353
ATL (attempt to locate), 349
audiometer, 191
averages questions (POST)
  overview, 44–46
  practice questions, 47–53

• B •

background, waiting periods for rechecking, 20
be on the lookout (BOLO), 349
behavior, for oral interview, 182–183
BKG (booking), 349
blood pressure, 192
blood test, 191–192
BOLO (be on the lookout), 349
bomb threat (10-79), 350
booking (BKG), 349
buildings, memorizing details about, 100
burglary, 347

• C •

calculators, 34
captain, role of, 352
captions, 107
cardiac stress test, 192
caution (10-0), 349
chain of command, 347
chain of custody, 347
chase in progress (10-80), 350
checking your work, 337
chest X-ray, 192
chief of police, role of, 353
choosing verb tense, 80–81
civil service test, 2
codes (law enforcement), 349–350
colorblindness, 190–191
comma splices, in Law Enforcement Essay Exam, 151
commander, role of, 353
comparative adjective, 86
complete sentences, identifying, 87–88
computerized voice stress analyzer (CVSA), 18
confiscate, 347
conventions in this book, explained, 2–3
corporal, role of, 351
county sheriffs, 21
course of actions, determining. _See_ problem sensitivity (NYC test)
crime, 348
crime in progress (10-31), 350
cross-multiplication, 42
CVSA (computerized voice stress analyzer), 18

• D •

DB (dead body), 349
dead on arrival (DOA), 349
deductive reasoning
  National Police Officer Selection Test (POST)
    overview, 56–59
    practice questions, 67–71
  New York City test (NYC test)
    overview, 64–67
    questions, 26
  overview, 16, 283
definition passages, 58–59

demonstrative pronouns, 85–86
denominator, 41
deputies, role of, 351
deputy chief, role of, 353
deputy commissioner, role of, 353
deputy inspector, role of, 352
deputy sheriffs, 21
deputy superintendent, role of, 353
detective, role of, 351
directional cues, 107
directions, following for Personal History Statement, 165
disqualification, 14
disregard last assignment (10-22), 350
division questions (POST)
  overview, 39–41
  practice questions, 47–53
DOA (dead on arrival), 349
documents, collecting for Personal History Statement, 163
domestic disturbance (10-16), 350
dress, for oral interview, 182
driving under the influence (DUI), 21
driving while intoxicated (DWI), 349
drowning (10-32), 350
drugs (illicit), 192
DUI (driving under the influence), 349
dummy drag test, 179
DWI (driving while intoxicated), 349

• E •

ears, testing, 191
ECG (electrocardiogram), 192
EDP (emotionally disturbed person), 349
electrocardiogram (ECG), 192
elimination during screening process, 20
Emergency Vehicle Operation Course (EVOC) training, 341
emotionally disturbed person (EDP), 349
employment outlook, 14

endurance exercises, 171
ETA (estimated time of arrival), 349
ethics
  questions, 185
  standards, 186
  training at police academy, 342
events (PAT)
  1.5-mile run, 176
  440-yard mobility/agility run, 176–177
  dummy drag, 179
  fence obstacles, 178
  modified squat thrust, 177
  one-minute push-ups, 175
  one-minute sit-ups, 174
  overview, 173–174
  stair climb, 178
  trigger pull, 178–179
  vehicle exit, 178
  vertical jump, 175–176
evidence, 348
EVOC (Emergency Vehicle Operation Course) training, 341
exam announcement, 9–10
exam success, tips for, 335–337
Example icon, 5
explosive leg power exercises, 171
eye test, 190–191

• F •

failure to appear (FTA), 349
familiarity with town, 185
felony, 348
fence obstacles test, 178
field training program, at police academy, 343
firearms training, 341
first-degree murder, 348
flexibility exercises, 171
following directions for Personal History Statement, 165
440-yard mobility/agility run, 176–177
fragments, identifying sentence, 87–88
fraud, 348
FTA (failure to appear), 349
future tense, 81

• G •

gastrointestinal disorders, 193
gathering information for
    Personal History
    Statement, 162–163
genitourinary disorders, 193
glandular disorders, 193
GOA (gone on arrival), 349
grammar
  adjectives, 86–87
  complete sentences and
      fragments, 87–88
  overview, 16, 25, 79–80
  pluralizing nouns, 88–90
  practice questions, 92–97
  practice test 1 (POST)
    answers and explanations,
        221–225
    practice questions, 216–217
  practice test 2 (POST)
    answers and explanations,
        249–253
    practice questions, 244–245
  practice test 3 (POST)
    answers and explanations,
        277–281
    practice questions, 271–273
  pronouns, 83–86
  spelling, 90–92
  subject-verb agreement,
      82–83, 151
  verb tense, 80–81
GTA (grand theft auto), 349
guessing answers, 337
gun involved (10-72), 350

• H •

harassment, 348
healthy diet, 336
hearing test, 191
heart tests, 192
hernias, 193
highway patrol officers, 21
homicide, 348
honesty
  importance of in Personal
      History Statement, 164–165
  during oral interview, 182
  in psychological exam, 194
human relations, at police
    academy, 343
hypertension, 192

• I •

icebreaker questions, 184
icons in this book, explained, 5
identifying complete sentences
    and fragments, 87–88
illicit drugs, 192
incident report writing
  National Police Officer
      Selection Test (POST)
    overview, 25, 129, 134–136
    practice questions, 140–144
    reading comprehension, 129,
        130–133
  New York City test (NYC test)
    overview, 137–139
    practice questions, 144–145
  overview, 16, 129, 348
  practice test 1 (POST)
    answers and explanations,
        221–225
    practice questions, 218–220
  practice test 2 (POST)
    answers and explanations,
        249–253
    practice questions, 246–248
  practice test 3 (POST)
    answers and explanations,
        277–281
    practice questions, 274–276
indefinite pronouns, 84–85
inductive reasoning
  New York City test (NYC test)
    overview, 62–64
    questions, 26
  overview, 16, 283
information ordering
  New York City test (NYC test)
    overview, 61–62, 110–113
    practice questions,
        26, 117–128
  overview, 16
inspector, role of, 353
intent, 348
Internet resources
  Commission on POST, 350
  CopCareer.com, 350
  Fire & Police Selection, Inc., 350
  LawEnforcement.com, 350
  LawOfficer.com, 350
  New York State Police, 350
  NYPD, 350
  Officer.com, 350
  PoliceEmployment.com, 350

PoliceLink.com, 350
PoliceOne.com, 10, 350
Selective Service, 11
U.S. Capitol Police, 350
U.S. Department of Justice, 350
USA Cops, 350
interview (oral)
  honing question and answer
      skills, 184–186
  image
    acting professionally, 182–183
    dress, 182
  overview, 19, 181–182
  preparing for, 27–28
  scenarios
    assessing, 187–188
    samples, 186–187
  speaking in front of others,
      183–184
  waiting periods for, 20
interview with psychologist,
    195–196
investigate, 348
investigator, role of, 351
involuntary manslaughter, 348

• J •

job applications
  acting professionally, 14
  disqualifications, 14
  overview, 10–11
  reviewing, 186
  sample, 12–13
  screening process. See also
      specific tests and exams
    elimination during, 20
    Law Enforcement Essay
        Exam, 18, 147–155
    medical exam, 19–20, 28–29,
        189–193
    Notice of Examination (NOE),
        9–10
    oral interview, 19, 20, 27–28,
        181–188
    PAT (physical ability test),
        18–20, 27, 169–179
    Personal History Statement,
        17–18
    psychological exam, 19–20,
        28, 194–196
    written test, 2, 15–17, 20, 23,
        24–27
juvenile, 348

• L •

labels (on maps), 107
language training, at police academy, 342
larceny, 348
last known address (LKA), 349
last name unknown (LNU), 349
law enforcement
 codes, 349–350
 other jobs in, 354
 promotions, 351–354
 resources, 350
 terminology, 347–349
Law Enforcement Essay Exam
 overview, 18, 147
 practice question and answer, 154–155
 sample prompts, 153–154
 scoring, 152–153
 steps
  overview, 147–148
  prewriting, 148–149
  proofreading, 150–151
  writing, 149–150
lie detector test, 18
lieutenant, role of, 352
listening to directions, 336
LKA (last known address), 349
LNU (last name unknown), 349
location (10-20), 350
lung tests, 192

• M •

major, role of, 352
man down (10-53), 350
manslaughter, 348
mathematics
 calculators, 34
 overview, 15, 33
 practice test 1 (POST)
  answers and explanations, 221–225
  practice questions, 203–206
 practice test 2 (POST)
  answers and explanations, 249–253
  practice questions, 231–234
 practice test 3 (POST)
  answers and explanations, 277–281
  practice questions, 259–261

questions
 addition, 34–36
 averages, 44–46
 division, 39–41
 multiplication, 37–39
 percentages, 41–44
 picking any answer, 46–47
 practice, 47–53
 subtraction, 36–37
medical exam. *See also* psychological exam
 blood test, 191–192
 gastrointestinal disorders, 193
 genitourinary disorders, 193
 glandular disorders, 193
 hearing, 191
 heart, 192
 hernias, 193
 lungs, 192
 muscular disorders, 193
 overview, 19–20, 189–190
 preparing for, 28–29
 skeletal disorders, 193
 urine test, 191–192
 vision, 190–191
memorization, 16, 283
missing person (10-57), 350
modified squat thrust, 177
moral standards, 186
motive, 348
multiplication questions (POST)
 overview, 37–39
 practice questions, 47–53
municipal police officers, 21
murder, 348
muscular disorders, 193

• N •

narcotics, 348
National Criminal Justice Officer Physical Ability Test (NCJOPAT), 169
National Police Officer Selection Test (POST)
 deductive reasoning
  overview, 56–59
  practice questions, 67–71
 defined, 2
grammar
 adjectives, 86–87
 complete sentences and fragments, 87–88

overview, 16, 25, 79–80
 pluralizing nouns, 88–90
 practice questions, 92–97
 pronouns, 83–86
 spelling, 90–92
 subject-verb agreement, 82–83
 verb tense, 80–81
incident report writing
 overview, 25, 129, 134–136
 practice questions, 140–144
mathematics
 addition questions, 34–36
 averages questions, 44–46
 calculators, 34
 division questions, 39–41
 multiplication questions, 37–39
 overview, 33
 percentages questions, 41–44
 picking any answer, 46–47
 practice questions, 47–53
 subtraction questions, 36–37
overview, 15–16
practice test 1
 answer key, 225
 answer sheet, 201
 answers and explanations, 221–225
 grammar questions, 216–217
 incident report writing questions, 218–220
 mathematics questions, 203–206
 overview, 199–200
 reading comprehension questions, 207–215
practice test 2
 answer key, 253
 answer sheet, 229
 answers and explanations, 249–253
 grammar questions, 244–245
 incident report writing questions, 246–248
 mathematics questions, 231–234
 overview, 227–228
 reading comprehension questions, 235–243
practice test 3
 answer key, 281
 answer sheet, 257
 answers and explanations, 277–281

grammar questions, 271–273
incident report writing questions, 274–276
mathematics questions, 259–261
overview, 255–256
reading comprehension questions, 262–270
reading comprehension
incident reports, 129, 130–133
overview, 25, 56–59
practice questions, 67–71
problem sensitivity questions, 67
structure of, 24–25
tips for, 25
NCJOPAT (National Criminal Justice Officer Physical Ability Test), 169
New York City (NYC) Police Department Police Officer Candidate Test
deductive reasoning
overview, 26
questions, 64–67
defined, 2
grammar
adjectives, 86–87
complete sentences and fragments, 87–88
overview, 16, 79–80
pluralizing nouns, 88–90
practice questions, 92–97
pronouns, 83–86
spelling, 90–92
subject-verb agreement, 82–83
verb tense, 80–81
incident report writing
overview, 137–139
practice questions, 144–145
inductive reasoning, 26, 62–64
information ordering
overview, 61–62, 110–113
practice questions, 26, 117–118
observation and memory
information ordering questions, 110–113
memorization questions, 100–104
overview, 26, 99
problem sensitivity questions, 113–114

recall questions, 115–117
spatial orientation questions, 114–115
visualization questions, 104–110
overview, 16–17
practice test 4
answer key, 332
answer sheet, 285
answers and explanations, 327–332
overview, 283–284
practice questions, 287–325
problem-sensitivity, 26
reading comprehension
deductive reasoning questions, 64–67
inductive reasoning questions, 62–64
information ordering questions, 61–62
practice questions, 71–77
written comprehension questions, 60–61
spatial orientation, 26
structure of, 25–27
tips for, 27
visualization, 26
written comprehension, 26
written expression, 26
NOE (Notice of Examination), 9–10
nouns, pluralizing, 88–90
number facility, 283
numerator, 41
NYC test (New York City Police Department Police Officer Candidate Test)
deductive reasoning
overview, 26
questions, 64–67
defined, 2
grammar
adjectives, 86–87
complete sentences and fragments, 87–88
overview, 16, 79–80
pluralizing nouns, 88–90
practice questions, 92–97
pronouns, 83–86
spelling, 90–92
subject-verb agreement, 82–83
verb tense, 80–81

incident report writing
overview, 137–139
practice questions, 144–145
inductive reasoning, 26, 62–64
information ordering
overview, 61–62, 110–113
practice questions, 26, 117–118
observation and memory
information ordering questions, 110–113
memorization questions, 100–104
overview, 26, 99
problem sensitivity questions, 113–114
recall questions, 115–117
spatial orientation questions, 114–115
visualization questions, 104–110
overview, 16–17
practice test 4
answer key, 332
answer sheet, 285
answers and explanations, 327–332
overview, 283–284
practice questions, 287–325
problem-sensitivity, 26
reading comprehension
deductive reasoning questions, 64–67
inductive reasoning questions, 62–64
information ordering questions, 61–62
practice questions, 71–77
written comprehension questions, 60–61
spatial orientation, 26
structure of, 25–27
tips for, 27
visualization, 26
written comprehension, 26
written expression, 26

• *O* •

object pronouns, 83–84
observation and memory
preparing your, 104
tips to improve, 116

observation and memory
(NYC test)
information ordering, 110–113
memorization, 100–104
overview, 26, 99, 100–104
practice questions, 117–128
problem sensitivity, 113–114
recall, 115–117
spatial orientation, 114–115
visualization, 104–110
officer, role of, 351
1.5-mile run, 176
one-minute push-ups, 175
one-minute sit-ups, 174
open-ended questions, 184
oral interview
honing question and answer
skills, 184–186
image
acting professionally, 182–183
dress, 182
overview, 19, 181–182
preparing for, 27–28
scenarios
assessing, 187–188
samples, 186–187
speaking in front of others,
183–184
waiting periods for, 20
organization
of municipal, county, and
state departments, 21
of this book, 4–5

• *p* •

pacing yourself, 337
past tense, 81
PAT (physical ability test)
events
1.5-mile run, 176
440-yard mobility/agility run,
176–177
dummy drag, 179
fence obstacles, 178
modified squat thrust, 177
one-minute push-ups, 175
one-minute sit-ups, 174
overview, 173–174
stair climb, 178
trigger pull, 178–179
vehicle exit, 178
vertical jump, 175–176
local test, 171
overview, 18–19, 169
preparing for, 27, 172

reasons for, 170
skill areas of, 170–171
tips for day of, 173
waiting periods for, 20
PC (probable cause), 349
people, memorizing details
about, 100
percentages questions (POST)
overview, 41–44
practice questions, 47–53
peripheral vision, 190–191
perpetrator, 348
Personal History Statement
completing
collecting necessary documents, 163
gathering necessary information, 162
information contained in,
158–161
overview, 17–18, 157
reviewing, 186
sample, 159–161
writing
checking work, 166
following directions, 165
importance of honesty in,
164–165
overview, 163
reading questions, 165
personal injury (PI), 349
personal questions, 185
personality test, 194–195
personality traits, 195
physical ability test (PAT)
events
1.5-mile run, 176
440-yard mobility/agility run,
176–177
dummy drag, 179
fence obstacles, 178
modified squat thrust, 177
one-minute push-ups, 175
one-minute sit-ups, 174
overview, 173–174
stair climb, 178
trigger pull, 178–179
vehicle exit, 178
vertical jump, 175–176
local test, 171
overview, 18–19, 169
preparing for, 27, 172
reasons for, 170
skill areas of, 170–171
tips for day of, 173
waiting periods for, 20

physical challenges, at police
academy, 340
PI (personal injury), 349
plainclothes officers, role of, 351
pluralizing nouns, 88–90
police academy
academic integrity, 341–342
ethics training, 342
EVOC training, 341
field training program, 343
firearms training, 341
human relations, 343
language training, 342
physical challenges, 340
rule enforcement, 339–340
strength training, 340
police officer, knowing role of,
185
polygraph test, 18, 20
positive adjective, 86
POSS (possession), 349
possessive pronouns, 84
POST (National Police Officer
Selection Test)
deductive reasoning
overview, 56–59
practice questions, 67–71
defined, 2
grammar
adjectives, 86–87
complete sentences and
fragments, 87–88
overview, 16, 25, 79–80
pluralizing nouns, 88–90
practice questions, 92–97
pronouns, 83–86
spelling, 90–92
subject-verb agreement,
82–83
verb tense, 80–81
incident report writing
overview, 25, 129, 134–136
practice questions, 140–144
mathematics
addition questions, 34–36
averages questions, 44–46
calculators, 34
division questions, 39–41
multiplication questions,
37–39
overview, 33
percentages questions, 41–44
picking any answer, 46–47
practice questions, 47–53
subtraction questions, 36–37
overview, 15–16

practice test 1
  answer key, 225
  answer sheet, 201
  answers and explanations, 221–225
  grammar questions, 216–217
  incident report writing questions, 218–220
  mathematics questions, 203–206
  overview, 199–200
  reading comprehension questions, 207–215
practice test 2
  answer key, 253
  answer sheet, 229
  answers and explanations, 249–253
  grammar questions, 244–245
  incident report writing questions, 246–248
  mathematics questions, 231–234
  overview, 227–228
  reading comprehension questions, 235–243
practice test 3
  answer key, 281
  answer sheet, 257
  answers and explanations, 277–281
  grammar questions, 271–273
  incident report writing questions, 274–276
  mathematics questions, 259–261
  overview, 255–256
  reading comprehension questions, 262–270
reading comprehension
  incident reports, 129, 130–133
  overview, 25, 56–59
  practice questions, 67–71
  problem sensitivity questions, 67
  structure of, 24–25
  tips for, 25
practice questions. *See also specific tests and exams*
grammar and spelling, 92–97
Law Enforcement Essay Exam, 154–155
National Police Officer Selection Test (POST)
  incident reports, 140–144
  mathematics, 47–53

reading comprehension, 67–71
New York City test (NYC test)
  incident reports, 144–145
  observation and memory, 117–128
  reading comprehension, 71–77
practice test 1 (POST)
  grammar questions, 216–217
  incident report writing questions, 218–220
  mathematics questions, 203–206
  reading comprehension questions, 207–215
practice test 2 (POST)
  grammar questions, 244–245
  incident report writing questions, 246–248
  mathematics questions, 231–234
  reading comprehension questions, 235–243
practice test 3 (POST)
  grammar questions, 271–273
  incident report writing questions, 274–276
  mathematics questions, 259–261
  reading comprehension questions, 262–270
practice test 4 (NYC test), 287–325
practice test 1 (POST)
  answer key, 225
  answer sheet, 201
  answers and explanations
    grammar, 223–224
    incident report writing, 224
    mathematics, 221–222
    reading comprehension, 222–223
  overview, 199–200
  questions
    grammar, 216–217
    incident report writing, 218–220
    mathematics, 203–206
    reading comprehension, 207–215
practice test 2 (POST)
  answer key, 253
  answer sheet, 229
  answers and explanations
    grammar, 251–252
    incident report writing, 252

mathematics, 249–250
    reading comprehension, 250–251
  overview, 227–228
  questions
    grammar, 244–245
    incident report writing, 246–248
    mathematics, 231–234
    reading comprehension, 235–243
practice test 3 (POST)
  answer key, 281
  answer sheet, 257
  answers and explanations
    grammar, 279–280
    incident report writing, 280
    mathematics, 277–278
    reading comprehension, 278–279
  overview, 255–256
  questions
    grammar, 271–273
    incident report writing, 274–276
    mathematics, 259–261
    reading comprehension, 262–270
practice test 4 (NYC test)
  answer key, 332
  answer sheet, 285
  answers and explanations, 327–332
  overview, 283–284
  practice questions, 287–325
practicing interviewing, 186
prepare to copy (10-63), 350
preparing
  importance of, 335–336
  for medical exam, 28–29
  for oral interview, 27–28
  for PAT (physical ability test), 27, 172
  for psychological exam, 28
  your memory, 104
present tense, 81
prewriting, in Law Enforcement Essay Exam, 148–149
prisoner in custody (10-15), 350
probable cause (PC), 349
probing questions, 184
problem orientation, 16
problem sensitivity (NYC test)
  overview, 67, 113–114, 283
  practice questions, 26, 117–128

process for screening
  elimination during, 20
  job application
    acting professionally, 14
    disqualifications, 14
    overview, 10–11
    sample, 12–13
  Law Enforcement Essay Exam
    overview, 18, 147
    practice question and
      answer, 154–155
    sample prompts, 153–154
    scoring, 152–153
    steps, 147–151
  medical exam
    blood test, 191–192
    gastrointestinal disorders,
      193
    genitourinary disorders, 193
    glandular disorders, 193
    hearing, 191
    heart, 192
    hernias, 193
    lungs, 192
    muscular disorders, 193
    overview, 19–20, 189–190
    preparing for, 28–29
    skeletal disorders, 193
    urine test, 191–192
    vision, 190–191
  Notice of Examination (NOE),
    9–10
  oral interview
    honing question and answer
      skills, 184–186
    image, 182–183
    overview, 19, 181–182
    preparing for, 27–28
    scenarios, 186–188
    speaking in front of others,
      183–184
    waiting periods for, 20
  PAT (physical ability test)
    events, 173–179
    local test, 171
    overview, 18–19, 169
    preparing for, 27, 172
    reasons for, 170
    skill areas of, 170–171
    tips for day of, 173
    waiting periods for, 20
  Personal History Statement,
    17–18
  psychological exam
    interviewing with psycholo-
      gist, 195–196
    overview, 19–20, 194

  personality test, 194–195
  preparing for, 28
  written test
    defined, 2
    lengths of, 23
    National Police Officer
      Selection Test (POST),
      15–16, 24–25
    New York City test (NYC
      test), 16–17, 25–27
    waiting periods for, 20
professional image,
    projecting, 14
promotions in law enforcement,
    351–354
prompts
  overview, 147
  sample, 153–154
pronoun-antecedent agree-
    ment, in Law Enforcement
    Essay Exam, 151
pronouns, 83–86
proofreading
  Law Enforcement Essay Exam,
    150–151
  Personal History Statement,
    166
prosecute, 348
psychological exam. See also
    medical exam
  interviewing with psycholo-
    gist, 195–196
  overview, 19–20, 194
  personality test, 194–195
  preparing for, 28
psychologist, interviewing with,
    195–196
push-ups (one-minute), 175

• Q •

questions and practice ques-
    tions. See also specific tests
    and exams
ethics, 185
grammar and spelling (POST),
    92–97, 216–217, 244–245,
    271–273
honing skills, 184–186
incident report writing
  National Police Officer
    Selection Test (POST),
    140–144, 218–220, 246–248,
    274–276
  New York City test (NYC
    test), 144–145

Law Enforcement Essay Exam,
    154–155
mathematics (POST)
  addition, 34–36
  averages, 44–46
  division, 39–41
  multiplication, 37–39
  percentages, 41–44
  picking any answer, 46–47
  subtraction, 36–37
National Police Officer
    Selection Test (POST)
  incident report writing,
    140–144, 218–220, 246–248,
    274–276
  mathematics, 34–53, 47–53,
    203–206, 231–234, 259–261
  reading comprehension,
    56–59, 67–71, 207–215,
    235–243, 262–270
New York City test (NYC test)
  incident reports, 144–145
  observation and memory,
    99–117, 117–128
  reading comprehension,
    59–67, 71–77
observation and memory
    (NYC test)
  information ordering,
    110–113
  memorization, 100–104
  overview, 99
  problem sensitivity, 113–114
  recall, 115–117
  spatial orientation, 114–115
  visualization, 104–110
oral interview, 184–185
practice test 1 (POST)
  grammar questions, 216–217
  incident report writing ques-
    tions, 218–220
  mathematics questions,
    203–206
  reading comprehension
    questions, 207–215
practice test 2 (POST)
  grammar questions, 244–245
  incident report writing ques-
    tions, 246–248
  mathematics questions,
    231–234
  reading comprehension
    questions, 235–243
practice test 3 (POST)
  grammar questions, 271–273
  incident report writing ques-
    tions, 274–276

mathematics questions, 259–261
reading comprehension questions, 262–270
practice test 4 (NYC test), 287–325
reading carefully, 337
reading comprehension (NYC test)
  deductive reasoning, 64–67
  inductive reasoning, 62–64
  information ordering, 61–62
  overview, 59–60
  problem sensitivity, 67
  written comprehension, 60–61
reading comprehension (POST), 56–59, 67–71, 207–215, 235–243, 262–270
reading for Personal History Statement, 165

• R •

reading
  directions, 336
  improving grammar skills with, 80
  questions for Personal History Statement, 165
  test questions, 337
reading comprehension
  overview, 15
  practice test 1 (POST)
    answers and explanations, 221–225
    practice questions, 207–215
  practice test 2 (POST)
    answers and explanations, 249–253
    practice questions, 235–243
  practice test 3 (POST)
    answers and explanations, 277–281
    practice questions, 262–270
reading comprehension (NYC test)
  overview, 59–60
  questions
    deductive reasoning, 64–67
    inductive reasoning, 62–64
    information ordering, 61–62
    problem sensitivity, 67
    written comprehension, 60–61
reading comprehension (POST)
  importance of, 58
  incident reports, 129, 130–133

questions
  overview, 25, 56–59
  practice questions, 67–71
recall questions (NYC test)
  overview, 115–117
  practice questions, 117–128
reflexive pronouns, 84
relaxing during test, 336
Remember icon, 5
repeat message (10-9), 349
report on file (ROF), 349
requirements
  one-minute push-ups, 175
  one-minute sit-ups, 174
researching job opportunities, 193
resources (law enforcement), 350
rest, importance of, 336
résumé, reviewing, 186
reviewing common interview questions, 185–186
robbery, 348
ROF (report on file), 349
rule enforcement, at police academy, 339–340
run-on sentences, in Law Enforcement Essay Exam, 150

• S •

samples
  job applications, 12–13
  Law Enforcement Essay Exam prompts, 153–154
  Notice of Examination (NOE), 10
  oral board interview scenarios, 186–187
  Personal History Statement, 159–161, 164, 165
scenario-based questions, 185
scoring in Law Enforcement Essay Exam, 152–153
screening process
  elimination during, 20
  job application
    acting professionally, 14
    disqualifications, 14
    overview, 10–11
    sample, 12–13
  Law Enforcement Essay Exam
    overview, 18, 147
    practice question and answer, 154–155
    sample prompts, 153–154

  scoring, 152–153
  steps, 147–151
medical exam
  blood test, 191–192
  gastrointestinal disorders, 193
  genitourinary disorders, 193
  glandular disorders, 193
  hearing, 191
  heart, 192
  hernias, 193
  lungs, 192
  muscular disorders, 193
  overview, 19–20, 189–190
  preparing for, 28–29
  skeletal disorders, 193
  urine test, 191–192
  vision, 190–191
Notice of Examination (NOE), 9–10
oral interview
  honing question and answer skills, 184–186
  image, 182–183
  overview, 19, 181–182
  preparing for, 27–28
  scenarios, 186–188
  speaking in front of others, 183–184
  waiting periods for, 20
PAT (physical ability test)
  events, 173–179
  local test, 171
  overview, 18–19, 169
  preparing for, 27, 172
  reasons for, 170
  skill areas of, 170–171
  tips for day of, 173
  waiting periods for, 20
Personal History Statement, 17–18
psychological exam
  interviewing with psychologist, 195–196
  overview, 19–20, 194
  personality test, 194–195
  preparing for, 28
written test
  defined, 2
  lengths of, 23
  National Police Officer Selection Test (POST), 15–16, 24–25
  New York City test (NYC test), 16–17, 25–27
  waiting periods for, 20
second-degree murder, 348
seize, 348

Selective Service, 11
sentence fragments, in Law
    Enforcement Essay
    Exam, 150
sergeant, role of, 352
shooting (10-71), 350
situational questions, 185, 186
sit-ups (one-minute), 174
skeletal disorders, 193
skills
  PAT (physical ability test),
    170–171
  question and answer, 184–186
social networks, 182
spatial orientation (NYC test)
  overview, 16, 114–115, 283
  practice questions, 26, 117–128
speaking in front of others,
    183–184
spelling, 90–92
squat thrust, 177
stair climb test, 178
stand by (10-12), 350
state police officers, 21
state troopers, 21
stop transmitting (10-3), 349
strength exercises, 171
strength training, at police
    academy, 340
subject pronouns, 83–84
subject-verb agreement,
    82–83, 151
subtraction questions (POST)
  overview, 36–37
  practice questions, 47–53
superlative adjective, 86
suspect, 348
suspected DUI (10-55), 350

• T •

ten-codes, 349–350
terminology (law enforcement),
    347–349
theft, 348

Tip icon, 5
town, familiarity with, 185
training
  ethics, 342
  EVIC (Emergency Vehicle
    Operation Course), 341
  field training program, 343
  firearms, 341
  language, 342
  strength, 340
trigger pull test, 178–179

• U •

unable to copy (10-1), 349
unable to locate (UTL), 349
undercover, 348
undersheriff, role of, 353
unranked police officer,
    role of, 351
urine test, 191–192
UTL (unable to locate), 349

• V •

vehicle exit test, 178
verb tense, 80–81
vertical jump, 175–176
victim, 348
vision test, 190–191
visualization (NYC test)
  overview, 16, 104–110, 283
  practice questions, 26, 117–128
voluntary manslaughter, 349

• W •

Warning! icon, 5
warrant, 349
Web sites
  Commission on POST, 350
  CopCareer.com, 350
  Fire & Police Selection, Inc.,
    350

LawEnforcement.com, 350
LawOfficer.com, 350
New York State Police, 350
NYPD, 350
Officer.com, 350
PoliceEmployment.com, 350
PoliceLink.com, 350
PoliceOne.com, 10, 350
Selective Service, 11
U.S. Capitol Police, 350
U.S. Department of Justice, 350
USA Cops, 350
writing
  Law Enforcement Essay Exam,
    149–150
  Personal History Statement
    checking work, 166
    following directions, 165
    importance of honesty,
      164–165
    overview, 163
    reading questions, 165
written comprehension
    (NYC test)
  overview, 17, 360–61
  questions, 26
written expression (NYC test),
    17, 26
written test
  defined, 2
  lengths of, 23
  National Police Officer
    Selection Test (POST)
    overview, 15–16
    structure of, 24–25
    tips for, 25
  New York City test (NYC test)
    overview, 16–17
    structure of, 25–27
    tips for, 27
  overview, 15, 23
  waiting periods for, 20

Notes

Notes

Business/Accounting & Bookkeeping

Bookkeeping For Dummies
978-0-7645-9848-7

eBay Business
All-in-One For Dummies,
2nd Edition
978-0-470-38536-4

Job Interviews
For Dummies,
3rd Edition
978-0-470-17748-8

Resumes For Dummies,
5th Edition
978-0-470-08037-5

Stock Investing
For Dummies,
3rd Edition
978-0-470-40114-9

Successful Time
Management
For Dummies
978-0-470-29034-7

Computer Hardware

BlackBerry For Dummies,
3rd Edition
978-0-470-45762-7

Computers For Seniors
For Dummies
978-0-470-24055-7

iPhone For Dummies,
2nd Edition
978-0-470-42342-4

Laptops For Dummies,
3rd Edition
978-0-470-27759-1

Macs For Dummies,
10th Edition
978-0-470-27817-8

Cooking & Entertaining

Cooking Basics
For Dummies,
3rd Edition
978-0-7645-7206-7

Wine For Dummies,
4th Edition
978-0-470-04579-4

Diet & Nutrition

Dieting For Dummies,
2nd Edition
978-0-7645-4149-0

Nutrition For Dummies,
4th Edition
978-0-471-79868-2

Weight Training
For Dummies,
3rd Edition
978-0-471-76845-6

Digital Photography

Digital Photography
For Dummies,
6th Edition
978-0-470-25074-7

Photoshop Elements 7
For Dummies
978-0-470-39700-8

Gardening

Gardening Basics
For Dummies
978-0-470-03749-2

Organic Gardening
For Dummies,
2nd Edition
978-0-470-43067-5

Green/Sustainable

Green Building
& Remodeling
For Dummies
978-0-4710-17559-0

Green Cleaning
For Dummies
978-0-470-39106-8

Green IT For Dummies
978-0-470-38688-0

Health

Diabetes For Dummies,
3rd Edition
978-0-470-27086-8

Food Allergies
For Dummies
978-0-470-09584-3

Living Gluten-Free
For Dummies
978-0-471-77383-2

Hobbies/General

Chess For Dummies,
2nd Edition
978-0-7645-8404-6

Drawing For Dummies
978-0-7645-5476-6

Knitting For Dummies,
2nd Edition
978-0-470-28747-7

Organizing For Dummies
978-0-7645-5300-4

SuDoku For Dummies
978-0-470-01892-7

Home Improvement

Energy Efficient Homes
For Dummies
978-0-470-37602-7

Home Theater
For Dummies,
3rd Edition
978-0-470-41189-6

Living the Country Lifestyle
All-in-One For Dummies
978-0-470-43061-3

Solar Power Your Home
For Dummies
978-0-470-17569-9

Internet
Blogging For Dummies,
2nd Edition
978-0-470-23017-6

eBay For Dummies,
6th Edition
978-0-470-49741-8

Facebook For Dummies
978-0-470-26273-3

Google Blogger
For Dummies
978-0-470-40742-4

Web Marketing
For Dummies,
2nd Edition
978-0-470-37181-7

WordPress For Dummies,
2nd Edition
978-0-470-40296-2

Language & Foreign Language
French For Dummies
978-0-7645-5193-2

Italian Phrases
For Dummies
978-0-7645-7203-6

Spanish For Dummies
978-0-7645-5194-9

Spanish For Dummies,
Audio Set
978-0-470-09585-0

Macintosh
Mac OS X Snow Leopard
For Dummies
978-0-470-43543-4

Math & Science
Algebra I For Dummies
978-0-7645-5325-7

Biology For Dummies
978-0-7645-5326-4

Calculus For Dummies
978-0-7645-2498-1

Chemistry For Dummies
978-0-7645-5430-8

Microsoft Office
Excel 2007 For Dummies
978-0-470-03737-9

Office 2007 All-in-One
Desk Reference
For Dummies
978-0-471-78279-7

Music
Guitar For Dummies,
2nd Edition
978-0-7645-9904-0

iPod & iTunes
For Dummies,
6th Edition
978-0-470-39062-7

Piano Exercises
For Dummies
978-0-470-38765-8

Parenting & Education
Parenting For Dummies,
2nd Edition
978-0-7645-5418-6

Type 1 Diabetes
For Dummies
978-0-470-17811-9

Pets
Cats For Dummies,
2nd Edition
978-0-7645-5275-5

Dog Training For Dummies,
2nd Edition
978-0-7645-8418-3

Puppies For Dummies,
2nd Edition
978-0-470-03717-1

Religion & Inspiration
The Bible For Dummies
978-0-7645-5296-0

Catholicism For Dummies
978-0-7645-5391-2

Women in the Bible
For Dummies
978-0-7645-8475-6

Self-Help & Relationship
Anger Management
For Dummies
978-0-470-03715-7

Overcoming Anxiety
For Dummies
978-0-7645-5447-6

Sports
Baseball For Dummies,
3rd Edition
978-0-7645-7537-2

Basketball For Dummies,
2nd Edition
978-0-7645-5248-9

Golf For Dummies,
3rd Edition
978-0-471-76871-5

Web Development
Web Design All-in-One
For Dummies
978-0-470-41796-6

Windows Vista
Windows Vista
For Dummies
978-0-471-75421-3

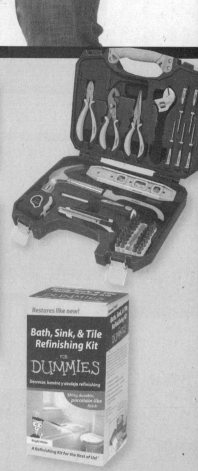
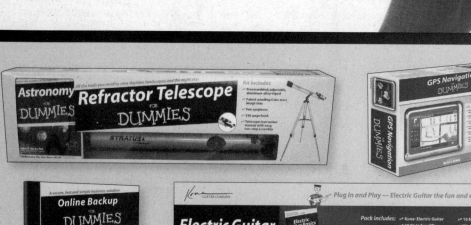